T0373160

GHOST CITIZENS

GHOST CITIZENS

Jewish Return to a Postwar City

LUKASZ KRZYZANOWSKI

Translated by Madeline G. Levine

HARVARD UNIVERSITY PRESS

Cambridge, Massachusetts & London, England

2020

Copyright © 2020 by Lukasz Krzyzanowski
All rights reserved
Printed in the United States of America
First printing

First edition published in Polish as
Dom, którego nie było: Powroty ocalałych do powojennego miasta,
by Wydawnictwo Czarne, Wołowiec, Poland, 2016

The right of Lukasz Krzyzanowski to be identified as the author of this
work has been asserted in accordance with the Copyright,
Designs and Patents Act, 1988.

Library of Congress Cataloging-in-Publication Data
Names: Krzyżanowski, Łukasz, author. | Levine, Madeline G., translator.
Title: Ghost citizens : Jewish return to a postwar city / Łukasz Krzyżanowski ; translated
by Madeline G. Levine.
Other titles: Dom, którego nie było. English
Description: Cambridge, Massachusetts : Harvard University Press, 2020. | "First published
in Polish as Dom, którego nie było: powroty ocalałych do powojennego miasta, by
Wydawnictwo Czarne, Wołowiec, Poland, 2016"—Title page verso.
Identifiers: LCCN 2019054730 | ISBN 9780674984660 (cloth)
Subjects: LCSH: Jews—Persecutions—Poland—History. | Holocaust,
Jewish (1939-1945)—Poland. | Antisemitism —Poland.
Classification: LCC DS134.55 .K7613 2020 | DDC 940.53/1809438—dc23
LC record available at https://lccn.loc.gov/2019054730

For Dorota

CONTENTS

GHOST CITIZENS

When I returned from the camp, our small town was completely empty. I observed houses that were non-houses, streets that were non-streets, and I saw people who were non-people. And there was a skinny goat that was not a goat, a skinny nag that was not a nag, flowers that were not flowers, and a sky that was not a sky. I walked down streets that were not streets, circled the market square that was not a market square, on which stood a church that was a not a church, a town hall that was not a town hall, and a lone bench that was not a bench. On Grobelna Street was a synagogue that was not there, but it alone existed for me, just as our two-story house did, that was no longer.

—Stanisław Benski, *Ocaleni*

There's no one here! But so many people are around.

—Samuel Puterman memoir, Emanuel Ringelblum Jewish
Historical Institute in Warsaw, 302/27

INTRODUCTION

ON AUGUST 17, 1950, a small group of Jews gathered in the center of Radom, an industrial city a hundred kilometers south of Warsaw. The square where they met was once home to the city's synagogue, a central place for generations of the city's Jewish inhabitants. During the German occupation, the synagogue stood at the center of the large ghetto. The building was torn down after the city was taken by the Red Army. On that warm, sunny afternoon, eight years after the ghetto was liquidated, the remaining Jews of the city mourned their murdered community and unveiled a monument dedicated to the victims of Nazi persecution (see Figure I.1). It was the last time the Jewish dwellers of Radom appeared together in public and acted as a community. Hence, the monument, which still marks the space, is a reminder of both the prewar community that perished during the Holocaust and the short-lived community of survivors who briefly came together in the early postwar period. The latter community is the main focus of this book. Targeted by violence and absent from the broader social and political picture of the city, Jewish survivors formed a small, isolated community, while attempting to rebuild Jewish life, their institutions, and networks in what used to be their hometown.

At the beginning of the road I traveled in writing this book lies a cruel crime. In 2008, I was hired by the Institute of Sociology at Jagiellonian University to organize materials in the files of Andrzej Paluch, a distinguished sociologist who had died in 2006, his work left unfinished.

Figure I.1 Monument commemorating Jews of Radom who perished during the
Holocaust. Photo taken soon after the monument was unveiled in 1950. Courtesy
Barbara Fundowicz-Towarek.

Among his papers were transcripts of interviews conducted by his students during their research trips. In these transcripts, recording the students' interviews with residents of towns and villages in what is today
southeastern Poland, I came across a laconic reference to two Jewish
women—a mother and daughter. The women had survived the Holocaust
in the local countryside and immediately after the war had returned to

their home village. There, some Poles whose identity is unknown took them to a secluded area near the village and raped and murdered them. When I read that story, I was not interested in the perpetrators or in the motives for this hideous crime. My attention was drawn entirely to the tragedy, the unimaginable suffering and loneliness of the two women. I was moved by the fact that we will never know who they were and what their lives were like. Today, even their names are forgotten.

The next impulse for thinking about Jews returning home immediately after World War II came from Jan Jakub Kolski's 1990 film, *Pogrzeb kartofla* (The burial of a potato). The main character, Mateusz Szewczyk (played by a renowned and very popular Polish actor, Franciszek Pieczka), returns from a concentration camp to his native town right after the war. Already, before arriving, he is making plans: "Finally—my home. My home, my home! Nothing special. I enter, exchange greetings, and that's all. I simply enter just as one enters one's home. After all, I am not the first . . . to return." It soon becomes clear that the return diverges significantly from Szewczyk's imaginings. No one is waiting for him. His wife and son are no longer alive, and the neighbors have stolen all his property. The returning man is met with enmity. One of the neighbors, throwing the things she had taken from his house at Szewczyk's feet, spits and mutters through clenched teeth, "Jew!" Although the main hero is not a Jew, which he proves by standing, trousers dropped, in a striped camp uniform before his neighbors, I read Kolski's film as a story about extreme isolation and rejection accompanying, above all, the postwar return of Jews to their hometowns.

When I first encountered these two stories, they made a huge impression on me, but at the time I did not think that soon I would devote several years to studying the fates of Jews who returned or attempted to return to their native places immediately after liberation. Most of their stories have not been recorded in history as anything special. They were ordinary people living in extraordinary times, whose fates, I am convinced, are worthy of being told. Studying the fates of ordinary people provides better insight into the wider social processes and daily life of a society than does focusing on privileged and exceptional individuals.

In 2009, in the State Archive in Radom, the city where I was born and went to school, I came across a large collection of documents describing

the life of Jews residing in the city immediately after World War II. It was
official documentation: the "institutional archive" of the District Jewish
Committee (Okręgowy Komitet Żydowski, OKŻ), which was active in
Radom in the years 1945–1950, and also was known by a shorter
name—the Jewish Committee. In many Polish cities and towns, similar
institutions sprang up after the war, but most often their documents did
not survive. That materials concerning the life of Jews in postwar Radom
were preserved was a matter of chance. At the beginning of the 1970s, in
the apartment in which the Jewish Committee was once located, new tenants took up permanent residence. Chaim Kamer, one of the last individuals connected with the committee, decided to transfer the archive to
a different place. He sent the documents, packed in three cabinets, two
chests, and several sealed parcels, to Zofia Wąsowicz, administrator of
the apartment house.[1] Wąsowicz placed the documents in a brick out-
building on the periphery of the city, in the Kaptur neighborhood. The
Security Police (Communist Poland's secret political police organization;
SB) found them there in 1974:

> On 4 May of the current year [1974], we received a signal through
> operational means that a favorable situation existed to access ar-
> chival materials, since a shed will be torn down, along with news
> that, taking advantage of the opening of the shed, pupils from the
> school located next to the shed and who lived in the vicinity had
> carried out Hebrew-language books to contribute to a scrap paper
> drive.
>
> As a result, after reaching the place and referring to a signal from
> the schoolchildren, we told Zofia Wąsowicz that we had learned there
> are some historical documents here that are inadequately stored and
> are succumbing to dispersal among and destruction by the neighboring
> inhabitants, therefore it would be necessary to secure them and transfer
> them to an appropriate institution, for example, the State Archive in
> Radom. At the same time, she was shown several documents obtained
> earlier from the unsecured part of the shed. Zofia Wąsowicz expressed
> her agreement to our having access to the archival materials and trans-
> porting them with the aim of securing them, which we accomplished
> on that very day.[2]

The Committee's documents were already incomplete when they were
retrieved by the Security Police. Some of the books and "liturgical ves-
sels and garments" were supposedly collected from the shed earlier by
Pola Zajdensznir, one of the survivors still residing in Radom.[3] It is unknown how many documents were turned in for pulping by the pupils of
the school or simply scattered by them throughout the area.

The Security Police handed over the documents found in the shed to
the State Archive in Radom, where they are preserved to the present day.[4]
Most likely, the Security Police found the majority of the Jewish Committee's materials to be useless for their work. The documents referred to
individuals who were long dead or residing permanently outside Poland.
The former Security Police officer who found the Jewish Committee's materials states that all the documents were handed over to the Radom archive.[5] However, in the archive there is no index card of Jews registered
in the Committee, although it was present among the archival materials
discovered in 1974. Several hundred certificates confirming registration
and certificates of name changes or changes of residency also are missing.[6]
It cannot be ruled out that the Security Police may have retained a portion of the documents for their own use. It is also possible that these archival items might have made their way into private hands.

Reading the materials of the District Jewish Committee in Radom, I
recognized in them places, street names, and addresses. At the same time,
I was looking at a reality completely unknown to me. The survival of a
large collection of Jewish Committee documents in a provincial Polish city
is highly unusual. Radom thus served as a model city for writing a case
study of the life of a postwar Jewish community in provincial Poland. This
study, although based on materials from a single city and steeped in local
context, allows us to understand phenomena broader than this single
case.[7] The fact that Radom was not a particularly important urban center
either before World War II or after, and that it did not stand out in any
respect, makes it possible to see it as a typical medium-sized city, one of
many such in central Poland. The social processes and phenomena taking
place in Radom immediately after the war were familiar to many other
Polish towns. Because part of my family was connected with this city from
prewar times and I myself spent the first seventeen years of my life there,
I possessed knowledge that would have been difficult for an outsider to

gain—for example, familiarity with the city's topography and its history of daily life, including locations of specific shops and enterprises and how the city changed over time.

Studying the postwar return of the Jews has particular significance for a better understanding of the processes taking place in Polish society right after the war. I am thinking here about the community of people who held *citizenship* in the Republic of Poland, not those identified by membership in a particular ethnic or religious group, despite my use of the terms "Pole" and "Jew," which I often treat in the book as distinct categories (for they functioned in that context). Some of the individuals I discuss would perhaps recognize as their own the words of the Polish World War II underground soldier Stanisław Likiernik, whose grandfather and parents consciously rejected all Jewish tradition and who was raised as a Pole: "I believe that people have a right to choose the nation to which they yearn to belong. Someone who denies this right to someone else is a son of a bitch. Damn it, I can't keep explaining to the end of time that I'm a Pole."[8] The phenomena I analyze contributed to the social change that led to the fact that Polish society today is almost entirely homogeneous. In this way, my study proceeds from Zygmunt Bauman's observation that "the experience of the Holocaust contains crucial information about the society of which we are members" and enlarges it to the period right after the Holocaust.[9] To consider the experiences of the people in this book as exclusively Jewish history would not only contradict the facts but would also contribute to reproducing the worst intellectual schemas that have already placed Jews outside Polish society. My goal is not the exclusion of the Holocaust survivors from the community of citizens. This book is an attempt at understanding human fate in all its complexity in specific social and historical conditions.

In the terminology I have adopted, a "survivor" is anyone who was exposed to repression in connection with being recognized under Nazi racial law as a Jew and who, despite this, managed to survive. My application of an external criterion (furthermore, one created by Nazi ideology) to determine whom, in this work, I consider to be a Jew, obviously presents a serious dilemma.[10] Among victims of the Holocaust as well as those who survived were people who identified themselves as Jewish, but there were also those with no affinity to Judaism or Jewish culture, those who considered themselves Polish, agnostic, or Christian. In between, there existed a huge space filled with intermediate or transitional identities—people who considered themselves both Jews and Poles at the same time. Although I keep this distinction in mind, I am also conscious of the fact that it is not entirely possible to take it into consideration when studying the community of Holocaust survivors. The subject that interests me is the group of individuals who, whatever their self-identification as Jews, Polish Jews, Jewish Poles, or simply Poles may have been, found themselves in mortal danger due to the Nazi policy of the "final solution of the Jewish question" during the German occupation of Poland and who managed to survive that nightmare.

American anthropologist Liisa Malkki, studying Hutu refugees in Tanzania, observed that in the face of large international humanitarian interventions, refugees cease being treated as individuals although each of them has a unique history, family, and emotions. They become instead a mass of people deprived of historical context who represent the universal figure of the refugee. According to Malkki, this phenomenon leads us to perceive refugees as mute victims and not as historical actors.[11] To some degree, this observation can also be applied to the survivors of the Holocaust. The reduction of the Jews living in Radom to traumatized victims might suggest passivity, and that would contradict the reality that emerges from the sources. Following the example of British historian Nicholas Stargardt, I do not construct my work around the category of trauma. I am more interested in the actions undertaken by the survivors of the Holocaust and their own interpretations of reality.[12]

In order to obtain the perspective of Holocaust survivors and to restore to them their own voice, a historian would naturally turn to personal documents (i.e., diaries or letters) produced by these people in the early postwar period. Such sources often allow for a view from within and thus facilitate a closer and more empathetic perspective. However, diaries and letters written immediately after World War II by the Jews who returned to Radom proved virtually nonexistent in the archival collections in Poland and elsewhere. Survivors who returned to the city were preoccupied with piecing back their lives from fragments—assuring themselves and their relatives (if they had any) of safety and securing their daily existence, searching for family members and information about their fates, getting back their property. Writing diaries and keeping letters was definitely not a priority for most of them. Furthermore, the vast majority of these people were ordinary men and women. A shoemaker or a seamstress, even when living in more peaceful times, hardly ever leaves any account about his or her life. The archival collection of the District Jewish Committee in Radom is thus of great value precisely because it offers insights into the life of the community and of individual survivors whose histories might otherwise remain untold.

Historical sources pertaining to the immediate postwar in Poland are often very fragmented. In addition, most of the people whose fates I wished to learn had left Radom and emigrated from Poland. They had settled in various parts of the world, often changing their country of residence and languages more than once. Therefore, documents that shed light on survivors' lives in Radom are scattered in multiple locations, including Canada, Israel, and the United States. On a few occasions, I was granted access to family documents still in private collections. Additional information about the return of Jews and their lives in the postwar city is provided by interviews recorded in oral history databases such as the Visual History Archive of the USC Shoah Foundation and the Fortunoff Video Archive for Holocaust Testimonies. Although I conducted my research more than six decades after the end of World War II, I was able to supplement the interviews available in the databases by conducting some thirty-five formal interviews, together with informal conversations—the majority of them with Jewish survivors, but a handful also with non-Jewish Poles. For obvious reasons, I was able to meet only those who were very young in the 1940s. Conversations with them facilitated my reading of the archival sources and were therefore very valuable, even though I rarely quote the interviewees. My Radom pedigree often served as an ice-breaker while interviewing former Radomers. Many of them had positive feelings toward the city of their youth even though most of them had left Radom many decades before a young Polish researcher appeared on their doorstep.

The history of Jews in Poland after the Holocaust—as opposed to the Holocaust itself—has been and to a certain degree continues to be located on the periphery of the main currents of scholarly interest. True, with the end of the Polish People's Republic, the attention of researchers began to be drawn more powerfully to the country's history after World War II, aided by the opening of archives and access to documents that were classified until that time. However, many historians studying this period have focused above all on political history and the history of the anticommunist underground. At the same time, the intense changes to which Polish society was subjected in the last decade of the twentieth century meant that many social scientists rarely looked to the period right after the war.

Furthermore, Poland still has a very complicated relationship with its past, and in particular with the Holocaust and the involvement of Poles in dispossessing and killing their Jewish compatriots. Nevertheless, there are scholars who have made inroads into tackling such difficult topics in Polish-Jewish history as anti-Semitism, violence during and after the war, and the restitution of Jewish property. The first scholarly work that touched upon these issues was *A Social Analysis of Postwar Polish Jewry*, written by sociologist Irena Hurwic-Nowakowska and based on extensive research of survivors living in Poland.[13] It earned a doctorate for its author at the University of Warsaw in 1950 but had little impact on developing the field, as it was not published until decades later. The landmark studies by Jan Tomasz Gross of anti-Jewish violence including *Neighbors: The Destruction of the Jewish Community in Jedwabne, Poland* and *Fear: Anti-Semitism in Poland after Auschwitz;* and the work of other scholars, including, prominently, David Engel and Joanna Tokarska-Bakir, not only initiated broad academic discussions and increased scholarly interest in the history of Jews in postwar Poland but also shaped the field in powerful ways.[14] Since then, a narrative of violence and emigration has dominated the historiography of the early post-Holocaust period in Poland. However, by focusing primarily on Polish anti-Semitism and violence—seen as factors pushing Jews out of Poland—most of the contemporary scholarship tends to pay little attention to the lived experience of survivors other than viewing them as passive victims fleeing racial hatred and violence.[15] Thus, the existing literature on the aftermath of the Holocaust in Poland paradoxically sheds little light on the everyday lives of individual survivors and their communities.

In her recent comparative study *Beyond Violence: Jewish Survivors in Poland and Slovakia, 1944–1948,* Anna Cichopek-Gajraj argues that in order to more fully understand survivors' experiences, one needs to look "beyond violence."[16] I extend Cichopek-Gajraj's argument even further by applying it to a case study of Jewish survivors who returned to the city of Radom. Using all available sources pertaining to this one location, I pursue an in-depth study of the everyday life of survivors and their interactions with the state and with non-Jewish citizens, as well as of Jewish individual and collective agency as manifested in the attempts to recover property and rebuild the community. Three topics turned out to be key for understanding the situation and experiences of the survivors: first, the violence people encountered immediately after the war, the meaning of that violence, and the impact it had on the Jewish community; second, the communal life of the Jews and their adaptive strategies as well as the dominant moods inside the community; and third, attempts at regaining property, which was one of the few kinds of contact many Jews had with Polish state institutions.

During the war and immediately afterward, non-Jewish Poles filled the empty spaces that had been left by the annihilated Jews. That emptiness and the intensive process of filling it were the backdrop for the return of the few survivors of the Holocaust to their hometowns throughout Poland. These people came back to an entirely different reality than the one they had known.

1
THE CITY

IN 1931, KIELCE PROVINCE, which at that time included the city of Radom, had a population of nearly three million people, over two-thirds of whom lived in the countryside. However, among the slightly more than 300,000 people who declared their mother tongue to be Yiddish or Hebrew, almost 78 percent were city inhabitants.[1] Radom was one of the larger urban centers in the province. According to the 1931 census, the city had 78,000 inhabitants. At the end of 1938, not quite a year before the outbreak of World War II, the number of people living in Radom had risen to 90,000.[2] About one-third were Jews.[3] They lived in various parts of Radom, but their religious and political life was concentrated in the center, where the Jewish district was located.[4] The majority of local Jews used Yiddish for the most part and maintained ties with Jewish tradition and religion. There was also a group of assimilated Jews in the city, but it was relatively small.[5]

As a large industrial center in the second half of the 1930s, Radom was included in the administrative sphere of the Central Industrial District. The most important plant in the city was the arms factory, which had been in existence since the mid-1920s. In addition to Mauser carbines and Nagant revolvers, the highly regarded semiautomatic VIS pistols and bicycles specially adapted for the military were produced there. During the 1930s, other factories produced carriages and chaises, bentwood furniture, gas masks, agricultural implements, shoes and saddlery, and cigarettes. There were numerous tanneries and foundries as well as many small manufacturing plants. Right before World War II broke out, an Ericsson telephone plant and a shoe factory belonging to the Polish shoe firm Bata S.A. in Kraków started up in Radom.[6] The latter's weekly production was 2,000 pairs of army boots and 5,000 pairs of workers' boots.[7]

Despite the existence in the city of several large factories, the majority of plants located in the city of Radom were small and barely modern. According to historian Sebastian Piątkowski, in the mid-1930s almost one-half of the inhabitants of the city who were actively employed worked in manufacturing. Most enterprises participated in the leather-and-shoemaking industry. The number of tannery workshops located in the city before World War II was as high as forty. The majority of them belonged to Jews.[8]

In the interwar period, a significant part of the Jewish population also participated in two other important sectors of the Radom economy—handicrafts and trade. Handicrafts were based primarily in small, one-person workshops. We have specific information about the percentage of participation of Jews in Radom handicrafts only from the years 1926–1929, but even from that fragmentary information it is possible to deduce that Jews represented a majority of the Radom craftsmen. Their traditional trades included cap making, leather stitching, shoemaking, tailoring, and also hairdressing, carpentry, and locksmith work. According to the data, only in metalsmithing were more Christians engaged than Jews, but only by one craftsman. By contrast, in Radom only Jews were engaged in making caps and hats.[9] As Piątkowski points out, "Jews dominated in both the wholesale and the retail trade. Probably around 60–70 per cent of the warehouses and shops belonged to them"[10] (see Figure 1.1).

Very few Jews occupied clerical positions in Radom, but they were represented in large numbers among professional occupations. In both these areas, Radom was not an exception in prewar Poland. Among the sixty-four physicians and dentists practicing in the city in 1932, people of Jewish origin constituted almost one-half (twenty-nine individuals). There were fewer Jews among the attorneys, five among the twenty-nine representatives of the Radom bar practicing in the city at the beginning of the 1930s. The Jewish intelligentsia in Radom were not numerous, but considering their high social capital, they played a crucial role not only in the life of the Jewish community but also of the entire city.[11]

Figure 1.1 Farmers market on Wałowa Street in the heart of the Jewish neighborhood before the war. In the spring of 1941, the street became a main artery of the large Radom ghetto. Courtesy Chris Webb.

As in other cities in interwar Poland, in Radom the most important Jewish institution was the Jewish religious community. As Jolanta Żyndul emphasizes, "The Jewish community in Poland never fulfilled an exclusively religious function; it always was occupied with a range of matters that were loosely connected with exercising their religious faith."[12] In the period immediately preceding World War II, the Radom Jewish community underwent a financial crisis. Exceptionally divisive internal conflicts in the community that arose from rivalry for power between the Orthodox and Zionist parties were certainly of no help in overcoming the crisis.[13] Before World War II, the Jewish community in Radom supported a synagogue and *beit midrash* (a house of study of the Torah and Talmud) located in the center of the Jewish district. It also administered a cemetery on the outskirts of the city and the Orthodox Hospital, which had two departments: surgical and internal medicine.[14]

Throughout almost the entire interwar period, the majority in the Radom City Council was held by socialists grouped around the Polish Socialist Party (Polska Partia Socjalistyczna, PPS).[15] The Jewish groups also had representation. Holding seats in the council were socialists (the all-Jewish Workers' Union Bund in Poland and Poale Zion Left), Zionists (various factions of the Zionist Organization in Poland), and Orthodox Jews (Agudath Israel, the so-called Aguda). Each of these groups collaborated with non-Jewish political factions. Throughout most of the interwar period, municipal politics were shaped by the Polish Socialist Party and the Jewish socialist groups allied with it. In opposition to their policies, an informal collaboration of Zionists and the Polish right arose. Orthodox Jews, in turn, supported the Sanacja camp, which had its origins in Józef Piłsudski's political supporters.[16]

Several demands put forward by council members representing Jewish groupings indicate that a large group of Jews in the city maintained a strong cultural distinctness. They used Yiddish mainly or exclusively, and lived in partial or even complete isolation from the community of Polish Christians residing in Radom. In 1927, the Jewish members of the council emphasized the need to make Yiddish the second official language in the city. Poale Zion Left advocated for the publication of city announcements in Yiddish, while the Bund called for the introduction of Yiddish in government offices. Representatives of both groups were equally in agreement on the necessity of educating children in the Yiddish language. Other demands focused on poverty, homelessness, and the lack of access to health care—problems with which many city inhabitants had to cope, not only in Radom but also in other cities of the Second Republic.[17]

One should certainly not infer from the presence of Jews among the city authorities that equal power was the rule in Radom. Demands formulated by the Jewish councilors from the socialist groups who collaborated with the ruling Polish Socialist Party testify to the existing inequalities between Christian and Jewish citizens of the city. In 1927, the Jewish councilors demanded among other things "that Jews be accepted to work in communal institutions" and "consideration of Jews in the allocation of apartments," making it possible for "the Jewish population to make use of city-provided social welfare services."[18] There is much to indicate that the Radom municipal council, perhaps seeking to save its resources, handed over responsibility for the care of the city's poor and sick Jewish citizens to the Jewish community.[19] Whatever the intentions of the city authorities may have been, as a result of their actions, the inhabitants of Radom who required help—Jews and non-Jews—were treated differently depending on their ethnicity. The councilors of the Jewish groups also put forward demands for proportional employment of Jewish workers on public works.[20] Not only was this problem not resolved, it only intensified in the following decade. In May 1938 the Radom weekly, *Trybuna,* a nonparty paper about municipal issues and the city's Jewish inhabitants, announced the following:

> A delegation of Jewish councilors intervened with Mayor [Józef] Grzecznarowski in the matter of hiring unemployed Jews on public works. The delegation argued that in the current season only 8 Jews were hired for city works projects among 500 laborers, despite the fact that the number of jobless Jews is continually growing because of the economic boycott.[21] That year, city authorities hired the smallest number of unemployed Jews over the past fifteen years. The delegation also interceded with the branch office of the Labor Fund [the institution responsible for fighting unemployment]. They asserted that the municipal authorities had not issued work requests for any of the Jews who were registered by the Fund as unemployed.[22]

As in other Polish cities, in Radom during the interwar period, there was a constantly deepening division between Jewish and Christian citizens. Certainly, economic crisis, mutual prejudices, and the growth of nationalist and anti-Semitic moods among the Christian population of the city all influenced the situation. Right-wing circles spread anti-Jewish propaganda within Radom, where both local and nationally distributed anti-Semitic press was available. In October 1937, *Trybuna* reported: "A group of teenagers distributed the periodical *Falanga,* devoted to the struggle with the Jews, on Żeromski Street [Radom's main street] on Sunday. The method of advertising this paper borders on inciting the mood of a pogrom, however. The distributors sang pogrom-style songs on the street and in the park, using offensive words in relation to Jews."[23]

Physical attacks on Jews also occurred in the city. Fights after soccer matches arising not only from sport rivalry but also from nationalist tensions were a frequent occurrence. The most serious incident took place on May 6, 1931, and is sometimes characterized as a pogrom. As in other parts of Poland, the largest number of attacks on Jews in the interwar period in Radom took place in the mid-1930s, and the majority of the perpetrators of anti-Semitic acts were never held responsible.[24]

Anti-Jewish moods were also revealed in the fight against Jews on the economic front. This activity sometimes was manifested in the devastation of Jewish shops through right-wing gangs, but much more often it relied on the distribution of flyers by activists or sympathizers of the National Party and the National-Radical Camp (Obóz Narodowo-Radykalny, ONR).[25] People were incited to boycott Jewish enterprises, and Christian residents of the city who made purchases in Jewish-owned shops were condemned. At times, activists would attach cards with the words "This swine shops in a Jew's store!" onto customers' backs.[26] Photographs of Poles making purchases in Jewish shops appeared in two papers, *Pod Pręgierz* and *Pod Kropidło*.[27] In the autumn of 1937, *Trybuna* reported that owners of rival "Christian" firms were behind the effort to stigmatize those who ignored the boycott:

> We have expressed the assumption in these pages more than once that the paper *Pod Pręgierz*, acting in concert with Endek [National Democratic] photo reporters, is an agency of city merchants.
>
> Our assumptions turned out to be true.
>
> In the last issue of that rag, dedicated exclusively to the boycott and struggle with Jews under the slogan *"Long live the Polish Army without Jews,"* we find advertisements of the following firms: W. Podstolski, Bazar Polski-Migałło, Antoni Szczepańczyk, Nowość tannery, Dom Handlowy-Miecznikowska [Miecznikowska Department Store], Edward Suchański, Maria Prokopowicz, St. Wancerz, Stanisław Schwarz, cukiernia [confectionary] M. Iwanowski, Stefan Kamasa, Ziętara, Stefan Wałowicz, Stefan Majewski (fuel), Kowalik (shoes), "Zdrój" (mineral water)—altogether over 40 advertisements.
>
> Next to them *Pod Pręgierz* places another 20 photographs of those who buy from Jews as the *only necessary payment* for the expensive advertisements. At last, it is no longer a secret which merchants in Radom are financing the boycott of Jewish trade.[28]

The call for a boycott was linked to an attempt to drive Jewish enterprises out of the market. In September 1937, the daily paper *ABC: Nowiny*

Codzienne [ABC: Daily News Items], published in Warsaw and connected to nationalist circles, carried a short report under a title that left nothing to doubt: "Take the tannery trade away from the Jews. Jewish tanneries in Radom are a hell for Polish workers." The anonymous author began the text with a subjective description of conditions in the city:

> I ride from the train station in Radom by droshky. The driver, like all owners of Polish droshkies, has a yellow metal band on his cap with the inscription: "Christian droshky." These inscriptions were a revolution. The Jewish droshky drivers, in despair, appealed to the county governor about removing the bands. They were met with unpleasantness: the county governor said, "Make your own cap bands, but in another color." Obviously, they did not. So, it is possible to recognize them at once from a distance, and on Saturdays they are the "Shabbos goys"—Poles who drove Jewish droshkies. And the fate of Polish droshky drivers improved. Until then there were as many of them as there were Jews: 70. Now, Jews are declining.
>
> But things are not going so well for Poles everywhere in Radom.
>
> The saddest part of Radom is the tannery industry, entirely controlled by Jews. As much as we observe progress in other fields—Polish shops are increasing, the inhabitants of Radom are starting to seriously boycott Jewish firms, a Polish Union is forming at present—still, in the tannery industry it is getting worse and worse.[29]

The piece ends with a summons: "It is high time to finally liquidate Jewish tanneries in Radom and give them back into Polish hands."[30]

As elsewhere in Poland, in Radom the process of creating various "Christian" organizations, which by definition excluded Jewish members, was an attempt at eliminating Jews from economic and public life. *Trybuna* reported in October on the provincial authorities' approval of a statute of the Association of Christian Real Property Owners; it differed from the association that had been active in the city since 1925 and had brought both Christian and Jewish members together. Such actions had as their goal breaking up existing organizations in which membership did not depend on ethnicity or religious affiliation.[31] Sebastian Piątkowski points out: "The Jewish press, already in 1936, was paying attention to the elimination of Jews from organizations and associations in which they acted together with Poles (the Work Fund, the Maritime and Colonial League, the Aerial and Anti-gas Defense League). . . . In 1939, the local branch of the Union of Noncommissioned Reserve Officers, to which two Jews belonged, and also the Union of Foresters, adopted a resolution instituting an 'Aryan' paragraph, i.e., denial of membership to individuals of the Jewish nationality."[32]

The Jews who lived in the city undertook efforts to oppose the boycott and their exclusion from public life, and protested against anti-Semitic speeches. Flyers were printed in Polish and Yiddish encouraging people to shop in Jewish stores, and lectures condemning anti-Semitism were organized. Activists from the PPS also joined the action.[33] After pogroms in nearby Przytyk in 1936 and a year later in Brześć nad Bugiem, the Radom Jewish community joined all-Poland strikes in protest against these events and the atmosphere that made them possible.[34]

Polish Christian individuals taking part in active anti-Jewish agitation, on picket lines outside Jewish shops, and in beatings were definitely a minority. In the minority, too, were the non-Jewish inhabitants of Radom who not only did not support the nationalist slogans proclaimed by the right but also continued sincere friendships with Jews. Most people probably adopted a posture of passive dislike while holding a politically or religiously motivated anti-Jewish attitude, but at the same time maintained correct neighborly and professional contacts with Jews. Here, one must agree with the view expressed by Marcin Kula: "Setting aside the case of the program of genocide accepted by the nation, I consider as most essential for characterizing inter-group relations not the extreme, but the average, behaviors. In the case of Poland they confirm . . . the distance between the Polish-Christian and Polish-Jewish communities and the relatively widespread dislike that arose against its background . . ."[35]

The distance between the two communities inhabiting Radom in the interwar period widened. Ben-Zion Gold, who was raised in the Orthodox family of a Radom merchant and city councilor, described in his memoir how Jews perceived it:

> Even our garments were different: religious Jews wore long black capotes and black flat hats with a short visor, whereas Poles dressed in European style. As religious Jews, we conceded that Poland belonged

to "them" and that we were in exile, waiting for God to redeem us. We were a nation "sojourning," living in Poland only temporarily. But being "strangers" in a country where our ancestors had lived for centuries produced complex feelings about ourselves and about Poles. Relations between Poles and religious Jews were burdened by prejudices on both sides. Just as our self-image was shaped by our religious tradition, so was our view of Poles. We were the descendants of Jacob, who, according to tradition, studied Torah and lived by its commandments. Poles, on the other hand, were the descendants of Esau, with all of the vile characteristics that our tradition ascribed to him: a depraved being, a murderer, a rapist, and an inveterate enemy of Jacob. This image of Esau, which developed two thousand years ago in reaction to the oppressive domination of the Romans, was transferred onto Christians who persecuted Jews. However, in our day-to-day contact with Poles these prejudices lay dormant until they were activated by anti-Semitic behavior.[36]

The divide between Christian and Jewish residents of Radom further deepened during the German occupation, which began in the city on September 8, 1939.[37] Before the Germans arrived, representatives of the local administration, government office workers, and police had left Radom. The majority headed east. Among those who fled were also private individuals, including Jews. After the Red Army invaded eastern territories of Poland on September 17, 1939, under a secret provision in the Molotov-Ribbentrop pact, some of these refugees returned to their native towns now occupied by Germans.[38] Others, of their own volition or forced to do so, remained in the territories administered by the Soviet Union. Many of them did not survive until 1945; others returned to Poland only after the war as repatriated citizens. Men dominated among the civilian escapees, as it was commonly believed that women and children faced no threat from the German army. The people of Poland, like those of other countries, drew on their experiences of World War I for their perceptions about what the new war would look like. The majority of them did not foresee that it would be an entirely different conflict.

After a short period of military administration, in October 1939 Radom found itself within the borders of the so-called General Government

(Generalgouvernement), the administrative unit established by Berlin under which most of central Poland was ruled (commonly known in Poland as Generalne Gubernatorstwo, Generalna Gubernia or simply GG).[39] This territory included around one-fourth of the Second Republic; about 35 percent of the prewar population of Poland lived in it.[40] Radom became the capital of one of the four districts of the GG (five, beginning in August 1941).[41] The heavily industrialized region remained an important industrial center during the German occupation. According to Wehrmacht data from 1940, five of the eight important arms factories in the General Government were situated in the Radom district.[42] In the city itself was an arms factory managed during the German occupation by Steyr-Daimler-Puch, a private Austrian firm. The largest shoe factory in the General Government was also located in the city—"Bata" Schuh und Lederwerke A. G. Zweigfabrik in Radom. (Before September 1939 the factory had belonged to the Polish shoe firm Bata S.A. in Kraków.)[43] Around 2,000 workers produced military and civilian footwear intended for the Germans.[44] The industrial firms active in the city were operated in conformity with the policy of exploitation introduced by the Nazis throughout the General Government. The occupying power intended that the GG be self-sufficient in an economic sense, and industry functioning in its territory was to serve the military needs of the Reich.[45]

Jan Tomasz Gross, in his sociological analysis of Polish society during World War II, states that there were four fundamental aims of the German occupation of Poland and all were dictated by racial ideology. First, the GG served as a "place of banishment" for individuals and groups considered undesirable in the Third Reich. Second, the aim of the occupation was to carry out the extermination of a population recognized by the Nazis as racially impure. Third, the occupation was to make possible the renewed Germanization of groups and individuals in whom the Nazis found "Germanic blood." Fourth, it was planned that all other people who remained alive were to be transformed into slave laborers for the Germans, which in practice often meant extermination through labor. These aims were realized with differing intensity depending on the time and region.[46] Radom was no exception to the German aims; in this industrial city economic exploitation rose to first place along with the extermination of Jews, who were almost one-third of its population.

The persecution of Jews began already in the first days after the arrival of the Germans and gradually grew more and more frequent and brutal, also acquiring an organized character. The process was described by Ichiel Leszcz, a prewar Jewish city councilor, in a testimony given immediately after the war:[47]

In the beginning the Wehrmacht entered Radom. The attitude toward Jews was still bearable. They were rounded up from time to time for jobs, ordered to wash a vehicle, to bring something. After the Gestapo arrived, everything changed. On Judgment Day [i.e., Yom Kippur] 1939[48] Gestapo officers entered the synagogues, dragged out Jews wearing tallises [prayer shawls], and brought them to the factory . . . "Arms Manufacturing Plant." They were beaten there, subjected to inhuman exercises, and let go. After that scene, Jews were constantly rounded up. They were humiliated. I, too, was caught by a German who asked me what I did before the war, saying, "You are a Jew, and that's all I need to know." People tried to avoid Germans. They began looting, collecting the most beautiful furniture, objects, beddings, jewelry. The local population immediately began demonstrating its hatred of Jews. Children would run after a Jew and call out, "Jude, Jude."[49]

In the General Government, as in many other parts of German-occupied Europe, the successive stages of the annihilation of Jews were introduced gradually. As Raul Hilberg observed, in many places the Holocaust proceeded according to a set pattern: the definition of the term "Jew" was the beginning; after it came expropriation, then the concentration of Jews in ghettos, and at the end the phase of annihilation relying on mass shootings of victims or deportations to extermination camps.[50] Concerning the course of the Holocaust, here, too, Radom did not differ from the cities of central Poland that became the territory of the GG. In July 1940, the occupation authorities issued a decree defining "Jew" that was binding throughout the General Government. According to Nazi law, a Jew was a person at least three of whose grandparents belonged to the Jewish religious community. If an individual having only two Jewish grandparents was in a marital union with a Jew or belonged to the Jewish community before September 1, 1939 (or enrolled in it after that date), that

Figure 1.2 A man moving into the ghetto assisted by a Polish carter. Courtesy
Łukasz Biedka.

person was also recognized as a Jew. A similar definition applied to
children born after May 31, 1941 from extramarital unions with a Jew.[51]
This definition was based on a racist ideology. The religious or ethnic
self-identification of the people it affected had no meaning. Earlier, starting
in December 1939, all individuals of Jewish descent who were more than
twelve years old and remained in the territory of the GG were ordered to
wear a white armband with a blue Star of David on their right arm (see
Figure 1.2).

The phasing in of the expropriation of Jewish property in Radom also
developed according to a scheme repeated in other localities. The German
administration demanded of the city's Jewish inhabitants both monetary
and material contributions. Jews were gradually deprived of almost all
their personal property, both real property and movable objects, with the
exception of objects of daily use under the condition that they did not have
any particular value.[52] At the same time, the German administration used
Radom Jews as forced labor. Initially, several hundred people were to report for work every day, but that number rose swiftly, and at the end it
included almost everyone.[53] In the spring of 1940, boys and men from

twelve to sixty years old who were physically capable of working were registered. As Sebastian Piątkowski reports: "Several months later, forced labor within the city was carried out daily by six thousand Jews, including six hundred specialists employed in military institutions and German offices."[54] Radom Jews, men and boys, and also women and girls, worked in the numerous forced labor camps in other localities in the Radom district (including Dąbrowa Kozłowska, Jedlnia, Lesiów, and Wolanów) and the Lublin district (among others, in Bełżec,[55] Mircze, and Cieszanów).[56]

By order of the occupation authorities, the creation in November 1939 of a Chief Council of Elders of the Jewish Population of the Radom district, generally referred to as the Judenrat, facilitated the organized exploitation of the Jewish population of the city and district. Headed by industrial entrepreneur Józef Diament, it was an expanded administrative apparatus, consisting of twenty-four members to whom several hundred employees reported.[57] Fundamentally, the Judenrat fulfilled two functions. On the one hand, it was obliged to execute the German authorities' regulations concerning Jews, including the collection of contributions, and fulfillment of labor force quotas and, later, quotas of people designated for deportation. On the other hand, it was the institution organizing the community life of the Jews. Unlike elsewhere in the General Government, the Radom Judenrat supervised not only the Jews in the city itself but also Jewish communities in surrounding localities.[58]

An important step on the road to the annihilation of the Radom Jews was the concentration of the population in two closed districts. On April 3, 1941, the Radom county governor, Hans Kujath, announced the creation in the city of two zones to be vacated by non-Jewish inhabitants during the following week, and in their place, no later than April 12, Jews who until then were living in parts of the city outside the designated areas were to move in. That is how the "closed residential districts for Jews in Radom"—the Radom ghettos—came into being.[59] The so-called large ghetto enclosed the part of the city center that before the war had been inhabited primarily by the Jewish population (see Figure 1.3). The Radom synagogue and ritual bath were located there. The center of the large ghetto was Wałowa Street. Unlike the Warsaw and Kraków ghettos, the ghetto in the center of Radom was not separated from the "Aryan" side by a wall; it was a demarcated area of dense development. The other closed

Figure 1.3 Main entrance to the large ghetto in Radom. On the right, an officer of the Polish "Blue" Police managing the traffic. Courtesy Łukasz Biedka.

district—the small ghetto—was created in the outskirts, in a poor, working-class part of the city called Glinice. How it was determined in which closed district—in the city center or Glinice—the Jewish inhabitants of Radom wound up is not clear. With regard to the two closed Radom districts, the term "ghetto compound" is sometimes used, which seems apt in that both districts were subordinate to the same Judenrat. However, contact between the large and the small ghetto in Radom was difficult and tightly controlled by the Germans.

Along with the order to reside in the ghettos, the Jews in Radom were forbidden to use the city's main streets and to leave the closed districts without special passes. At the end of September 1941, in both Radom ghettos nearly 26,000 registered people had barely 4,000 apartments (6,500 residential rooms) at their disposition. Jews from surrounding localities were also resettled in these closed districts, among them escapees from other cities and individuals expelled from the Polish territories that had been incorporated into the Reich.[60] In the first half of 1942, around 33,000 people lived in the small and large ghettos together. The conditions of life there gradually worsened. There were not enough apartments. Crowded conditions prevailed. Hunger and diseases (primarily, typhus) spread. Many people lived in extreme poverty (see Figure 1.4). Repres-

Figure 1.4 Open-air market on Wałowa Street in the ghetto. Radom, between April 1941 and August 1942. Courtesy Łukasz Biedka.

sive measures by the occupiers intensified. Initially, they had affected mainly representatives of the intelligentsia and individuals capable of playing a leadership role in organizing a resistance movement against Nazi policies, but in time they applied to larger and larger groups of the population. Between April 1941 and August 1942, around 700 individuals were arrested. The largest number of arrests took place in April 1942 and were part of an operation carried out throughout the GG and aimed at representatives of the intelligentsia and individuals suspected of communist activity. Many Radom Jews were taken into custody then, among them the chairman of the Radom Judenrat, Józef Diament. His place was taken by a laryngologist and prewar political and social activist, Ludwik Fastman.[61]

Two extremely brutal liquidation actions in August 1942 put an end to the existence of the Radom ghetto. They were the first deportation of Jews to the extermination camps carried out in the Radom district of the GG under Operation Reinhard—a mass annihilation of the Jewish population in the GG. In the territory of Radom and the entire Radom district, the operation was overseen by then-fifty-two-year-old deputy commander of the SS and police for the Radom district, Wilhelm Joseph

Blum.[62] On the night of August 4, 1942, an SS division aided by the Polish "Blue" Police (a collaborationist auxiliary formation in the GG, composed of Poles and subordinate to the German Ordnungspolizei, Order Police) carried out a deportation action in the small ghetto in Glinice.[63] A selection was made on the spot. Eight hundred men and nineteen women capable of working were transferred to the large ghetto.[64] The remaining 8,000 inhabitants of the small ghetto were driven to the train station and loaded into cattle cars. A second group designated for deportation, consisting of around 2,000 individuals, was brought to the train from the large ghetto in the city center. It is likely that the men directing the action badly overestimated the number of individuals subject to deportation from Glinice, and therefore people from the second closed district were added to the transport. Some of them certainly died during the transport or perished during escape attempts. Those who made it to the train's destination were murdered in the extermination camp at Treblinka. During the first deportation of Jews from Radom, around 100 to 150 individuals perished in the city itself; they were mainly children and older persons shot to death in the small ghetto and on the way to the railway station.[65]

Two weeks later, the liquidation action in the large Radom ghetto was carried out. At that time, around 25,000 people were living there. The deportation of the Jews from Radom began on the evening of Sunday, August 16, 1942, and lasted two nights.[66] The action was carried out similarly to the deportation of the ghetto in Glinice but was even more brutal. The ghetto was surrounded by a detachment of Polish Blue Police, while German forces assisted by Ukrainians from auxiliary formations and by the Jewish police carried out roundups in the ghetto. At least twice, large groups of people were herded across the city to the railway station. During the liquidation of the large ghetto in Radom, about 18,000 to 20,000 Jews were deported to the extermination camp at Treblinka. It is difficult to determine precisely the number of individuals murdered in the city itself during the action. There were at least 800 to 1,000 such victims. Among them were patients of two hospitals belonging to the ghetto and many individuals killed in their own homes, as well as in the streets when they were being driven to the railway station.[67] In the freight cars into which the inhabitants of the ghetto were crammed, there was such a crush that people were dying even before the train left Radom or during the journey. At a stop at the railway station in Siedlce, about one hundred bodies were removed from the transport.[68] The people who survived the trip perished in gas chambers shortly after arrival.

After the majority of the inhabitants of both Radom ghettos were deported, about 3,000 individuals remained who worked in the SS workshops on the territory of the vestigial ghetto created in a part of the former large ghetto, now transformed into a forced labor camp for Jews on Szwarlikowska Street.[69] Around 2,000 prisoners from the camp on Szkolna Street, employed in the Radom arms factory, made up the second group of Jews in the city. On November 8, 1943, the camp on Szwarlikowska Street was liquidated and the prisoners transported to the Szkolna Street camp.[70] In January 1944, the SS took over supervision of the Szkolna Street camp from the Wehrmacht; it became a subcamp of the Lublin concentration camp (known colloquially as Majdanek).[71] In connection with the Red Army's offensive, on July 26, 1944, the German authorities ordered the closing of the factory and evacuation of the camp. The 2,867 prisoners in it were led out from Radom ninety kilometers on foot to the town of Tomaszów Mazowiecki. From there they were transported by train to Auschwitz-Birkenau. After the transport's arrival at the camp on August 6, 1944, the 450 women in the train were detained on the spot and a selection was conducted among the men. About a hundred were immediately murdered, while those the Germans considered fit for labor were loaded into the freight cars again and taken to an SS-run labor camp in Vaihingen near Stuttgart.[72]

There are many testimonies describing the sequential stages of the annihilation of the Radom Jews and documenting individual crimes. The testimonies of Polish railroad workers employed at the station in Radom during the war seem particularly important. These were the Christian Poles who witnessed the deportation from a very close distance. In 1947, several railroad workers gave testimony during the trial of Wilhelm Joseph Blum, the liquidator of the Radom ghetto:

Witness Władysław Czerniacki, railroad worker, age 51, son of Michał and Ludwika . . . Polish, Roman Catholic . . . residence: Radom . . . testified: "I saw how during the liquidation of the Ghetto the Jews were beaten and driven out. They were driven into freight cars that were fenced in with barbed wire and sprinkled with chloric lime, 80 to 180 individuals jammed into a single car in which only 40 individuals could fit. It was forbidden to give them water in that situation because doing so was punishable by death."

Witness Bolesław Kazimierski, age 52, son of Antoni and Rozalia, residence: Radom . . . railway worker . . . Polish, Roman Catholic . . . testified: "One day, ordered by my German superior at the time of the liquidation of the Ghetto I stayed on after work. Then fifty freight cars arrived, we wired the windows, and [we] reinforced the doors with screws from the opposite side. After completion of these jobs the cars were moved to a different place, floodlights were set up, and then after 23:00 lights came on where the Ghetto was. Uniformed police were walking from the direction of the station, SS-men stood beside the sealed cars on one side, one of them ordered that a board be place up to the car, 140 people went into the first car, on one side the car was surrounded by SS-men wearing black berets, [and] they were beating the Jews with rubber truncheons. If someone stumbled, he fell down as a corpse; after the car was filled up the screws were tightened. Some of the cars were sprinkled with lime; a few were clean. I remember this fact, that smoke was escaping from one of the sealed cars, it was difficult to unscrew the doors, [and] the interior was already just corpses."

Witness Władysław Bielawski, age 50, son of Jan and Maria, residence: Radom . . . KPK worker [sic; it should say PKP—an acronym for Polish State Railways] . . . Roman Catholic, Polish . . . testified: "In the summer of 1942 my German superior informed me that I would be employed after work. Then 48 freight cars arrived, maybe even more, and we were told to tighten screws on the car doors. Then Jews were brought and loaded into the cars. I recall that during the loading Jews were beaten and shot in the back of the head. In one car, after it was opened, it was confirmed that no one remained alive."

Witness Stanisław Badowski, son of Wincenty, age 31, residence: Radom . . . traffic controller, railroad worker . . . Polish, religion:

Roman Catholic . . . testified: "In the summer of 1942, working at the railroad station in Radom, I received a dispatch about preparing freight cars from Skarżysko. I was on duty that day and at 7:30 I received an order from an inspector to check if the train was ready to be dispatched, [so] I went outside and saw the loading of Jews into the cars. They were horribly beaten during this, if someone fell off the plank he was not allowed to go in a second time, they finished him off on the spot, and the next people went in. After the loading an order arrived to pull the cars from the work tracks to the station tracks, and next the trains were pushed out in the direction of Dęblin. Those cars came from Skarżysko, already wired shut and fitted with screws on the city side. I saw in one of the cars, which was loaded with Jews, that when the door was closed an arm that hadn't fit inside the car was crushed. The arm was cut off and hung there in the shirt. From 140 to 180 people were loaded into the car then. In the second transport, on the other hand, on the siding in Marywil, they loaded from 250 to 280 in a single car. Children were thrown onto the heads of the people who were standing in the cars."[73]

The Polish railroad workers who gave these testimonies were as close to the Holocaust as possible. At the same time, they were not prisoners; they were not confined to barracks—they lived in the city and moved around in it relatively freely. Certainly, after work they maintained contact with their families or friends.

The testimonies of the railroad workers and the fact that columns of Jews destined for the death transports were driven through the "Aryan" part of the city, and that many individuals were murdered along the route to the station, prove that the non-Jewish inhabitants of Radom must have known about the cruel fate of their Jewish fellow citizens. The annihilation of the Radom Jews almost in their entirety played out before the eyes of their non-Jewish neighbors. Without a doubt, this had an influence not only on the stance of Polish Christians toward Polish Jews during the German occupation but after it as well.[74] In 1988, in one of the first articles concerning the views of the Holocaust of Poles as witnesses, the sociologist Antonina Kłoskowska attempted to construct a typology of Polish attitudes. Stressing that the sole quantifiable criterion of an attitude is behavior, Kłoskowska distinguished five types which, in her opinion, can be observed when analyzing the attitude of Poles toward Jews during the occupation: active sympathy (aid), sympathetic passivity, total indifference, unfriendly passivity, and finally, active hostility.[75] According to the author, "Making use of statistical terms, it is possible to accept hypothetically, and only hypothetically, that unfriendly passivity and sympathetic passivity were situated within a range of the most frequent attitudes characteristic of the Polish community in general. It is impossible to estimate the quantitative mutual relation of these two so different attitudes."[76] The results of studies carried out over the past two decades by historians, sociologists, and literary scholars concentrated predominantly (but not only) around the Polish Center for Holocaust Research of the Polish Academy of Sciences' Institute of Philosophy and Sociology suggest that the conclusions formulated by Antonina Kłoskowska might have been too optimistic.[77] In his analysis of the phenomenon of saving Jews for money, Jan Grabowski asserts, "Anti-Jewish feelings did not diminish or disappear over time. Quite to the contrary, everyday scenes of mass murder and the constant barrage of the German propaganda tended to reinforce and strengthen the existing prejudice. The anti-Jewish attitudes were also not limited to the poor or uneducated."[78]

A factor that played an unusually important role in the process of the Holocaust, not only in Radom, was the increasing isolation of the Jews from the non-Jewish Polish population and deepening of the distance between representatives of both these groups. The Nazi racial policies and differentiation of citizens by the law and practice of the German occupying administration found a receptive ground of profound differences between Jews and Polish Christians that already existed before the war, along with layers of aversion and anti-Semitism. During the occupation, a true abyss formed between most of the representatives of the Polish Christian and Jewish populations of Radom. It often made attempts of rescue impossible and led the Jews to their death. Accounts by individuals who broke through that distance testify to the isolation. One of them was Bogdan Kowalski. A postman from western Poland, he had escaped to the GG before a threatened arrest and had been living in Radom since the summer of 1940. There, he befriended a Jewish woman and her family who lived nearby. In his memoir, Kowalski described a seemingly trivial scene from the Radom street at the beginning of the occupation:

Once, I remember, I'm walking down Kelezkrauz Street [actually, Kelles-Krauz] in Radom with a Jewish woman, Pola Blatman, whom I know from way back; she was wearing the "star" [i.e., the armband with the Star of David] and as we got ahead of a German with a woman, he immediately shouted "halt!" and immediately turned to me, where's my armband—I'm not one, I'm a Pole, why should I have an armband—and he in response: so a Pole is walking with a Jewess, and I reply to that in German: "If she's pretty, why not?" I really caught it for those words, but what of it, I was young. Then we walk on, and she says to me, "My God, it's so lovely in the world, and I have to die." I comforted her in my own way, but it was hard to say something to her because she was depressed, because in addition, as we went further, now children were shouting behind us, "A jude climbed onto a stall, the stall began to fall, the jude could only bawl." . . . [79]

Had the encounter with the Polish children taken place a year later, when Kowalski's friend was already hiding on the "Aryan" side, the woman might have paid with her life.

Violence directed against Jews from the German side must have had an influence on the attitudes of the Polish inhabitants of the city toward the Radom Jews. Poles saw it not only during the liquidation actions in the ghetto but already from the very first days of the occupation when it was still assuming less murderous forms of humiliation, of symbolic violence, the cutting off of beards and the beating of those dressed in the traditional garments of religious men. Jan Tomasz Gross writes:

. . . *violence changes the geometry of the space of interpersonal relations.* Violence—at any rate in the framework of Judeo-Christian tradition, although it is perhaps a cultural universal as universal as the incest taboo—obligates people and institutions which are its witnesses to get engaged, and concretely, to oppose it. Which obviously does not mean that everyone adhering to a cultural norm will react in one particular way. Nevertheless, all people who find themselves in an area where violence is being enacted are bound by such an obligation, and in order not to engage must adopt an appropriate decision. In other words, being "nearby," "non-interested," "not-engaged" and so forth in relation to the Holocaust is a posture demanding a justification from which it is necessary to explain oneself, responding to the question (at least in one's own conscience): "Why did you do this?" "Did you do this?"— because not-doing-anything in the face of the Holocaust is also acting.[80]

Nothing suggests that the attitude of the Christian inhabitants of Radom toward their fellow-citizen Jews at the time of the Holocaust stood out in any way from what was going on throughout the entire General Government. The mechanisms of assisting or harming Jews by their Polish neighbors were exactly the same here as throughout German-occupied central Poland. Radom differed from large cities like Warsaw or Kraków in that it was more difficult to hide or "disappear" here for a long time. Therefore, one can speculate that fewer individuals, especially those from Radom itself, survived there on so-called Aryan papers— pretending, that is, to be Polish Christians and moving around freely in the streets. Such a possibility remained open probably only for individuals who did not have earlier ties with Radom. A student of medicine from Lwów, Ada Birecka-Jaworska, née Auerbach, was in such a situation. The young woman, an arrival from far away, whose Polish was flawless and who possessed the real baptismal certificate of a deceased woman, succeeded in keeping her identity secret from everyone, including the father of her child, a Pole she met while looking for work in Radom.[81] In a city like Radom, aside from knowledge of the Polish language and Catholic customs, having contacts on the "Aryan" side and so-called good looks in order to hide "on the surface," it was also necessary to be a stranger, someone from the outside. Max Goldman, a specialist in the leather business, who as Marcin Galas escaped to Radom from the Kraków ghetto with his wife and children, was in a similar situation. He was employed as one of the directors of the Bata factory, where he was the only non-German in such a high position.[82] In the case of Radom citizens born in the city, the risk of recognition on the street and denunciation was too great, and this in itself closed off the possibility of living with "Aryan papers" for an extended time even if one possessed the appropriate material means for doing so, the cultural competence, and contacts. The few Radom Jews who survived on the "Aryan" side in their native city were forced to remain in hiding for almost the entire time. This made them totally dependent on the willingness of non-Jews to help.

In the *Encyclopedia of the Righteous among the Nations,* published by
the Yad Vashem Institute, thirteen individuals are mentioned who were
honored for aiding Jews in Radom.[83] Six of them are members of two families. One of the awarded was Dr. Jerzy Borysowicz, a doctor who ran a
psychiatric hospital in Radom during the war. The Yad Vashem website
lists approximately thirty Righteous who provided aid in Radom.[84] These
numbers should be treated with caution, of course, since not all those who
helped were honored, among other reasons because not all those who were
hidden lived until the end of the war and submitted their stories. However, even taking into consideration the fact that the data included are incomplete, aid for the Jews from the non-Jewish inhabitants of Radom
during the Holocaust was in general a relatively rare phenomenon. During
the occupation, the majority of contacts between Poles and Jews—not only
in Radom but also in other places in German-occupied Poland—were
constrained by circumstances, and their character can be described as
instrumental. Without a doubt, a shared place of work played an essential
role. The factories in which Jews who were brought in from the ghetto,
and later from the camp, worked together with non-Jewish inhabitants of
the city became sites for trade and exchange of information, and sometimes spaces for providing assistance.

Years of war meant the experiences and fates of Jews and Christian
Poles were different, often extremely so. The wedge between the Jewish
inhabitants of Radom (and, broader still, of the General Government) and
their Polish-Christian neighbors was driven not only by the racist laws
and policies of the occupier but also by social processes and phenomena
that arose (or acquired an extreme form) due to the German occupation
but did not develop directly from it. The Jewish experience is expressed
by unimaginable personal suffering and the suffering of one's loved ones,
loss of family and home, of social status and all property, and hunger—
or several years of living in a state of extreme danger caused by it. The
Polish-Christian experience had a more ambivalent character. On the
one hand, the life of non-Jewish Poles under German power also was
marked by death and daily terror, but on the other hand, new possibilities came into being. They opened up precisely in connection with the
German occupation and Holocaust, and some portion of the non-Jewish
inhabitants of the country eagerly profited from the opportunities. The
Polish literary scholar Kazimierz Wyka, in an essay written in 1945,

referred to this as the "passive and automatic entrance of Poles into positions from which the Jews had been driven."[85] The systematic extermination of Jews by the Nazis was used by some Poles to improve their own material and social situation—as occurs wherever the crime of genocide takes place. Non-Jewish Poles, although persecuted by the Nazis, were in a privileged position compared with their Jewish fellow citizens. That position was sometimes used to bring aid to Jews, and sometimes to do them active harm: exploiting, denouncing, blackmailing, and in extreme situations, murdering them. The German occupation broke Polish society into two almost completely disconnected groups: Polish Jews and Christian Poles. The distance that had existed between them before the war became an abyss. Those Polish citizens who survived—Poles and Jews both—entered the new postwar reality with all their wartime baggage.

The Postwar City

On January 16, 1945, detachments of the First Belorussian Front of the Red Army entered Radom. Not much earlier, the last German military units and administration had retreated from the city. Tadeusz Kotarbiński, a prominent professor of philosophy, who had been living in Radom after the collapse of the 1944 Warsaw uprising, described these events in his diary:

21.01.1945
A breakthrough. We won a great fate. The military front rolled through us and we are living, at least those of us here, and Wandzia, and Adaś.[86] Bah, the house where we are living survived; not a single window pane in it fell out. On Monday the 15th, impeded by the roadblocks that they themselves had erected across the road to make enemy attacks more difficult, a detachment of Germans packed Mleczna Street Concrete columns stand there, leaving only a narrow opening in the roadway. Truck after truck right here, tanks, cars, in two columns, horses, men on foot milling in a crowd. They were moving in an orderly fashion, but crowded and fast. [illegible] that march-past ended on the 15th at five in the afternoon [illegible], then began again in a new form [illegible] at seven in the morning. . . . The night from Monday to Tuesday in clothing . . . Booming all around. I thought it was the Germans firing

their cannons [*illegible*]. But it was the explosions of shells falling on
the city.

. . . On Rwańska Street and Constitution Square [*illegible*] the
corpses of several Kalmyks [*illegible*] who served with the Germans . . .
The Russians captured the German commandant of the city and [*illegible*] are holding him in a cage. . . . The city park is open to Poles [*illegible*]. In the morning Adaś goes to buy bread and brings back half a
loaf. . . . [*illegible*] The moderate winter is holding. Today there was
slightly more frost. [*illegible*] The Soviets are pushing forward rapidly.[87]

Jan Jasek, an officer in the prewar State Police in Radom and during
the war a member of the Blue Police, subordinate to the Germans, in
memoirs written after the war noted the atmosphere right before the liberation of the city:

I wasn't in a particular hurry to return to the police station, suspecting
that at any moment there'd be the final flight of the Germans, and
fearing at the same time that the Germans, fleeing, could force the police to escape with them, or even shoot them.

When I got back, already at dusk, I found the police station locked
and I learned that the Germans, at the last minute, had organized a
gathering of all the Polish policemen in the courtyard of 5 Rej Street
where the German police were located.

After receiving this information, I flew out of my house and waited
in hiding for further events.

I found out from observers that already that evening the Germans
had vacated Radom and driven all the Polish police in front of them.

On the night of January 15–16 we sat in the cellars, since the artillery was thundering and shells were flying over our building with a
whistle.

The next day, at dawn, the Soviet Army was already in Radom.

The policemen who had been taken away by the Germans came back
one by one after a couple of days and, as they told it, the Germans were
so thrown off balance that they were no longer interested in them and
it was possible to escape at any opportune moment. Several policemen
did not return, however.[88]

The passage of the front was accompanied by terror. As in other locales, here, too, people were preparing for the worst. No one knew how long the shelling of the city would last and how the invading Red Army would behave. Maria Fołtyn, twenty-one at the time, and her brother lived through the liberation of Radom buried under coal by their mother. The woman most likely was afraid that her daughter's beauty would arouse dangerous interest from the front-line soldiers.[89]

Mieczysław Wośko, a teenager at the time, traversed emptied Radom along with his friends in search of food. In an interview, he recalled that the artillery shelling began toward evening on the day preceding the entry of the Red Army. According to his telling, several hours passed between the flight of the Germans and the entrance into Radom of the Soviet army. During that time, the inhabitants threw themselves into plundering the abandoned German apartments and stores.[90] Tuwia Frydman, a survivor who lived through the city's liberation, writes in his memoir about the looting of property left behind by the Germans: "Meanwhile, the Polish population, emboldened by the general chaos and confusion, threw themselves into looting shops and storehouses. Furious fights erupted; everyone took whatever and as much as they could. Not only adults took part in that looting, but little children did, too, helping their parents. Even very old people didn't sit at home then, but plundered as best they could."[91]

Right after the liberation of Radom, a report arrived at the state-level leadership of the ruling communist party—the Central Committee of the Polish Workers' Party (Komitet Centralny Polskiej Partii Robotniczej, KC PPR). Its author stated: "Part of the population is thoroughly supplied with goods and foodstuffs acquired by looting. The civilian population ransacked and plundered the furnishings of virtually all offices."[92]

Individual patrols of the Red Army were soon followed by the front troops. The military command assumed power in Radom. The problem of the local population looting properties left unattended was by no means limited to the hours preceding Soviet entry to the city, and it took on dimensions that forced the military commandant of Radom county and city, Colonel Ivan Volkov, to issue a special edict a month after liberation:

> On the first days after liberation of the city of Radom by the Red Army much property discarded by the retreating German divisions was plun-

dered by the local population. We are aware of incidents when individual people illegally assumed ownership of automobiles, leather goods, foodstuffs, and so forth. However, they are all war trophies and cannot belong to anyone other than the Red Army. I therefore order the inhabitants of the county and city of Radom to hand in to the Military Headquarters of Radom city (7 Moniuszko Street) or to Community Military Headquarters all illegally held items that previously belonged to the German army, German institutions, or individual people of German extraction. I warn you that individuals who do not obey the present regulation and conceal looted trophies will be brought to justice according to military law.[93]

It seems likely that the above regulation had little impact on the behavior of the city inhabitants.

In the days immediately following liberation, troops were passing through Radom all the time. Mieczysław Wośko remembers the inhabitants rejoicing at the sight of a large column of shoeless German prisoners of war led down the main street of the city and soldiers in Polish uniforms singing the Polish national anthem in front of the city park. Two days after the liberation of Radom, on January 18, 1945, announcements appeared in the city signed by Kazimierz Kiełczewski, the new mayor from the Polish Workers' Party (Polska Partia Robotnicza, PPR). He announced that he had taken office at the behest of the Provisional National Government. He summoned the citizens of the city to "loyal collaboration at normalizing public life," "renewal of work in all fields of community and economic life," and "the immediate cessation of mindless stealing and the destruction of social welfare."[94] Upon assuming civilian authority in Radom, the communists began building their political base in the city. Four days after liberation, the Radom PPR counted barely twelve members; by the middle of May 1945 it had 2,200. The communists brought to life the Municipal National Council (Miejska Rada Narodowa, MRN)—a collective body responsible for implementation of the new government's policies at the local level. The MRN was based on the communist underground structures that existed during the German occupation.[95]

The joy felt by many inhabitants of the city at the end of the German occupation mixed with uncertainty about tomorrow and daily worries.

The approximately 60,000 residents lacked everything.[96] As in other Polish cities at that time, it was difficult to procure food and basic necessities. For the first two days after liberation, Mieczysław Wośko and his entire family ate only potatoes—nothing else could be found.[97] The food situation did not improve significantly in the following weeks and months: ". . . local production and service structures were in no condition to satisfy the immense needs of the population even for goods of prime necessity—food, for example. . . . The continually rising price of food with the concomitant necessity of supplying oneself on the free market was an enormous problem. The supply situation in Radom was still deemed 'catastrophic' in 1946."[98]

In early 1945, acquiring food and other high-demand goods was made more difficult by the exchange of currency carried out in the territories taken by the Red Army. This contributed to a deepening of "the economic chaos, the stopping of cash turnover, and support of profiteering habits."[99] In accord with the January 6, 1945, decree issued by the State National Council (Krajowa Rada Narodowa, KRN) about the deposit and exchange of banknotes of the Bank of Issue in Poland, beginning on January 10 the currency that was in circulation during the German occupation was no longer valid. Until February 28, 1945, every adult citizen who was not an entrepreneur could exchange 500 złotys at the rate of one to one.[100] However, in the Radom region even the new banknotes were in short supply, and acquiring them did not guarantee the possibility of purchasing goods. Under the date January 29, 1945, Tadeusz Kotarbiński wrote in his diary: "Nothing can be purchased because value has been removed from our former money [*illegible*] since January 11, and despite long standing in lines it's practically impossible to get the new money. We already have two five hundred notes, but I can't acquire even a blade of grass for them [*illegible*] because no one [*illegible*] wants or is able to give me change due to the absence of smaller banknotes in circulation. And there's a directive to open all stores immediately."[101]

By the end of 1945, not many more than 500 of the 2,000 shops operating in the city before the war had resumed business, in part because a very large share of the retail trade before September 1, 1939, had been held by Jews, the majority of whom perished during the Holocaust.[102] The difficulties in obtaining food in the territories controlled by the communists, the poorly organized currency exchange, and the wide-spread uncertainty that at times reached the dimensions of a market panic contributed to a dramatic rise in prices. Peasants were less eager to supply the cities with food. If items were traded, it was usually through barter. There was a growing demand for gold and dollars, with a con-comitant rise in the exchange rate.[103] Inflation set in, and the price of goods was still rising many months after liberation. In March 1946, the Municipal Department of Information and Propaganda noted:

> Every Thursday provisioning teams from factories or the Unions or Head Offices [state-owned industrial organizations] drive in to Radom (to the market) and paying no attention to prices, buy up all the goods available. At the same time, groups of "wholesale looters" who have ve-hicles (often official trucks) are also operating—buying foodstuffs for the West [i.e., for the Western Territories]. As a result, prices shoot up by about 20 percent every week. Butter, which used to cost 330–350 złotys, costs around 420–450 złotys today. The most dangerous thing is that these newcomers operate with enormous sums in cash and take everything, often even spoiled goods. . . . There is almost no meat at all in the city, while products from butcher shops have escalated in price by about 30 percent . . . The city community was unpleasantly aston-ished to read notes in *Głos LUDU* [The voice of the people; a daily pub-lished by the KC PPR] about the arrival in Warsaw of a great quantity of flour, 80 percent of it from the Lublin and Kielce areas. In an irony of fate, instead of sending flour to the Kielce region for the population which for four months now has not received bread on their ration cards, flour is still being exported beyond the provincial borders.[104]

Inflation was also increased by the irregular delivery of coal, which did not satisfy demand. In Radom, these difficulties were felt by both industry and household economies. The Municipal Department of Information and Propaganda reported: "The matter of supplying the population with fuel appears most tragic. Coal, insofar as it is available, presently costs 4 złotys per kilo on the open market."[105] The lack of coal and the poor tech-nical condition of the municipal power plant also caused frequent inter-ruptions in the supply of electrical energy that was burdensome for

everyone. The outages led to increased dissatisfaction among the inhabitants of Radom, felt most powerfully on October 30, 1945, when youth
from the Radom schools organized a demonstration. Its main slogans
were "We want to study," "We want light."[106] After the protests, Radom's
mayor issued a ban on appliances that used a great deal of power (heaters,
irons, cookers) during the hours of highest energy demand. Also, apartments were to be illuminated with no higher than fifty-watt bulbs. However, the inhabitants of Radom had to wait several more months for ame-
lioration of the energy situation. The city's supply of electric power was
upgraded only at the beginning of 1946.[107]

Even though the city did not suffer serious damage during the battles,
Radom industry endured significant difficulties immediately after liberation. Preparing for withdrawal, the Germans moved out of Radom the
equipment of many factories, machinery, and stocks of raw materials.[108]
Because of this, half of the 133 plants that existed in the city before the
war could not resume work after liberation.[109] The arms factory, the largest
industrial plant in Radom, presented a lamentable sight:

> In this factory bare walls remained: floors, windows, window frames
> had been torn out one after the other; 90 percent of the fittings on the
> premises were demolished. In nine of the buildings, roofs and upper
> floors were blown off by the explosion of stock-piled explosives in-
> tended to destroy the entire factory. Laboratory and technical equip-
> ment, all machine tools and materials had been taken. At the same time,
> approximately 480 15-ton freight cars and 500 trucks were driven away.
> The entire electricity, water distribution, and heating grid was disman-
> tled. . . . The railroad maintenance shops . . . had been evacuated to
> Germany in 1944. The evacuation was so thorough that not only were
> the machinery and fittings removed, but also the sidetracks and roofs
> on the buildings were torn out.[110]

The destruction of many Radom industrial plants contributed to the
rise of high unemployment in the city, which only intensified with the arrival of repatriated citizens from the east and the economic slowdown at
the turn of 1945–1946. The situation was difficult throughout Kielce
province—from September 1945 to July 1946, the number of registered

unemployed individuals rose as much as 500 percent.[111] Those who found work despite the difficulty often earned so little that their wages did not cover living expenses.[112]

Aside from problems getting work in Radom, it was just as difficult to find an apartment. In 1946 there were on average 2.1 people for every room, while the rate for the country as a whole was 1.7. Considering the relative size of their populations in need of housing, the availability of residential rooms was only slightly better in Radom than in destroyed Warsaw and in Lublin, initially the center of political life. In both of those cities, there were on average 2.2 people for every available room. It was even harder to get a room of one's own in Radom than in Łódź, the largest Polish city in this period.[113] In addition to postwar migrations, the fact that many people had come to the city over the course of the war also had an influence on population density in Radom. A large number of people had flooded into the city from the capital in the autumn of 1944 after the collapse of the Warsaw uprising. Many representatives of the intelligentsia arrived then. Not all of them left the city immediately after liberation. Some of them took part in the rebuilding of municipal institutions, community organizations, and industrial plants: "The city authorities conducted a registration of engineers and technicians living within the city limits. It turned out that Radom had the largest concentration of technical intelligentsia at the time. The majority of those who were registered came from Warsaw and had found themselves in Radom after the collapse of the Warsaw Uprising. In response to the appeal by the authorities, around 600 people pledged participation in the work of teams concerned with industry."[114]

Among the intelligentsia living in Radom right after the war were excellent humanists and scholars from Warsaw University, such as professor Tadeusz Kotarbiński. Film and theater director Andrzej Wajda, who as a youth had also come to Radom during the war and after the liberation studied in one of the high schools there, recalled that the city was living through a period of unusual liveliness at the time.

Only once did Radom become an intellectual center, a cultural center. . . . Immediately after the war. It was the most beautiful period of my life. Who didn't appear there then [or live there]? It was in Radom that Tadeusz Kotarbiński wrote and delivered public lectures on his "Treatise on Good Work" [which was to become one of his most influential books]. Julian Przyboś came, Jerzy Andrzejewski, Jan Parandowski. There were lectures about Polish literature; it was only then that I found out who Tuwim was, Słonimski, Staff, Broniewski. . . . These talks were organized by the city library; I also organized a variety of exhibits there.[115]

Radom's intellectual liveliness did not last long. Individuals who had settled in the city, forced by circumstances during the occupation, gradually returned after liberation to wherever they had come from or moved on to other places. At the end of April 1945, Kotarbiński noted in his diary: "Soon it will be necessary to leave Radom. I could demand to remain here for two more months, teach my course on logic until the end, give exams to those who are interested. . . . Although continually there's one of us leaving the city and departing—Sawicki, Górnicki, Śliwczyński. . . . But what will determine our departure is the visit of Mr. Bieńkowski,[116] Vice Minister of Education, who dropped in by auto the day before yesterday, in the evening. . . . A long conversation over tea. . . . At a meeting of professors and lecturers from Warsaw composed of individuals who are living here a committee was elected from among the assembled professors to [engage with] Warsaw University matters. . . ."[117] Kotarbiński himself left Radom in May 1945 to take up the post of rector of the university being organized in Łódź.

It is not easy to describe unambiguously the emotions accompanying the end of the German occupation. Roman Loth, who was a teenager at the time, described the atmosphere years later in his memoir: "The predominant feeling was excitement and joy, that it's over. But together with that—uncertainty and anxiety. Paradoxically, when the military activity was moving away from us, when it was possible to count on a peace of sorts, we felt at a loss, trusting in a foggy hope, lost in the new world that was looming up from Chaos as in the first days of Creation."[118]

As in other places in Poland, life in Radom, aside from joy at the end of the German occupation and the daily difficulties in acquiring provisions, also had a much darker side. Immediately after the Red Army en-

tered the city, arrests began of individuals suspected of collaboration with
the Nazis; prewar officials and members of Polish underground organizations were also being arrested. Jan Jasek, the former Blue Policeman
who was detained just a few hours after liberation, belonged to the first
group of arrestees:

> January 16, 1945, when the Soviet forces were already in Radom, I went
> into the city in the morning dressed in civilian clothes to buy bread in
> a bakery somewhere. I had gone about 100 meters from the house when
> two Soviet soldiers armed with automatic rifles approached from the
> other direction, and in front of them was a 12- to 14-year-old boy who,
> passing me, turned around to the soldiers, saying, "Oh, that one also
> served in the police." The soldiers stopped me, asking where I work
> and where I live, after which they ordered me to lead them to my apart-
> ment where they checked my papers and then conducted me to 4a
> Moniuszko Street, taking along two other policemen who were my
> neighbors. . . ."[119]

After being held for twenty-four hours in the cellar of the building occupied by the Soviet security police (NKVD) and a brief interrogation,
the men were ordered to return home. Several days later, the NKVD summoned all the policemen and then released them. The situation was repeated in the following days. Jasek then decided to hide at his brother's
home in a small town thirty kilometers from the city. When it turned out
that the trains were not running, he returned to his home. From there,
he was taken by the NKVD on January 29. This time, the officers interrogating him were interested not only in his service in the Blue Police but
also in the political organizations with which Jasek had had contact before the war, during the time when he worked for the State Police. Along
with a large group of people arrested in Radom, Jasek was deported into
the depths of the Soviet Union at the beginning of February.[120] Most likely,
the cause of the arrests and deportation to the east was simply that their
service in the prewar State Police or, during the occupation, in the Blue
Police, had come out into the open. Franciszek Troll, the police lieutenant
and former commander of one of the police stations of the Blue Police in
the city, a man who at the time of the liquidation of the Radom ghetto had

allegedly saved a dozen or more individuals, was among the group of deported policemen.[121]

There were many more stories in Radom like those described in Jasek's
memoirs. Ivan Serov, the official in charge of NKVD work with units of
the First Belorussian Front, conducting activity in the Warsaw and Radom
region in January 1945, informed Lavrenti Beria, the NKVD chief, that
during the dozen or so days of the offensive,

> . . . operational groups and NKVD units active in the zone of the First
> Belorussian Front carried out the following work:
> Arrested in total 2,219 people, including: 63 spies and saboteurs,
> 345 [individuals] from the commanding cadre of the ROA [Russian
> Liberation Army][122] and traitors of the Fatherland, 661 active members
> of underground enemy organizations (the Home Army [Armia Kra-
> jowa, AK], the Peasants' Battalions [Bataliony Chłopskie, BCh], the
> National Armed Forces [Narodowe Siły Zbrojne, NSZ] and others), 60
> [individuals] from the commanding-operational cadre of the police,
> prisons, camps and punitive organs, 16 [individuals] from the execu-
> tive cadre of the prosecutor's office, judges and military tribunals, 57
> mayors and the executive cadre of the organs of power, 9 directors of
> large administrative and economic organizations, 99 [individuals] from
> among the remaining enemy element.[123]

According to the author of the report, the largest ethnic group among
those arrested was Poles—1,562 individuals. As Marcin Zaremba writes,
"The arrests embraced landowners, managers, the administrative and
self-governing apparatus, the forest service, railway workers, teachers, the
clergy. Soviet counterintelligence arrested many Radom judges, attorneys
and administrative employees of the judiciary."[124] Although it is difficult
to find approximate data, it appears that the number of individuals detained in Radom in the first days and weeks after liberation was very high.
"One constantly hears that someone was arrested, held, studied, very
often—let go in the end," Kotarbiński noted in his diary toward the end
of January 1945.[125]

As the front moved farther west, the new authorities' security organs
focused on defeating the opposition and the armed anticommunist under-

ground. Radom and its surroundings were the site of especially intensive actions by partisan groups against the communists. The two largest divisions of the armed underground fighting against the new regime operating in 1945 in the surroundings of Radom were led by Antoni Heda (pseudonym "Szary" [Gray]) and Stefan Bembiński (pseudonyms "Harnaś" and "Sokół" [Chieftain and Falcon]).[126] The anticommunist partisans generally operated outside the city, but sometimes were present in Radom itself. Such situations were described by an official of the Municipal Department of Information and Propaganda in a report from September 1945: "On September 22, 1945, in the evening, thugs from the NSZ got away with checking the identity cards of passersby for an hour and a half on dark side streets in the city center, searching for members of the PPR. . . . Incursions took place in the private apartments of members of the PPR and Security Service [UB]. Beatings were made note of. . . ."[127]

The strength of the armed underground in the region is attested by the fact that the linked divisions of Heda and Bembiński, numbering about 150 individuals, managed to break open the prison in Kielce on the night of August 4–5, 1945.[128] One month later, Bembiński's division briefly took control of the Radom prison and freed the individuals detained in it. Kielce's vice provincial governor, Henryk Urbanowicz, informed the Ministry of Public Administration (Ministerstwo Administracji Publicznej, MAP) about the attack:

On September 9 of the current year [1945], at 21:40, there occurred an attack by a group of people composed of approximately 60 individuals wearing uniforms of the Polish and Soviet Armies, armed with automatic weapons, against the prison and the Second Police Station in Radom. As a result of this criminal action the attackers succeeded in freeing 310 prisoners (among this number many "Volksdeutsche") and in taking control of the above-mentioned Police Station, where they stole guns and many other items belonging to the policemen's equipment. During the shooting 8 individuals (including 5 civilians) were killed. The attackers took the 310 freed prisoners with them.[129]

That detachments of the armed underground operating in Radom and the surrounding vicinity were able to successfully carry out such actions in the centers of cities bears witness to their large numbers, good supply of arms, and strong local support. The relatively large losses on the side of the new authorities also indicates the strength of the anticommunist divisions of the armed underground operating in the region. According to data supplied by the Provincial Office of the Security Service (Wojewódzki Urząd Bezpieczeństwa Publicznego, WUBP) in Kielce, in the second half of 1945 in Kielce province twenty-three officers of the Security Service, fifteen policemen, fourteen Red Army soldiers, and two soldiers of the Polish Army (Wojsko Polskie, WP) perished. Three members of the PPR, two members of the Peoples' Party (Stronnictwo Ludowe, SL), and four state officials lost their lives.[130] At the same time, sixty-three soldiers of the WP, fifteen UB officers, five policemen, and one Red Army soldier were disarmed. Thirty-six attacks were carried out against police stations, headquarters of the Security Service (Urząd Bezpieczeństwa, UB) were attacked twice, and Railroad Security Police (Służba Ochrony Kolei, SOK) stations were attacked eight times. One hundred sixty incidents were characterized as terrorist attacks, which in the language of the documents from the time means that they were recognized as political acts, and their perpetration was ascribed to organizations conducting armed struggle against the communists.[131] These data point to a very violent ongoing conflict in the Radom region, at times resembling actual civil war. Even in Radom itself, there were battles of policemen and UB officers with members of groups that were difficult to identify. In October 1945, the Municipal Headquarters of the Citizens' Militia (Komenda Miejska Milicji Obywatelskiej, KM MO; that is, Municipal Police Headquarters) reported that a patrol from one of the Radom police stations was twice shot at in the course of two days by people whose identity cards they wished to check.[132]

Analyzing these events, it is unusually difficult to distinguish acts of armed political struggle from ordinary criminality. On one hand, the postwar underground often slipped into banditry. On the other hand, right after the war ordinary criminals often pretended to be various army formations, policemen, or UB officers. They wore uniforms and possessed automatic weapons.[133] In addition, in most of the attacks the perpetrators were never caught or even identified. When looking through the statistics of attacks from immediately after the war, one is struck by the huge number of incidents, especially armed robberies, acknowledged by the security authorities as common crimes. Both business offices and the apartments of private individuals were almost always robbed in the presence of their residents and under threat of gunfire. The violence was worst in 1945. In Radom and its surrounding vicinity alone, the number of robberies exceeded well over one hundred. Several dozen murders were also recorded.[134] If one adds to this the fact that many crimes were certainly not reported to the police, a horrifying image emerges. To be sure, as the new authority became established and the intensive actions of its institutions grew progressively stronger, the level of criminality dropped, but in the following years the situation in Radom was also far from ideal. In the period from June to the end of July 1946 alone, five attacks on institutions and six on private apartments took place in the city. There were also two attacks on pedestrians in the streets.[135] The number of attacks carried out in Radom gradually fell, but still in December 1947 as many as ten incidents were recorded.[136] At the same time, fewer and fewer crimes in the city were committed out of political motives. Detection was increasing. At the end of December 1947, the commander of the police in Radom and the chief of the Section of the Criminal-Investigative Service of the police both reported that "the major cause of crime is alcoholism, which is extensively widespread within the city of Radom. With the aim of reducing intoxication, drunks are placed under arrest to sober up, after which they are fined. Criminal reports are filed with the County Governor of the city about addicts and trouble-makers."[137]

The overconsumption of alcohol and the general availability of firearms led to frequent recourse to guns while resolving conflicts and quarrels. According to data from the Provincial Department of Information and Propaganda in Kielce, on the night of New Year's Eve 1945, in Radom alone, "as a result of fights arising from excessive consumption of alcohol and a state of drunkenness, 16 individuals lost their lives, and of those, according to widespread rumors in the city, 9 were shot by officers of the Security Service."[138] High unemployment also played a role, as did the fact that right after liberation the region was full of individuals whom sociologist Stefan Czarnowski, writing about them in 1930s, had called "superfluous people"—demobilized men accustomed to a "military lifestyle," deserters, tramps, the unemployed, speculators.[139]

A separate group of crimes were acts carried out by soldiers or deserters from the Red Army. In the second half of 1945, together with the march of Soviet armies across Kielce province, a wave of sexual violence and other crimes rolled across the region. The Kielce County governor in his report to the Provincial Authority in Kielce informed them about the unusual brutality of acts committed by Soviet soldiers:[140]

> . . . rapes, robberies and thefts committed by soldiers of the Red Army are a daily and mass phenomenon.
>
> In the community of Niewachlów 7 Soviet soldiers raped a 15-year-old girl, the teacher's servant, who is seriously ill and in a life-threatening condition. In Cedzyna, 5 Soviet soldiers raped a 35-year-old woman who, after the attack, is seriously ill. In Łopuszno, an 80-year-old woman was raped by several Soviet soldiers and died immediately afterward. . . . In Snochowice, Kukulski Stefan, age 24, was killed by Soviet soldiers when he defended his sister, whom the Soviet soldiers wanted to rape. . . .
>
> In Kielce recently, there were a dozen or more incidents of rape carried out in relation to both older women and very young girls; in the act they bit their victims in a bestial way, literally tearing out pieces of their flesh, and even in one case biting through the larynx. Throughout Kielce county, the army is terrorizing the population and destroying its belongings.[141]

According to information from the mayor of Kielce, in the summer of 1945 soldiers of the Red Army raped about thirty women in the city itself. Half of them became infected with venereal diseases.[142] It is unlikely that Kielce, eighty kilometers from Radom, was an exception along the route of the Red Army's march. As Marcin Zaremba writes,

> One was most frequently exposed to attacks at railway stations and in their vicinity, and in trains, from which it happened that Soviet soldiers, even while a train was moving, would throw out passengers who were unwilling to hand over their baggage. On July 28, 1945, in a train on the Radom-Skarżysko line, they raped a woman, slit her throat, and then threw her onto the tracks. Before she died, the woman managed

to indicate who the perpetrators were. Also toward the end of July, drunken Soviet soldiers threw out of a moving train (between the Jedlnia Letnisko and Radom stations) a Polish railway worker and his wife. The man's hands and one leg were cut off by the wheels; the woman died on the spot.[143]

When attempts at stopping the Russian marauders were undertaken by the police, the Security Service, the Polish Army, and even other Soviet soldiers, they often ended in shooting. One such incident occurred at the train station in Radom on September 26, 1945:

> . . . at 9–10 o'clock, when passenger train No. 717 from Dęblin en route to Skarżysko arrived at the Radom station, Soviet soldiers were traveling in the center cars; three of them, in a drunken state, began robbing Polish civilian passengers, taking their packages, money, and things.
>
> On the platform, SOK [Railroad Security Police] supervisor Rajski and second lieutenant Pryciak from the Municipal Office of the Security Service [MUBP] in Radom, having heard the cries of the passengers, entered the car with the goal of intervening. They brought out onto the platform a Soviet soldier who was holding in his hand a watch taken from a passenger and who hadn't yet managed to conceal it. As they steered him in the direction of a security patrol, other Red Army soldiers, seeing this, leaped out of the cars with the intention of physically freeing their colleague and surrounded Rajski and second lieutenant Pryciak. At this time a Russian patrol from the garrison, led by the garrison captain, came up to them. The commander approached the struggling Russian soldier and wanted to take the revolver out of his hand; then the Russian soldiers jumped on the captain and started to choke him. The captain began shooting and threw a hand grenade at the soldiers, as a result of which one soldier was wounded. Shots rained onto the soldiers from the patrol's side, after which they set about disarming them. One killed and four wounded Soviet soldiers were counted.[144]

As they rode through the region, the Red Army men felt complete impunity and did not recognize the authority of Polish institutions responsible for maintaining order. Their disarming and even murdering of Polish policemen (that is, members of the Citizens' Militia; Milicja Obywatelska, MO) bears witness to this.[145] In a confrontation with well-armed groups of drunken and aggressive Soviet soldiers, the Polish services often remained powerless. No one was able to restrain the Red Army from plundering and destroying the territory across which it marched. It is in this context that a letter sent in May 1946 to the Department of Agricultural Education by the director of a school in Zwoleń, thirty kilometers from Radom, must be read: "In connection with the outset of the passing of Soviet armed forces and the driving of cattle, the Managing Board of the Agricultural High School in Zwoleń respectfully requests the issuance of appropriate regulations insuring school property in the event of probable losses."[146]

The Return of Jews

In the postwar reality, joy at the end of German occupation mingled with despair over scarce provisions, unemployment, and the destruction of industry. Fear increased as bloody conflict between the new authorities and the anticommunist underground intensified, common crime exploded, and deserters and Soviet soldiers roamed the country. In this tense environment, gradually Jews started to reappear. Sometimes, the first disillusionment hit them even before they reached their hometowns. Henryk R., nineteen years old at the time and a native of Radom, encountered this as he and a friend were returning to Poland from Germany. When they reached the registration point for returnees in the Poznań train station, a young woman working there asked Henryk for his Jewish first name. He replied "Heniek" (colloquial form of "Henryk") but that he did not understand why she was asking about his Jewish name. Her answer was, "Because you are a mangy Jew!" From Poznań the men, riding atop a train that was packed to the limit, made it to Łódź, where they decided to go their separate ways. Henryk arrived in Radom alone. At the station, two boys recognized him and directed him to the Jewish Committee, which ran lodgings. There, Henryk learned that none of his family members had yet returned to the city. Along Żeromski Street, on which Jews had not been permitted during the occupation, he could walk on the sidewalk like a man again. He set off to see what his parents' apartment looked like and who lived there now. As he stood in front of his family home, one of the tenants opened a window. Henryk involuntarily shouted, "Papa!" A stranger's voice informed him that he was not his father and ordered him to get lost. Henryk recalled that he was flooded with pain. He was nineteen years old and completely alone. A few years before, his family and friends were living in Radom; now, at most, he met a few neighbors there.[147]

There are no exact data concerning the number of Polish Jews who survived the Holocaust, and the estimates of historians vary widely. There is no doubt that the greatest number survived in the territory of the USSR—most likely more than 300,000.[148] Among the survivors in the Soviet Union were also escapees from central Poland who primarily managed to flee east at the beginning of the war, and Polish citizens living in the eastern parts of the Polish Republic that were occupied by the Red Army in September 1939. The overwhelming majority of individuals from both groups survived due to evacuation into the heart of the USSR or, often, due to imprisonment in labor camps there. Estimates of the number of individuals who survived the Holocaust in the Polish lands also vary. These figures range from 30,000 survivors within the borders of Poland from 1945 to 80,000 or even 120,000 survivors in the entire expanse of the republic that was occupied by the Germans.[149] According to Barbara Engelking and Jan Grabowski, the most common estimate is that between 40,000 and 50,000 Polish Jews survived in the occupied territory.[150] These people had had very different experiences. Some had lived to see liberation in German camps. Others held out in hiding: in attics, cellars, barns, or rented apartments or behind an adopted non-Jewish identity. Far fewer individuals survived by hiding in forest bunkers or fighting in partisan units. Overall, the number of survivors—those who managed to flee the occupied territory or lived through the genocide on the occupied soil—amounted to approximately 10 percent of the population of Polish Jews before September 1939.[151] Locally, the percent of Jews who survived the Holocaust may have been much lower. The means by which those individuals survived also differed widely and was influenced by a variety of circumstances, including social and natural environments, as well as different policies implemented regionally by the German administration.[152]

Regardless of the area, however, one can state with confidence that the surviving Jews were by no means a representative group of the prewar Jewish community.

In the first days after liberation across the country, lone individuals began to appear, then groups of people who had survived the Holocaust in hiding or with "Aryan" papers. These people had had to overcome the least geographical distance. In a second wave, freed prisoners from German concentration and forced labor camps arrived. Only later did individuals arrive who had survived in the USSR, the largest wave between February and August 1946 as the result of the so-called repatriation from the Soviet Union, which was organized by agreement between the new Polish authorities and Moscow. As a result of the "repatriation" of the prewar Polish citizens from the USSR, over 100,000 Jews appeared in postwar Poland.[153] The actual number of people who arrived from the USSR exceeded the official "repatriation" statistics since, as historian Natalia Aleksiun writes, "an unknown number of Polish Jews crossed the new eastern border of Poland either by passing the organized repatriation or prior to its start."[154]

The majority of survivors who emerged from hiding or arrived in Poland immediately after liberation found themselves in an unusually difficult position. First of all, most of them were entirely alone, without family or friends. They were carrying the burden of often extremely traumatic experiences. Many of them were seriously undernourished and sick, incapable of taking up work. Bereft of all property, they had no means to support themselves. As a group the survivors were in a singular situation in Polish society, where they found themselves in a social vacuum. Jewish self-help committees that arose spontaneously in various cities in Poland almost immediately after liberation gradually filled that void. As early as November 1944, the Central Committee of Jews in Poland (Centralny Komitet Żydów w Polsce, CKŻP) was created. At first, it was active in Lublin, the political center at the time, but at the beginning of 1945 it was transferred to Warsaw. It was a central institution to which locally active communities of survivors reported and that was supposed to take care of securing the daily existence of all Jews staying in Poland and to represent their interests before state authorities.[155] Until the communists took total control of the CKŻP in

1949, Jews enjoyed partial autonomy in postwar Poland.[156] Provincial, district, and city Jewish committees scattered across the country were subordinate to the CKŻP. Those institutions represented the communities of survivors in Poland. Although in a legal sense the Jewish Committees existing after the war were not a continuation of the prewar Jewish denominational communities, in practice they were often perceived as such by the Jews themselves and by government representatives. Sometimes that is obvious even in the language of official correspondence, when departments addressed their letters to the Jewish community—the Jewish *gmina*—and in fact sent them to the Jewish Committees.[157] As in many other cities, in Radom, right after liberation the Jews staying in the city organized a committee that reported to the CKŻP. The District Jewish Committee in Radom was an institution with central significance for survivors returning to the city and surrounding localities. Not only did it represent the Radom Jews before the authorities, it also ensured basic assistance for survivors in the city.

The introduction of registries of survivors was among the activities undertaken by the CKŻP, so its data offer numbers concerning Polish Jews present within Poland's new borders in the first postwar years. At the beginning of May 1945, there were close to 43,000 survivors in Poland, among them around 4,700 individuals in Kielce province. Until the end of 1945, the number of Jews staying in Poland almost doubled. The number of survivors staying in the Kielce region likewise rose initially. In August 1945, it reached almost 5,100 individuals, but in the second half of the year the number fell to around 1,000. Most likely, this change was caused by the numerous acts of violence in the region to which Jews fell victim in the late summer and autumn of 1945. The largest number of Jews in postwar Poland, around 244,000, was recorded toward the end of the "repatriation" action from the USSR, at the beginning of the summer of 1946, before the Kielce pogrom.[158]

Some of the survivors who appeared in Polish cities and towns immediately after liberation actually were on their way to other places. Traveling around the country was very difficult. There was total chaos on the railways; initially, in many areas trains were not running at all or ran on an irregular schedule. As a rule, only the army and representatives of the authorities and organizations traveled by cars or trucks. Private individuals, who often had far to travel, were compelled to hitch rides on trucks and peasant wagons, to cover large distances on foot, or to camp out in train stations, waiting for a train on no schedule at all. This forced people to stop in places they had not planned on stopping in, and sometimes to travel by way of localities that otherwise would have been completely out of their way. Writing about Polish society immediately after the war, Marcin Zaremba compares it to magma.[159] As he notes:

> Poland became the arena of a great wandering of peoples: Poles, Germans, Ukrainians, Jews, and representatives of other nations. The returning began immediately after the end of fighting. Concentration camp prisoners, POWs, and forced labor workers returned to the country. Eight hundred thousand Poles returned from Germany before August 1945. Until the end of 1947 a total of around 1,600,000 were repatriated. Poles also came from England, Hungary, Italy and other countries where the war had flung them. Around 285,000 Poles and Jews deported to Siberia and Kazakhstan in 1940 decided to return. The greatest wave, around 200,000 individuals, flowed into the country in the spring of 1946. It is worth remembering that the first half of that year was also the time of the most intensive phase of the expulsion of the German population from Poland.
>
> The end of the war began not only the return of many millions of people to their homes, but also a new stage of resettlements dictated by the political decisions of the victors.[160]

Many Polish citizens, as forced laborers, in camps, or in hiding, had lived with the hope of returning home. It might have seemed that the end of the German occupation had created the possibility of realizing those very natural yearnings. Police officer Jan Jasek, who had been arrested by the NKVD and deported to a work camp in the Urals, described the moment in early November 1947 when he arrived in Radom from the USSR together with a group of Poles who, like him, had been deported to the Soviet Union: "From the train station in Radom we all headed straight to the N.P.M. [Holy Virgin Mary] Church[161] to pray for a while and then we went our separate ways to our homes." Jasek related the emotions and uncertainty accompanying his return home:

I was not certain if I would find my family in the old place; I even doubted in general that I would find them in Radom, if they would all be alive. Approaching my house, however, (and it was already dark), I observed with joy the same flowers and curtains in my windows; I was certain then that my family was where it should be; the next moment was to be my most joyful or most despairing—and so, would I find them all alive and healthy, or not. And it was in truth the most joyous moment in my life when thanks be to God I found everyone from my closest family alive and well.[162]

Virtually none of the thousands of Polish Jews returning after the war to their native places could be so happy. True, many of them, especially in the first weeks after liberation, lived with the hope that someone among their loved ones had survived, but in general they were met with great disappointment. Even if returning Jews, just like the Polish policeman, recognized their curtains in the windows of their family home, most often those curtains, like the entire apartment, had a new owner. The recollections of Jan Jasek returning to his city from a Soviet labor camp depict the stark difference between the experiences of the postwar return of Polish Christians and Polish Jews. Whereas the former in general returned in both a physical and a social sense to the places they had been forced to abandon, the latter most often returned to a social void, even if they recognized the walls and streets of their native city.

A feeling of profound isolation accompanied the survivors. Lea (Łaja) Pines, a forty-year-old teacher, informed the Emigration Department of the CKŻP in June 1946, "At present I am living in Radom and I am completely alone, because during the war I lost everyone. I support myself by giving French lessons to Christian children, since there are no Jewish children in our city."[163] Many survivors fully comprehended the enormity of their loss only after their return or, to be more precise, at the time of their attempt to return home.[164] Aleksander Wajselfisz, a medic in the Polish Army, visited Radom in the late spring of 1945. He wanted to see his native city. There he met Józef, the custodian of the apartment house in which he had lived before the war. According to Wajselfisz, the custodian asked him, "Where are you staying, sir?" When the man replied that he was stopping at the Hotel Europejski, Józef said, "You won't stay there.

It's not safe there. You'll stay with me, sir, in the custodian's quarters."
However, Wajselfisz wanted first to visit the grave of his father, who had
died before the war. When he and the custodian reached the Radom
Jewish cemetery located at the outskirts of the city, the medic had a
shock—on the land where there once was a cemetery, cows were now
grazing. He recalled that his first reaction was that he wanted to shoot
the cows; he didn't know what to do with himself. That same day, he left
Radom and returned to his military unit. Wajselfisz was in Radom three
more times. He returned twice to meet his surviving relatives. The last
time, he came to the city in 1948 to sell his family's real property. Each of
these three visits lasted barely a day. He never spent the night in Radom.[165]

Disillusionment deepened even more as Jews emerging from hiding
often met with aversion on the part of the Polish inhabitants of the city.
Tuwia Frydman and his friend were not the only ones to experience this.
In the last days before liberation, they found shelter in an abandoned
building in the center of Radom, where they awaited the appearance of
the Russians. Both went out into the street to look at detachments of the
Red Army entering the city. In his memoir, written in a third-person re-
portage style, Frydman reported, "Rotsztajn [Frydman's friend] straight-
ened up and went closer. Seeing his Semitic looks, a woman called out,
'O! Look! Even a little Jew has appeared . . . !' Rotsztajn wasn't the least
offended, but on the contrary responded with pride, 'I am not a little
Jew . . . I am a Jew . . . !'"[166]

Both men wandered around the streets in hopes that there were other
surviving Jews, but they did not meet anyone they knew. Frydman wrote
that "many Poles looked back at them as if having caught sight of some
phantom or wild beasts which had escaped from a circus cage."[167]
Henryk R. also remembers the unfavorable attitude, full of disbelief, of
Poles he encountered. During an interview, he said that when he returned
to Radom, people looked at him as if he were an animal that had escaped
from the zoo.[168] Survivors in other localities also had similar experiences
in the first days after liberation. Marceli Najder, a pharmacist from Galicia,
wrote in his diary, "O, Freedom—only he is able to value You, who has
lost You. . . . We are drunk with freedom. We go out into the streets, they
look at us as if we're freaks—for two years no 'nasty little Jews' seen (may
the devil take them—not the nasty Jews, but the ones who are staring)."[169] It

was possible to hear hostile remarks about Jews everywhere. Mietek
Pachter, a survivor from the Warsaw ghetto, related conversations of individuals standing in a line for food in Łódź:

> These conversations began on the topic of food rations, what are they
> giving today, or on the theme of children, but they ended about Jews.
> I was standing in line and eavesdropping on these conversations which
> wounded my heart. The speakers did not know that I'm a Jew, so they
> spoke openly about everything. Most often I heard the following con-
> versations: "To think that so many of them remained, where did that
> garbage hide? They beat them, gassed them, held them in closed
> ghettos, and there are still so many left . . . ," "You know, neighbor,
> each of them gets ten thousand złotys per person from their committee,
> and if one of them has a whelp of a child, he gets fifty thousand . . . ,"
> "A person thought we'd finally be done with them, but look at it, they're
> proliferating across our Poland . . . ," "And they've given them category
> one cards [that is, better food rations] to boot. Even the Germans
> couldn't put an end to them."[170]

Pachter also described his reaction to what he heard: "My soul bled,
because the unhealed wound reopened, and it was very painful."[171]

The moment when the war ended was also a moment of extreme loneliness and feelings of guilt for many survivors when they realized the enormity of their loss. Maria Orwid describes such an experience. Then fifteen years old, she was in Kraków at the end of the war: "I stood in the
surrounding crowd completely alone and semi-conscious. Then I fell into
terrible despair. I began to cry. I sobbed for a long time and could not
calm down. Thoughts were rattling around in my head: 'Too late! What
am I doing here when I don't have my daddy or my whole beloved family!
Why do I have to go on living?'"[172]

Mietek Pachter, too, recalled the bitterness accompanying the moment
of exit from the liberated Nazi camp: "Here is where our tragedy began.
Here we came to our senses—who are we, whom do we have, where will
we go? No one is waiting for us; we won't find any of the people we hold
dear."[173] A feeling of great estrangement and experience of dislike on the
part of non-Jewish inhabitants became for many Holocaust survivors

markers of their return to their native city. Not only in Radom, but in other places in Poland, they met everywhere a "greeting" that Jan Tomasz Gross sketched out: "'Moszek—or Abramek, Josiek, Szlomek, Szewek, how did it come about—so you are alive?'—that as a rule is what the sentence of greeting sounded like at the first meeting of acquaintances from school or neighbors. Except that in the tone of voice there was no sympathy to hear, rather surprise, and sometimes also a hidden threat."[174]

A few weeks after liberation, at least 281 Jews were in Radom.[175] That is the number of individuals who reported to the Jewish Committee as of February 2, 1945. The majority were young or middle-aged, which was typical in the Polish lands previously occupied by the Germans. Older individuals and children had less chance of surviving the Holocaust.[176] Among the survivors registered in Radom immediately after the entrance into the city of the First Belorussian Front were almost twice as many men as women. Barely one out of three originally came from Radom. These people were in the city or its nearest surroundings toward the end of war, and the arrival of the Red Army caught them there. Almost 300 individuals is a relatively large number if one considers that many camps were not yet liberated and communication in the territories occupied by the Red Army left much to be desired. Some of these survivors surely had escaped when in the summer of 1944 the Germans liquidated most of their labor camps in the Radom district.[177] While the majority of inmates were shipped to other concentration and labor camps, the evacuation of prisoners brought opportunities to escape. Emil Karpp was one of the people who ran away from the camp at Szkolna Street: "In June 1944 during the last deportation I escaped. I took shelter in an isolated house. Later, I hid for a time at the home of a Polish man I knew, after that at the home of a Polish woman acquaintance."[178] The future head of the Jewish Committee in Radom, Mojżesz Bojm, was also an escapee. With three colleagues, he escaped from a labor camp in Bliżyn, some fifty kilometers from Radom: "Unobserved, we walked away during work, broke through a wall and escaped to the forest. Because the front was close, we did not encounter any partisans. We wandered around in the forest until the arrival of the Red Army, i.e., until January 18, 1945."[179] Already in February 1945, both Karpp and Bojm were in Radom and had provided their testimonies about their wartime experiences.

Right after liberation, Jews appeared who had lived through the occupation in the city, on the "Aryan" side. After the entry of the Red Army,
Aron Hendel (who would be a victim of one of the postwar murders) and
his three brothers emerged from their paid-for hiding place in the home
of a Polish married couple.[180] Individuals who had been hiding in localities
in the vicinity of Radom also arrived in the city. Among these survivors
were Icek Heider and Zelik Karpman. The two men were related to each
other and had lived through the last months with three other family members in a bunker dug out beneath the barn of Polish peasants in Biejków,
a village about forty kilometers from Radom.[181]

In the first months after liberation, the number of Jews arriving in
Radom grew continually (see Figure 1.5). In mid-February there were 490
individuals, and not quite one month later, 596.[182] It is difficult to determine the exact number of survivors actually residing in the city. Their
numbers most likely never exceeded several hundred individuals. Among
the cities in Kielce province, only in Częstochowa were there more Jews,
but it was the only location in the whole district where the forced labor
camps had not been evacuated and the prisoners remained in the camps

Figure 1.5 Survivors visit the Radom Jewish cemetery in late summer or autumn
of 1945. Courtesy Barbara Fundowicz-Towarek.

until their liberation.[183] The largest number of survivors were in Radom in the summer of 1945. Lucjan Dobroszycki, basing his estimate on CKŻP data, gives the number as 959 individuals in Radom in the first half of August 1945.[184] Mass departures of survivors from the city occurred in late summer 1945, connected with the escalation of violence against Radom Jews. At the end of October 1946, only 111 survivors were living in Radom, of whom barely a dozen had been there since winter 1945.[185] Almost all Jews living in Radom in the autumn of 1946 had some earlier ties with the city—they were born there or lived there before the war. By the end of the 1940s, the majority of survivors had left Radom; some no doubt merged into the non-Jewish community and broke off contact with members of the Jewish community. According to Security Service data, at the beginning of 1950 only thirty Jews lived in Radom.[186]

Of the survivors who stayed in Radom, most were artisans. Many fewer representatives of the intelligentsia and workers returned. Most likely, this was because artisans as a professional group were less mobile in comparison with other professions such as physicians, lawyers, and laborers. Artisans were powerfully connected with the concrete, physical space of the city—with their workshops and the tools inside them. It was significantly more difficult for them to start life anew in a strange place.[187]

Among the Radom survivors, it is necessary to distinguish people who registered with the Jewish Committee from those who actually lived in the city in the postwar period. Until December 1949, the Jewish Committee registered at least 1,756 individuals in the city, but most of them never lived in Radom after the war.[188] They came to the city to take care of matters or to search for surviving relatives or friends, and while there they reported to the Committee. Especially in the first period, registration was a way of leaving a trace for individuals seeking contact with survivors. The majority of those who registered left immediately—for Łódź or Warsaw or the Western Territories, or they emigrated from Poland. Others who lived in the city never registered with the Committee. Some of them maintained contact with the community of survivors in Radom or with its individual members. Others, though, continued their life as non-Jews, which they had begun during the occupation, and never established contact with their prewar Jewish identity; for obvious reasons, it is impossible to estimate the scale of this phenomenon.[189]

The survivors' joy at liberation and hopes of finding their loved ones and rebuilding in the city their lives that had been interrupted by the war collided with a wall of human indifference, dislike, and often enmity. Disillusionment quickly gave way to fear. The reactions Jewish survivors met with from their Polish neighbors were not limited to unpleasant looks and verbal taunts. At times they also encountered a much more dangerous manifestation in acts of violence. In provincial Polish cities, the atmosphere of enmity and violence had a fundamental impact on the shape of the local communities of survivors.

2

VIOLENCE

WRITING ABOUT ANTI-JEWISH violence in the postwar context presents one with particular difficulties. The broader issue of anti-Jewish violence has been studied many times in recent years, yet it remains highly politicized. One must be aware of at least two serious risks in analyzing its post-Holocaust occurrence. The first is extreme reductionism, the attempt to ascribe to Jews' ethnic origins every act of violence to which they fell victim.[1] But after all, Jews, like Poles, Americans, or Chinese, can be attacked, battered, or murdered for many reasons, not only because of their ethnicity. The second danger is acceptance of the opposite position—the explanation of anti-Jewish violence solely as postwar, ordinary criminality. Such an approach is disqualified by the simple finding that for some attackers the ethnicity of their victims did matter fundamentally. In the case of many attacks on Jews carried out immediately after the war in Poland, the Jewishness of the victims was unquestionably the chief, if not the sole, motive for the crime.

Another obstacle in researching postwar violence against survivors is that after seventy years, documents and testimonies that would allow the indisputable characterization of these events often are not available. An additional difficulty arises from the fact that already in the 1940s, these crimes and their perpetrators' motives have been subjected to interpretation by the victims, their loved ones, or members of their community. Thus, we are condemned today to wading through source material in which the separation of the dry description of events from subjective opinions can be exceptionally difficult. This is especially so because for many postwar crimes there is very limited information about both those motivated by anti-Semitism and ordinary crimes.

Robberies

The plague of robberies in Poland in the first years after the end of the German occupation did not pass by Radom. In reports about crimes sent by the Radom police (Citizens' Militia; Milicja Obywatelska, MO) commander to his superiors in Kielce, the prevalence of robberies committed in the city jumps out.[2] They can be divided into two types. The first are robberies in the offices of various institutions. In October 1945 alone, attacks in Radom were carried out against the mill, the Railway Workers' Cooperative, the freight office of the Polish State Railways, a leather warehouse, and a tannery; twice against the State Alcohol Monopoly store; and against the offices of two commercial enterprises.[3] On average, the bandits' loot from each of these crimes came to less than 100,000 złotys in cash. These were large sums for private individuals, but not staggeringly high. An exception was the attack on the Elgold tannery on October 18, 1945, when thirty attackers stole skins with a combined value of approximately two million złotys.[4] The large number of assailants involved and the unusually high value of the stolen goods suggest that one of the armed underground groups operating in the territory of Radom county was behind this robbery. Attacks on institutions connected with the leather industry were especially prevalent in Radom. The several dozen tanneries in the city presented a compelling target for attackers, considering the high price of skins and the demand for them. In a time of postwar inflation, skins and other expensive objects had a higher value than money. The second type of crime common in Radom right after the war was robberies of private individuals. As emerges from the police reports, the average value of the goods taken did not differ significantly from that stolen in attacks on institutions, but aside from cash and objects universally considered valuable—wedding bands, rings, and watches—criminals often stole clothing, bed linens, lengths of fabric, and other items that were in short supply right after the war.

Reports by the Municipal Headquarters of the Citizens' Militia (Komenda Miejska Milicji Obywatelskiej, KM MO) make possible a generic description of a typical robbery of a private individual in Radom in 1945. With very few exceptions, these robberies took the form of an apartment invasion. In the police materials, there is little information about robberies carried out against passersby in the street. These were linked to a greater risk of failure—it was easier for the victims to flee, as accidental witnesses or police patrols might appear. In addition, street robberies were no doubt less remunerative than robberies in a victim's apartment, where not only cash and personal valuables were found but also household goods. In a typical apartment invasion, two to five attackers took part. When there were three or more criminals, one usually stood watch nearby and gave a signal to the rest of the group to withdraw in case danger threatened.

Considering the low crime detection rate, not much can be said about the perpetrators. It is clear from the police reports that they were without exception men, mainly young men. The majority of the robbers did not wear masks. The attackers would often present themselves to their victims as officers of the police or the Security Service (UB): "On October 23, 1945, a robbery was carried out against P[*illegible*] Aleksander in Radom on Górna Street . . . by three unknown individuals, armed, who represented themselves as officers of the UBP [i.e., UB] from Kielce, conducted a search of the home and stole 50,000 złotys and jewelry worth 150,000 złotys."[5] It is unknown whether the individuals who carried out this attack really worked for the Security Service, as it is possible that criminals claimed to work for the service with the aim of more easily overcoming any refusal to carry out their orders. Sometimes the perpetrators maintained that they were members of the Home Army (Armia Krajowa, AK), the main resistance movement during the war. As Franciszek Gaworek, who was attacked on November 13, 1945, testified:

> . . . into my apartment on Podwalna Street . . . three individuals dressed in civilian clothes with a "Vis" handgun, who, after terrorizing the people there, proclaimed that they were AK and were going to search for weapons because apparently members of the Polish Workers Party live here. These individuals went into the room and conducted a

search of the wardrobe and other furniture, flinging everything in them onto the floor.

From a woman's handbag lying on a table they took around 700 złotys. Whereas my wife voluntarily gave them 1,000, and they took 800 from my daughter's bag. In all, they collected around 2,500 złotys. I should mention that the individuals had demanded 10,000 złotys after entering the apartment. Having gathered up the money the perpetrators of the attack fled in an unknown direction.[6]

In the investigation documents, there is no information as to whether Franciszek Gaworek or any other resident was a member of the Polish Workers' Party (Polska Partia Robotnicza, PPR). Such information, had it been correct, most likely would not have been omitted in a report prepared by the investigators. There is also nothing in the files other than the testimonies of the victims that would point to participation of people connected with the underground in the invasion of the apartment on Podwalna Street. This crime was not classified by the police as an attack with a political background. Most likely, it was an ordinary robbery, and its perpetrators, wanting to look more serious, represented themselves as members of an anticommunist partisan group. Taking into account, however, the considerable activity of the armed underground in the vicinity of Radom, it cannot be excluded that some attacks on private apartments really did have a more political underlying basis. The actual connection of these groups with the AK remains a separate question. As Jan Tomasz Gross points out, in the years 1944–1956, there existed at least fifty-two armed detachments using AK in their name, and the term was "commonly used long after the dissolution of the AK to refer to any kind of anticommunist formation. Similarly, 'boys from the forest,' [partisans] who continued some form of underground activism on their own, often referred to themselves as AK".[7]

Some attacks were committed by detachments of the underground, but there is also no doubt that impersonation of AK members (as also of MO and UB officers) was a strategy employed by common criminals and relied on to eliminate possible resistance and to terrify victims. In addition, by representing themselves as the armed underground, the bandits could throw investigators off the trail, leading them in a false direction. In

general, however, painstaking covering of one's tracks proved unneces-
sary, since in the immediate aftermath of the war the police often were
unable to pursue perpetrators and conduct investigations carefully and
effectively.

A clear feature of postwar robberies was the attackers' use of firearms
(handguns, as a rule, but submachine guns also might be used). Access
to firearms was universal at the time. People still had them from the war
years or came into possession of them during the Germans' hasty retreat.
Although the new authorities attempted to limit the number of weapons
in private hands, their efforts did not bring the expected results.

On Boxing Day 1945, the Radom police together with the Security Service carried out an action aimed at discovering individuals who possessed weapons illegally:

> . . . at 17:00 all cinemas were surrounded simultaneously and a personal
> search of all individuals was carried out, along with identity checks.
> The result: 4 handguns were confiscated and 9 individuals suspected
> of carrying out attacks on a political basis were detained. From 19:00
> to 24:00 on that day, four flying patrols of 12 people each were sent into
> the streets of Radom city; they checked the identity of male passersby
> and also conducted personal searches of individuals suspected of pos-
> sessing a weapon. The result: several people were detained and 2 hand-
> guns were confiscated.[8]

Although the result of this action was not impressive, just the fact that
the police and the Security Service were frisking casual passersby in
search of weapons testifies to how common it was for unauthorized individuals to carry guns in the city.

Despite the fact that in virtually every attack on private individuals the
perpetrators employed weapons, very rarely, according to the police reports, were victims wounded or killed at the time of the robberies. If they
carried out the attackers' commands, were not defending themselves, and
were not representatives of the communist regime, they suffered no physical harm. In the vast majority of these cases the very threat of using a
gun brought the intended result. In 1945 in Radom, however, there were
at least two attacks during which the victims of the apartment invasion,

who were not affiliated with the authorities and who, without resisting, did exactly as ordered by their attackers and yet they were killed. Both murdered men were Jews.

Robberies That Went Wrong? Ludwik Gutsztadt and Aron Hendel

On the springtime afternoon of June 16, 1945, Ludwik Gutsztadt, the proprietor of a jewelry store in Radom, accompanied by his wife, entered his apartment on the third floor of an apartment house in the city center, on Żeromski Street. An unknown man followed them. He pulled out a revolver and ordered Gutsztadt to hand over the briefcase the jeweler had brought home. The owner gave the briefcase to the attacker, who ordered him to go into the second room. When Gutsztadt turned to go, the man shot him in the back of the head and fled. Nothing happened to Eugenia, Gutsztadt's wife, who was in the same room and was the only eyewitness to the crime, which she recounted to her older son.[9]

Gutsztadt's two sons were out of the house at the time of the attack. Someone approached the elder of them, thirteen-year-old Eli, who was playing in the street, and said, "Go home quickly; they've shot at your father."[10] When the boy reached home, he found a group of gawkers standing in the street. In the courtyard of the apartment house, his unconscious father, his head wrapped in a bloody towel, was being carried into a horse-drawn cab. Gutsztadt was taken to the municipal hospital. He did not regain consciousness and died three days later, on June 19, 1945. Right after the shooting of her husband, Eugenia sent her sons to the Praga district of Warsaw, to the people who had hidden one of the boys during the war. The day after his death, Gutsztadt was buried in the Jewish cemetery in Radom, which had been devastated during the war.[11] There is no information about Gutsztadt's murderer; nothing indicates that the attacker was caught, let alone put on trial. The victim's son maintains that Eugenia Gutsztadt reported the attack to the police.[12] I did not come across any documents, however, from an investigation. It is likely one was never conducted.

It is worth looking closely at who the murdered jeweler was and what he was doing in the city before that tragic June afternoon. Ludwik Gutsztadt

Figure 2.1 Ludwik Gutsztadt during
his service in the Polish Army before
World War II. Date unknown. Courtesy
Eli Gat.

descended from a family of merchants long settled in Radom. Before
September 1939, he managed a jewelry store in the city center. He specialized in the sale of watches, gold, and diamonds. His wife, Eugenia,
came from a wealthy family. Her father was a grain merchant and the
owner of several large properties in the center of Radom. Ludwik and
Eugenia Gutsztadt and their two sons, Eli and Henryk, survived the
Radom ghetto. All four managed to cross over to the "Aryan" side from
the ghetto thanks to help from Józef Dolecki, Ludwik's friend from the
time of their service in the Polish Army[13] (see Figure 2.1).

After escaping from the ghetto, the family split up. Ludwik Gutsztadt
had "good looks"—he was a blond with blue eyes and a pale complexion.
He stayed in Warsaw and in 1944 took part in the Polish uprising there.[14]
His wife and two sons also hid in the capital, in two different places in
Praga, a left-bank district of Warsaw. Already in 1944, immediately after
Praga was taken by the Red Army, his wife left for Lublin with the boys.
Ludwik found them there at the end of January 1945. Soon afterward, all
four returned to Radom. Ludwik's mother and brother also survived.
They, too, came back to their native city. The Gutsztadts returned to using
their real surname. "In Radom, we were so well-known, that there was
no point in remaining on our 'Aryan' papers," the jeweler's son told me

during the course of his interview.[15] Already in the winter of 1945, Gutsztadt again opened a store in the city. He traded watches with Soviet soldiers, and sold rings and small pieces of jewelry.[16] What emerges from his son's account is that the business was developing well, and the family could afford, among other things, to hire private tutors for their sons.

The prospering shop of Ludwik Gutsztadt, a Jew who had only recently returned to the city, must have attracted attention, particularly as the majority of survivors living in Radom not only were in no condition to return to their prewar occupations, they were, for the most part, destitute.[17] Also, many non-Jewish inhabitants of the city were living in poverty, and the presence among them of a prospering Jew certainly aroused envy in many individuals. But if the main aim of the attack on Gutsztadt was robbery, the attacker did not prepare well for it. The jeweler did not walk down the street with a great deal of cash; he had installed a safe in his store. In the briefcase taken from Gutsztadt, most likely there was nothing especially valuable.[18]

It is also unlikely that the death of Gutsztadt was the result of a personal settling of old scores. Nothing suggests that Gutsztadt attempted to get back property lost by him or his relatives during the war or that he had gotten involved in some kind of conflict. There is also no information about his political activism. True, in February 1945 Gutsztadt joined the Jewish Committee created in Radom, but he appeared there as a nonparty individual and filled no administrative role.[19] Although robbery undoubtedly was part of the attack on Gutsztadt, it was not the reason for the jeweler's death. He did not defend himself. He fulfilled the demands of the attacker without resisting. Gutsztadt was shot in cold blood—with a bullet to the back of the head from a close distance. This makes the crime recall an execution more than a fatal shooting of a robbery victim.

Another robbery during which a Jew was killed took place in Radom on November 6, 1945. Two armed men, dressed in civilian clothes, broke into an apartment located in a small apartment house on an out-of-the-way side street, Zacisze. The attackers checked the identity cards of Aron Hendel, who was staying there, and shot him on the spot. The sister-in-law of the murdered man, Anna, also was wounded. The bandits took their time and remained in the apartment for three quarters of an hour, vandalizing it. When the police arrived, they sealed the apartment and secured Aron Hendel's body there. Anna Hendel was taken to the hospital. The perpetrators of the murder were not discovered. That much is known about the crime from a laconic report prepared by the chief of the Investigative Department of the Municipal Headquarters of the MO in Radom.[20] A somewhat more detailed description of the attack was presented three months later by Anna Hendel. Then living in Germany, the woman presented her testimony:

> On November 6, 1945, at 15:30, into the apartment at 8 Zacisze Street where I was living with my family, two attackers in civilian clothing with revolvers in their hands burst in. In the apartment 4 individuals were present: I, my brother-in-law Hendel Aron, 30 years old, and two Christian women we knew. The attackers demanded money from us, assuring us that they will do nothing bad. One stayed with us, and the other searched the apartment. They took all the valuable things from the apartment. The search lasted about 45 minutes. After that much time had passed, a third individual knocked at the door and said something into the ear of one of the attackers, to which he replied, "Fine, in a moment." At the same time, the light went out and until now it has been impossible to determine if that was accidental, or deliberately caused by the attackers.
>
> One of them then led both Polish women out of the apartment, and the other ordered us to go into the second room; he ordered me to pick up my child, then shot at my brother-in-law, hitting him in the temple and producing instantaneous death, and then at me, wounding me in my right hand, since I managed to dodge the bullet, after which he ran out of the apartment. As a result of the wounding, parts of the third and fourth fingers of my right hand had to be amputated.[21]

From the woman's account, it becomes clear that two phases can be distinguished in the attack against the apartment on Zacisze Street. The first would have been the robbery. Two attackers entered the apartment. One watched over the individuals inside, while the second searched for valuable objects. The second stage of the attack was the murder of Aron Hendel and the shooting of his sister-in-law.

The moment of transition between the two phases appears significant. It is then, in Anna Hendel's account, that the reference to a third attacker positioned outside the apartment, no doubt as a lookout, appears. He entered the apartment and discreetly conversed with the bandit who was already inside. It is not clear if the attackers had prepared an action plan previously or if they established it only then. What is certain, however, is that this was the turning point at which the attack in the apartment on Zacisze Street ceased being an ordinary robbery, one of many such in Radom in 1945.

At the point the third man entered, the light went out in the room. As Anna Hendel admitted, it was unknown if the bandits disconnected the power or if a temporary interruption in the supply of electricity occurred, not an unusual problem at the municipal electric plant. Darkness must have reigned in the apartment, since it already gets dark at that time in November. The attackers led the two Christian women, the Hendels' acquaintances, out of the apartment, thus separating the non-Jewish and the Jewish victims. What happened to the two women is not known. It does not appear that any harm befell them. Perhaps the bandits, who became aware that two non-Jewish women were in the apartment, decided it would be safer to remove them from the place.

From the moment the two Polish women and the bandit escorting them left the apartment, the attack on the Zacisze Street apartment resembled the murder of Ludwik Gutsztadt. There was now only one attacker in the apartment, who ordered Aron and his sister-in-law with the child in her arms to go into the other room. Then shots were fired. Aron Hendel was killed on the spot by a bullet to the head, and then Anna Hendel was wounded. Taking into consideration the course of the event and the fact that the attackers clearly were not in a hurry, one can speculate that the murderer may have deliberately let Anna Hendel live. That her injuries were not life threatening—a shot to her right hand—also suggests this. Perhaps, as Anna Hendel suggests in her account, she succeeded in dodging the attacker's bullet. If so, then why did he not shoot again?

The Jewish Press Agency (Żydowska Agencja Prasowa, ŻAP) released information about the attack on the Hendels in a short notice in its bulletin: "On November 6, 1945, unknown perpetrators committed an

attack in Radom on a private apartment on Zawisza [sic] Street. . . .
Citizen Hendler [sic] was murdered by the attackers, one woman was
gravely [sic] wounded."[22] The incorrect street name and changed surname
of the victim can be attributed to carelessness or an error on the part of
the individual preparing the notice, who certainly did not know Radom;
the ŻAP Bulletin was published in Łódź. It is more difficult to explain
where the information in the text about the grave condition of the
wounded woman came from. The news certainly refers to Anna Hendel.
The wounds she sustained, although no doubt painful, were not life-
threatening. Most likely, the ŻAP notice was prepared on the basis of
incomplete information and its author (or informant) assumed that a
shooting in an apartment must be linked to serious injuries.

The robbery during the attack on the Hendels is a separate issue. The
police report mentions the vandalizing of the apartment and the taking
of "several items" from it.[23] Theft is completely absent from the notice
in the ŻAP Bulletin, which confirms that the writer was relying on im-
precise information on the events in Radom. Theft of property during
attacks against Jews decidedly was in ŻAP's field of interest, so it likely
would not have gone unreported. On the same page of the bulletin,
next to the information about the attack against the Hendels, was an
equally brief notice about an attack on an automobile transporting Jews
from Kielce to Siedlce; the murder of one of the women passengers was
mentioned together with robbery.

Considering that the theft during the attack on Zacisze Street is only
touched upon in the police report and not mentioned at all in the ŻAP
notice, Anna Hendel's account develops this thread. According to her,
the exit of the attackers did not mean the end of the robbery. Some of the
items in the apartment were stolen later by police who were summoned
to the scene: "The police conducting the investigation sealed the apartment, first taking advantage of the opportunity to steal many valuable
items of clothing and other things. . . ."[24] From Anna Hendel's testimony,
it appears that the behavior of the policemen left no doubt that the murderers of her brother-in-law would not be captured and would remain un-
punished: "[the police] created difficulties in issuing permission for
burying the corpse. The police wanted to convince us that it was Jews
who committed the murder."[25]

During my archival search, I did not come across a single trace that would allow me to believe an investigation was conducted after the attack on the Hendels. Most likely, nothing at all happened. Although the circumstances suggested a crime motivated by anti-Semitism, and the policemen were obligated by order of the head commander of the MO to meticulously investigate such crimes, it appears this order was seldom adhered to.[26] The theory advanced by the police, that Jews killed Aron Hendel, is unlikely. It may, however, explain why policemen who were not eager to apprehend the perpetrators would propose such a theory. If someone from the victim's circle committed the murder, then the crime would have been a community matter, not a political crime motivated by racial hatred.[27] Presenting the Hendel murder in such a light could serve as justification for minimizing the crime and a reluctance to capture the attackers.

Why, then, and by whose hand did Aron Hendel die? Most likely, no proof exists to make possible a definitive answer. Perhaps Aron Hendel perished only because he was a Jew, and his murderers were Polish nationalists. Even had they not known who was living in the apartment (which is hard to believe), all doubts would have been dispelled after the check of the victims' identity documents. Checking documents during attacks was a quite common practice immediately after the war. It allowed perpetrators to get their bearings, to determine if there were policemen or members of the PPR among those they were attacking. Such practice additionally helped to terrify the victims. In the case of the apartment on Zacisze Street, it also allowed the attackers to determine the ethnicity of the victims. Another possibility is that the death of Aron Hendel was the result of an unfortunate confluence of circumstances. If the electricity shutdown was not planned, then the shocked (and perhaps also inexperienced) attacker may have begun shooting out of fear that the victims were attempting to mount a resistance. It is also possible, however, to find other motives for the murder of Aron Hendel. In order to discover them, it is necessary to look closely at Aron Hendel's past.

Aron Hendel was born in 1909 as the second child of Jakub and Rachela. The Hendel family was religious and moderately wealthy. Aron's father had an iron materials warehouse. He was also a partner in an enamelware factory. Aron had five siblings: three brothers (Naftali, Berek,

Figure 2.2 Building at 7 Wałowa Street in which the Hendel family lived before
World War II. Photo by Lukasz Krzyzanowski.

and Chaskiel) and two sisters (Judit and Topcia). Right before the war,
the Hendels lived in the center of Radom, in a district inhabited primarily
by Jews. They occupied a large, five-room apartment on the second floor
of an apartment house on Wałowa Street (see Figure 2.2). In 1941, this
building was at the center of Radom's large ghetto. Therefore, after the
creation of the closed Jewish district, the Hendel family could remain in
their apartment, to which they brought their relatives.

  Of Aron Hendel's nuclear family, only he and his brothers survived the
liquidation of the ghetto in August 1942. The men were most likely moved
to the labor camp for Jews on Szwarlikowska Street. In the summer of
1943, with the help of an acquaintance, they found a hiding place on the
"Aryan" side. It was a small room separated from the apartment occupied
by a couple named Szubiński and their three children. One additional
person was already there. The room was crowded and had no toilet. The
people hiding there had mattresses, chairs, and a lot of books. They had
to maintain silence, since the youngest Szubiński daughter did not know

there were Jews living in the apartment. At some point, Naftali Hendel's wife, Chana (Anna), her mother, and a third woman joined the men in hiding.[28] From a postwar list of the Jewish population in Radom located among documents of the District Jewish Committee, we learn that in April 1944 Chana gave birth to a daughter, Emilia.[29] What was done with the child before liberation is not clear. Taking into consideration the danger of discovery, it is hardly likely that the infant stayed in the hideout with her parents. Perhaps she was placed with some Christian family in the city. Perhaps the child's mother also moved there.

Every week, the Hendels paid for their place in the hideout and the food supplied to them by the Szubińskis. Chana, who had "good looks" and spoke Polish without an accent, would go out into the city from time to time to sell jewelry, earning money to pay for the hideout. Not long before the Red Army entered the city in January 1945, the Hendels' host informed them that he already had enough money and they should find a new "hole" for themselves.[30] It is obvious that they succeeded in either convincing or buying off the man, since the Hendels stayed on in the Szubińskis' apartment until liberation. After the Russians occupied the city, the Hendels did not come out of hiding for another week. Only then did they move to the apartment belonging to their relatives.[31] In the documents I found, there is no other postwar address for the name Hendel than the apartment house on Zacisze Street. It can be assumed, then, that that was where they moved directly from their hideout in the Polish couple's apartment.

The story of the survival of Aron Hendel, his brothers, and his sister-in-law is one of only a very few examples of the survival of so many individuals from one family, hiding in Radom on the "Aryan" side. If one also takes into consideration the minuscule chances of success of long-lasting concealment for money, the story of the Hendel family must be seen as exceptional.[32] In their wartime fates, however, there is nothing obvious that might have given cause to murder Aron Hendel. A possible motive probably should be sought in the ten months between the liberation of Radom and the murder on Zacisze Street.

Jan Tomasz Gross states that attempts at recovering property by Jews returning to their native localities were the most frequent context for postwar murders whose victims were survivors of the Holocaust. Such anti-Jewish violence stemmed from the determined opposition to Jews' attempts to recover property that had wound up in the hands of their Polish fellow citizens during the occupation or immediately after it.[33] In the documents of the City Court in Radom and in the court registries, there are no records, however, concerning a case connected with the apartment house on Zacisze Street where the Hendels lived after the war. It is doubtful, then, that one of the Polish tenants in the building was behind the murder of Aron Hendel or that it was some third individual wishing to take over ownership of the real property.

A potential motive for the murder could, instead, be found in a case, which was before the City Court in Radom, concerning recovery of a different property. On June 6, 1945, an attorney acting in the name of Aron, Naftali, Berek, and Chaskiel Hendel filed a complaint in the Radom court about the return of movable property: 3,100 kilograms of nails, 2,850 kilograms of casts, 1,630 kilograms of enameled cast-iron pots, 2,400 pitchforks, 315 kilograms of spades, 360 padlocks, 600 kilograms of chains, 315 kilograms of wire, and 475 kilograms of enamelware dishes or other goods of the same value.[34] In the fragmentary documentation of the case, there is no appeal to the court that presents in detail the foundation of the Hendels' claims. Judging from the listed goods, they came from the warehouse of iron materials managed by the Hendels' father before the war. During the occupation, that property was confiscated and handed over to the warehouses of the German firm Webendorfer Brothers.[35] The estimated value of the goods included in the Hendels' appeal exceeded one million złotys, at the time a very large sum. Although in theory the disputed goods, as part of the property of the "post-German" enterprise, were under state administration, as the case unfolded, it became clear the authorities had no idea where to look for them. The institution administering property over which owners had lost control during the war, the Provisional State Administration (Tymczasowy Zarząd Państwowy, TZP), determined that "the contents of the warehouses according to the account of the local caretaker was driven away by unknown individuals or the authorities in an unknown direction."[36] Later, the TZP representative suggested that the goods belonging to the Hendels might have already been taken by the Germans.[37] However, a few months later, in October 1945, the TZP confirmed that the contested property had been appropriated by the central government.[38] These changing versions by the TZP could have arisen from the chaos that reigned in the office's documentation as well as the impeded circulation of information in the initial period of its functioning. It is also likely that the goods from the warehouse belonging to the Hendel brothers' father had been embezzled, and the convoluted explanation by the TZP bureaucrats aimed to conceal the misuse of Hendel property. If that were so, the Hendels' appeal would have been a serious threat, as the court would have begun to investigate what had happened to the contested goods. The case of the return of the property to the Hendels did not, however, have a legal continuation. "Due to the death of one of the petitioners," the court suspended action on November 21, 1945.[39] If in fact the property belonging to the Hendels had been embezzled, then the death of Aron Hendel certainly was convenient for any individuals mixed up in the embezzlement. The remaining Hendel brothers could have submitted a new appeal to the court for the return of the property, but it was obvious that the men, terrified by Aron's murder, would not take that step.

There is at least one other reason why Aron Hendel might have died. Exactly one week before the murder, he was witness to a crime. On the evening of October 29, 1945, five attackers armed with machine guns and a handgun broke into an apartment in a house in the very center of Radom, on Rwańska Street. The apartment was occupied by two surviving Jews: fifty-six-year-old sheet metalworker Eliasz Birenbaum and his twenty-eight-year-old relative, Maria Cyna. During the liquidation of the ghetto, the owner of a Radom brewery, Jan Saski, had hidden Birenbaum in his attic.[40] Later, Birenbaum was in Pionki, most likely in the labor camp for Jews at the gunpowder factory located there. From there he wound up in Auschwitz.[41] Maria Cyna was also in the Radom ghetto and, after its liquidation, in the Szkolna Street camp, from where she was deported to Auschwitz.[42] In 1945, on the October evening when the attack occurred, two other people—acquaintances of Maria Cyna—were also in the apartment. One was Bogda Jasińska, a Catholic nurse from Gdańsk who was staying with Cyna, having come to Radom on leave.[43] The other person was Aron Hendel.[44]

The victims' testimonies containing a detailed description of the attack on the Rwańska Street apartment were preserved. It is therefore possible to reconstruct the course of the attack and to recognize the role Aron Hendel played in it. According to Maria Cyna's testimony, after entering the apartment, the attackers, dressed in civilian clothing,

> . . . ordered us to go into a second room and keep our arms up. They searched the men, looked at their identification papers, and threw them onto the floor. . . . These individuals took three watches from us. A gold watch from Jasińska Bogda, a man's watch from Chendel Aron, and an Anker "double" watch from me.[45] They also took a gold ring with a small diamond in it from my friend and began taking from the apartment . . . , they pulled 2 wool blankets off the beds, opened the wardrobe and took all the personal linen and around 70 meters of white cloth from it. 2 lengths of leather weighing around 11 kilograms, 1 pair of brown women's shoes, 2 pairs of new stockings, 1 brown purse . . . , 4 pairs of black shoe uppers, 1 electric iron, 1 leather jumpsuit, 1 short leather jacket, 2 pairs of leather gloves and they took around 2 thousand złotys from a handbag, 1 man's watch and a gold signet ring and many other trinkets. They packed all of this into the blankets.[46]

The losses were estimated at 100,000 złotys, a substantial sum.[47] Considering the value of the loot, it was one of the largest attacks that took place in Radom in the autumn of 1945. At the time, the value of stolen cash and objects during an attack on private individuals was estimated to average no more than 50,000 złotys. The police reports for October 1945 list only one attack on an apartment when the bandits stole goods worth more than those taken during the attack on the apartment of Eliasz Birenbaum and Maria Cyna. In that attack, a significant quantity of jewelry was stolen.[48]

The escape of the bandits after plundering the apartment on Rwańska Street was described by Birenbaum in his testimony: "The individual standing in the corridor shouted an alarm; the individuals with the loot wrapped up in blankets left the apartment. I jumped out the window and saw those individuals who headed for the dark lane that leads to the Lutheran church. One individual, when I raised the alarm, threatened me with a revolver, that he'll shoot, and the rest took off. . . ."[49]

Fleeing the apartment, the attackers divided into two groups that ran in opposite directions. Perhaps they were acting according to a prepared plan. Nothing in the witnesses' testimonies suggests that the perpetrators were members of the armed underground. Quite the opposite; it appears that they were "civilian" bandits driven not by political motives but only by an ordinary desire for profit. Probably, the attack on the apartment of Birenbaum and Cyna was not the only crime this group had on its account, and Christian Poles were equally its victims. Three days after the incident on Rwańska Street, on November 1, 1945, another attack took place on an apartment in the center of the city, when Tadeusz Imieński, who lived at Third of May Square, was robbed. This crime was nearly identical to the incursion into the apartment of Birenbaum and Cyna. The robbery did not succeed, as the attackers were scared off by several officers of the Polish Army (Wojsko Polskie, WP) who were relaxing in a nearby restaurant and reacted to the cry for help. The perpetrators of this particular robbery probably were aware that they were invading a "Christian" apartment. We cannot exclude that the same criminal group was responsible for both attacks—against Birenbaum and Cyna, and against Imieński.[50]

That the nature of the attack on the apartment of Birenbaum and Cyna was exclusively robbery is indicated by the fact that in Cyna's testimony she mentions a brief conversation with the attackers, in which there is no anti-Semitic tone: "In a casual conversation with the individuals in the apartment one of them explained that 'it's all the same to him, in any case he had enough enemies.'"[51] The other two witnesses also did not testify about any signs of anti-Semitism on the part of the perpetrators. True, it cannot be excluded that the victims were not honest with the police interviewing them and kept certain details to themselves, but it seems probable that the invasion of the apartment occupied by the two survivors had robbery as its motive. Holocaust survivors were an easy mark for attackers driven by a desire for profit; Jews were without a doubt the most defenseless and most vulnerable inhabitants in the postwar city.

During the attack on Rwańska Street, it was dark in the apartment, and the attackers used flashlights.[52] Nonetheless, Maria Cyna managed later to give the police a sketch of two of the attackers. Eliasz Birenbaum also insisted during his interview that he would be able to recognize the bandits, since he had managed to get a good look at them, but they were not people previously known to him.[53] One individual is missing from the testimonies of the victims—Aron Hendel. He had used the commotion of the attack to flee. The bandits knew his personal details and knew where he lived; his identity had been checked by them earlier, after all. It cannot be ruled out that Aron Hendel recognized one of the bandits and was murdered one week later as an inconvenient witness to the attack on the apartment of Birenbaum and Cyna.

Most likely, it will never be possible to establish definitively the motives that drove the murderers of Ludwik Gutsztadt and Aron Hendel. However, as noted above, their murders were exceptional when considered against other attacks carried out in Radom in 1945. Both men had not acted politically in the postwar period, they did not collaborate with the communist authorities, and they offered no resistance during the attacks, and yet both were shot. It is difficult to say what role their ethnicity played, but there is no doubt that the perpetrators were aware they were shooting at Jews. Ludwik Gutsztadt had returned to using his real name and was well known in the city. Aron Hendel also used his real name, and his identity was checked by the attackers. I believe that in the case of the murders of Gutsztadt and Hendel it would be appropriate to note a theory formulated in November 1945 by Tadeusz Jan Woleński, then mayor of Częstochowa, who, analyzing other acts of violence against Jews, wrote in a letter to the Kielce provincial governor: "Perhaps in both attacks matters of illicit trade and the reckonings and claims connected with it played a part, but I do not rule out that these matters would have caused different consequences if only Poles themselves were involved."[54] In the context of the Radom events analyzed here, it would be necessary only to replace "illicit trade" with robberies or attempts to thwart the restitution of property to survivor Jews.

The Death of a Policeman: Bolesław Gaut

Regardless of the difficulty in pointing to the motives behind the murders of Ludwik Gutsztadt and Aron Hendel, one thing can be excluded with certainty: they were not murders arising from the political activity of the victims or their work for the new authorities. The same cannot be

Figure 2.3 Building at 11 Żeromski Street where Bolesław Gaut lived and where he was killed. Photo by Lukasz Krzyzanowski.

said about another murder of a Jewish inhabitant of Radom. On July 14, 1945, in his apartment on Żeromski Street, the main street of the city, police sergeant Bolesław Gaut, a former partisan known as "Bolek," was shot (see Figure 2.3). Three weeks after the murder, the Municipal Headquarters of the MO drew up a brief report for the Provincial Headquarters in Kielce: ". . . 3 individuals armed with handguns . . . at 21:00 broke in to the apartment of Sgt. Gaut Bolesław, an officer of the Investigative Department of the MO Municipal Headquarters in Radom. . . . These characters, one of whom wore a military uniform, while the other two were dressed as civilians, stole 2 revolvers from Gaut, after which they killed him with a shot into his mouth. Immediately, an investigation was begun by the Investigative Department of the Municipal Headquarters of the MO, which, after determining that the murder had a political character, was turned over to the Municipal Office of the Security Service [Miejski Urząd Bezpieczeństwa Publicznego] in Radom."[55]

More light is thrown on the circumstances of Gaut's death by the testimony of Zofia Siwiec, who at the time of the murder was working as a typist for the Radom police:

On Saturday, July 14 [1945], returning from work, I met an acquaintance in the street, "Orion," who stopped and asked me if I knew Gaut. I replied that I did, since we work at the same institution. After my answer, "Orion" smiled and proposed that if I would come to Gaut's in the evening I would see his execution. I was very surprised and treated those words with great disbelief. After a brief conversation, I took leave of "Orion" and, walking on, I met Gaut, who first proposed that I go to a party in the District Military Recruitment Office with him and then asked me to come since he has news for me from a woman friend of mine from Poznań. I arrived at Gaut's around nine o'clock. I found him alone and he told me with a smile that he had nothing for me from Poznań, and began pressing me again to go with him to the party at the District Military Recruitment Office. I replied to this with a smile and wanted to leave. On the threshold I met three guys and recognized one as "Orion." I wanted to leave, but one of them, whom I did not know, turned me around and ordered me to sit down. They began a conversation with Gaut in the course of which another policeman came into the apartment. They showed him the chair next to mine, disarmed him, and checked his identity papers. Then they ordered Gaut to remove his uniform, at which he began asking them not to do that. When Gaut spoke his pleas too loudly, they yelled at him to be quiet. Gaut took off his uniform but did not agree to removing his trousers and shoes, crying and continuing to beg them to leave him in peace. I observed the impatience of the arrivals and saw "Orion" raise his gun to shoot. I was running automatically in the direction of the door when one of them grabbed me by the arm, walked out with me into the entranceway and there, holding a pistol in his hand, said that I had seen their work, their execution, and threatened me that I have to maintain silence because for them one bullet more is nothing. I was terrified since it was the first time I encountered such an event and hurried home. On July 15 I gave testimony at [MO] Headquarters and the Security Service, not giving in it the information that I

knew "Orion." I kept that secret because of fear of the threat that I
have to maintain silence.[56]

Most likely "Orion" was Władysław Kozłowski, active until autumn
1945 in a detachment under the command of Stefan Bembiński, one
of the local partisan leaders during the war and early postwar.[57] After
the arrest of his commander, Kozłowski formed his own detachment,
which joined the Freedom and Independence organization (Wolność i
Niezawisłość, WiN). In 1946, he was the deputy to the commander of the
Inspectorate of the Union of Armed Conspiracy, Franciszek Jaskulski
("Zagończyk") and was one of the more important soldiers of the anticommunist underground in the vicinity of Radom. Together with his entire
detachment, he came out to the communist authorities in September 1946
as a member of the underground.[58] Although the surname of the man who
used the pseudonym "Orion" does not appear in Zofia Siwiec's testimony
about Gaut's murder, the statement on the other side of the document indirectly indicates that people connected with Bembiński's detachment
were behind the murder. This other side contains another testimony by
Siwiec. There the woman describes in detail her participation in the wedding of her friend Halina Łudczak and Stefan Bembiński one month after
Gaut's murder.[59]

There are also other documents directly ascribing to Władysław
Kozłowski participation in the murder of the policeman. In the 1970s
and 1980s, the Security Police (Służba Bezpieczeństwa, SB) drew up reports on armed detachments of the postwar anticommunist underground
that had been active in Kielce province. The materials were intended for
internal use by the Security Police, and certain of the original items on
which the reports were based no longer exist.[60] These reports appear to
be genuine, because they appeared several decades after the events they
described, so it is unlikely that the officers would have added or invented
information in order to incriminate the underground. It is hard to sup-
pose that after so many years, the SB had some kind of goal in ascribing
to detachments that had not existed for a long time (and partly to dead
underground activists) deeds they did not commit.[61] Written in 1985, *Report
No. 94 of the Terrorist-Robbing Illegal Organization "Freedom and Independence" (WiN) under the Leadership of Stefan Bembiński, Pseudonyms*

"Harnaś" [Chieftain] *and "Sokół"* [Falcon] does not leave any doubt as to the identity of the two individuals who took part in the murder of Bolesław Gaut. In addition to Władysław Kozłowski, also mentioned is Eugeniusz Cichoński (pseudonym "Strumień" [Stream]). Cichoński, like Kozłowski, was not a rank-and-file member of the armed underground. He joined Bembiński's detachment in June 1945. At the moment of Gaut's murder, he most likely was in a small group protecting the detachment's leader. These were the most experienced and trusted people, who also carried out special assignments.[62] Cichoński later led one of the subdetachments of a group subordinate to Bembiński.[63] The third attacker was not identified and appears in the SB materials as N.N. (nomen nescio).[64]

It seems that Zofia Siwiec, the police typist present in the apartment at the time of Gaut's murder, was not only an unwilling witness to the crime. The 1985 report names her as a mole from Bembiński's detachment in the Radom police. She was to take care of issuing false documents and supplying the underground with information, and she was aware of the plan to murder Gaut.[65] Furthermore, after Bembiński's arrest and the liquidation of his detachment, Siwiec became a member of the group led by Władysław Kozłowski.[66] Gaut's card in the officers' index—such cards were created for each police officer in service—also carries an annotation that a woman collaborated on his murder: "the bandits were led into the apartment by an employee of the 1st police station, Citizen Siewcówna [*sic*]—a member of an illegal organization."[67] Nothing more is known about the role played in the entire event by the second police officer who entered Gaut's apartment when the attackers were already there. His name does not appear in any of the documents I discovered. The attackers disarmed the man and checked his identity papers, but he was not ordered to take off his uniform. Everything indicates that nothing bad happened to him.

Several factors clearly differentiate the murder of Bolesław Gaut from the murders of Gutsztadt and Hendel. Gaut, as a police officer, was linked to the new, communist authorities in an obvious way. Of these three murders, it is only in connection with Gaut's murder that the attacker is described as wearing a military uniform. What is more, it seems possible to identify the particular unit of the anticommunist underground responsible for the killing and to name two of the three perpetrators. What distinguishes Gaut's murderers from those of Gutsztadt and Hendel is also the fact that the attackers were not robbers and according to the records the only items they stole were the officer's handguns. Therefore, it is clear, this crime was not motivated by a simple desire to profit.

If the murder of Gaut was carried out by three individuals among whom two at least—Władysław Kozłowski and Eugeniusz Cichoński—filled important roles in the anticommunist underground operating in the Radom region, it makes sense that it might have been a political murder. Such motivation is also suggested by the talk among the killers about an "execution"—if the testimony of Zofia Siwiec is to be believed. The historian Ryszard Śmietanka-Kruszelnicki states that Gaut was murdered by a detachment of the underground, and that the murder might have been connected to the victim's work in the Investigative Department of the MO.[68] Śmietanka-Kruszelnicki does not, however, offer proof confirming the alleged zealous engagement of Gaut in police work. Also, I did not come across any information on this topic in the archives. Most likely, Gaut's personnel files were not preserved. The only documents referring to Sergeant Bolesław Gaut are the card in the officers' index which mentions his service in the People's Army during the war and in the police after the war, and the documents directly tied to his death.[69] Śmietanka-Kruszelnicki concludes that the murderers knew that their victim was a Jew and that the murder might have arisen also from the fact that "on the basis of the activity of several officers and undercover agents of Jewish descent, observed by the underground's intelligence, individuals directing the underground structures could decide to apply the so-called principle of collective responsibility."[70] Concealed in this sentence is the assumption that Bolesław Gaut might have perished as an officer-Jew for the sins of other police employees of Jewish descent working in Radom. This thesis by Śmietanka-Kruszelnicki implies that in the territory of Radom there were multiple officers of the police and Security Service who were Jewish and particularly active in combating the anticommunist underground. What is more, in order to justify Śmietanka-Kruszelnicki's thesis, the ethnic background of these officers would have to be a commonly recognized fact. Although in the city there really were several Jewish MO police and at least one, and most likely a few, UB officers of

Jewish origin (their personnel questionnaires contain information about religion—"Mosaic," or nationality—"Jewish"), still my research did not allow me to identify individual Jews who were particularly active in combating the anticommunist guerrilla forces.

Śmietanka-Kruszelnicki himself did not supply proof of his, in my opinion, controversial thesis. If, then, his assertion is to be accepted as true, it should be taken with a warning that it may apply not so much to the actual activity of officers of Jewish origin but to their visibility, to the presence of Jews in positions they had not occupied in Poland before 1939.[71] If that were the case, then what was important was the perception, not the reality, of participation by Jews in the MO and UB. The belief that Jews overwhelmingly populated those forces was very common in Polish society right after the war. Even Nikolai Selivanovsky, the main Soviet adviser in the Polish Ministry of Public Security, believed it. In October 1945, he "wrote that in Radom 82.3 percent of the UB personnel are Jews."[72] An attentive reading of the Radom officers' personnel questionnaires unequivocally refutes this assertion.

As it was with the murders of Gutsztadt and Hendel, it is impossible to discern with absolute certainty the motives of the murderers of Bolesław Gaut. Perhaps it was a matter of sowing terror among the Radom police; and Gaut, who had no family and was an acquaintance of a woman collaborating with an underground detachment, seemed an easy mark. The crime also displays a certain similarity with a murder committed in March 1946 in Lublin. The victim there was Chaim Hirszman, a former UB officer and one of two surviving prisoners of the Nazi extermination camp in Bełżec. That incident was analyzed in detail by Dariusz Libionka, who determined that most probably Hirszman did not particularly apply himself to his work, and at the time of his death he was no longer in the service of the UB. Therefore, this death, too, cannot be seen as revenge against an allegedly cruel officer-Jew fighting with the anticommunist underground. Attempting to understand the actions of the perpetrators, Libionka came to a conclusion that, to a certain extent, also applies to the murder of Gaut in Radom: that the perpetrators ". . . could not be unaware of Hirszman's Jewish origins, and it would seem that their perception of reality was informed by antisemitism. Still, as is evident in the investigation and the trial records, ideology played a less important part in their actions. Their major goal seems to have been the desire to obtain weapons."[73]

The murderers of Gaut may also have been after his police uniform. However, there are two essential differences between the deaths of Hirszman and Gaut. First, the perpetrators from Lublin were high school students, fantasizing about forming their own underground organization. But all the evidence about the Gaut murderers indicates that he was killed by soldiers of the anticommunist underground, at least two of whom occupied important positions in the hierarchy of the conspiracy. These people did not need to take such a significant risk in order to obtain just two revolvers and a single police uniform. Second, Gaut, unlike Hirszman, was still a serving officer at the time of his death. The murder of Gaut also differs from all the other deaths of Radom police in 1945. Most probably, in the first year after the war, no other policeman working in Radom was killed while off duty in his apartment.[74] Other incidents of policemen's deaths in 1945 were directly connected with the service duties they were carrying out: patrolling the street, checking identities of passersby, participating in actions against the underground and common criminals.[75] A question without an answer is why among more than 370 policemen serving in Radom in July 1945 was it Bolesław Gaut, a Jew with a partisan's past, who was disarmed and shot. Was this only a coincidence, and if so, then why did nothing happen to the other policeman who entered the apartment during the attack?

Nowhere in the materials I found is there information suggesting that the authorities considered the killing of Gaut to have been a murder with an anti-Semitic background. It is difficult to say how members of the Jewish community living in the city in 1945 viewed it. The name Gaut does not appear in any of the accessible documents of the District Jewish Committee in Radom or in correspondence with the CKŻP. Yet the Radom Jewish Committee knew about the murder. It even engaged in organizing the policeman's funeral: "The Deputy Commander of the Municipal MO for Political-Educational Affairs, 2nd Lieut. Fularski, communicated about the matter of the funeral for murdered Sgt. Gaut with the President of the Jewish Committee in Radom, who requested burial of the remains according to rituals of the Mosaic faith and in the Jewish cemetery."[76]

It is fruitless to search for any information related to the murder of Gaut
in the collected interviews and published memoirs of individuals who
were in Radom in 1945. The complete lack of information about Gaut's
death in documents created by survivors living in the city might indicate
that they did not consider the policeman a member of their community
and so his death was not recognized as a "Jewish" death. It is worth
noting, however, that the Jewish Press Agency, which had its office in
Łódź, published a short piece about the situation of Jews in Radom at
the end of August 1945 that not only included the murder of Gaut but
also presented it in the context of a wave of anti-Semitic violence flooding
the city.[77]

It was not only the ŻAP Bulletin that mentioned the death of the policeman. Bolesław Gaut was most likely the *only* Jew killed in Radom right
after the war about whose death the local press wrote at the time. The
Radom-Kielce *Dziennik Powszechny* (The universal daily), published by
the Provincial Office of Information and Propaganda, printed on July 18,
1945 a brief informational note titled "Felled by a Treacherous Hand."
The text is, however, above all a report from the funeral of the murdered
policeman. The murder itself was described in just one sentence:

> On the 16th of this month, the funeral of Bolesław Gałut [*sic*], an of-
> ficer of the Municipal Headquarters of the MO in Radom, was held.
> He was murdered in a deceitful and treacherous manner in the night-
> time hours in his own apartment. Employees of the Citizens' Militia
> and representatives of political parties and community organizations
> participated in the funeral.
>
> In a speech over the grave one of the dead man's friends emphasized:
> "Our tragically dead colleague is one among the first who stepped up
> to active struggle against the partitioner [i.e., the German occupier].
> Already in 1942, he is in a partisan detachment. His courage and
> bravery earn him universal respect. His helpfulness and collegiality—
> universal love. After the achievement of Independence, he does not rest
> on his laurels, does not try for an easy, comfortable life, but immedi-
> ately takes on demanding and selfless service in the Police. In the forest
> he fought for Independence, in the ranks of the Police for the preser-
> vation of that Independence. To preserve independence—that means, to

establish Democracy. Our colleague Bolesław fights for Democracy—
and perishes at his post.[78]

Readers of *Dziennik Powszechny* did not learn from the article that
the funeral took place in the Jewish cemetery in Radom. In this text,
saturated with the language of propaganda, the ethnic background of
Gaut and the place of his interment were passed over in silence. Perhaps
this information was considered beside the point. Probably, however,
the omission was deliberate. Had the press written that Gaut was a Jew
or that he had been buried in the Jewish cemetery, readers unfavorable
to the authorities could have read that as confirmation of the conviction,
universal in Poland at the time, about government by *żydokomuna*
("Judeo-Communism"). For pragmatic reasons, the communists, who
in 1945 were continually forced to court support in society, considered
it essential to demonstrate that the new authorities were Polish, and not
"Jewish."

Perhaps these same reasons also determined the private character of
the funeral ceremony for the murdered policeman. As a former partisan,
Bolesław Gaut had a right to a state funeral, but he did not get one. The
lack of a state ceremony even caused the Provincial Headquarters of the
MO in Kielce to launch an investigation. Two months after the funeral,
the vice governor of Kielce province, Henryk Urbanowicz, demanded explanations from Provincial Headquarters and identification of the institutions responsible for the offense.[79] What answer he received is unknown.
Immediately after Gaut's murder, the MO commander and the chief of
the Investigative Department—the murdered man's superiors—were away
from Radom on official business. The deputy commander of the MO for
political-educational matters organized the funeral. It was he who con-
tacted the Jewish Committee about the burial and ordered the obituary
notices and flowers. He also made the arrangements for a vehicle to transport the body to the Jewish cemetery, which lay on the outskirts of the
city, and delegated seven police officers to participate in the funeral. Perhaps the deputy commander was afraid to make the decision about a state
funeral in the absence of his superior. Perhaps this omission was the result of ordinary carelessness or haste. Taking into consideration the mood
among several of the Radom policemen, it is difficult to exclude another

possibility as well. The lack of a state ceremony might have been an expression of contempt for their fellow officer who was a Jew.

Documents pertaining to Zygmunt Mazur, the MO commander in Radom, shed additional light on the attitude of the Radom police leadership toward Gaut's murder. Mazur was in charge of the Radom police from mid-February 1945. When he assumed the post, he was barely twenty-four years old, and like many officers at the time he had a past as a partisan. In 1947, the Special Department of the Provincial Headquarters of the MO in Kielce (responsible for internal supervision) initiated an investigation of him. In addition to being accused of using his position to obtain unauthorized profits (sending policemen out on looting expeditions to the Western Territories, appropriating for personal use property of the Municipal Headquarters of the MO), the commander was also charged with the theft of the private belongings of Bolesław Gaut after his death. The policeman who put together the report in this case also mentioned the lack of a state funeral: "In 1945 in the spring Sgt. Gaut Bolesław (pseud. Bolek) was killed by bandits; an employee of the MO in Radom, of Mosaic faith, he deserved an honor platoon and escort to his final resting place with certain honors and to have his remains buried as a hero who perished for the State and Democracy at the hands of bandits—and yet, he did not have that; instead his domestic property was looted by the Commander of the Municipal MO Capt. Zygmunt Mazur and for his own reasons."[80] This information was confirmed in the course of the investigation by another police officer serving in Radom. He testified, "It wasn't enough that Capt. Mazur did not accompany him to his place of eternal rest as a hero with honors . . . but also thoroughly looted the apartment of the murdered man in an agreement with the investigative department."[81]

It is difficult to say what influence the fact that Gaut was a Jew may have had on what happened to his belongings after his death. It may have come down to a simple financial question. Throughout the country, the official earnings of policemen were very low at the time. Recalling the beginnings of the police, an officer from Kalisz wrote, ". . . MO police received their first wages only in May 1945 [that is, four months after the organization of the MO in the city]. . . . They were each paid 500 złotys a month; a kilogram of butter cost 450 złotys."[82] The situation was even worse in Wałbrzych, where the police did not receive a salary until September and did not have matching uniforms until the end of 1945.[83] A very strong sense of material deprivation was characteristic of the MO police. If one adds to this that many were used to the lawlessness of wartime and were highly demoralized, it is not surprising that some of them sought illegal ways to improve their daily life.[84] As becomes evident from the investigation of the commander of the Radom police, he frequently made use of his position to earn money on the side. Appropriating for his personal use the belongings of the murdered policeman could have been simply one more opportunity to enrich himself, all the easier as Gaut did not have a family that might have inherited his property. However, the fact that the commander of the MO took items left behind by a murdered policeman-Jew and even traded them—"he sold a leather coat the property of Gaut Bolesław" to another officer—brings to mind the fates of the property of Jews murdered during the Holocaust.[85] The comparison is all the more justified by the fact that Captain Mazur did not hide his dislike for Jews.

"Pogrom" in Radom

Among the murders carried out against Jews in Radom right after the war, one was exceptionally cruel in its violence. Committed on the night of August 10, the murder of four people in rooms at the Jewish Tailoring-and-Gaiter-Making Cooperative "Praca" (Work) differed from all the other murders in almost every regard.[86] First, the murders were not accompanied by theft of property. According to the report of a survivor living in Radom at the time, neither cash nor valuable goods disappeared from the premises of the cooperative. As the investigative procedures were being carried out, "800 marks were found [in] a wardrobe; many skins and clothing belonging to the cooperative turned up in that room. The investigation demonstrated that nothing was missing from among these items."[87] Thus, although in reports about the crime the term "attack" often appears, it was not a typical robbery, nor was it murder accompanied by theft, like the murder of Bolesław Gaut, when the victim's weapons were taken.[88]

Another circumstance distinguishing this event from other murders of Radom Jews is the number of victims. Four Jews were murdered, among them airman Aron Getłach, a first lieutenant in the Red Army, and three civilians: Bela Apel, Józef Gutman, and Tanchem Gutman.[89] At the time of his death, Getłach was thirty-three years old. He was buried in the military section of the Radom Christian Orthodox cemetery in the city.[90] Bela Apel and Józef Gutman had married right before their death. There are even reports that they perished on the evening immediately after their nuptials.[91] On July 15, 1945, the District Jewish Committee in Radom announced that twenty-year-old Józef Gutman and nineteen-year-old Bela Apel intended to wed. Before the war she had lived in Warsaw, and during the occupation she was in the forced labor camp in Skarżysko-Kamienna; he was a native of Radom.[92] Tanchem Gutman, a thirty-four-year-old men's tailor by trade, the oldest of the murdered individuals, lived in Radom before the war. During the occupation, he was in the camps. At the end of the war, he was working in an airplane-parts factory in Germany. After liberation, he returned to Radom. In May 1945, Gutman explained to Henryk R., whom he encountered on a street (they knew each other from a camp), that he had opened a tailoring shop on Żeromski Street at the address where the cooperative was housed. His clients were to be Polish and Soviet officers for whom he would make uniforms. Even several decades after this encounter, the man emphasized that Gutman was dressed in a suit. Evidently, this had made a big impression on him; a suit must have been a sign of particular success at a time when the majority of returning survivors were wearing rags, sometimes even the same ones in which they had left the camps.[93]

Additional information about the victims and the circumstances of the murder is supplied by Mojżesz Kirszenblat's testimony. It was he, probably, who was the last to see the victims alive:

being . . . in Radom, in the evening I dropped in as a guest to Gutman Tanchen residing on Żeromski Street. . . . The four of us sat there, conversing: I, Gutman, Birenbaum Luba, and a first lieutenant from the Red Army (an airman). I left at 5 minutes past 10. The next day, at 6 in the morning news spread about a murder in the above-mentioned place of 4 individuals: 1) Gutman Tanchen, who was stabbed with knives in the throat, abdomen, and near the heart. 2) The first lieutenant, who was lying in the corridor, his hands tied behind his back and shot with a bullet in the nape of the neck. 3) A married couple who lived in the adjoining apartment: Mrs. Gutman lay in the corridor with her hands bound, slashed with a knife above her calves and shot with a bullet in the nape of the neck. 4) Her husband, Gutman, was taken to the hospital that night with a bullet wound where he died the next morning, not having regained consciousness.

. . . .

The bodies of two of the murdered people I myself saw after the unsealing of the apartment on August 14. The body of the oberlieutenant [first lieutenant] was taken away on August 13.[94]

Eliasz Sznajderman, a relative of Józef Gutman and a witness at his wedding, found the mortally wounded man in the city hospital. He was lying on a stretcher on the floor. Sznajderman asked a doctor for help, but he was told there was nothing to be done. An hour later, Gutman died. When the dead man's relative returned to the apartment where he lived with his wife, he found under his door a card with a threat that if they didn't leave the city in three days, they would share the murdered people's fate. Eliasz and Mania Sznajderman organized the burial of Józef and Bela Gutman the next day in the Jewish cemetery and immediately left Radom. According to Sznajderman's testimony, in an interval of a few days he had accompanied the young couple on their "entry into a new path of life" and sent them off to the place of their eternal rest. In an interview he gave in 1995, he remembered that he had photographed his cousin's wedding. Perhaps it was he who made the only known photograph from that event (see Figure 2.4).[95]

The perpetrators of the murder in the Jewish cooperative were not concerned with maintaining silence. In addition to a knife, they also used firearms. That the murders were committed in an apartment building located scarcely a few dozen meters from the headquarters of the Radom authorities and not far from a police station testifies to the brazenness of the attackers. The murderers acted quickly: "The murders were discovered at 10:30, so the entire action lasted around 20 minutes."[96] The testimony by Mojżesz Kirszenblat from January 1946 is the most complete description of the crime discovered to date. My search for documents from the investigation Kirszenblat mentions brought no results. It is possible

Figure 2.4 Nuptials of Bela Apel and Józef Gutman. Radom, summer of 1945.
Voice of Radom.

that since one of the victims was a Soviet officer, the investigation was
taken over by the NKVD.

It is difficult to understand the exceptional cruelty of the crime described in Kirszenblat's report. In my review of crimes committed in the
second half of the 1940s in Radom and its environs, I did not encounter
an equally bestial murder. News about the bloodshed in the apartment
house on Żeromski Street spread very fast. In a letter intercepted by the
Military Censor's Office, sent from Radom on August 18, 1945, someone
wrote, "You can imagine that last week, from Saturday to Sunday,[97] there
occurred in Radom a fact such as has not happened even in Kraków.
Imagine, that next to the MO police station 4 individuals (Jews) were murdered in a building; they didn't shoot, but slashed, them. They cut their
throats and punctured their chests, including a Soviet major, also a
Jew. . . ."[98]

In testimonies by survivors from Radom, information about a pogrom
in Radom appears frequently, followed by a description of the murders
in the Jewish cooperative.[99] The fact that the murder of four Jews in Radom
took place a night before the pogrom in Kraków, which occurred on
August 11, 1945, certainly is not insignificant. The two events were often

referred to together, and the Radom crime was seen as part of the same phenomenon as the outburst of collective violence targeting Jews in Kraków. Traces of people's assumptions about links between the Radom crime and the Kraków pogrom can be seen even in fiction. One of the heroes of the short novel *Ocaleni* (The saved) by Stanisław Benski, himself a survivor, published in 1986, poses this question: "I know that in Radom they murdered a Jewish family on Żeromski Street. I know that Mr. Drobner said at a protest meeting in Kraków that someone threw a hand grenade at the Jewish orphanage in Rabka. . . ."[100] Bolesław Drobner, vice chairman of the Head Council of the PPS, delivered his speech in the course of a demonstration condemning the Kraków pogrom.[101] Information about the crime in Radom in connection with the news about the pogrom in Kraków also reached beyond Polish borders. In August 1945, the Jewish Telegraphic Agency published a press notification pointing to Radom and Kraków as centers of anti-Jewish activity in Poland. It also reported that in Kraków, 120 individuals were murdered, and in Radom, four. While the number of victims of the Kraków pogrom was greatly inflated (only one fatality is well documented), the information about the victims of the murder in Radom was exact.[102] Even representatives of the authorities began to speak of the events in Radom as a pogrom. During the August 16, 1945, session of the secretariat of the KC PPR, Roman Zambrowski noted that an attempted pogrom had taken place in the city. This information appeared in his speech concerning the Kraków pogrom and other acts of anti-Jewish violence that had taken place at the time in Miechów, Chrzanów, and Rabka.[103]

Although referred to as such, the fourfold murder committed in the "Praca" Cooperative cannot, however, be placed in the category of a pogrom. The three pogroms of Jews in postwar Poland—in Rzeszów (June 11–12, 1945), in Kraków (August 11, 1945), and in Kielce (July 4, 1946)—had a mass character and were drawn out in time and in public view. During the three pogroms the violence was committed by multiple perpetrators and was witnessed by crowds who often were not indifferent to it. As opposed to these events, the murder of the four Jews in Radom was a crime executed swiftly, quietly, and without witnesses. Among the attackers during the events in Rzeszów, Kraków, and Kielce were soldiers and policemen, while it remains unknown whether there was direct

participation of people representing the authorities in the murder in
Radom.[104] Also, it is not known if the murder in the cooperative was pre-
ceded by a rumor accusing Jews of the ritual murder of Christian
children (the so-called blood libel), but that is what accompanied the
three acts of collective violence in the other cities.[105] There is no way to
prove that the murder committed in Radom was a pogrom. It is very likely,
however, that it arose out of an atmosphere similar to that surrounding the
mass anti-Jewish violence in Rzeszów, Kraków, and Kielce. In the light of
available records, one cannot point to anything other than hatred of Jews
as the motive that drove the perpetrators of the Radom murder.

Against the Jews: The Anticommunist Underground

The survivors of the Holocaust saw the crime committed in the "Praca"
Cooperative as an anti-Semitic act directed against their entire community. This interpretation was supported by the fact that not quite two
weeks before the murder, flyers had appeared in the city and surrounding
areas ordering Jews to leave the region:

TO
THE JEWISH COMMUNITY IN_____
   It is confirmed that Jews are working collectively in the intelligence
service in behalf of the present regime brutally imposed on us, thereby
acting to the detriment of Polish Society.
   As a spokesperson for the voice of Polish Society, I advise all jews
to get out beyond the borders of Radom county and the city of Radom
by August 15, 1945.
   I warn [you] that overstaying the deadline or requests for help directed to the present authorities will be ruthlessly punished.[106]

Flyers with identical contents also appeared in Jedlińsk, a small town
thirteen kilometers from Radom. It was most likely a planned propaganda
action calculated to terrify Jews in the region and force them to leave. The
Jews living in Radom treated the flyers very seriously. A meeting was
called in the District Jewish Committee about the matter. According
to testimony by Henryk Griffel and Mendel Goldberg delivered in

January 1946 before the historical commission in Stuttgart (a local branch of the Central Historical Commission of the Central Committee of Liberated Jews—a Jewish institution documenting the Holocaust, active in the American zone of occupied Germany):

> . . . around August 7, 1945 we were summoned to the Jewish committee in Radom to a meeting of a group of Jewish citizens, called with the aim of discussing the situation of Jews in Radom in connection with the ultimatum of a certain organization demanding the abandonment of Radom city by Jews. At this conference the president of the committee presented several copies of the flyer, the so-called Ultimatum. . . . [107]

To the submitted testimony Griffel and Goldberg attached the text of the flyer. Unfortunately, there is no information if the meeting in the Jewish Committee ended with any proposals on how to improve the security of the Jews in the city.

For the survivors living in Radom, it was clear that some kind of armed organization was behind the flyers calling for their removal. The official style of the flyers led survivors to believe that the author or authors were not amateurs. The anti-Jewish flyers distributed in Radom and vicinity were not created by a lone-wolf actor. Similar documents, after all, appeared in various parts of Poland at the time. Under "Radom ultimatum," the author signed "D.O.W.S." According to Ryszard Śmietanka-Kruszelnicki, it was an acronym for "Dowódca Oddziału Wolności Sokół" (Leader of the Freedom Force, Falcon) used by the local leader of the anticommunist underground, Lieutenant Stefan Bembiński. In mid-1945, Bembiński commanded one of the largest groupings of smaller partisan units in the Kielce region, subordinate to the Armed Forces Delegation for Poland, an anticommunist underground organization formed from the Home Army.[108] The hypothesis ascribing the ultimatum to Stefan Bembiński's division active in the Radom area seems even more likely to be accurate in that this group was very engaged in propaganda. Anti-Jewish accents appear also in other flyers widely distributed in the region in the summer of 1945, and signed with "D.O.W.S." or "D.O.W. Sokół."[109] The contents of these printed materials lead us to place the ultimatum delivered to the Jews in the context of the division's broader propaganda activity. A flyer titled "To Soldiers of the Army of Żymierski" (i.e., the Polish Army subordinate to communist authorities) reads:

> Soldiers. Your officers are primarily russians or jews. They tell you that you are serving in a Polish army, but that is a lie, for the spirit of that army is jewish-bolshevik. They tell you that you have Free Poland, but that is a lie, for in Poland the NKVD is ruling and the security police staffed with communists and jews. They tell you that you fought and now you are establishing democracy, but that is a lie, for in Poland a bloody and cruel regime of bolshevik dictatorship rules. A venal clique of Judeo-Communists carrying out precisely the commands of the red tsar Stalin has seized power. . . . Here, in our country, the disciplined ranks of soldiers of the underground organization are disbanded, but they keep on. In Siberia and here beside you in the prisons the best sons of the Fatherland are perishing amid the hideous agonies imposed on them by communist thugs and jews![110]

This flyer had as its goal to encourage the opposition of rank-and-file soldiers of the Polish Army to their leaders and political management. Worth noticing is the argument the author used to undermine the respect of the Polish soldiers for their superiors. The officers are "foreigners"— Russians or Jews—and Poland is ruled by communists and Jews or, "Judeo-Communists." At the end, the author clearly contrasts Polish patriots and their executioners—"communist thugs" and Jews. True, one can point to the logical inconsistency of the argument contained in the flyer—after all, it is not clear if Jews are condemned as communists or only because they are Jews—but the myth of Judeo-Communism appearing here is, after all, not in itself consistent.

Also, in one of the last flyers signed "D.O.W.S.," under the heading "Soldiers of the Żymierski Army. Soldiers of the Security Police and Citizens' Militia," there is an appeal to those fighting on the side of the communists not to act "against the best Poles" and become "a blind tool of Judeo-Communism."[111] The anti-Semitic contents of printed matter distributed in Radom and its vicinity express an opposition between "Judeo-Communism" and "the Polish Nation." Joanna Tokarska-Bakir detected this by analyzing numerous dispatches and appeals published by divisions of the Polish anticommunist underground.[112] In these texts, Jews are presented as an element that is extremely alien and hostile to everything Polish. The juxtaposition of Jews and communists in this context turned out to be useful for the underground's propaganda. It made every Jew into a communist, and every communist into a Jew—a stranger, an enemy, a non-Pole, and a nonpatriot. Such an intellectual operation was based on at least two assumptions: "Since there are Jews among the Communists, all Communists are Jews," and "A Pole who is a Communist thereby ceases being a Pole."[113] The account that appears in the flyers published by the underground can therefore be seen as an expression of their authors' anti-Semitism and propagation of ethno-cultural nationalism, and their attempt to gain support for their political struggle by appealing to emotions that were widely shared within Polish society— namely, dislike, and often simply hatred, of Jews. It can be assumed that if one of the flyers fell into the hands of someone who did not identify with its political program, that reader would likely agree with the creators of the flyer on one point: the perception of Jews as alien and also, perhaps, as enemies. As the research conducted by Joanna Tokarska-Bakir and by Jan Tomasz Gross shows, right after the war representatives of various milieux, often otherwise hostile to each other, displayed anti-Jewish views and positions.[114] Paraphrasing the words of Jan Karski, one can say that anti-Semitic clichés created "something like a narrow footbridge on which there came together in agreement" broad strata of Polish society, independent of their differing views on other matters.[115]

Against the Jews: The Police and the Security Service

Anti-Semitism was universal in Poland, both among employees of the police (Citizens' Militia, MO) and the Security Service (UB)—the forces supposed to uphold the law immediately after the war, and among the anticommunist underground and the civilian population. According to Marcin Zaremba, for MO policemen in the first postwar years anti-Semitism was the common ground "for an understanding with society, manifesting their distance from the authorities, while at the same time it was safer [than an anti-Soviet posture], because (at least in the beginning) it did not threaten to bring down severe official consequences."[116] Throughout the country, there were numerous acts of anti-Semitic violence committed with the participation of policemen, officers of the Security Service, and soldiers.[117] Jan Tomasz Gross argues that the participation of men in uniform was "a characteristic feature of aggression against Jews in Poland immediately after the war."[118] The incursion of soldiers into the building at 7 Planty, which was occupied by Jews, is recognized as the beginning of the Kielce pogrom.[119] The participation of police officers and the army in the pogrom met with the raucous approbation of the crowd that gathered in Kielce. Cheers rang out: "Long live our army and the MO!," "Bravo militia! [the police],"[120] "No need to fear the army, the army is with us!"[121] Analyzing the Kielce events, Joanna Tokarska-Bakir points out that "in the cries of the mob gathered at 7 Planty Street there gradually emerged an alliance of the militia [the police] and the army with the mob."[122]

The participation of representatives of the uniformed services in anti-Jewish violence in Poland immediately after the war was not limited to pogroms. In the first postwar years, one can point to numerous examples of murders of Jews in which the murderers were police officers. From the report of Dr. Szloma Herszenhorn, director of the Office for Matters of Aid for the Jewish Population attached to the Presidium of the Council of Ministers, it appears that in March 1945 alone at least five Jews were murdered by officers of the MO. In an even greater number of incidents, the police refrained from action or even protected the murderers.[123]

For the second time since 1939, Jews became citizens excluded from the protection of the law. Mojżesz Rubinstein, an official in the Department for Jewish Minority Affairs in the Ministry of Public Administration, noted in February 1945: "There were incidents in Częstochowa of various offenses by the Citizens' Militia in relation to the Jewish population which were reminiscent of the time of the German occupation."[124] Just as under the Nazi rule, several crimes committed by policemen had an almost public character: "In Ćmielów, Opatów County, one Jew was murdered. From the testimonies of Jews from Ćmielów submitted to the Central Jewish Committee, it appears that the murderers are local MO policemen. The corpse of the murdered man lies, it appears, under a garbage pile not far from the police office."[125]

At times, the officers themselves boasted of their participation in a crime: "On the evening of the 18th of the present month [March 1945] the Jew, Lt. Leon Wiślicki of the Polish Army, was murdered in Ryki on his way to the mill. The day after the murder in the apartment of Citizen Kwiatkowska there were several members of the Citizens' Militia, one of whom declared: 'Boy, did we drink at his expense'; these words were uttered when there was talk about the murder committed against Lt. Wiślicki. Present at this conversation was Citizen Steinbruch Nela, residing in Irena on Starowiejska Street."[126]

Definitely more frequent, however, were incidents of negligence, when the police or other services did not act to protect Jews and to discover the perpetrators of violence. On June 14, 1945, in Starachowice, barely fifty kilometers from Radom, ". . . four individuals armed with handguns attacked the house of Waldman [?] Hersz. One entered the apartment and terrorized the eight men there. Six managed to flee, and two were killed. The event took place near the police station. Not far away several MO policemen were sitting in a store and despite the gunshots they did not intervene. Enesman Izrael and Brotbeker Chil were killed."[127] In Jedlińsk, thirteen kilometers from Radom, on July 8, 1946, Alter Frymer aka Wulf Waserman, who arrived in the city to inquire about his property, was killed at midday at the police station. Frymer came to the station to request police intervention. The murderers allegedly fled with the victim's body. A brief police statement does not provide any information regarding the attackers' identity. It also does not mention any action undertaken by officers serving at the station during the attack.[128]

Examples of the police not acting on crimes against Jews can most likely be identified in Radom as well. The only focused documentation I found in the Radom MO files pertaining to a crime against Jews was related to the investigation of the attack on the apartment of Eliasz Birenbaum and Maria Cyna in October 1945. Everything indicates that there are no extant files created during the investigations into any of the postwar murders of Jews in Radom. It is possible that documents were discarded or are still awaiting discovery. It is more likely, however, that, in general, investigations were not undertaken at all—even if the crime scene was secured at the outset and other initial investigative procedures were performed. The wife of Ludwik Gutsztadt reported the shooting of her husband to the police. Officers appeared when the injured man was still in the hospital, but the victim's son recalls that he never heard anything about an inquiry.[129] Investigations aimed at discovering the perpetrators of postwar murders of Jews as political matters could have been conducted by the Security Service. However, I also could not find any documents in those files that would allow me to state that the UB actually undertook such actions. It is easier to understand this state of affairs when one studies the moods that were prevalent among some of the Radom law enforcement employees. Insight is made possible by the personnel files and disciplinary cases of police officers serving in Radom immediately after the war. In those documents, one can find examples of expressed aversion and even open enmity toward Jews.

In one such investigation into a matter of abuse, Zygmunt Mazur, the commanding officer of the Radom MO, was accused of not allowing a woman to be called to account who, in the summer of 1947, verbally attacked Sergeant Jan Wac, a policeman in the municipal headquarters and senior arresting officer in Radom. As he was leaving his house with his wife, Wac had helped his neighbor Nowakowski, also a policeman, detain a brawling drunk. At that point Nowakowski's housekeeper got involved. In the presence of her employer, she began screaming at Wac: "You hymie mug, why are you detaining Poles" and "The present Government in Poland is Jewish."[130] Wac arrested the woman, but Commanding Officer Mazur ordered her release and informed his subordinate that Wac had no right to arrest women.[131] It is difficult to determine if the commanding officer's decision was influenced by the fact that he shared the views expressed by the housekeeper or if it was motivated by his desire to avoid problems—to avert an explosion of anti-Jewish disturbances in the city. A conversation between Wac and his direct superior, Chief of the Investigative Department Henryk Compała, may suggest the latter possibility. After consulting with Commanding Officer Mazur, Compala informed Wac: ". . . if we are going to deal with such matters in this way, then the same thing will happen in Radom that took place in Kielce on July 4, 1946."[132]

In the files of the disciplinary investigation of Zygmunt Mazur, there is also information showing unambiguously that the commanding officer of the Radom MO was disdainful of Jews and shared the prevalent belief in the myth of "Judeo-Communism." While talking with his subordinate, who spoke positively about the situation in the Soviet Union, Mazur was supposed to have said "that he'd heard that things are not at all as good [in the USSR] as I say; on the contrary, *if fewer Jews were in charge, then maybe it might be pretty good.*"[133] According to this same witness, the commanding officer also expressed his disdain for Jews immediately after the Kielce pogrom. The question of evacuating Jews residing in Radom was discussed at the time: "I was summoned by Commanding Officer Mazur, who ordered me in a way that was contemptuous of the Jewish population to take two vehicles and remove 'it' for me [the commanding officer] from Radom to Warsaw so that the same thing that happened in Kielce shouldn't happen here and so that I [the commanding officer] shouldn't have to sit in prison for them later."[134]

Analyzing Commanding Officer Mazur's stance and the anti-Jewish moods dominant in the ranks of the police, it is difficult to refute the finding that the example came from above. The attitude of the superior had to have had an influence on the behavior of his subordinates. Even if it did not encourage open dislike of Jews, it certainly strengthened the belief that anti-Semitism was met with acceptance in the MO's ranks and that impunity was all but guaranteed.

Later, it did happen that members of the Radom police were relieved of duty for voicing anti-Jewish slogans. This was the case with Rifleman Bolesław Żuraw. He was discharged on disciplinary grounds at the beginning of 1949. In the decision issued by the Special Department of the Provincial Headquarters of the MO in Kielce, in addition to the charge of nurturing a hostile attitude toward the political system of Poland, the Soviet Union, and the Red Army, as well as promoting reaction and having contacts with "foreign class elements," was the assertion that Żuraw ". . . acts according to nationalistic prejudices, sowing hostile antisemitic propaganda among the officers of the MO, directing it against employees of the MO, not only those who are of Jewish descent, but it's enough if they look Semitic. . . ."[135]

It is possible that the reference to the officer manifesting an anti-Semitic attitude toward the fellow policemen he perceived as Jews, but who were in fact not Jews, made Żuraw's offense appear even more serious in the eyes of his superiors. In addition to his demonstration of enmity toward

"real" Jews, the policeman "imputed" Jewishness also to his Polish coworkers. If this officer actually was an anti-Semite, it is hard to believe
that in displaying his prejudices he limited himself exclusively to other
policemen. That is even less probable because Żuraw, as the officer on
duty in the Second Police Station in Radom, had contact with Jews living
in the city. It was he who in October 1945 took the report of Eliasz Birenbaum and Maria Cyna about the robbery attack.[136] Perhaps civilians
did not feel safe enough to inform the policeman's superiors about expres-
sions of dislike and enmity on his part. Two factors might have been decisive: an elevated sense of threat and the fact that dislike of and verbal
aggression directed at the survivors were so universal that only the most
drastic instances were reported.

There are also reasons to assume that accusations of anti-Semitism
could sometimes be used by MO officials to discredit coworkers, especially after the Kielce pogrom, when at least officially the leadership of
the police and the central authorities had begun to combat anti-Semitic
attitudes among their subordinates. In the summer of 1946, the previous
assistant to the commanding officer of the Radom MO for political-
educational affairs, Stefan Skałbania, was charged with anti-Semitism.
This occurred when, in the wake of the pogrom in Kielce, Skałbania was
named acting chief of the Political-Educational Department in the Provincial Headquarters of the MO in Kielce. His competitor for that position
informed their superior that Skałbania was "a demagogue, a member of
the PSL [Polish People's Party], and an anti-Semite."[137] News about the
anti-Jewish attitude of a high MO official in Kielce appointed immediately
after the pogrom undoubtedly could have damaged him. Most likely, there
was nothing in the accusation of anti-Semitism but a dirty struggle for pro-
motion. In the end, other reasons were decisive in Skałbania's dismissal
from office.

A particular insight into the anti-Jewish mood prevalent in the Radom
MO is provided by documents from the trial of aforementioned Jan Wac,
a police officer charged in the spring of 1949 with taking bribes. While
defending himself, Wac testified about the enmity he encountered from
other policemen. He insisted that the accusation against him resulted from
one of his colleagues' dislike of him as a Jew:

Kiliańczyk Andrzej . . . has been hostile toward me since he found out that I am a Jew, this is, since 1947, he has constantly pestered me about whether I am circumcised, repeating "show me what it looks like." He has made fun of me in various ways, saying that I don't have children because I have a sawed-off dick and "your wife is a Pole and needs a longer one"; that Kiliańczyk Andrzej was always pestering me and didn't give me a moment's peace. I would answer him, "Why are you pestering me like this, did I take your property or your wife, am I taking your salary, I survived the occupation and you twist my words all the time and affect a Jewish accent."[138]

Jan Wac had remarried in 1946. His first wife and three young children had perished during the Holocaust.[139] Even if Kiliańczyk did not know this, he must have been aware of the context. This was not ordinary verbal sparring between coworkers. Kiliańczyk was abusing a Jewish colleague. Probably with the aim of frightening his fellow policeman, Kiliańczyk told one of Wac's female acquaintances that Wac had died. Kiliańczyk supposedly told the woman that ". . . Wac drove his wife to the hospital and he himself was supposed to go to Busko for treatment. Wac had an altercation with a guy in the train carriage and they dragged the yid out of the car, murdered him, and no trace of him remained."[140]

Kiliańczyk held this conversation in September 1948, a year and a half after the last documented incident in the so-called railway campaign—the forcing out of Jewish travelers from railroad cars and their murder by members of the underground or ordinary bandits. Such incidents occurred throughout Poland at least until late 1946 and claimed approximately 200 lives.[141] Only a dozen or so months later, the memory of those events must still have been alive. The threat contained in the rumor was sufficiently obvious that Wac reported it to his superior, who summoned Kiliańczyk for a discussion. Unfortunately, it is not known how that meeting went. However, the attempt to turn for help to the chief apparently did not have much effect. In the opinion of the policeman who made the complaint, all that happened was that "all of this got broadcasted around Headquarters that Wac is a Jew."[142]

The witness to Kiliańczyk's dislike of Wac was the cleaning lady in the Municipal Headquarters of the MO, whom Kiliańczyk reproached for her friendship with his Jewish colleague:

> Kiliańczyk Andrzej kept picking on me, "You . . . have relations with Wac, couldn't you find a Pole, only you have to take up with a Jew," and she answered him: "what business is it of yours who I have relations with, with a Pole or a Jew, or is a Jew not a man, stop picking on me." Kiliańczyk answered her: "sure, stop picking on me—you want to have relations with a Jew because now the Jews are in charge."
>
> "In the government, too," he said, "we have Jews," he even used names, "in our Headquarters, too, there's also a Jew, Wac Jan, who has an assumed name; after all his name is Brezel Aron and not Wac Jan; he pretends he's a great Pole. I [Kiliańczyk] have reported this."[143]

As can be seen from this exchange of opinions as related by Jan Wac during his investigation, Kiliańczyk suggested the woman befriended a Jewish officer in hope of profit. Believing in the myth of "Judeo-Communism," Kiliańczyk was convinced that with the communist government Jews came to power in Poland. He also treated Wac's adoption of a more Polish-sounding name as an offense that had to be reported to his superiors. Kiliańczyk felt sufficiently immune to punishment that he showed enmity toward Wac in the presence of other police officers and even in front of the commanding officer of the Radom MO himself, who knew the persecuted Wac from their time as partisans. According to Wac:

> . . . in 1949, on Christmas Eve, I came to the City MO Headquarters and found the Commanding Officer of the City, Lt. Strzelecki Edward and Skiba Jerzy, also Lt. Murawski Józef; also Kiliańczyk Andrzej was with them. I walked up to the Commanding Officer, Lt. Strzelecki, because he is my colleague from the forest, and greeted him with a kiss, and when Kiliańczyk noticed that I was exchanging a kiss with Commanding Officer Lt. Strzelecki, Kiliańczyk said in the presence of those who are named above: "Judas, how nicely he kisses; only a Judas can do this." I, Wac Jan, asked him, "Explain to me what Judas means, you

antisemite." He, instead of answering what Judas means, answered me, "Don't worry; they," pointing upward, "won't give a fuck."[144]

In fact, his superior did rebuke Kiliańczyk, but it is difficult to see that as a serious intervention in defense of the bullied policeman. It was not the only time Wac met with the behavior of superiors that he could interpret as granting permission for others to openly abuse him.

From the documents created at the time of the bribery investigation and trial of Wac, one cannot determine for certain that, as Wac held, Kiliańczyk had made up the corruption accusation to ruin the hated colleague. It is possible that Wac did take a bribe, but without a doubt it was the anti-Semitism of another policeman that made it possible for him to mount the line of defense described above. Wac's argument aimed at demonstrating that the entire affair was the result of a conspiracy of anti-Semites. Pronouncing on the matter, the court clearly made a similar interpretation. The Military Regional Court in Kielce sentenced Wac to one and a half years in prison, suspended. Among the factors taken into consideration in meting out the relatively light punishment was "the fact of persecution of him as a Jew by Policeman Kiliańczyk Andrzej."[145] In the documents of the investigation and judicial hearings, there is no information that would point to rational causes for Kiliańczyk's hatred of Wac. Only one of the witnesses testifying during the trial mentioned a possible reason: "I heard from Kiliańczyk that the accused is a Jew and receives better civilian rations than he does; . . . he does not receive such."[146] Many Jews, like other individuals who were particularly persecuted during the German occupation, qualified to receive better food rations—first category food ration cards. This often aroused envy among individuals who did not receive such rations. It is difficult, however, to see this as the real cause of Kiliańczyk's tormenting of Wac. According to Wac, one of the individuals mixed up in accusing him supposedly said that Kiliańczyk talked him into incriminating their Jewish colleague, arguing that "Wac is a Jew; it's not necessary for him to work here where he can harm Poles."[147]

Wac himself asserted, "I had a lot of enemies against me, because I was the only one of my heritage who was employed there."[148] His case was reopened and Wac petitioned the court to drop it. Wac urged the court to understand how tragic his life had been until then:

> Because I am of Jewish descent, I remain without any family, like a single finger. During the time of my arrest my wife died [the second wife, the one he married after the war]. I have had a tragic and difficult life. . . . I politely ask the High Court for *dismissal* of the charges, because I am alone like a finger, so that I would have no one to give that piece of bread to me. I have already yearned for it for weeks and even slept in tombs [reference to hiding during the Holocaust]—so heavy was my life.[149]

In the second trial, the Military Regional Court in Kielce sentenced Wac to one year in prison.[150] Wac and another police officer sentenced in the same case appealed. In the end, the Supreme Military Court over-ruled the judgment and dropped the case against the two policemen on the grounds of lack of sufficient proof of guilt, the good reputation they enjoyed as police officers, and the contradictory testimonies of the witnesses.[151]

Based on other records, we can assume that individuals hostile to Jews could be found in the Security Service, too. In the first period after the war, many police and officers of the UB were recruited from partisan de-tachments, primarily from the People's Army (Armia Ludowa, AL). As Joanna Tokarska-Bakir demonstrates, the AL partisan detachment "Świt" (Dawn), active in the Kielce region, was responsible during the war for at least several murders of Jews in hiding. After the war, many of its mem-bers took up work in the Kielce region in the UB and the MO, and in or-gans of the state administration. Among those with ties to this detach-ment were the later chief of the Provincial Office of the Security Service (WUBP) in Kielce Władysław Sobczyński and the Kielce provincial gov-ernor Eugeniusz Wiślicz-Iwańczyk. Both were in office in July 1946 when the pogrom occurred in Kielce. Other former members of the de-tachment worked in the police in Skaryszew fifteen kilometers from Radom, and in Częstochowa.[152] At least two former partisans directly participating in murdering Jews during the German occupation found employment after the war in the County Office of the Security Service

(Powiatowy Urząd Bezpieczeństwa Publicznego, PUBP) in Radom.[153] One of them was Adam Bakalarczyk (pseudonym "Dulka"). He worked in the UB from January 1945 as a section director and later as the deputy chief of the PUBP in Radom.[154] The majority of the members of the Dawn detachment who took part during the war in executions of Jews never answered for their acts. Only Tadeusz Maj, the commander of the detachment, was sentenced to eight years in prison in 1954. Immediately after the war, he was an employee of the Polish Workers' Party (PPR) in Radom. Later he served in a special-purpose military formation subordinate to the Ministry of Public Security—the Internal Security Corps (Korpus Bezpieczeństwa Wewnętrznego, KBW) in Lublin and worked in the Provincial National Council (Wojewódzka Rada Narodowa, WRN) in Kielce and the Special Commission for the Struggle against Excesses and Economic Sabotage.[155] In the course of his trial, he attempted to explain the motives for the murders committed against Jews as orders received from his superiors. He also spoke about his attitude toward Jews: ". . . I still had prejudices against Jews from before the war as speculators, exploiters. . . . Also, my attitude toward Jews was contemptuous and I considered that there cannot be a place for such people in the new Poland."[156] Another time, Maj admitted: ". . . I treated Jews as enemies of the new order and I did not want them to come to power in Poland." In the course of the hearing, he confessed that he was an adherent of the view that "Jews are a people of a lower character."[157]

Obviously, having only the detachment leader's confession to murdering Jews out of anti-Semitic motives, we cannot come to any definite conclusions about the attitudes his subordinates held toward Jews. However, many things indicate that their attitude toward Jews in hiding whom they encountered during the occupation did not diverge significantly from the approach presented by Maj himself. Many members of the detachment came from the same milieu and even from the same village as Maj and had similar experiences during the occupation. The testimonies of members of the Dawn detachment that were collected during the investigation spoke indirectly to their negative attitude toward Jews. There is nothing in the testimonies to indicate that any of the partisans questioned the legitimacy of the murders they committed. One can find, on the other hand, numerous hints that the murders of the Jews served to enrich the members of the detachment, even supplementing their partisan wardrobes: ". . . On that day I observed that some of our people have different clothes and shoes. For example, I distinctly recognized the trousers that Tracz Wacław, pseud. 'Skóra,' was wearing, they were a bit too tight on him. Anyway, he himself, i.e., Tracz Wacław, showed me those trousers with a laugh, saying, 'Look, they belonged to those Jews.' . . ."[158]

It is unlikely that the hostile attitude toward Jews that the members of the Dawn detachment held during the war disappeared the moment the German occupation ended. Entering the new postwar reality, they must have carried the baggage of their old prejudices. That former partisans involved in murders of Jews during the occupation were assigned to positions in the UB, the MO, and government offices proves that (at least right after the war) there were those among the new authorities who approved admitting into service people whose anti-Semitic posture was generally known, for the killings committed by the partisan detachment during the war were not tightly kept secrets. The enmity toward Jews felt by some in the Security Service might have influenced their slowness in conducting inquiries.

The Radom Citizens' Militia and the Security Service there in the first postwar years were not institutions that in any real sense could (or wanted to) protect the Jews living in the city from violence. The greatest obstacle was most likely not the universal lack of trained people or of weapons at the time, but rather a lack of goodwill and the anti-Semitism of the officers. When it came to their attitude toward Jews, a segment of the MO and, most likely, of UB employees, had more in common with the soldiers of the anticommunist underground who believed in "Judeo-Communism" and with the new owners of "post-Jewish" property than with the officially stated slogans voiced by the new authorities about the equal rights of all citizens—without regard to their ancestry.

The Local Administration and Representatives of the Catholic Church

The lack of equal treatment of Jews was also noticeable in contacts with the local administration. Immediately after the Red Army entered the territory of central Poland, there began to appear information about dis-

crimination against Jews by civil servants. This phenomenon did not bypass the Kielce region. Already in February 1945, an official in the
Department for Jewish Minority Affairs in MAP, Mojżesz Rubinstein,
wrote, "After the liberation of Kielce province from the German occupier,
rumors reached the Department about harassment of the Jewish population by local government circles."[159] With the goal of verifying these reports, Rubinstein visited Częstochowa, Kielce, and Radom on February 10–20, 1945. In his report about the trip, he noted, "The city of
Radom authorities (the top leaders) relate very well to the matters arising
from the needs of the Jewish population. There are incidents, however,
where various links in the administrative apparatus (the lower level) de-
ploy antisemitic methods."[160] The conclusion of his report in relation to
the two other visited cities was the same. Also, Dr. Szloma Herszenhorn,
director of the Office for Matters of Aid for the Jewish Population attached
to the Presidium of the Council of Ministers, noted in the same month:
"In Radom one notices an unfavorable and even hostile relation of the ex-
ecutive organs for the needs of the Jewish population, paying no heed to
the positive attitude of the authorities of a higher instance. . . ."[161]

Poor treatment of Jews by lower-level officials of the Kielce regional administration must have happened often, as just a month after the arrival
of the Red Army, in February 1945, the Provincial Authority addressed
this message to the county governors and administrators of *miasta
wydzielone* (larger cities with dual local- and county-level governance) in
Kielce Province:

> It has come to the attention of the Ministry of Public Administration
> that citizens of Jewish nationality living in the territory of the province
> are not received appropriately and assisted by particular authorities and
> offices.
>
> In consideration of the above . . . the Provincial Office asks the Cit-
> izen County Governors and Municipal Administrations of the *miasta
> wydzielone* to provide the office personnel who report to them with ap-
> propriate instruction so that all clients coming to their offices will be
> received and treated appropriately and with due speed, and their af-
> fairs concluded matter-of-factly. Those who violate the above rules must
> be held to official account.[162]

The letter and the orders of provincial authorities appeared to have no great impact on how the county governor in Radom served Jewish petitioners. A fragment of correspondence from the Radom District Jewish Committee to the county governor bears witness to this:

> . . . we inform you that since the beginning of August, 1945 in connection with the appearance of anti-Jewish flyers on the walls of small towns and villages belonging to Radom county and in Radom city, a delegation of the District Jewish Committee in Radom turned to the citizen County Governor with the aim of informing him and demanding possible protection. After checking in at the secretary's office of the Citizen County Governor and reporting that it is about a matter of safety, the delegation was informed after a two-hour wait that the time had passed, and they should return on the next day.
>
> The delegation made an appointment for 10 o'clock and was assured that they would definitely be received. Despite showing up and requesting a reception they were informed the next day in the secretary's office that the Citizen County Governor had left and there was no possibility of being received.[163]

In this case, the Ministry of Public Administration intervened with the Kielce provincial governor regarding his subordinate: "The county governor in Radom behaves hostilely to the citizens of Jewish nationality [and] constantly refuses to receive a delegation of the Jewish population of the city of Radom. The Political Department of MAP requests that you remind the Citizen County Governor that as a government official he must have an equal attitude toward the needs of citizens whatever their nationality, race, religion, in accordance with the spirit of state democracy."[164]

It is unknown whether this intervention brought any results. Only the answer of the county governor has been preserved. He stated that he receives all petitioners and on the occasion under question he was unable to interrupt an important meeting or forgo an official trip.[165] Even if the county governor's explanation was truthful, what is essential is how his behavior would have been interpreted by Jews in Radom given the difficulties survivors of the Holocaust were encountering in other locales in the region: "In Jędrzejów, county governor Felis takes care of all Jewish matters negatively. A similar situation exists in Chęciny and Chmielnik. In Ostrowiec, the Municipal National Council [MRN] summoned representatives of the Jewish Committee from whom they demanded that all Jews be directed to work in the mine."[166] An appeal to direct Jews to perform hard labor and attempts occurring in the country to mark Jews by stamping their identity documents or issuing distinctive registration cards call to mind the repressions employed after the war toward the Volksdeutsche (i.e., the prewar Polish citizens who during the war declared themselves to be German).[167] While the treatment of the Volksdeutsche was a punishment for their wartime treason (real or perceived—some people were forced to declare German nationality), the postwar treatment of Jews signified a continuation of practices known from the German occupation. That it was seen as such by some civil servants is confirmed by information presented by a delegate of the Jewish committee from Ostrowiec Świętokrzyski (a town seventy kilometers from Radom) during a conference of Kielce Province committees in May 1945: "Recently, civil servants were still expressing their belief that in relation to Jews, German laws apply."[168] This conveys the mentality of some of the workers in the government administration and their attitude toward the Jews returning to the Kielce region immediately after the conclusion of World War II.

The unfavorable attitude of the local authorities created a climate permitting all sorts of open dislike and even enmity toward Jews. The posture of the Catholic Church also contributed to this atmosphere. The second important actor on the postwar stage (perhaps even the most important at a moment when the new authorities had barely achieved legitimacy), the Church did not take a decided stand against anti-Semitism. The Kielce pogrom revealed explicitly the indifferent or thoroughly negative attitude of numerous priests and officials of the Roman Catholic Church in Poland toward the question of violence against Jews. At the same time, one can assume that the position (more often the lack of one) of representatives of the Church had a significant influence on the attitude of society as a whole toward the Jews. According to Bożena Szaynok, until July 1946 the topic of the safety of Jews "was mentioned [only] a few times in speeches by the clergy and in the Catholic press."[169] Representatives of the community of survivors turned to Church officials with pleas for official condemnation of murders and anti-Jewish violence. The answers of the Church dignitaries to these appeals allowed Szaynok to reconstruct the dominant attitude among Polish clergy on the topic of postwar violence against Jews: "All of them in more or less open fashion let it be understood that attacks against Jews, about which they were informed, are not the only example of bandit-like behavior in postwar Poland. Another element of the Church's position in this matter was a conviction about the strong connections of Jews with the communist power and a conviction about their [i.e., the Church's] lack of real influence on the existing situation."[170]

Both before and even after the pogrom in Kielce, voices unambiguously condemning crimes against Jews and the accusations of ritual murder that cropped up in various parts of the country were unusually rare among the officials of the Catholic Church in Poland. On July 11, 1946, the Polish primate, Cardinal August Hlond, published a statement defining the position of the national church in relation to the Kielce pogrom and Polish-Jewish relations right after the war.[171] He declared that the events in Kielce had no racist underpinning. He pointed clearly to the guilty tensions in Polish-Jewish relations: ". . . this good attitude [of Poles toward Jews] is spoiled, for which to a large extent the Jews bear responsibility, occupying as they do in Poland leading positions in public life, and aspiring to impose structural forms, which an enormous majority of the nation does not desire."[172] In this way, the primate suggested that Jews were murdered in Kielce not because they were Jews, but because other Jews were communists. In his declaration, the head of the Church in Poland also pointed out that the Jews killed in Poland were victims of a political struggle in the country in which "proportionately more Poles are perishing."[173] Jan Tomasz Gross asserts that the majority of Catholic Church officials in Poland most likely shared the position expressed in Cardinal Hlond's declaration. It appears that the position of many representatives of the clergy toward anti-Jewish violence right after World War II can be characterized as condemnation of the murders themselves with an accompanying absence of condemnation of the pogroms and negation of the fact that enmity toward Jews as Jews did exist. A significant exception was the position adopted by the Częstochowa bishop, Teodor Kubina, who openly condemned anti-Semitism and disavowed all rumors about the ritual murder of Christian children by Jews. However, Bishop Kubina's stance met with public criticism on the part of the episcopate.[174]

Among the opinions expressed by Church officials after the Kielce pogrom, it is also possible to point to voices suggesting that there was no place for Jews in postwar Poland. Such a position was to be presented by then bishop of Lublin Stefan Wyszyński during a meeting with delegates of the Jewish community in Lublin that took place one week after the pogrom in Kielce. The delegates turned to Bishop Wyszyński

> with an appeal that he addressed to the clergy and faithful of the diocese a pastoral call which, by its contents, might contribute to a calming of minds and cessation of anti-Semitic acts in general and murders in particular. Bishop Wyszyński, after listening to the petition, refused to adopt any sort of positive position. He explained this evasively as the apolitical nature of the Church, etc. Finally, he advised that it would be better for Jews if they would just clear out of Poland, to Palestine, for example, or buy some kind of colony or island for themselves.[175]

As of this date, it has not been possible to discover any church sources documenting the course of this meeting.[176] There is, however, a report from early 1954 of a secret informer who reported on Wyszyński, (at the time already Poland's primate), when he was interned by the communist authorities. According to this document, Wyszyński told the informer that when he was a bishop of Lublin he was visited by a Jewish delegation that worked closely with the government. Bishop Wyszyński asked them whether they were a political delegation, hoping to reject their visit, as he was afraid of a provocation sponsored by the communists. The delegation, however, stayed and asked Wyszyński to support their protest. According to the informer, the bishop did not remember details and was not sure whether it pertained to the Kielce pogrom or something else. The bishop did not sign the protest, since he had reservations about the quality of the text. Afterward, another Jewish delegation paid a visit to the bishop and asked him to instruct the worshippers not to destroy Jewish cemeteries.[177] Indeed, in August 1946 Wyszyński addressed a letter to the clergy of his diocese. In the letter, the bishop urged priests to teach the worshippers to respect all cemeteries, sites of mass executions, and grounds of the former concentration camps. The bishop condemned devastations taking place in multiple cemeteries—Catholic and others. He urged the clergy to combat the "Nazi prejudice" that aimed at destruction of Jewish cemeteries: "We shall remember that once this rule is violated—the right of the deceased to rest in decent peace—it will backfire on us in the long run."[178] It seems that he reasoned if people kept destroying Jewish cemeteries, there would be nothing to stop them from doing so to Catholic ones in the future. Hence, the protection of Jews and their cemeteries clearly was not in the center of the bishop's concern.

Dislike for Jews was certainly held by part of the lower clergy, too. In the pronouncements of several priests, it is even possible to come across encouragement for a settling of accounts with the Jews. In one of the main sanctuaries of Radom, the Holy Virgin Mary Church, the priest proclaimed, "take brooms to swiftly clean out this riffraff, the sooner, the better; Jews are our enemy."[179] It is necessary to remember, as Szaynok emphasizes, that Church documentation touching upon the attitude of the Catholic Church in Poland on the safety of Jews after the war is fragmentary, frequently is in no order, and generally continues to be difficult to access.[180] It seems, however, that on the basis of even this incomplete information, one can assert that the Church did not act as a barrier to the hostile mood toward Jews prevalent in the society.

Anti-Semitism in the Region and Jewish Interpretations of Violence

An attempt at a full explanation of the murders of seven Jews in Radom in 1945 and identification of the perpetrators of the crimes and their motives leaves us with more questions than answers. However, in order to comprehend the position of the Jewish community living in Radom immediately after liberation, it is not necessary to ascertain the perpetrators' motivations. As American sociologist Robert K. Merton, referring to William Isaac Thomas's theorem, has observed: "Men respond not only to the objective features of a situation, but also, and at times primarily, to the meaning this situation has for them. And once they have assigned some meaning to the situation, their consequent behavior and some of the consequences of that behavior are determined by the ascribed meaning."[181]

Although it is possible to point to multiple differences between the murders committed in Radom right after the war, these crimes were part of a larger context of anti-Semitism and anti-Jewish violence in the city, the region, and almost the entire country in the second half of the 1940s (and were perceived by survivors as such). As Andrzej Żbikowski asserts: "These murders, irrespective of whether they were committed on racial (antisemitic) or political grounds, or even if they occurred during the course of armed robberies were, of course, only the apex of a broad-based pyramid of torment, humiliation, blackmail, and extortion committed against the unwanted Jews."[182] In the archives and survivors' testimonies, information about the murders has been preserved above all else. There are fewer references to crimes that did not leave fatalities in their wake, to daily manifestations of enmity and dislike for Jews residing in the territory of Radom right after the war. In her report describing the murder of Aron Hendel, his sister-in-law enumerated, matter-of-factly, other attacks in Radom whose victims were survivors: "After this attack there were another several attacks on Jews, fortunately ending without victims, namely on Maria Cyna, Urbach, the Den family, Mumek Heller, Mrs. Fuks. After all these attacks not only were the police regulations not strengthened, on the contrary, the curfew was lifted."[183] Her words indicate that she perceived the murder of Aron Hendel as simply one of many anti-Jewish events.

Although there is no proof that a single, organized group was responsible for the crimes against Jews in Radom, or that the murders were directly connected in some other manner, to survivors residing in the city these incidents formed a sequence of events. The survivors perceived them not as individual acts of violence but as manifestations of the same phenomenon—Polish anti-Semitism. Joseph Freeman, who returned to Radom in 1945, wrote in his memoirs: "The Polish, still hating us and having seen the Nazis kill millions [of Jews], tried to finish off our community. In Radom the killing of Jews was a daily occurrence, and I witnessed several while there. Mr. Gudstat, inside his jewelry store, had his head chopped off by a Polish man who then flung the severed head onto the street. That same day the city's only Jewish tailor, who lived in his shop across from the police station on Zeromskiego Street, was also killed."[184]

Freeman is speaking here about the murder of Ludwik Gutsztadt and no doubt the murder in the Jewish "Praca" Cooperative. It is obvious that Freeman mixed accurate information about the crimes committed in Radom with rumor. According to Gutsztadt's son, a witness to the transport of the victim to the hospital, his father died only three days after being hospitalized. This rules out the version reported by Freeman. Perhaps he believed a rumor circulating in the city about Poles decapitating a locally well-known Jewish jeweler. The report by another survivor proves the existence of similar rumors. Having returned to Radom, this woman learned that Poles had already killed several Jews and cut off their heads.[185] On the one hand, the references to mutilation of the bodies of Jewish victims appearing in the memoirs of both these individuals can be a sign of the panic prevalent among the survivors; on the other hand, it recalls the murder in the "Praca" Cooperative when numerous knife wounds were inflicted on at least two of the victims. Most likely also referring to the crime in the cooperative is the report by Bertha G., a survivor who, along with two colleagues, was staying in the home of a young Jewish couple in Radom. After she had left the apartment, Bertha G. learned that the couple was murdered the following night. In an interview deposited in the Fortunoff Video Archive for Holocaust Testimonies, she stated that Poles had cut off their heads.[186] Information and rumors about cruelly mutilated victims of postwar murders committed against Jews in Radom fell on fertile soil. The majority of survivors who found themselves in the city had still vivid memories of the German occupation. Many of them had seen acts of extreme cruelty during the liquidation of the ghettos, in the camps, during the death marches, or while hiding on the "Aryan" side. Lejzor Fiszman described the Radom ghetto in the course of the deportation: "The streets were sown with corpses. Limbs torn from bodies were scattered about, a severed head lay not far from its torso, there were puddles of blood everywhere, objects, clothing, bundles, feathers strewn everywhere, rising up in the air quite thickly."[187] While it seems unlikely that cold weapons (i.e., knives or axes) were commonly used during liquidation of ghettos, there is plenty of evidence of human blood literally flowing on the streets. After what many survivors had seen during the Holocaust, it was easy to believe the rumors about the cruel mutilation of the victims of postwar murders. There are even reasons to believe that the Jews living in the city perceived postwar violence as a continuation of the violence from the time of the German occupation. Four days after the murder in the "Praca" Cooperative, one of the survivors in Radom sent a letter to a relative or an acquaintance who was still living in the Soviet Union at the time: "The situation of Jews is strained, they are attacking and robbing them. In Radom 4 Jews were killed. At night, Jews walk in the street until nine o'clock; they are afraid of the night, *they are experiencing such a life for the second time.* Fascist bands, soaked through with the spirit of Hitlerism, remain in the forests. There are pogroms throughout Poland. They want to kill off the remainder. Don't come. . . ."[188]

That many events in the city must be recognized as undoubtedly motivated by racist hatred was conducive to perceiving individual acts of violence as a series of anti-Semitic acts. There is no other explanation than anti-Semitism for the attempts at break-ins or the attacks on the Jewish shelter in the city. References to several such events are preserved in the documents of the District Jewish Committee: "On the night of the 28th–29th of the present month [August 1945] an attack was carried out against the Jewish shelter in Radom, as a result of which there were several people wounded and roughed up. As a corpus delicti of this attack, a cap of one of the attackers remained behind . . ."[189] The material proof sent to the Municipal Office of the Security Service (Miejski Urząd Bezpieczeństwa Publicznego, MUBP) did not help in capturing the perpetrators of the attack. I did not come across any information indicating that anyone was charged for the attack on the shelter.

The frequent tormenting of inhabitants of the Jewish shelter terrified the survivors. At the end of October 1945, the District Jewish Committee informed the MO commander in Radom that "almost daily unknown individuals break the window panes in . . . the shelter, and even stage attacks."[190] Such incidents were still occurring at the beginning of 1946. In February, there were two attacks on the Jewish shelter in Radom.[191] Each time it happened at night, and the residents of the shelter were helped by a unit of the fire department located across the street: "On the night of February 14–15, 1946 at 1:00 am an unknown individual began banging at the shelter, attempting to force open the door. Asked who he is, he answered that he is sent from Security to check identity cards. The residents of the shelter escaped through the windows in a panic to the neighboring

Fire Department, phoning the police at the First Station. After not quite an hour the police appeared and arrested the intruder."[192]

One week later, on the night of February 21, 1946, unknown individuals again attempted to break into the shelter, but because of the intervention of the Fire Brigade the attack was unsuccessful. Although from the short descriptions of these incidents it is not clear that these were attacks, there is no doubt that that was how the residents of the Jewish shelter and the District Jewish Committee interpreted the events. There is a lack of information as to whether the man banging on the shelter door on the night of February 14, 1946, really was from "Security," or whether he was only pretending to be a UB officer. It is also not known why it took the police almost an hour to reach the location of the incident. The building that housed the First Police Station was a few hundred meters from the Jewish shelter. Perhaps help arrived more quickly, since the MO policemen arrested the man. It also cannot be excluded that the intruder was drunk. His fate is not known.

Many times, the perpetrators probably were more interested in terrifying the Jews in Radom than in doing them real physical harm. The vandalizing of the grave of Gutsztadt by unknown perpetrators should be counted as one such incident. As Anna Hendel observed in her report, "At present there are only 7 graves in this cemetery—it's all victims of murders by Poles after the end of the war. Not one grave of someone who died a natural death. It is worth noting that the only monument erected on the grave of one of the victims, Ludwik Gutsztadt, was defiled and damaged the day after it was erected"[193] (see Figure 2.5).

The destruction of the jeweler's grave must have made a great impression on the survivors living in Radom at the time. Photographs documenting the demolished tombstone are found not only in the family archive of Gutsztadt's son, who today lives in Israel, but also in the hands of a private person in Poland and in the Clara Thomas Archives at York University in Toronto.[194] It is hard to interpret the destruction of the grave as an act of hooliganism. In 1945, the symbolism of this event must have been clear: in the postwar city there was no room for Jews or for any traces of their presence. Survivors who remained in Radom were not safe not only in their lifetime but also after death. Even the dead could not sleep peacefully.

Figure 2.5 Group of survivors at the vandalized tombstone of Ludwik Gutsztadt in the Radom Jewish cemetery. Summer of 1945. Courtesy Eli Gat.

The attacks on the Jewish shelter in Radom and the difficult conditions inside it made the survivors try to avoid the place. Whoever could, lived somewhere else. Seventeen-year-old Halina Wajsbord, who returned to the city along with her mother and two other women from a camp in Germany, spent the first several nights in lodgings managed by the Jewish Committee.[195] Sometime later they met an acquaintance in the streets. The man insistently advised them against spending more nights in the shelter. The women transferred to an abandoned building of a Jewish school. That same night, several armed men appeared. After ascertaining that there were only women in the building, they withdrew. Halina Wajsbord and her mother managed to stay in the abandoned school for several months until their departure from the city.[196]

Among attacks on individuals were crimes of an obviously anti-Semitic character. The robbery and severe beating of Aron Łęga, who worked as a supervisor in a Radom sawmill, should be counted in this category:

After the end of the war I worked in the state sawmill as a manager. On August 27, 1945, at 3:00 in the afternoon, when I was standing in the hall . . . with a cashier, an individual whom I didn't know walked up to me holding a revolver and asked if I am a Jew. I answered affirmatively and he then asked if I own a weapon. I replied that I do not. Then he shouted, "Hands up!" and ordered me to walk ahead of him, conducting me to the sawmill office. In the office there was another individual, who informed me that in Poland there is no place for Jews, that every Jew is a Bolshevik, a communist, after which he started beating me on the face and head with the revolver, causing 3 wounds on my head and knocking out several teeth.[197]

This attack was not only aimed at the injured man himself but also meant as a warning to other Jews living in the city. This crime had as its aim above all else terrifying Łęga and other survivors. "After this they advised me to inform all the Jews in Radom that there is no place for them in Poland and that Poland [is] only for Poles."[198] Although in this attack, too, there was an element of robbery, perhaps what was more important was humiliating the victim and complicating his life: "After the beating they ordered me to undress until I was naked and left me only in my torn and bloodied shirt; they took all my documents and proofs of property ownership, as well as my change, leaving me without a cent. . . ."[199]

The indifference of their non-Jewish fellow citizens and city authorities to anti-Semitic acts of violence had a great influence on the general feeling of threat prevalent among the survivors living in Radom. The beating of Aron Łęga, as distinct from many of the crimes described in this chapter, was carried out in the presence of non-Jewish witnesses: ". . . they ordered me to lie on the floor and forbade me to notify the police, then left, not detained by anyone, although the attack took place in front of all the workers. However, not only did no one react, but even after the attack not one of the workers who knew me from before the war offered me the slightest help."[200]

The passivity of the victim's coworkers might have arisen from several causes. First of all, the workers may have feared for their own safety; the attackers were armed. This does not explain, however, why even after their escape no one helped Łęga. During the attack, the bystander effect, well known in social psychology, may have come into play: "The greater the number of bystanders who witness an emergency, the less likely any one of them is to help the victim."[201] It is also very likely that none of the workers intervened because the witnesses were separated from the victim by too great a social distance. No one wanted to give any reason to be accused of sympathy for Jews. Perhaps the fact that Łęga was a member of a different, universally disliked ethnic group played a greater role in the decision not to help. It is possible that the lack of intervention on the part of the sawmill workers, both during the attack and after it, was due in part to the lack of social integration between the Holocaust survivors living in Radom and the non-Jewish community inhabiting the city. Finally, the nonreaction of the witnesses could also have arisen from the fact that they (or some of them) shared the anti-Semitic attitudes manifested by the attackers.

Given the passive stance of his coworkers, Aron Łęga must have felt extreme isolation and rejection by people whom, he stressed in his report, he had long known. These feelings were common among survivors. Having returned to the place of their origin, they encountered enmity on the part of their former neighbors. Like many other Jews, Łęga was able to count neither on informal support from non-Jewish acquaintances nor on assistance from his employer or the UB: "When I reported the attack in the head office of the State Forests' Office, to which the sawmill belonged, they informed me that I could no longer work there. The officer on duty at the Office of the Security Service informed me that Jews have nothing to do in Poland and advised me to emigrate."[202]

It is not known what intentions lay behind the reaction of Łęga's employer or the UB officer. Perhaps, in advising emigration, the officer was admitting that the government was in no condition, or did not wish, to ensure the security of Jews staying in Radom. It is easy to imagine, however, that seeing the reactions of the State Forests' Office and the UB employee, Łęga must have experienced an even greater feeling of abandonment and rejection. The situation described by the Jewish sawmill supervisor conveys very well the extreme helplessness of many survivors who fell victim to crimes right after the war. There was no force able and willing to protect Łęga from the next beating. So it is not at all surprising that he decided to leave Radom. He gave his report, from which we know his story, four months later, before a Jewish historical commission in Stuttgart, in Allied-occupied Germany.

Insight into the attitude of the Radom street toward Jews is offered by
reports of the Municipal Office of Information and Propaganda drawn up
in July 1946, immediately after the pogrom in Kielce: "In the current
month, very powerful anti-Jewish moods have revealed themselves, especially among the intelligentsia. The fact of the pogrom of Jews in Kielce
met with the moral approbation of many groups in our community. The
opinion that a ritual murder had actually taken place was generally prevalent. This conviction was prevalent not only among non-party members,
but even some members of the workers' parties gave themselves over to
the collective psychosis. Despite this, with this background there was no
threat of riots in the city."[203]

Someone also started a rumor that Jews in the city were taking revenge
on Poles for the events in Kielce: "Information was circulated that in
Radom a massacre of prisoners had taken place in revenge for the Kielce
pogrom."[204] This rumor was disseminated in an underground newspaper,
which reported in the summer of 1946, ". . . Jews have received from the
security authorities permission to 'execute' well over a hundred Poles as
compensation for Kielce. The crimes were committed in the cells. They
hung people on butcher hooks."[205]

As in other cities in the region, in Radom the authorities organized a
protest action to condemn the pogrom. As the local Radom-Kielce *Dziennik Powszechny* (The universal daily) reported, on July 14 during a rally
in the hall of the Wisła movie theater a resolution was adopted condemning "the instigators and all those who carried out the Kielce crime," and
predicting active opposition to similar actions "in the name of the ideals
of Christian ethics, respect for the dignity of man, his position in the
family of democratic [peoples] of the world." An appeal was also made to
the state authorities to adopt decisive actions aimed at ensuring the peace
and safety of citizens.[206]

The description in the newspaper of the Radom meeting condemning
the pogrom does not, however, present the whole truth about this assembly. The report of the Municipal Office of Information and Propaganda contains a less optimistic image of the meeting:

"The Kielce events forced the adoption of a more active stand; the
weight of the action in connection with the Kielce pogrom fell on both

workers' parties. They organized with the collaboration of the Branch [of the Office of Information and Propaganda] over twenty mass meetings at work places and one public rally. As was reported in a special letter, *the Labor Party and the Polish Peasant Party did not take part. So they turned into completely unsuccessful events, attendance was very low, despite the strong propaganda activity* preceding the meeting."[207]

The low attendance and lack of representatives from the two officially acting political parties can testify to the fact that many individuals did not think it at all appropriate to condemn the pogrom in Kielce. That this was a common attitude is confirmed, additionally, by what happened in other mass meetings, where agreement was not reached on adopting the resolutions: "in the brewery in Radom the workers opposed an anti-pogrom resolution. Also in the cooperative of the State Forests' Office the resolution condemning the Kielce crime was opposed. . . . In Radom some of the railroad workers opposed the resolution condemning the pogrom."[208]

Simply put, the Kielce pogrom met with approbation in many circles. Additionally, reports arriving from analogous rallies in localities not far from Radom confirm this response. In Dęblin, speeches were interrupted with cries met with applause: "Away with the Jews," "They came here to defend the Jews, shame on them," "The Jews murdered 13 Polish children and they . . . came to defend them," "Jews are at the head of the UB," "We want democracy, but without Jews."[209] In Skarżysko-Kamienna, a "stormy mood" prevailed during two mass meetings—in the "Kamienna" factory 500 people gathered, and in the mechanical department of the Polish State Railways, 150. During both assemblies, resolutions condemning the pogrom in Kielce were rejected.[210] In Ostrowiec Świętokrzyski, a representative of the PPR, appearing at a rally called to condemn the pogrom, began delivering anti-Semitic slogans himself: "What is going on; we slave like horses and the Jews in Ostrowiec live as if they're cozily seated near the Lord God's hearth; they buy butter and chickens; where were they when we were fighting in the partisan detachments?"[211]

The comparison of anti-Jewish violence in postwar Poland to the tip of an iceberg (Andrzej Żbikowski writes about "a pyramid of persecutions") seems appropriate.[212] True, the most noticeable are acts of physical violence directed against Jews, but more common in postwar society was general dislike and hostility toward the survivors that created an atmosphere of consent to violence and virtually guaranteed impunity. As is characteristic of icebergs, a broad base was located under the surface, and only occasionally did a visible trace appear in the archives. The atmosphere had, however, immense influence on the lives of survivors living in Poland right after the war and occupies a great deal of space in their testimonies and memoirs.

3

COMMUNITY

THE PREWAR JEWISH communities and organizations they knew had ceased to exist. Having lost everything and everyone, Jews naturally sought companionship. Together, they felt safer. Together, they found it easier to endure their isolation, to celebrate holidays without their families. On March 28, 1945, a young soldier named Michał Guzawackier came to the Jewish Committee in Radom for the seder dinner (see Figure 3.1). Most likely, he was passing through Radom, as he hailed from Przasnysz, a town 200 kilometers away. During the war, he had wound up in the USSR, where he served in the Polish Army.[1] The numerous medals Guzawackier pinned to his uniform bear witness to the combat he saw. In a room decorated for the holiday, paper stars of David hang on the walls. Approximately sixty individuals are gathered around two candlelit tables, modestly set, women in dresses and men in jackets, while a few, like Guzawackier, wear uniforms. There are no children or older people among them. The majority are not smiling; they remain serious. Perhaps they are thinking about those with whom they will never sit down again to a holiday dinner.

THE JEWS WHO took up residence in Radom immediately after liberation met daily with antipathy from the non-Jewish inhabitants of the city. Many testimonies about their return include references to former acquaintances' unfriendly "greetings." Their inhospitable welcome, coupled with information that was circulating about violent attacks against

Figure 3.1 Seder organized by the District Jewish Committee in Radom in 1945.
Michał Guzawackier is the third man seated on the right. Yad Vashem Photo
Archive, Jerusalem, 6622/3.

Jews, led the returnees to perceive Radom as an extremely hostile and
dangerous environment. Jews who fell victim to attacks could not count
on help from their non-Jewish neighbors. The war had loosened ties and
increased the distance between people, particularly the distance between
Polish Christians and Polish Jews. The life-and-death concern of the
Radom community of survivors was how to function in that hostile reality.
At least two strategies for coping with the danger and daily hostility the
survivors encountered can be discerned: flight (meaning, most often,
emigration) and defense.

It is difficult to grasp the true scale of postwar departures of Jews. Immediately after the war, Polish society was living out of suitcases. This
was true particularly of Polish Jews. Without a doubt, the greatest wave
of migration of survivors from Radom occurred in August 1945 after the
appearance of the "D.O.W.S." flyers ordering Jews to abandon the city
and the murder of four individuals in the "Praca" Cooperative. The Municipal Office of Information and Propaganda in Radom noted that in
August 1945, a total of 2,097 individuals left the city for the Western
Territories (i.e., part of postwar Poland that before the war belonged to

Germany).² Some percentage of them were certainly Jews, but many of the survivors' departures, most likely the majority, were not included in the official statistics.

Halina Wajsbord and her family left Radom immediately after the killings in the Jewish cooperative. Years later, she recalled that when they reached the railroad station the day after the crime, the platform was full of people who wanted to flee the city.³ Some left Radom for a short time, intending to stay away until after August 15—the date designated in the flyers as the deadline for Jews to vacate the city.⁴ However, many of them never returned. Most of the survivors living in Radom right after the war had already left before the summer of 1946 when, in the wake of the Kielce pogrom, there were mass departures of Jews throughout Poland.

Those who, at least initially in 1945, decided to remain in Radom had no choice but to turn to the authorities for help. There were no informal channels for influencing the non-Jewish inhabitants of the city to suppress attacks against the Holocaust survivors residing there. Social control had weakened greatly after the war and at times, for all practical purposes, it did not exist at all. Thus, the Holocaust survivors, finding themselves in a threatening situation, requested assistance from the authorities in the hope that they would be treated seriously and without prejudice—although on the local level it was often difficult to count on that. The reluctance of officials was not the only danger to which the survivors exposed themselves by asking for intervention and defense. Their open appeal to the authorities for help, and especially to the Security Service (Urząd Bezpieczeństwa, UB), a branch of the new government that was arousing fear and hatred among so many Poles, risked being perceived as clear confirmation of the stereotype that Jews were communists and were in collusion with the UB. Reinforcement of this belief, prevalent in Polish society at the time, could only cause more harm to the survivors by stoking anti-Semitic sentiments among non-Jews.

The community of survivors attempted to exert pressure on the government through the CKŻP. In the case of the incidents in Radom, such intervention was attempted at least once—after the appearance of the "D.O.W.S." flyers and the murders in the "Praca" Cooperative. However, the chief motivation for the CKŻP appealing to the central authorities was that a pogrom had taken place in Kraków and the sanatorium for

Jewish children in Rabka had been attacked. The CKŻP representatives also pointed to the murders in the Radom cooperative to bolster
their case with the government. The matter was discussed at the highest
level, and the Radom Jews received assurances of government help. A
CKŻP circular from August 17, 1945, sent out to each Provincial Jewish
Committee (Wojewódzki Komitet Żydowski, WKŻ) in the country,
stated: "An intervention with the Prime Minister and the Minister of
Public Security was made; it resulted in the dispatch of immediate
orders to the Provincial Security Commands [i.e., Provincial Offices of
the Security Service] in response to which several companies of troops
were sent to Radom."[5]

It is not known whether the army detachments intended to protect the
Jews actually reached Radom. If they arrived there immediately after the
attack on the "Praca" Cooperative, most likely they did not remain in
the city for long. Already at the end of that same month, on the night of
August 28, there was an attack at the Jewish shelter in Radom in which
several individuals were assaulted. During that same period, in broad day-
light, Aron Łęga was beaten up and there was an attack in the Słowacki
Street apartment of a man named Lewental.[6] There is no information confirming the protection of Jewish institutions in the city by "several companies of troops." Had there been troops in Radom with orders to protect the
Jews, most likely the attacks would have stopped for a time.

After the appearance of the anti-Semitic flyers in Radom and its environs, the District Jewish Committee (Okręgowy Komitet Żydowski, OKŻ)
also appealed directly to the authorities for help. In August 1945, letters
with identical contents were addressed to the Kielce provincial governor,
the county governor of Radom City, and the mayor:

In connection with the flyers that were widely distributed by various
dark, reactionary fascist elements ordering the Jewish population to vacate the territory of Radom county and the city of Radom under threat
of repression, a certain percentage of the Jewish population, in fear for
their own life, temporarily left Radom, leaving their places of residence
to the mercy of fate.

Various individuals are profiting from this and petitioning the
Housing Commission in Radom to assign to them the temporarily

abandoned Jewish apartments. The Housing Commission is accepting such applications and sending out agents, *which arouses in the Jewish population the impression that the entire society sympathizes with similar efforts by the dark elements and increases the panic among the Jewish community even more.*

Considering that the spreading of panic by the improper behavior of lower government offices certainly does not accord with the intentions of the Central Authorities, and considering that at present, after the easing of tensions and the calming of the situation, the Jewish population is gradually [returning] to their apartments, we respectfully request that an order be issued forbidding the Housing Commission in Radom to accept this kind of application.[7]

In this letter, one's attention is drawn to the contrast between the central authorities' declaration and the practices of the local administration. Most likely, in order to heighten its effect, it was sent both to the provincial governor, that is, to the government's representative, and to the local authorities at county and municipal levels. What results this intervention may have had are unknown. Even if steps were undertaken with the aim of exercising better control over the Housing Commission in Radom, they could not have contributed to reducing the panicky mood among the Jews in the city.

After the attack on the "Praca" Cooperative and other attacks on Radom's Jewish inhabitants in August 1945, the District Jewish Committee applied to the Municipal Office of the Security Service for prosecution of the perpetrators. In October 1945, in connection with the smashing of windows at the Jewish shelter and the attacks, the chairman of the Radom Committee appealed to Zygmunt Mazur, the police commander in Radom, asking him to post guards in front of the shelter. The letter is an urgent plea for help: "Considering the danger our charges are in, we ask that you not reject our request because it is a matter of life or death."[8]

A week later, Commander Mazur replied in writing that he had given the staff of the police station near the shelter "an order to send out patrols to the extent possible and to extend help in case of need."[9] This is one of just a few responses by the authorities to appeals for help that can be found in the archives of the Radom OKŻ. The Committee came forward again with a request for protection in February 1946, after two attempted break-ins at the shelter by unknown individuals. In a letter addressed to the Municipal Headquarters of the Citizens' Militia in Radom and the Provincial Headquarters of the Citizens' Militia in Kielce, they again proposed "posting guards in front of the shelter with the aim of protecting the residents of this shelter from attacks."[10]

The requests for assistance and security submitted by the Jews residing in Radom city to authorities at the local and provincial level usually brought no results at all. Jan Tomasz Gross, describing the lack of response by government officials during the Kielce pogrom, observes: "It was entirely clear to the leading figures of the regime—whether in the Party, in the police, in the Security Service, or in the military—that political expediency allowed no course of action that the general public might construe as benefitting the Jews. In lieu of rushing to the defense of imperiled citizens—the Jews of Kielce who were being murdered—the guiding concern of the authorities was to persuade the public that they were not unduly preoccupied with safeguarding the Jews."[11] Gross's observation applies not only to the events in Kielce but more broadly to the lack of decisive action by the authorities in response to the majority of violent acts against Jews immediately after the war. Probably the sole chance for Jews to obtain assistance was to represent assaults against Jews not as racial but as antigovernment. Such a strategy is evident in several petitions and requests by the Jewish community for intervention. However, such appeals, too, usually did not fulfill the hopes placed in them.

On the basis of scraps of correspondence conducted by the Jewish Committee in Radom with the local security authorities, we can argue that in this situation the Radom Jews resolved to defend themselves. Three days after the plea that guards be stationed in front of the shelter, the chairman of the Jewish Committee requested that the MO commander issue him a firearms permit: "Considering the frequently repeated attacks on our shelter located in Radom . . . , we respectfully request that you authorize one rifle, one tommy-gun, and 10 grenades for the Committee office located in Radom. . . . Considering that it is difficult for us to ascertain the permanent residents of the shelter, we respectfully request that you grant permission in such a manner that every time a weapon is entrusted we might know and have control over whose hand it is to be found in."[12]

In mid-February 1946, eight residents of the Jewish shelter also petitioned for the distribution of weapons: "We take this opportunity to emphasize that the shelter, as a gathering of Jews, is often the object of hoo-
ligans' excesses and in light of this we ask that one tommy-gun and ten
hand grenades be given to our shelter."[13] These were not the first requests
for access to weapons that were addressed to the security authorities by
Jews in Radom. Already in May 1945, the Jewish Committee had turned
to the Municipal Office of the Security Service with a request that "permission be granted for individuals guarding the premises of the Jewish
Committee in Radom . . . and the 'Praca' Cooperative Work Society in
Radom" to possess and carry weapons. Later in its request, the Committee
clarified the reasons it was calling for weapons:

> On the premises of the Jewish Committee there are various articles of
> food and clothing that are a public good and designated for sharing
> among individuals who need help, first among them the camp inmates
> who are returning from various concentration camps.
>
> On the premises of the "Praca" Cooperative Society there are work-
> shops and sewing machines as well as various materials that are the
> property of the Cooperative Society and private individuals.
>
> The possession of guns by individuals guarding these premises is
> essential both in connection with the security of the public good en-
> trusted to them and also in consideration of their personal safety.
>
> It is necessary, therefore, to give the individuals guarding those
> premises the possibility of defense in case of an attack by asocial indi-
> viduals and social outcasts.[14]

The request referred to an allocation of two rifles. It is not known how
this appeal was treated by the Radom UB. Probably the committee received some kind of weapons from the Security Service or managed
somehow to get them on its own. In its files is a handwritten receipt drawn
up by a UB officer testifying to the fact that in December 1948, when the
security situation had improved in the city, the Jewish Committee had
handed in to the local UB two Mauser rifles and two tommy-guns. If those
weapons were in the possession of Radom Jews already in 1945, they
would most likely have been located on the premises of the Committee

itself and not in the "Praca" Cooperative or the shelter. Perhaps it was due to this protection that the premises of the District Jewish Committee were never attacked, unlike the shelter, which was located on the same street, and the nearby cooperative.

Several Jews living in Radom managed to arm themselves with guns. This is borne out by a report published at the beginning of 1946 after a visit to Radom by Samuel Margoshes, a delegate of the World Jewish Congress and reporter for the New York Yiddish daily *Der Tog* ("The Day"). Margoshes met with survivors living in the city and spoke with the Committee's chairman:

> "We cried out to the authorities, we begged them to have mercy and to surround us with protection. They calmed us down, but what was the effect? One hundred Jews were torn from their beds and four were shot. The remaining Jews fled immediately. We were left with nothing!"
>
> He stretched out his arm, pulled out a revolver, and laid it on the table. A dozen or so Jews did the same thing. The table was covered with revolvers.
>
> "It's the end!" a middle-aged man with a mild, sad look on his face lamented. "This is how we live now—with a gun at our side. In my building, every Jewish neighbor keeps an ax under his bed. But will that help? A week ago, two Jews were murdered."[15]

After that meeting, Margoshes had to spend the night in the city. He bolted his door and got into bed. He writes, "I wanted to sleep, to rest, to forget, but my fear of death was too powerful. It choked me throughout the entire night I spent in Radom."[16]

The American journalist was not the only Jew in the city experiencing panicky fear. Right after the war, fear was a constant companion to Polish Jews in Radom, as in other places. The postwar anxiety had many faces. Each of the survivors living in Radom at the time had a personal history of fear. Bertha G., for example, a young Jewish woman wounded in a vehicle accident near Radom, was brought, unconscious, to the Radom hospital. When she regained consciousness, her shock after the accident was exacerbated when she learned about the killing of a Jewish couple (the murder in the Jewish cooperative about which she later testified).

Bertha G. kept repeating that Poles were murdering Jews. Her relatives began to worry that she might be killed in the hospital, as there were only Poles there. They quickly brought her back to her home in Białobrzegi near Radom and arranged for a private doctor to take care of her.[17] Their fears about Bertha G.'s safety in the hospital were not completely unfounded. In June 1945 in Lublin, two armed attackers broke into the Sisters of Charity hospital and opened fire on the Jewish patients.[18] Fear was without a doubt the strongest emotion Jews lived with in the social reality of Poland after the Holocaust.

The panicky mood among the survivors was intensified even more by their loneliness. Those who decided not to flee had little chance of an active defense. They therefore had to elaborate a model of passive defense, a means of functioning in society that minimized threats. The Jews residing in Radom, and probably also in other medium-sized Polish cities, created a model of mimicry and withdrawal. Some of those individuals were still living with an "Aryan" identity assumed during the occupation. Others, like the policeman from Radom, Jan Wac, changed their surnames right after liberation. Often, the motive for the change was the desire to legalize the only documents they possessed, identity papers from the period of the occupation.[19] Usually, it was also a matter of concealing their Jewish origin. Very often their parents' first names and their mothers' maiden names were also changed so as not to arouse anyone's suspicion about whether they really were Christians.[20] For many people, the process of "domesticating" their assumed identity meant the complete breaking of ties with Jewish circles and Jewish tradition. As a rule, these individuals do not figure in any postwar documents held by Jewish institutions, but that does not mean that they were not recognized as Jews in the non-Jewish environment in which they lived.

Survivors living in the provinces in Poland right after the war (except for those in the Western Territories) who decided to maintain ties with the Jewish world, or return to it, created closed communities. Within their communities' boundaries, the members fulfilled most of their social needs. Right after the war, living in an environment that seemed to them (often correctly) like a sea of hatred, Jews were fundamentally invisible in the social landscape. They were ghost citizens—physically present, but socially nonexistent for the majority of the city's inhabitants.[21] At the same time, in their closed communities the survivors undertook efforts to re-build life under new conditions, in a reality whose every aspect was marked by the Holocaust.

The District Jewish Committee in Radom

The survivors in Radom lived in constant fear and uncertainty. Some left; others arrived. If we compare data from February 1945 and October 1946, it turns out that in the course of twenty months not only did the number of Jews residing in the city diminish by almost two-thirds but there was also almost a complete change of the people in their group. Only a dozen or so individuals who registered right after liberation were still living in Radom in the autumn of 1946.[22] Despite the unusual mobility of Jews in postwar Poland, the survivors residing in Radom were not only a group of individuals with a common origin or experience; they formed a community. For the entire period of its existence, there was one organization at its center: the District Jewish Committee. In the first postwar years, other Jewish organizations were also present in Radom: the Jewish Religious Association (Żydowskie Zrzeszenie Religijne), known after June 1946 as the Jewish Denominational Congregation (Żydowska Kongregacja Wyznaniowa); a unit of the Union of Zionist Democrats, "Ichud"; a committee of the Jewish National Fund (Keren Kayemeth LeIsrael); the local committee of the United Israel Appeal (Keren Hayesod); the District Jewish Historical Commission; and the Committee for Honoring the Memory of the Jewish Martyrs of Radom. However, none was more active than the District Jewish Committee, and their actions were organizationally and personally linked to the work of the Committee. Thus, the life of the community of survivors in postwar Radom was centered on the District Jewish Committee.

The Committee arose immediately after the liberation of the city. Already on January 27, 1945, it turned to the municipal authorities with a request for one hundred kilograms of bread for "The Shelter of Jews in Radom," and it received that allotment.[23] As Sebastian Piątkowski writes, the first head of the Committee was "a former partisan surnamed Obstler, sent especially from Lublin to fulfill this function."[24] Obstler's signature and a round seal denoting "Central Committee of Polish Jews—Radom

Branch" can be seen below the request for the bread allotment, the earliest of the discovered Radom Committee documents. It is also possible that the founding of the Committee was the grassroots initiative of the survivors living in Radom at the moment of liberation. As Natalia Aleksiun notes: "Some of the committees in the provinces arose spontaneously and only later were they included into the structure of the CKŻP."[25] Irena Hurwic-Nowakowska characterized the social milieu in which, after the war, Jewish committees like the one in Radom arose in Poland:

> All were frightened, wandering, and unable to settle down. They could not return to their homes or their families, for there weren't any. They were people who had survived catastrophe. Persons of vastly different backgrounds felt in their common Jewishness the impact of their shared national fate. The most basic physical needs of former camp inmates and repatriates needed to be met.
>
> The Jewish institutions which operated at this time had great vitality. Jewish committees formed to provide financial assistance and other services. Immediately these committees became the focuses of Jewish life.[26]

A proposal to officially create a District Jewish Committee in Radom was raised during a session of the CKŻP Presidium only on February 21, 1945, when the Committee was already active in the city.[27] Several days before, the official in the Department for Jewish Minority Affairs in the Ministry of Public Administration, Mojżesz Rubinstein, had traveled to Radom. In his report, he asserted that the composition of the Jewish Committee in Radom was inappropriate for personal and political reasons and that the CKŻP had already taken steps aimed at reorganizing the committee.[28] It is hard to say what gave rise to the reservations voiced by Rubinstein. He might have had in mind the absence of representatives of the Polish Workers' Party (Polska Partia Robotnicza, PPR) on the Committee. True, Obstler, the chairman, had declared his party membership, but in the report this information is placed in doubt (in a notation: "so he says").[29] In the first known makeup of the Committee's board, among the fourteen members were six not affiliated with any party, two members of the Bund, two Zionists (noted as "P[oale] Z[ion] Left" and "Zionist"), and one representative of Orthodox Jews ("Agudath").[30] Individuals who were able to pass as supporters of the new authorities were definitely a minority. Aside from the chairman, there was one "Democrat" and one former member of the prewar Communist Party of Poland (Komunistyczna Partia Polski, KPP) on the Committee. For comparison, at the same time, as many as five out of the twelve activists on the Jewish Committee in Częstochowa belonged to the PPR.[31] Perhaps in criticizing the Radom Committee, what concerned Rubinstein was the necessity of ensuring support for the new authorities in an organization representing the community of Radom survivors.

A few days later, at the beginning of March 1945, there were serious changes in the Committee in response to instructions from the CKŻP. The board was reduced to seven individuals. After a no-confidence vote, the board that had been serving until then resigned. In its place, a new chairman, Engineer Mojżesz Bojm, was appointed, along with a three-member board, a secretary, and an auditing commission.[32] It is difficult to determine whether the changes in the Committee made it more trustworthy from the point of view of the authorities. True, in the report cited earlier, the new chairman, Mojżesz Bojm, was labeled a sympathizer of the Bund, and almost two years later his membership in the PPR is noted beside his name, but there are no signs of his having engaged in any sort of political activity.[33] In the archival materials, there are no documents at all suggesting that the Jewish Committee in Radom or its members participated in party politics. The Radom community of survivors concentrated on survival above all. There was no place for politics—not Jewish, not national. There was a branch of the Union of Zionist Democrats "Ichud," but in the light of the documents its activity seems very limited.[34] The General Jewish Labor Union "Bund" most likely was not reborn at all in Radom after the war. There was never a cell of the PPR in the Jewish Committee. This was not due to a rule—in Kalisz, where the community of survivors was not much larger than in Radom, in November 1947 a PPR organization was established within the local Jewish Committee.[35]

What is known of the beginnings of the Radom Committee appears to confirm the thesis by David Engel that although Holocaust survivors often organized themselves spontaneously on the local level, the institutions created by them were subjected, after a short time, to reorganization in connection with guidelines from the CŻKP.[36] In accordance with the hierarchy chart of the CKŻP, the District Jewish Committee in Radom reported to the Provincial Jewish Committee (Wojewódzki Komitet Żydowski, WKŻ) in Kielce.[37] This dependence ended, however, with the death of the chairman of the WKŻ, Seweryn Kahane, in the Kielce pogrom and the liquidation of the Committee in Kielce by the CKŻP at the end of July 1946.[38] After the pogrom, the District Jewish Committee in Radom became the most important Jewish institution active in the northern part of Kielce province. However, one cannot say that it wielded all the powers of the liquidated WKŻ. The Jewish population cluster in the Kielce region contracted dramatically because of the mass flight of survivors from the region.

From the very beginning of its activity, the Radom Jewish Committee occupied a six-room apartment in a three-story building in the center of the city, at 45 Traugutt Street (see Figure 3.2).[39] In the autumn of 1946,

Figure 3.2 Building at 45 Traugutt Street, where the Radom District Jewish Committee occupied an apartment between 1945 and 1950. Photo by Lukasz Krzyzanowski.

the board of the Committee, the secretariat, the bookkeeping office, the storehouse, and a day room occupied the space.[40] At a later time, a prayer room was also set up in one of the six rooms.[41]

In 1945, the Jewish Committee also made use of an apartment in a building located at 27 Żeromski Street, where a library was organized. Its book collection was composed of Yiddish books received from the Municipal Public Library, which had come into possession of them during the war. The Committee also strove to get back books in Polish that had come from the prewar Zionist library.[42] These efforts probably did not bring any results, however. In addition, meetings organized by the committee took place in the 27 Żeromski Street space.[43] Right after the liberation of the city, the Committee also ran an outpatient clinic. Survivors needing medical help were seen there by a doctor and a nurse.[44] The clinic was established in the second half of 1945 and ceased to operate in late 1945, probably due to the departure from Radom of a physician, Ludwik Fastman.[45]

The history of the Radom Jewish Committee fully reflects the fates of the community of survivors there. The Committee was a relatively large organization only in the first months of its activity when it was divided, like the CKŻP, into departments (social welfare, evidence and statistics, culture and propaganda, productivization, and health). The extensive organizational structure turned out to be impossible to maintain in the relatively small and continually changing community of survivors. The membership of the Committee changed many times. Among the at least thirty-eight individuals active in the Committee during its existence, that is, in the years 1945–1950, only a few served longer than several months. The preserved documents make it clear that the local authorities did not devote much attention to the Committee. Perhaps they saw it as a not particularly important self-help organization acting on behalf of barely a handful of the city's citizens. Despite everything, though marginal from the perspective of society as a whole, the importance of the Committee's role in the lives of survivors residing in Radom immediately after the war cannot be overestimated.

A majority of the activities undertaken by the Committee were focused on providing help for Jews returning to Radom as well as for those only passing through the city on their way to other regions of the country. Those who returned from the camps required special help: "children recently returned from the concentration camp in Oświęcim [KL Auschwitz];

they are completely exhausted and physically underdeveloped, in light of which allotting them appropriate nutritional substances is a matter of life for them."[46] At the beginning, the most important matter was organizing food for the survivors. Under requests addressed to the Municipal Administration's Department of Provisioning, the following remarks were sometimes added: "for the purpose of distribution among the poor Jews of Radom city,"[47] "for the purpose of distribution to the local Jewish population and those passing through,"[48] or "In consideration of the very serious situation in which our wards find themselves, we request a prompt allotment of the named products."[49] The Committee's assistance had great significance, since many of the survivors arriving in the city were extremely undernourished, had neither money nor ration cards, and could not obtain food on their own:

> Lately, the number of individuals returning from the German concentration camps has been constantly rising. These camp inmates are physically and materially utterly exhausted. Our obligation is to organize for them immediate food aid. Due to a lack of funds we are in a simply hopeless situation and we cannot meet our obligations. True, we received ration cards on the basis of the list of registered people we presented, but this list does not include individuals who recently arrived. Until the formalities are taken care of we always have to provide food aid for several days. Every day new individuals are arriving who turn to us for aid.[50]

The second elementary need of many of the survivors was at least a temporary roof over their heads, and the Radom Committee undertook this as a first order of business. That is why, already from the first weeks of its activity, the Jewish Committee ran a shelter.[51] Formally, however, the hostel was opened only in March 1945 in a small one-story building assigned to the Committee by the city authorities.[52] But the building was not adapted to the function it was supposed to fulfill. Therefore, the Committee appealed to the Housing Commission to change the assigned space:

> We respectfully request that you kindly allot to us the premises at 23 Kiliński Street for the establishment of a soup kitchen and shelter for

the people in our care. This place completely meets all the conditions needed for this type of institution.

The premises assigned to us for a shelter at 52 Traugutt Street are inadequate, for they require a great investment for which we do not have the funds. Therefore, we would gladly give up those premises.

Considering that it is a matter in this instance of providing additional nutrition for individuals who returned from concentration camps completely exhausted, we ask that you make possible for us the establishment of a soup kitchen and shelter and the favorable execution of the present submission, particularly since the proposed premises are empty and unused.[53]

Attempts at changing the premises clearly were not successful, since the Committee eventually opened a shelter and soup kitchen in the unsuited 52 Traugutt Street building, which was not suitable for those purposes.[54] In the spring of 1945, the shelter rapidly filled with survivors who found themselves in the city and had nowhere to go. In May the Committee turned to the municipal Housing Commission for additional assignments of space in light of the situation they faced: "We submit that at this time we have no available rooms, and considering the continually growing number of Jewish camp inmates returning to Radom, the housing issue is becoming very urgent, since the shelter at the Committee cannot house all the Jews who have returned so far."[55] A few days later the Committee additionally explained:

The housing problem in relation to the Jewish population in Radom has not been resolved despite our numerous interventions and most of our charges are deprived of a roof over their head and must remain in the shelter, which is designed as only temporary housing for former camp inmates.

Over the past few days 78 women returned to Radom from concentration camps in Germany. Additional transports are en route. We have found ourselves in a simply hopeless situation, for we do not have at our disposal rooms in which to accommodate these camp inmates, who for the most part come from Radom.[56]

That same month, the Committee estimated the housing needs of Jews returning to the city as at least fifty rooms, which seems a large number. In the documentation, there is no evidence that the Housing Commission acceded to any of the Jewish Committee's numerous requests for assigning additional premises.[57] Many survivors found their former apartments occupied by new tenants who, most often, had taken up residence during the occupation or in the first weeks after the liberation of the city. For many Jews, the problem of finding their own corner in the city of their birth (or their prewar residence), where they or their families had owned apartments or even homes and townhouses before the war, was a source of additional trauma and frustration, and consequently a reason to leave. People who managed to find somewhere to stay often were living in private apartments or workplaces with other survivors not related to them. It was easier for them to deal with daily difficulties together, and sharing an apartment with other tenants created a substitute for family life. Only as a last resort did survivors make use of the shelter run by the Committee. A critical view of the conditions in the shelter at the end of May 1945 was taken by an inspector for the CKŻP, Henryk Zeliwski:[58]

> . . . at the time of inspection, the shelter was occupied exclusively by former Auschwitz camp inmates (10 women mainly over 40 years old, 7 men among whom were two cases of tuberculosis—17 individuals in total)—it offers a clear image of the entirety of attitudes and work conditions of the Committee in place. . . . Acceptable accommodations, running water, electricity. Maintenance is sloppy despite a fixed monthly budget of 2,000 złotys (for the shelter manager). The fundamental, unacceptable negligence on the part of the Radom Committee and its social welfare officer is the utter lack of a kitchen for cooking in the shelter. Due to this lack on average 20 inhabitants of the shelter are deprived of even the most primitive possibilities for cooking their food collectively, so they do this with great difficulty, individually and by taking turns, which is uneconomical and causes internal discord.[59]

The CKŻP envoy, incredible as it may seem, ordered the elimination of the post of shelter manager. He also obligated Committee chairman Mojżesz Bojm to immediately put into operation a Jewish people's soup kitchen in the city. In addition to the appropriate preparation of the premises, the Committee had to arrange for food products and fuel. To this end, at the beginning of June 1945, letters were sent to the Department of Provisions and Trade and to the Department of Industry of the Municipal Administration in Radom: "The preparatory work for the soup kitchen, which at the moment will supply 300 meals daily, and with the influx of camp inmates will have to increase the quantity of meals, is already completed and the distribution of meals is dependent only on the necessary quantity of fuel being allocated."[60]

Throughout the entire time of its existence, the soup kitchen was dependent on help from the outside. In the initial period, it received food products from the city authorities. Later, it functioned only thanks to financial and material aid provided by foreign Jewish organizations primarily from North America. The aid was allocated by the American Jewish Joint Distribution Committee (known as the Joint) and CKŻP acting as intermediaries. Correspondence of the District Jewish Committee shows that running the soup kitchen meant constant wrestling with problems related to provisions. Particular difficulties arose in the summer of 1945 when the largest number of survivors arrived in Radom. In July and August, the Committee turned to the municipal authorities three times with requests for supplies for the kitchen, ending their letters with the same formula: "In light of the exhaustion of all the nutritional items possessed by us, we respectfully request your kind, swift resolution of this matter so that we will not be forced to stop distribution of the meals which are the sole source of nourishment for the majority of those who make use of the soup kitchen."[61]

In July, the Radom Committee sent a dramatic telegram to the Provincial Jewish Committee in Kielce: "We are without money. Threat of soup kitchen closure."[62] Ultimately, the cafeteria did not stop functioning, but in the second half of 1945 the demand for meals dropped as a consequence of the mass departures of Jews from the city and the gradual stabilization of the lives of those survivors who remained.[63] In May 1946, the issue of the soup kitchen's continuing operation was debated at a joint session of the Radom District Jewish Committee and the local Jewish Religious Association. Representatives of both organizations agreed that the soup kitchen was still necessary. It was decided that the meals would be kosher. It was also agreed that the Jewish Committee and the

Jewish Religious Association would run the kitchen together and cover the costs connected with it. Free meals were to be given to the poorest survivors.[64] I believe it is significant that these arrangements were undertaken in the period of intensified repatriation of Polish Jews from the USSR. The soup kitchen was closed in October 1946.[65]

The Committee also provided survivors with material assistance, which consisted mainly of clothing sent by the Joint or by Radom landsmen organizations active abroad (i.e., organizations of people originating from the city). At times, the Committee also gave monetary assistance to individuals under its care. That activity was insufficient, however, and most likely also inefficient. In a community that remained in constant motion and where all assistance was distributed centrally, actual needs were difficult to estimate. In addition, totally inappropriate, unusable items were occasionally sent to the Committee:

> . . . The District Committee, considering the insignificant quantity of materials allocated to it for distribution, is unable to supply and satisfy everyone appealing for aid. One bale of clothing received by the District Committee in September 1946 contained the following unusable objects, namely: 412 pairs of socks that were mainly worn out and unmatched, 135 assorted children's bonnets, 80 worn-out scarves, 25 pairs of old, mostly unmatched gloves, 80 ties, worn out; tailors' cloth trimmings, stiff men's collars, women's belts, punctured balls for children, and single buttons.[66]

The District Jewish Committee in Radom also served as a contact point for Jews returning to the city or passing through it who were looking for relatives. A similar function was fulfilled, in fact, by all the Jewish committees active in the Polish territories. They registered survivors and collected information about them. Registration in the committees meant an act of formal confirmation of one's Jewish descent, which made it legal to receive aid offered by the committee. As Natalia Aleksiun observes: "In the first months after liberation registration was a universal phenomenon since the Jewish committees organizing it were a source of information about relatives and material assistance received by them as intermediaries."[67]

Thanks to registration by the Committee, survivors left behind a trace in documents and noted their (often only temporary) presence in the city after the war. Lists of the people registered with the Jewish Committee were available to individuals searching for their relatives. The Jewish Committee also acted as an intermediary for contact between survivors and relatives who resided abroad. In this respect, too, the Jewish Committee in Radom did not differ from institutions active in other cities. It is not known exactly how the registration process in Radom proceeded. Presumably, the writing down of survivors' surnames (especially in the first months) took place when shortly after their arrival in the city Jews visited the Committee's office. That is what Henryk R. did when he arrived in Radom from a camp in the spring of 1945. He recalls that in the shelter he was advised to go to the Committee and register in case someone might be looking for him. Henryk, who was nineteen at the time, was entered into the Committee's card file and received some modest financial help and coupons for food. Handing him money, one of the clerks said, "Listen, Heniek, we don't want to insult you, but everyone receives two hundred złotys." According to Henryk's story, that sum allowed him to buy two loaves of bread.[68] At least for a certain period, individuals registering with the Committee could count on such small, but in those circumstances always needed, financial support.

The desire to leave information for one's relatives and the hope for aid on the part of the Committee likely caused even individuals who were only passing through Radom to register, too. Registration with committees in several cities was a relatively universal phenomenon. The CKŻP estimated that 10 to 15 percent of individuals were registered more than once.[69] At the same time, it is difficult to determine precisely the number of people who did not register at all. Some survivors, certainly not many, managed without the Committee's help. Others did not want to have any contact with Jewish institutions or feared revealing their ethnic origin to society at large. Not included in the records are also some number of Jewish children who remained after the war in the custody of non-Jewish families and institutions.[70]

At a time when many survivors still hoped that they would find someone from their family alive, the committees were a natural place for people arriving in cities to meet and exchange information. One should not be surprised, therefore, that many of the returnees made their way to precisely these institutions immediately after their arrival. Sara Zyskind described her first contact with the committee in Łódź:

> When we reached the Relief Committee Office, we were welcomed joyfully and shown a typed sheet listing the names of all those who had survived in the ghetto itself. My heart would not stop thumping as I scanned the list, but there was no mention of Genia or Rysia. Then I looked at the list of returnees. None of the names on it was familiar to me or to any of my friends. The members of the committee told us not to give up hope: the war had only just ended, and very few survivors had managed to return so far. Many thousands must still be on the roads trying to get back. We must have patience—someone was sure to turn up eventually.
>
> Our names were added to the list of returnees. . . . On our way out of the office building, we noticed all the names scratched on the walls of the hallway; they were the names of survivors and people who had returned to Lodz. I picked up a nail from the floor and scratched my name in large block letters on the wall near the staircase. When my relatives came back, they would see my name—a sign of life—even before they looked at the list of survivors.[71]

Zyskind also recalled that in the following days she would go to the building in which the committee was housed several times a day to observe the returning Jews. She counted on finding one of her relatives among them. The Radom Jewish Committee was much smaller and what it could accomplish was more limited than the committee in Łódź, the center of postwar Jewish life in Poland. But it was the sole Jewish institution active in the city, and as such had great significance for individuals searching for family and wanting contact with other Jews.

The Committee also served as the meeting place for survivors and representatives of Jewish organizations who were visiting the city. In January 1946, Sam Lipshitz, a journalist from Canada, arrived in Radom. He was from Radom, but he had emigrated across the ocean before the war. In one of his articles, Lipshitz described the situation he found in his native city at the start of 1946: "It is quiet in the Committee's offices.

Two young girls and Engineer Mietek [Mojżesz] Bojm, the chairman of the Radom Committee, welcome us. They already know that a delegation will be visiting them. They also know that one of the members of the delegation is a Radom native. So they are even happier. Before we realize it, it's growing noisy in the Committee building. News of the arrival of a delegation runs through the city at lightning speed and people start arriving—some to greet us, others to hand over a letter, to see a fellow countryman, and still others, to complain."[72]

Another form of the Jewish Committee's help for survivors was its assistance in finding work for Jews staying in the city. Encapsulated in a propaganda term, "productivization of the Jewish population," this activity was linked with the aim of making the Jewish population "productive" citizens working in industry or craft, a goal that had been set by the communist authorities. It was in third place among the goals that the CKŻP had set for itself (after the struggle with fascism and participation in building a "democratic" Poland).[73] August Grabski points out that there was an essential propaganda dimension in "productivization of the Jewish population": "It was supposed to overturn anti-Semitic stereotypes about Jewish speculators and usurers (to a lesser degree, about so-called *luftmenschen*—people without a steady source of income), and to serve the stabilization of the Jewish community in Poland."[74] It was also a question of a practical goal: the CKŻP and the Jewish Committees reporting to it were undertaking efforts for Jewish survivors to resume paid work, sometimes also to return to their prewar occupations. In contrast to distributing food and clothing, or securing a place to sleep for the night, this form of activity was not just temporary assistance, but rather a structural one. At a time when many Jews were without the means to keep themselves alive, making possible their return to the workforce seemed essential. It can be viewed as a social dimension of return, which some survivors achieved and many more were attempting to achieve. The CKŻP and the local Jewish Committees were supposed to facilitate these returns.

The occupational situation of Jews in Radom immediately after liberation was very difficult. "Only a slight fraction of citizens of the Jewish nationality is working; the majority live on the aid they receive, and a certain portion is involved in illegal trading and speculation," noted

Mojżesz Rubinstein of MAP after visiting Radom in the second half of February 1945.[75] In a community in which, in the first period, craftsmen predominated, an essential problem was to create conditions that would make it possible for them to return to their crafts. This was even more difficult because the Jewish craftsmen had all lost their workshops and tools as a consequence of the war. After liberation, most were not successful in recovering their shops. Assistance was indispensable if they were to return to their prewar occupations. Already at the beginning of January 1945, the CKŻP Presidium turned its attention to the necessity of starting up individual craftsmen's shops and organizing Jewish work cooperatives.[76] However, as can be seen from the report of an emissary of MAP, in February 1945 they encountered serious difficulties in Radom: "The Jewish Committee has done very little in the area of productivization. In this period only one tailors' workshop was organized where 7 workers are employed. The lack of space, work tools, and machines makes the swift organizing of cooperatives difficult."[77] Despite this, in the spring of 1945 in Radom there were already three tailors' and three watchmakers' workshops; one workshop each for a bootmaker, jeweler, shoemaker, barber, capmaker, and upholsterer; also, a dental technicians' laboratory and a butcher's shop.[78]

The artisans who possessed professional qualifications could, through the Committee's intervention, apply for a loan to start up their own shop. Financial as well as material support (in the form of tools and machinery) was supplied by the Treasury for the Productivization of Jews in Warsaw. However, most likely some potential applicants could not profit from such a loan because one of the conditions for receiving it was the presentation of two solvent guarantors.[79] In a situation in which most survivors had very limited means, the demand for loan insurance could be a serious obstacle for individuals desiring to obtain help. After almost a year of activity of the Treasury for the Productivization of Jews, the CKŻP sent the following circular to the Jewish Committees:

The results to date of our assistance to individuals for creating independent workshops have not been satisfactory.

Quite frequently there are instances of the exhaustion of allocated credit, sale of the machinery installed for the use of people working on their own, abandonment of the place of residence shortly after obtaining a loan or receiving a machine.

This proves that the Committees are insufficiently monitoring the loan applications, are not informed as to whether the loan that was granted actually can contribute, and in what time period, to the borrower's becoming independent.

. . . .

The unsatisfactory means of paying interest on the loans is proof that the Committees are not in contact with the borrower, are not interested in their fate, do not know if the loan that was granted served its purpose.[80]

The devouring of aid received for organizing one's workshop indicated how great was the poverty many survivors lived in immediately after the war. At a time when their fundamental needs were not met, the question of returning to their trade was a secondary matter. It is also likely that some of the survivors who had planned to emigrate used the loan to support their travels. The problems to which the CKŻP turned the committees' attention make one aware of the difficulties linked to the creation of workplaces within the survivors' community. A support system assuming relative stability and constant contact between a Jewish committee and a borrower was doomed to failure at a time of postwar migrations.

For those artisans who did not have the possibility of opening individual workshops, joining a Jewish work cooperative was the sole chance of returning to their profession. Michał Grynberg, the author of a work about the Jewish cooperative movement in postwar Poland, also points to other essential factors arguing for the creation of a cooperative: "After all, that form of employment had to create the conditions for concentrating in specific localities larger groups of people for cooperative work; at the same time, these institutions had to fulfill the function of centers for psychological rehabilitation and also for instructing individuals who did not have a trade."[81] The Jewish cooperatives, in addition to being places of work, gave the survivors a sense of belonging to a collective; it was one more dimension of the return to normality.[82] In the spring of 1945, two Jewish cooperatives were functioning in Radom—a tailoring and a bootmaking coop.[83] Both were located at the same address, in an apartment house on Żeromski Street. Most likely, it was a single cooperative shop employing mainly cobblers, bootmakers, and tailors. Available information suggests it was organized by the Committee in March 1945.[84] That cooperative, functioning under the name "Praca," had only nine members in May 1945.[85] The Radom Jewish Committee succeeded in leasing from the government for the cooperative's use machines that had belonged to Jewish artisans before the war. The development of the "Praca" Cooperative was interrupted, however, by the murder committed in August 1945. As a result of the panic that erupted in the wake of the crime, the majority of the cooperative's members left the city, apparently that month.

To be sure, the development of a Jewish cooperative created the possibility of a return to one's occupation, but it was limited by at least two factors. The Committee had to convince artisans—the potential members of the cooperative—of the idea of cooperative work and overcome the aversion of the local authorities overseeing the trade. Most Jewish artisans were not accustomed to working in a cooperative; before the war, they ran their own one-person workshops. As Sebastian Piątkowski notes: "In 1927, among the 81 carpenters, tailors of 'traditional garments,' and butchers belonging to the Jewish Artisans' Club in Radom there were only 30 hired employees."[86] Although before September 1939 there were several Jewish craftsmen's cooperatives in Radom, it seems that they did not play an important role in the economic life of the Jewish community or, indeed, of the entire city. The disapproving attitude of the authorities toward the cooperatives being organized by survivors was manifested in the difficulties created by the Radom Audit Federation of the Cooperative Society of the Republic of Poland, to which all cooperatives active in the region reported in 1945. In May 1945, CKŻP inspector Henryk Zeliwski pointed to both factors that were complicating the creation of Jewish work cooperatives in the Kielce region:

> The Audit Federation in Radom is creating all kinds of difficulties in recognizing the appropriateness of Jewish cooperatives that are being newly founded. It takes months to resolve applications; they are playing for time (it should be admitted that this system turned out to be highly useful and effective in its negative outcomes). In rejecting the registration of a bootmakers' and leather accessories cooperative of 8 qualified

craftsmen, they submitted that Jews can join the already existing (only nominally!) cooperative society of this branch, without taking into consideration the fact that in the very name of that cooperative these words are clearly included: "Christian cooperative society."[87] This method of dealing with the matter leads to an easily understood disinclination, distrust, and a certain anxiety about engaging in one's craft and making one's earnings dependent on the institutions which so unrealistically and unpardonably treat people, a significant majority of whom find the idea of cooperative work to be completely new and even entirely foreign. Instead of encouragement and assistance, interested people are met with difficulties and obstacles that are predominantly purely formal, to be sure, and thus bureaucratic.

The situation described above automatically and unavoidably causes a loss of interest in the possibility of cooperative work, resentment against the initiators (the boards of the Committees) for time wasted in vain (informational, organizational, reporting meetings, etc.), for efforts made and trouble taken, sometimes even financial investments (trips, etc.). As a result, the craftsmen move away from a given locality, seeking a more grateful location for *independent* and entirely *autonomous* utilization of their craft, or—what is most common—they grasp at engaging in trade as the easiest means of earning income, which is successful everywhere.[88]

The Radom "Praca" Cooperative Society experienced difficulties in gaining approval from the Audit Federation. Most likely, the attempt at registering another Jewish cooperative in the city was not at all successful, which is why the boot-making and leather accessories cooperative began business in the spring of 1945 as a handicrafts enterprise.[89] It appears that it was incorporated later into the "Praca" Cooperative. As Michał Grynberg notes, most survivor-craftsmen could not afford to wait for the authorities' decision, "which is why the delay in starting up workplaces in cooperative societies ended in many instances with resignation" on the part of potential cooperative society members.[90]

Jews in many provincial localities in Poland encountered similar problems while establishing production cooperatives. A letter that the Main Administration of the Audit Federation of Cooperative Societies of the

Republic of Poland addressed to its local branches throughout the country in April 1945 bears witness to this:

> The Provisional Central Committee of Polish Jews [i.e., CKŻP] has turned to us with a complaint that the Jewish committees in provinces are meeting with immense difficulties on the part of the local authorities in establishing Manufacturing Cooperatives.
>
> These difficulties are created by the administrative authorities and branches of "Społem" [national consumers' cooperative], or Branches of the Audit Federation.
>
> Considering the problem, the Main Administration of the Audit Federation recommends that the Jewish issues of the manufacturing cooperatives be treated in a cooperative fashion, the same way the issues of Polish cooperatives are treated, without singling them out and without obstructing them.[91]

Probably, in order to make the initiatives undertaken by survivors independent of the Audit Federation of the Cooperative Societies of the Republic of Poland, the CKŻP began efforts to create a central organization that would supervise Jewish cooperative societies exclusively. In February 1946, the Central Economic Office "Solidarność" (Solidarity) was established in Warsaw.[92] This had no impact on the situation in Radom, since by that time the "Praca" Cooperative no longer existed. Also, everything indicates that there were no attempts to organize new Jewish cooperatives in the city.

Many Jewish craftsmen in Radom could not return to the occupations they pursued before the war. They were forced to leave the city or to seek other work. An inspection carried out by the CKŻP in the autumn of 1946 indicated that already at that time the Radom Committee was not engaging in any organized fashion in creating places of work for the people in their care, and there were only three Jewish craftsmen's enterprises in the city (one tailor's shop and two bootmakers' shops).[93]

When one analyzes the entire aid activity of the District Jewish Committee in Radom, the utter lack of information about possible collaboration with non-Jewish organizations is striking. It was different in Kielce, where the Jewish Committee concluded an agreement with the local branch of the Polish Red Cross about providing health care for the Jewish population in the city.[94] In the files, there is no trace of a similar agreement between the Radom Jewish Committee and any of the non-Jewish organizations active in the city. The Committee's correspondence with the city authorities testifies, rather, to its complete dependence on external help rather than collaboration on equal, partnership principles. The Committee (along with the Jews who found themselves in Radom) occupied the position of a client of the authorities and of non-Jewish institutions, and thus had no influence on their decisions and activities. At the same time, after the war the Radom Jewish community was too weak to be self-sufficient. Before the war, when there was a large Jewish population, they could function in almost complete isolation from non-Jewish institutions, in a microcosm whose center was the Jewish community. Many of the Jews living in Radom immediately after the war were familiar with such a life. However, in the new landscape, ideas turned out to be more enduring than reality. The small size and constant fluctuation of the community of survivors together with its isolation from the non-Jewish world, as well as the community's distance from the centers of Jewish life in postwar Poland, meant that the District Jewish Committee had to act in unusually difficult conditions. Thus, a great deal depended on the individuals who could assume the role of leaders.

Discrediting Surviving Members of the Prewar Elite

After the war, Jewish society in Poland was characterized by a ruptured continuity of elite society. Many individuals who were especially active politically and socially did not survive the Holocaust. Representatives of the Jewish intelligentsia as well as various types of leaders had been met with particular repression on the part of the occupying German power. Considering their position in prewar society, these individuals were marked by the Germans as potentially dangerous. The specific repressions aimed at the Jewish intelligentsia and prewar activists did not bypass Radom. In the second half of 1941, the occupying authorities conducted roundups of people connected with the communists and the Bund in the Radom ghetto. According to an account given by Ichiel Leszcz, one of the Jewish members of a prewar Radom city council, sometimes just being related to political activists or even having the same surname meant a death sentence: "They searched for communists like Frydman and Grosman who were on their list, but they were no longer there, so they found other Frydmans and other Grosmans. A certain Margolis was executed whose cousin had been a communist activist thirty years earlier, prior to the cousin's emigration to America. All the Bund activists were shot, people who belonged to no party were shot. People were sent to Auschwitz. As a councillor I was afraid to sleep at home."[95]

Before the launch of the Final Solution that destined all Jews in Nazi-controlled territories for death, Leszcz and others with similar backgrounds were particularly endangered due to their prewar political activism. There is also evidence about the actions targeting the Jewish elite society even after the majority of the Radom Jews had been murdered in the Treblinka extermination camp. At the beginning of 1943, the German administration of the camp on Szwarlikowska Street that was created for Jews after the liquidation of the Radom ghetto announced the possible exchange of several of the Jews in Radom for German citizens interned in Palestine. The camp prisoners' trust was probably boosted by the conviction prevailing among the Radom Jews that in late autumn of the previous year, a dozen or so individuals holding foreign passports had been sent from Radom to Palestine. In 1943, only Jews with higher education, doctors, engineers, and members of their families would qualify for an exchange.[96] This account appears to confirm Sebastian Piątkowski's thesis that in announcing the creation of a list of people for an exchange, the German authorities were intent on unmasking "intelligentsia who were now concealing their former social status" and also "potential creators of resistance."[97] Ichiel Leszcz's words also leave no room for doubt that the goal of the action was the elimination of the remaining members of the best educated stratum of Radom Jews: "The Purim action against the Jewish intelligentsia took place in a particularly subtle manner. They were fooled into believing that they were to be sent to Palestine since there was an order to deport the Jewish intelligentsia to their country. One hundred fifty individuals from among the intelligentsia and other strata signed up for the list. This was on March 21, 1943. Instead of Palestine, they were sent to the Szydłowiec cemetery."[98]

Among the approximately 130–150 volunteers selected for departure were many factory owners, civil servants, and physicians. Toward the end of March 1943, these individuals were transported from Radom by truck. Almost all who had declared their desire to participate in the prisoner exchange were shot in a mass execution in the Jewish cemetery in Szydłowiec, a town some thirty kilometers from Radom.[99] The victims of this execution whose names Leszcz mentioned can be counted as members of the intelligentsia or as belonging to intelligentsia families: "Mothers had to undress their children. The wife of Engineer Korman undressed her own child and the children of her sister, who was the wife of Attorney Salbe. Dr. Frich grabbed a knife from a Ukrainian [guard] and attacked him. He [i.e., Dr. Frich] was murdered in a cruel fashion along with his family. Prof. Dr. Szicer perished at that time along with his wife."[100]

The Nazi authorities' policy reaped a bloody harvest among the Jewish elites. Many among the small number of those who managed to survive never returned to where they had lived before the war. Some of them had to struggle with controversies stemming from their activities during the war. In accordance with an order from Reinhard Heydrich, individuals who enjoyed respect within the Jewish community were conscripted into Judenrat staffs. Saul Friedländer observes that this regulation probably derived from two assumptions: the Jewish elites would become agents of submission to the occupying authorities rather than leaders of resistance; and as people universally respected they would enjoy great authority among the Jewish population. Therefore, wherever possible, individuals known mainly for their prewar public activism became members of the Judenrats.[101] The Jewish council of elders, created in Radom in 1939, was no exception. As Sebastian Piątkowski observes, the council arose from the transformation of the Jewish Social Self-Help Committee, an institution created spontaneously by Jews with the aim of helping city residents in the first months of the war. Thus, social and political activists, doctors, city councilors, civil servants, and factory owners entered the ranks of the Radom Judenrat.[102]

At least two high-ranking bureaucrats of the Radom council of elders, both physicians, survived the war and returned to the city: Ludwik (Lipa) Fastman, a laryngologist and "a well-known social activist, city councilor in the second half of the 1930s, and member of the Jewish Committee for Promoting the National Loan"; and Naum (Norbert) Szenderowicz, a dermatologist and venereal disease specialist, "a long-term trustee of the Jewish Orphans' Home in Radom."[103] Szenderowicz completed his medical studies in Prague at the beginning of the 1920s and had been practicing in Radom since 1924.[104] Fastman studied in Vienna. He had worked in Radom from 1929 as a physician for the Social Insurance Company and the Jewish and city hospitals. Both men were already well known in the city before the war. In the spring of 1942, Fastman became the head of the Radom Judenrat after the arrest of Józef Diament, who had held the office until then. After the liquidation of the Radom ghetto and the creation of the labor camp, Fastman fulfilled the function of intermediary between the camp authorities and the Jews imprisoned there. According to Piątkowski, he was a kind of "Jewish camp commandant."[105] In January 1943, Fastman was replaced by Szenderowicz. In the spring of 1946, Szenderowicz described his activities since the outbreak of the war in a letter to the president of the Main Board of the Society for Safeguarding the Health of the Jewish Population (Towarzystwo Ochrony Zdrowia Ludności Żydowskiej, TOZ):

In September 1939 I was fleeing the Germans and thus I was . . . absent from Radom, and when I returned in October, I was coopted into the Council of Elders, which was composed of 30 members, including in that number all the Radom doctors [Jews].

In December 1939 the Radom doctors met with the goal of undertaking the work of the TOZ and at that meeting I was elected leader of the organization.

In the summer of 1941, after the so-called Chamber of Health was established, I was recognized by the Authorities as director of the Jewish chamber of health, subordinate together with the Polish doctor who was the director of the Polish chamber of health to the German doctor who was the director of the general chamber of health.

After the liquidation of the ghetto and the relocation of the Jews who were still alive into the Radom forced labor camp, I became director of the medical department in the camp.

In the beginning of January 1943, Dr. Fastman, until then the president of the council of elders, was arrested, and on January 10, 1943
I was named the camp elder in his place and fulfilled that function for
three months until the day of my arrest, i.e., until May 1, 1943.[106]

From May 1943, Szenderowicz spent half a year in the Radom prison,
after which he was a prisoner in the Auschwitz, Sachsenhausen, and
Dachau concentration camps. In June 1945, he arrived in Radom, where
he reopened his private medical practice.[107] A photograph of Szenderowicz shows a gentleman in his fifties, dressed in a suit, gazing outward
(see Figure 3.3). Large, round eyeglasses in dark frames obscure his bushy
eyebrows. He is almost completely bald. The photograph was undoubtedly taken soon after his return to Radom from the camp. On the reverse
is the stamp of the renowned Radom photographer Stanisław Sybilski.[108]
One month after Szenderowicz's return, Ludwik Fastman also came
back to the city. After his arrest by the Gestapo at the beginning of 1943,
he was in the Auschwitz concentration camp. He survived the death
march and was liberated by American forces in Austrian territory, in
Ebensee camp, a subsidiary of the Mauthausen-Gusen concentration
camp.[109] Both doctors announced their return to Radom in the local press.
In the summer of 1945, in the Radom-Kielce *Dziennik Powszechny* (The

Figure 3.3 Dr. Naum Szenderowicz. ID
photo taken in Radom in 1945. Emanuel
Ringelblum Jewish Historical Institute in
Warsaw, TOZ, 754.

universal daily), the following announcements appeared: "Dr. Med. N. Szenderowicz, dermatological and venereal diseases (formerly of Piłsudski Street . . .) has returned. Radom, Moniuszki Street . . . ,"[110] and "Dr. Med. L. Fastman, specialist in diseases of the ear, nose and throat (formerly of Sienkiewicz Street . . .) has returned. Radom, Piłsudski Street . . ."[111] Announcements of this kind were common at the time. On the day that, most likely, the first announcement submitted by Fastman appeared, Dr. Stefania Perzanowska, who also had been a prisoner in concentration camps, likewise announced in the pages of *Dziennik Powszechny* her return to the city and the reestablishment of her practice. However, the announcements by Fastman and Szenderowicz served more than merely as advertisement and information for former patients. They served notice that two Jewish doctors, whom many of the survivors remembered as important officials of the Radom Judenrat, had returned to the city. As Sebastian Piątkowski writes, "Already at the time of the occupation, as also after the end of the war, the opinions held by Radom Jews who survived the Holocaust about the activities of the Radom Council of Elders were uniformly negative. The members of the Judenrat were considered collaborators who contributed substantially to the tragedy of the Jewish population, among other things by profiting from the misery of their brethren."[112]

The view expressed by Piątkowski requires some refining. There was no agreement among survivors about how to evaluate the extent and ultimate role of the Judenrats as institutions and of their individual officials in the Holocaust. Arguments about the councils of elders have also been reflected in the historiography. Hannah Arendt wrote of the Jewish elites' compliance with the Germans and their assistance in the Holocaust: "To a Jew this role of the Jewish leaders in the destruction of their own people is undoubtedly the darkest chapter of the whole dark story."[113] Saul Friedländer argued against this view, observing: "This largely unsubstantiated thesis turned Jews into collaborators in their own destruction. In fact any influence the victims could have on the course of their own victimization was marginal, but some interventions did take place (for better or worse) in a few national contexts."[114] Raul Hilberg, in turn, focused attention on the ambiguous role the Judenrats played during the Holocaust: ". . . the Jewish leadership both saved and destroyed its people, saving some Jews and destroying others, saving Jews at one moment and destroying them at the next. Some leaders refused to keep this power; others became intoxicated with it."[115]

Considering the differences among survivors in interpreting the role of the Judenrats, it would be best to separate evaluation of the institution (in general, uniformly negative) from evaluations of the individuals working in them, whose attitudes often varied greatly. After the war, this question was considered by the CKŻP. At the end of June 1945, the topic was discussed during the Presidium's meeting:

> Citizen Zelicki: Frequently, people who played an active role in the work of the Judenrats come forward and wish to insinuate themselves into work in Jewish institutions. Also, letters arrive from Provincial and Municipal Committees focusing attention on such individuals. We should probably return to the resolution adopted by the Presidium already in Lublin [i.e., at the very start of the CKŻP's activity] in the matter of compiling a "black list" of such individuals and sending a copy of that list to all branches throughout the entire country.
>
> Citizen Bitter is of the opinion that we must approach the above matter very cautiously. Not all Judenrat officials, after all, acted to the detriment of Jews. There were among them also those who, as much as their strength and possibility allowed, helped Jews. He is in favor of addressing all the branches in a circular, asking them to compile a list of Jewish vermin in a given locality, to submit such lists to the Central Committee, which will examine the matter through a specially selected Commission. The Central Committee will also publish an appeal on this matter in the press.[116]

The diversity of positions taken by survivors of the Holocaust toward former members of the Jewish councils of elders illustrates very well the example of the two Radom doctors. I did not come across any information indicating that the activity of Ludwik Fastman as a high official of the Radom Judenrat was considered controversial. For obvious reasons, it is impossible to rule it out entirely. Information about probable accusations might not have been preserved in the archives; some people might have considered just the fact of participation in the Judenrat as compro-

mising. But the thesis that Ludwik Fastman was not controversial is supported by the fact that during his several-months stay in Radom after the
war not only did he conduct a private practice, he also worked as a physician in the outpatient clinic organized by the District Jewish Committee,
where he interacted on a daily basis with other survivors.[117] We should
also note, however, that Fastman did not renew his social and political
activity while in Radom after the war. He was not a member of the District Jewish Committee's leadership despite being one of the few survivors in the city who was knowledgeable about and had a great deal of experience in social work. He was one of the few Jews who returned to
Radom truly prepared to play a role as leader of the community of survivors. Fastman's attitude during his stay in Radom in 1945 might have
arisen from personal reasons, from a reluctance to be engaged after his
work in the Judenrat, but it might also have been the effect of an unvoiced
charge of collaboration with the Nazis that potentially hung over the
Radom laryngologist's head. Perhaps, as a former member of the Judenrat,
he did not enjoy the trust essential for taking up a key position in the
postwar society of Radom Jews. In December 1945, Fastman left for
Wałbrzych (city in Lower Silesia region where Polish citizens were newly
settled and German inhabitants were expelled), where he began work as
a physician in the Society for Safeguarding the Health of the Jewish Population and was involved in building the local health service.[118]

In contrast, the return of the second Radom doctor and former president of the municipal Judenrat, Naum Szenderowicz, aroused significant
controversy among the Radom survivors. Immediately after his arrival in
the city in June 1945, accusations appeared about the abuses he was said
to have committed when, first as chief physician in the Radom Judenrat's
Health Department, he was responsible for medical care and headed the
infectious diseases hospital in the ghetto, and later, as the president of the
council of elders. In that same month, Szenderowicz reacted to the accusations with an appeal to the District Jewish Committee in Radom for
an official rehabilitation trial. The doctor described his efforts to cleanse
himself of the charges weighing on him in a letter to Mojżesz Bojm:

> I have nothing to add to my request for a court trial addressed to the
> Committee on June 29, 1945, i.e., immediately after my return from

Dachau. You have probably not forgotten that I pushed for that request of mine to be granted both in the secretariat, in person to you, to president Kahane of blessed memory, even to Wajngort, my personal enemy since 1936, and have constantly requested that I be investigated.[119] I also heard from you: "We summon people to court, but you are pushing yourself forward"; you probably have not forgotten my reply, that that is precisely the difference between me and those who fear the court.

Despite my immensely difficult living conditions in Radom (one small room with an even smaller kitchenette—7 people) I did not want to leave Radom, although I have had splendid proposals to go to Olsztyn, Szczecin, Jelenia Góra. I kept waiting for that court hearing.[120]

One month after Szenderowicz's first request, on July 28, 1945, the chairman of the Provincial Jewish Committee in Kielce, Seweryn Kahane, appointed judges in the District Jewish Committee in Radom who were to examine the rehabilitation case of the Radom doctor. Aron Fridenthal (Friedental), chairman of the Jewish Committee in Ostrowiec Świętokrzyski, became the leader of the judges empaneled for the case. Two representatives of the Radom Committee, its chairman, Engineer Mojżesz Bojm, and Ichiel Leszcz, were also to judge Szenderowicz. The committee, however, did not hold the former Judenrat official's rehabilitation procedure, explaining that since no formal denunciation of him had been received, there were no grounds for initiating an investigation.[121] It is not known what precisely was alleged or who exactly made accusations against Szenderowicz immediately after his return to Radom.

After five months of residency in the city, in the autumn of 1945, Szenderowicz left for Wałbrzych, where he organized a division of the Society for Safeguarding the Health of the Jewish Population and even became its director. It is difficult to determine the causes of his relocation to Lower Silesia. The former German territory there was continually receiving new settlers, and many survivors relocated there, including Szenderowicz and Fastman. From Szenderowicz's own words, it appears that he was living in difficult conditions in Radom. It cannot be ruled out, however, that a great role in his decision to leave was played by accusations against him and the consequent social isolation of this once well-known doctor and

activist in Radom. It is impossible to say if in going to Wałbrzych Szenderowicz was running away from his wartime past. There is a testimony
by one of the Radom survivors that concludes: "I stress that after the war
Szenderowicz was living in Radom, but because the Jews treated him with
enmity and harassed him, he moved to Lower Silesia."[122] Even if the doctor's move was an escape, it was not a successful one. Accusations connected to Senderowicz's behavior in the ghetto reached him in his new
place of residence, too. In the spring of 1946, he addressed the presidium
of the Society for Safeguarding the Health of the Jewish Population "about
the initiation of a rehabilitation procedure in connection with my social
work during the occupation."[123] That request also was not granted: "Due
to a lack of competence and a relevant mechanism, TOZ neither took up
this matter nor conducted an investigation of it."[124]

The situation in which Szenderowicz found himself had to have been
exceptionally difficult for him. The stain of a traitor weighed on him, but
his guilt was neither confirmed unambiguously nor even officially named.
In addition, two institutions with the authority to effectively cleanse him
of suspicions about collaboration with the Germans—the District Jewish
Committee in Radom and the board of TOZ—rejected his appeals for a
rehabilitation procedure, thus making a defense against the accusations
impossible. Finally, an institution qualified to adjudicate in instances of
this sort, the Citizens' Tribunal of the CKŻP (also referred to as a Citizens' Court or Jewish honor court; Sąd Obywatelski; Sąd Społeczny),
established in September 1946, took up Szenderowicz's case.[125] This
action, however, most likely was not undertaken in response to Szenderowicz's appeal, but resulted from a denunciation that came in to the
Provincial Jewish Committee in Wrocław at the beginning of November 1946.
The first person to formally step forward with an accusation against
Szenderowicz was a twenty-five-year-old nurse, Bela Frydman, who
had returned to Radom from a camp in 1945. Frydman accused Szenderowicz of accepting bribes in exchange for taking care of various matters
in the ghetto, attempting to force sexual contact, having direct responsibility for her mother's and sisters' deportation, publicly slapping her
face in the bath house, and exercising arbitrariness and self-interest in
creating the "Palestine list"—the list of ghetto inhabitants who supposedly were to be exchanged for German citizens interned in Palestine by

the Allies. In her deposition submitted on November 3, 1946 in Radom, she stated:

> Because I was in Radom throughout the entire period of the occupation, I am very well informed about his *coarse* behavior toward people. As he was the representative of the Jewish community, they were all forced to turn to him on various matters. Alas, there was no chance that the Doctor would do anything disinterestedly for anyone. Whoever was not in a position to ransom himself could perish. Women who were forced to turn to him for help or for intervention had a terrible fate: he would behave outrageously in those instances. I myself can affirm this, since more than once I was the victim of his wild instincts, obviously defending myself, and he promised me that he would take his revenge at the first opportunity. He kept his word.—During the general expulsion [i.e., the main liquidation of the ghetto in 1942], being together with him by coincidence at the station during the deportation of the children and elderly, I caught sight of my mother and sister in the crowd. Addressing a German officer with a request that he help me, he [the officer] informed me that Dr. Szenderowicz, as our representative, could take care of this officially. I turned to him with my burning request, begging him for at least a few words of intervention. I knew that if he wished to, he could take care of the most important matters; after all, he had the closest contact with the German authorities. Alas, he was deaf then to my weeping and pleas. After all, I did not promise him payment for it, and, after all, he had promised me he would take his revenge at some time! My pain was even greater when, in my presence, with no effort, he saved a different individual—the current wife of Dr. Fasknaus [Fastman].[126] He did not want to help my poor mother, unfortunately. Him alone I can thank for the cruel death of my mother and sister—since there was that occasion to save them. . . .[127]

Ten days later, Bela Frydman confirmed her accusations against Szenderowicz, testifying in Warsaw at the Citizens' Tribunal of the CKŻP. The record of the hearing casts additional light on the accusations against the Radom doctor:

Szenderowicz was a very zealous executor of the occupier's commands. The Jews were terribly afraid of Szenderowicz. He was implacable, he sometimes rendered certain services, but only for people who had a great deal of money and paid appropriately; at any rate, he listened to their requests. Toward others who did not have money, he behaved boorishly, did not want to hear them out at all and the Jews were immensely afraid of him because after all he was quick-tempered and violent. The first time I encountered Dr. Szenderowicz was at the end of 1940. I turned to him with a request to be taken on as a nurse at the Hospital for Infectious Diseases. During our conversation Dr. Szenderowicz behaved very aggressively toward me as a woman and I could eventually receive work only at the cost of giving myself to him. Understandably, I protested categorically against such behavior, and Szenderowicz told me "if you begin this way with me, it's no good, I will take my revenge against you." I note that even before the war, Dr. Szenderowicz had the reputation of a man who "doesn't let a woman go." During the occupation, when he was a kind of lord of life and death within the ghetto, that character trait of his distinctly came to the surface and making use of his position he behaved unusually aggressively toward women subordinate to his authority.[128]

Bela Frydman attested that Szenderowicz attempted to force sexual contact also at another time when the young nurse wanted to include herself, her fiancé, and her brother in the "Palestine list":

During registration, Szenderowicz made use of his position in this manner, that being placed on the list was dependent on who will pay more. Whoever did not have money could not count on being placed on the list. At that time, the Jews considered placement on the list as salvation, because it seemed that they would evade deportation in that way. In the matter of being registered I knew that I was completely dependent on Szenderowicz, but despite that I could not muster the strength to go to him. But since it was a matter not only of myself, but also my brother and fiancé, at the urging of my friends I managed to go to Szenderowicz. Szenderowicz behaved horribly toward me. He was already practically undressed. I defended myself fiercely, and when he realized that his efforts were unsuccessful, he ordered me to leave with the words, "get out of here immediately." Then I succeeded in arranging registration through Dr. Fastman.[129]

In the materials of the trial held before the Citizens' Tribunal, there are no testimonies allowing one to challenge the accusations brought forward by Bela Frydman. Among those who gave testimony, however, there are also no eyewitnesses to the events described by the young nurse. This is not surprising, if one takes into consideration that some of the crimes of which Szenderowicz was accused had a sexual character, and such crimes are usually not witnessed, even in more peaceful times. Aside from Frydman, during the court proceedings there was only one other individual who insisted that he had experienced personal harm from Szenderowicz. Fifty-eight-year-old Pinkus Zyskind testified: "[Szenderowicz] personally beat me in 1943 in the Radom camp because I allowed a Jewish carter, who brought in potatoes from the Aryan side, to take 6 or 10 kilograms of potatoes for his family."[130] Other than the testimonies of Bela Frydman and Pinkus Zyskind, the testimonies of the remaining prosecution witnesses appear to rely on overheard opinions or on what they were told by Frydman or someone else who had supposedly fallen victim to Szenderowicz but who at the same time did not personally take part in the judicial procedure. Some of the witnesses informed the court directly that their knowledge came from Bela Frydman, including a man who visited Radom in the spring of 1946 during the Passover holiday. A letter written by him was included in the case file:

And now I will tell you about a certain Jewish girl, Bela Fridman [sic], who lives in Radom on Rywańska St. [Rwańska]. . . . She was a hospital nurse. . . . She told me terrible things about Szenderowicz as head of the Judenrat and as a doctor. Szenderowicz attacked her, and in response to her resistance threatened her with these words: 'you'll regret this, Bela.' And when the expulsion started, he sent her mother and sister away, despite an SS-officer wanting to rescue them. All the Radom Jews speak very positively about Bela. Even the SS-men respected her despite the fact that she often incited the Jews. Her aunt Dina, I don't remember her surname, says that Szenderowicz ripped Bela's blouse on her. The girl is ashamed to talk about that. The girl, her hair disheveled, fled from him.[131]

In the documents of the prosecution, some of the testimonies are based, it seems, almost exclusively on secondhand opinions. Maria Nadel, a former office worker in the ghetto, repeated most of the accusations made by Bela Frydman. The exceptional generality and impersonal form of Nadel's breathless testimony merit attention:

I did not know Szenderowicz at first, *I only heard in the ghetto, that people did not speak well* of Szenderowicz, that he blackmailed, that he took money or presents, and so forth. *People were terribly outraged* that, for instance, during the time of the expulsion action on 13 January 1943 instead of being in the square where he could help people, he was sitting in his apartment with SS-man Szipers [Schippers], who was the executioner of the ghetto after the expulsion.[132] . . . *Some Jewish policeman, I don't remember his name,* told me that he was standing outside the door of Szenderowicz's apartment and heard Szenderowicz's daughter tell her mother "to delete someone else from the list." . . . *It was known everywhere* that Szenderowicz vulgarly said, "if you want to be on the list—then pay." The expulsion action that I have already mentioned, on 13 January 1943, applied particularly to those who were not registered on the list; all of them were expelled and transported to Treblinka, if during the time of reading out the names Dr. Szenderowicz had been in the square, he could have been of help even at the last minute because there were clerks from the Judenrat who, when they were reading out the list of people who were registered and therefore did not have to be deported, read out names that were not on the list in order to save people. *After this I heard about Szenderowicz* that he behaved very boorishly to young women and attempted to use his position in such a way that when one of them asked him for something, he promised that he would take care of the matter, but under the condition that she would "go to bed" with him. Dr. Szenderowicz was exceptionally unhelpful and merciless, as a doctor he could have served the population on many occasions, for example there were occasions when someone was employed at hard labor and could have, with a

medical certificate, freed himself from that job and transferred to an
easier one, Dr. Szenderowicz never gave anyone such a certificate
without money, not even the very ill, *that's what the workers said
where I was working and that was the general opinion in the ghetto.*[133]

It is not only the impersonal form that makes Nadel's testimony barely
convincing. The woman did not cite any scene she herself had witnessed.
Additional doubt should be raised, perhaps, by the fact that Nadel lived
in the same apartment house, possibly in the very same apartment, as Bela
Frydman. (The woman lived with other survivors, but the documents do
not include the apartment numbers.) Obviously, the circumstances do not
settle the question as to the groundlessness or truth of the accusations lev-
eled against Naum Szenderowicz. However, in the eventual resolution of
the case, the court might have had doubts about the reliability of the prosecution witnesses and their testimonies.

Bela Frydman's brother, Tuwia, also testified against the Radom
doctor. He testified that Szenderowicz, as the leader of the commission,
had to have contributed to his being sent to the Bełżec labor camp.[134]
Tuwia Frydman accused Szenderowicz also of much graver acts—
fraternizing with the Germans and responsibility for the deportation of
the Radom Jews: "Dr. Szenderowicz drank vodka at home with Untersturmführer Schippers, known as the Radom ghetto executioner. Drunk,
Schippers beat and did not admit Jews who were the representatives of
the work posts. He beat them with the leg of a chair. He beat Tempelhof
among others. Schippers' drunken condition contributed among other
things to his not permitting the reading of the complete so-called 'Palestine' list, due to which several hundred . . . individuals who were on the
list were deported at the time."[135] Frydman also mentioned Szenderowicz
taking bribes to arrange matters for ghetto inhabitants: "Dr. Szenderowicz in the form of bribes for assigning better work, as Älteste took two
diamonds from Bencjon Szajnberg (presently Sławiński Bolesław, domi-
ciled in Radom . . .)—doctor of dentistry."[136]

There is no documentation that would confirm Tuwia Frydman's accusations. Information about the doctor's friendly meetings with Germans
appears in other testimonies as well, including that of Maria Nadel.
Whether truthful or not, such rumors were undoubtedly compromising

for Szenderowicz. He was directly accused of fraternizing with the enemy in its worst incarnation, the SS. Even if the Radom doctor did drink alcohol with the Germans, intimate friendship with them does not seem very likely, and, after all, Szenderowicz could not be responsible for their later behavior as Tuwia Frydman suggested in his testimony.

Bolesław Sławiński, mentioned by Tuwia Frydman as one of Szenderowicz's victims, himself was among the individuals testifying in support of the doctor. Even before Tuwia Frydman gave his testimony, Sławiński, who was unable to appear in person at the hearing, wrote a letter in which he informed the Citizens' Tribunal about the Radom doctor's conduct:

> He used his influence on the Germans, judging from his behavior toward my wife and me, for the good of the Jews.
>
> On 13.1.1943 a new deportation of the remaining Jews from various work posts took place—it was the so-called "Palestine action." At my request, on that critical day Dr. Szenderowicz at the moment the party was moving out onto the "path of death" pulled my wife out from that group and saved her by doing that. Out of gratitude I gave him 2 diamonds and my wedding ring so that with those items, as I heard, he was able to ransom the life of other Jews, because, as I know, there were instances when Dr. Szenderowicz would give the Germans gifts in the form of gold or jewelry with the aim of saving the life of unfortunates, which he often succeeded in doing.
>
> Considering the above, I personally make no accusations against Dr. Szenderowicz.[137]

This is one of the few instances in the entire Szenderowicz trial when the testimony of a defense witness directly refutes the interpretation of events presented by a witness for the prosecution. The majority of those defending the Radom doctor limited themselves to citing examples of his positive behavior, without reference to the concrete charges.

Szenderowicz denied almost all the accusations. He admitted only to "slapping Bela Frydman in the so-called filthy section of the bathhouse and delousing room as she was the person responsible for order and cleanliness in the bathhouse, which I [Szenderowicz] did not observe at that time despite my warning that 'the commission is coming.'"[138] The defendant presented correspondence from people testifying to the help he gave them during the occupation, and he requested that the court call witnesses including Mojżesz Bojm, the president of the District Jewish Committee in Radom; Dr. Ludwik Fastman and his wife; from Łódź, the director of the Society for Safeguarding the Health of the Jewish Population in Poland; a judge from Poznań; and a doctor from the UB sanatorium in Kudowa Zdrój. These witnesses for the defense certainly would have made a good impression on the court. It is not known, however, if all the people named by Szenderowicz were questioned. If they were, some of the testimonies are missing from the trial documents.

Among the documents Szenderowicz presented to the court are the letters of Rózia Rywan and Celina Nasielska, former workers in the health service in the Radom ghetto. These testimonies originated in April 1946, thus before the initiation of proceedings in the Citizens' Tribunal. Most likely, the women wrote them at the request of Szenderowicz himself, who was counting on TOZ initiating his rehabilitation. Rózia Rywan testified:

> It is known to me from the time of my work in Radom in the surgical hospital in the Radom ghetto, that during the occupation Dr. Naum Szenderowicz, carrying out the duties of director of the Health Center, in addition to fulfilling his purely professional duties worked with devotion and dedication for the common good of the Jews, in particular, for the doctors and medical personnel in the hospital where I was employed, and also for other people.
>
> In the period of his work until the moment of his arrest no one from among the doctors and medical personnel fell victim to deportation from Radom.
>
> I know about the above both on the basis of my personal knowledge and also from frequent contacts with colleagues in my profession.[139]

Several weeks later, Celina Nasielska wrote a letter to Szenderowicz: "Dear Doctor! News about you and your Family afforded me so much joy, as if I had found my Father. After all, you were that for me and in general for all the nurses during so many terrible years. I remember very well everything that you did for me and for Rózia, Doctor. I am full of contempt for all those who now dare to say a bad word about you. Please forgive the tone of my letter, but in writing to you, Doctor, I forget that you are my boss."[140] In his testimony, the president of the Radom Jewish Committee, Mojżesz Bojm, described the selfless help that the defendant, making use of his position, gave him in the ghetto: "I have Dr. Szenderowicz to thank for extracting me from the German armaments factory where I was in very bad shape and giving me employment in this workshop in the ghetto.—At that time it was a kindness for me.—I paid Dr. Szenderowicz nothing for that."[141] Bojm also referred to the matter of the "Palestine list," the crossing out of names, and taking of bribes. He suggested that the money accepted for being added to the list might have been designated for activity serving the inhabitants of the ghetto:

> I know that there were instances when people who volunteered for the Palestine list and ought to have appeared on it did not, however, appear on that list.—I assume that Dr. Szenderowicz had influence on the construction of the list.—I personally appeared on the Palestine list.—If Szenderowicz contributed to people being deleted from the Palestine list, I don't know it, because obviously that all took place behind closed doors.—I heard from people that they paid to remain on the Palestine list.—I do know that there was a so-called "phony cashbox" in the Judenrat from which means were drawn for bribes and presents for the Germans.—There was even a designated cashier for the "phony cashbox."—It was Dr. Żabner (no longer living).—How far everything was carried out reliably, whether the money actually went to the cashbox or to a personal pocket, that I do not know.[142]

Accepting payment from the inhabitants of the ghetto and designating it for the provision of additional assistance was also mentioned in Ludwik Fastman's testimony. The former president of the Judenrat, who held the office prior to Szenderowicz's appointment, testified: "I remember that the Jews gave rather large sums for being inscribed on the Palestine list. I entered them into the general income with the purpose of assistance. What was done in that area in 1943 and how the related amounts were entered in the books, that I do not know."[143]

The attorney's widow who married Fastman immediately after the war testified in favor of Szenderowicz. Romana Fargotsztejn-Fastmanowa, making use of her prewar acquaintances, wrote three letters to attorneys capable of influencing the course of the trial, including the lawyer Ludwik Gutmacher, the prosecutor (the so-called speaker of the prosecution) on the Citizens' Tribunal. Fargotsztejn-Fastmanowa insisted that Szenderowicz "undeservedly became the victim of malicious slander. I owe my life to this man; he pulled me out of a transport that was going to Treblinka."[144] In another letter, she wrote, "You will say, sir, that perhaps Dr. Szenderowicz was moved by some particular views as to my person. But no, because just as he did for me, he rescued from the first deportation my servant (she is living in Radom now; her name is Jadzia Markowicz)."[145] Fargotsztejn-Fastmanowa referred directly to the accusations advanced by Bela Frydman. She described in detail how Szenderowicz pulled her out from among people who, during the deportation, were on the ramp of the Radom railroad station. The woman declared that everything happened so quickly there was no question of saving her husband, Henryk Fargotsztejn, who was also among the people destined for deportation. Fargotsztejn-Fastmanowa in a letter attached to the trial documents affirmed: "It is out of the question that at that moment someone could have spoken to Dr. Szenderowicz or pleaded with him for anything."[146] The woman also tried to discredit the accusation of the attempted rape of Bela Frydman, writing that that was yet another charge advanced by the same individuals: "It is only vulgar picking on someone."[147] Fargotsztejn-Fastmanowa also made reference to the act Szenderowicz had admitted— slapping Bela Frydman's face in the bathhouse—and presented her interpretation of this event: "Do you know, sir, what keeping the bathhouse in Jewish hands meant and whose job it was? It was the job of Dr. Szenderowicz, who wanted to show the Germans that we are not a breeding ground of spotted typhus, that we are not a filthy, slovenly people as they said we were. If Dr. Szenderowicz went so far as to aim a slap at a person who, whether consciously or unconsciously, wanted to discredit in front of the German commission the efforts of Jews and his work as a medical doctor, then that act ought not be brought under the criminal code."[148]

The files of the trial before the Citizens' Tribunal of the CKŻP reveal the extremely varied opinions and interpretations held by Radom survivors concerning Naum Szenderowicz's behavior during the occupation—from the decidedly negative to the unequivocally positive. There were people who considered the former Judenrat president to be guilty of the death of their relatives and of "destroying the Jewish intelligentsia of Radom."[149] Many stated, on the other hand, that they survived thanks to the selfless help rendered them by Szenderowicz. These people considered the accusations against the Radom doctor as ridiculous slander. As Rachela Wajsbrot described it: "He was too great a community worker and had and has too great a Jewish heart to be capable of doing such a thing.—Dr. Szenderowicz himself was arrested and tortured by the Gestapo many times.—He was arrested under a charge of sabotage and under a charge of sending Jews out to underground work."[150]

It is difficult to say what the verdict of the Citizens' Tribunal of the CKŻP would have been in the case of Szenderowicz. Due to the lack of proof, and the fact that the testimonies of the witnesses were often contradictory and mixed facts with opinions, the case of the Radom doctor was complicated. The trial did not conclude with a sentence. In the middle of January 1947, Naum Szenderowicz committed suicide by taking an overdose of medicine. There is no doubt that the doctor's death was connected to the accusations made against him.[151] "His great self-respect could not bear such an insult; he no longer had the strength to explain himself when he had expected to hear words of gratitude; he preferred to stand before God's Judgment and find understanding there. A great community worker, a man with a Jewish soul, was dismissed from his work to satisfy libels and calumny," wrote the doctor's widow, Irena Szenderowicz, several days after her husband's death.[152] She turned to the Citizens' Tribunal for posthumous rehabilitation of her husband. The court did not initiate such a procedure, however, and only allowed the woman to have access to the trial documents. In July 1947, legal action was undertaken against Irena Szenderowicz herself in the Citizens' Tribunal in connection with allegations that she had assisted her husband in putting together the "Palestine list" and even personally drew it up.[153] The proceedings were suspended because by then the widow had left the country with her daughter.

There was also no resolution in the third of the Radom trials, in which an individual connected with the Judenrat was charged with abuse in connection with the creation of the "Palestine list." In November 1948, the Citizens' Tribunal of the CKŻP suspended proceedings against Henryk (Hersz) Zameczkowski, who was living in Warsaw and at the time was an employee of the Joint.[154] He was charged with having taken enormous bribes for inclusion on the "Palestine list" and drinking alcohol with Germans while he was director of the population registry department in the Radom ghetto.[155] He was also charged with having given the Germans the addresses of Jewish communists or of individuals who had the same family names as political activists. The accusations against Zameczkowski also touched upon sexual exploitation of women:

> He did favors for women who gave themselves to him, and took vengeance upon those who rejected his offers. This actually happened to my wife. When she offered him a diamond or money to have a definite place on the list, Zameczkowski said that from women he did not accept payment in money, only in nature. At the time of the action [i.e., the deportation] he did not read out her name and in that way my wife was deported with 7 individuals. My wife's last words still echo in my ears: "I am going to the oven because I did not want to give myself to him." I will add that if one or more individuals is found who state that Hersz Zameczkowski did them favors, then they were ransomed by the sacrifices of hundreds of other Jews.[156]

Just as during the trial of Szenderowicz, many witnesses were found who maintained that Zameczkowski had no influence on the tragic situation in the sealed Jewish quarter or that, on the contrary, he helped its inhabitants. As in the trial of Szenderowicz, the only proof in the case was the testimony of witnesses who most likely relied for the most part on rumors and overheard opinions. Sometimes the witnesses who gave evidence in favor of Szenderowicz held Zameczkowski accountable for exploiting the "Palestine list." Such a version of events was presented by the dentist Bolesław Sławiński. Several other witnesses, in their turn, questioned the validity of the accusations against Zameczkowski, blaming Szenderowicz for everything. The surviving Radom Jews sought in their own circle those who were guilty of the tragedies and misfortunes during the occupation. Although the judicial proceedings against Szenderowicz,

his wife, and his colleague Henryk Zameczkowski did not end in definitive judgments, the accused were also not cleared of all suspicion.

The cases of these former officials of the Radom Judenrat appear to
demonstrate that some surviving representatives of the Jewish intelligentsia
aroused controversy in postwar Jewish society. Neither of the two Radom
physicians who served as chairman of the Jewish council of elders,
Ludwik Fastman and Naum Szenderowicz, remained in the city. They
both were deeply involved in to providing healthcare for the Jewish population in Wałbrzych. Everything indicates that the former director of
the population registry in the Radom ghetto, Henryk Zameczkowski,
did not return at all to Radom after the war, but worked in the Joint office
in Warsaw. Thus, Fastman, Szenderowicz, and Zameczkowski, three
surviving high-placed officials from the Radom ghetto, continued to fill
important positions in the postwar Jewish communities, but none of
them worked in Radom. It is possible that resuming their lives once again
in the city with which their wartime past was connected struck them as
impossible. One of the witnesses appearing in Szenderowicz's case
ended his testimony with the assertion "In my opinion and that of all the
Radom Jews . . . he [the accused] should not occupy any community
position."[157]

"A Leader's Power over People Remains
a Great Mystery": Accidental Leaders

The majority of prewar Jewish social and political activists and members
of Radom's Jewish intelligentsia perished during the Holocaust. A few
survivors from among these groups did not return to the city, or their return was entangled with controversies related to their position and their
behavior during the occupation. In the community of the survivors living
in Radom, new leaders therefore emerged. The longest-presiding
chairman of the District Jewish Committee in Radom and, at the same
time, the most significant figure in the postwar Jewish community in the
city was Mojżesz Bojm (see Figure 3.4). When he assumed his position,
at the beginning of March 1945, he was not quite forty-three years old.
He was older, however, than the majority of survivors in the city and was
one of the few who had higher education.

Figure 3.4 The office of the District Jewish Committee in Radom. Committee
chairman Mojżesz Bojm is seated in the middle. Standing on the left is Jakub
Zajdensznir; the woman with dark hair is most likely Nella Gutman. Courtesy
Barbara Fundowicz-Towarek.

Although Bojm was a native Radom citizen and had lived in the city
right before the outbreak of the war, he was actually not a well-known
figure in the prewar Jewish community. He had completed his engineering
studies in France, and prior to September 1939 he worked as a technical
manager in a plant that produced brass goods—the Bliska foundry.[158] He
was a co-owner of this small company.[159] No records indicate that Bojm
held a high position in the Jewish community or that he participated in it
socially or politically before 1939. He did, however, belong to the relatively small stratum of Radom's Jewish intelligentsia. Although in this milieu, too, he was not in any way distinguished. Most likely, that is precisely the reason why very little information about his life before the
outbreak of war was preserved. The one thing that is known is that in
1936 he married Rywa (Rywka) Gutsztadt, who was two years older
than he was and also a native of Radom.[160] At the time of their marriage,
both were in their thirties. They were, then, people who in prewar Poland would have been considered as having married relatively late in life.
Neither the bride nor groom appears to have come from a well-to-do

family. They did not sign a prenuptial agreement, although it was common practice among wealthy individuals at that time. Nonetheless, they were not badly off. Two years after their wedding, the couple moved to an apartment in a fashionable building on the city's main street. They were representative of prewar Radom's Jewish middle class.[161]

Mojżesz Bojm's wartime fate is relatively well documented. Even before he was selected chairman of the Jewish Committee in Radom, at the beginning of February 1945 he gave testimony about his experiences during the occupation. He also recalled his experiences when testifying as a witness in the trials of Naum Szenderowicz and Henryk Zameczkowski and, in the summer of 1949, at the trial of Herbert Böttcher, the former SS and police leader in Radom district. On the basis of those testimonies, it is known that from the beginning of the war until the spring of 1943, Bojm was living in Radom. While in the ghetto, he continued to work at the Bliska foundry. After the liquidation of the ghetto, he was one of the prisoners employed at the Radom arms factory, where he was a metalworker. From October 1942 to March 1943, he was the foreman of a "metal-work and electrical repair workshop in the Radom ghetto" (most likely this refers to the vestigial ghetto or the camp on Szkolna Street).[162] In March 1943, Bojm was transferred to a labor camp for Jews sixty kilometers from Radom, in Bliżyn. He was supposed to construct a sewer system there. In the summer of 1944, when the front was approaching, there were rumors of a planned transport of camp prisoners to the Auschwitz concentration camp. Bojm worked out a plan of escape: "I resolved to break through the sewer and flee. There were thirty-six Jewish men and five Jewish women remaining. I proposed a joint escape. They hesitated; they believed that the trip to Auschwitz was still not death. Only three men decided to escape with me: the Jewish Engineer Sieradzki, who was formerly the vice-director of the Piotrków power station, Żółtowski from Tomaszów Mazowiecki, and a chauffeur, Grinfeld."[163] The four men succeeded in fleeing the camp and surviving in the forest, where in January 1945 the Red Army offensive found them. It is not known when exactly Bojm returned to Radom, but it appears that it was almost immediately after the city was taken by the Russians.

Although several documents reporting the wartime fate of Bojm exist, there is not much one can say about his personal experiences. The testimonies given at the time of the court procedures naturally touched upon concrete questions and the roles of the defendants in the events under discussion. Also, however, in Bojm's testimony given right after liberation the impersonal language is striking, producing the impression of a man for whom the most important thing was telling the story of Radom Jews at the time of the Holocaust and not his personal experience. This can also be observed in many other early testimonies by individuals coming from Radom (and other places)—the personal experiences and sufferings of the authors are only the background to the annihilation of the entire community. Many survivors, as if feeling morally obligated to testify above all on behalf of the dead, gave few details about their own experiences. Also, by not speaking about themselves, they avoided touching on their most painful memories.

Little is known about the fate of Mojżesz Bojm's wife. This is what appears in the certification of personal data opening his testimony: "Family status: He remains alone. Wife deported to Oświęcim [Auschwitz]. Her fate is unknown."[164] Rywa Bojm most likely survived the war but did not return to her husband and her native city. In the files of the District Court in Radom, there are documents on the Bojms' divorce proceedings conducted in 1948 in the absence of the engineer's wife. The suit brought by Mojżesz Bojm attests:

> In 1942 after the liquidation of the ghetto in Radom the respondent [Rywa Bojm] was transported to a camp and from March 26, 1943 she was in Auschwitz, from which she regained her freedom after the camp was liberated. In these conditions, from the moment war activities had ended, all sorts of obstacles that had made her return impossible disappeared, and since the continuing absence of the respondent is in no way justified, the plaintiff [Mojżesz Bojm] assumes that the respondent has maliciously abandoned him and therefore he desires a divorce because of her culpability.[165]

Rywa Bojm's place of residence could not be determined, so her interests in the divorce proceedings were represented by a court-appointed attorney. Mojżesz Bojm presented two witnesses. One of them testified that he had seen a letter from the woman to her husband sent from Stuttgart, and the other declared:

I knew the respondent before the war and was liberated with her in Germany. As Radom natives we stayed together and that is how I know that she received news that the plaintiff was alive. I know that the plaintiff occasionally sent her valuable items. When I was leaving for Radom, the respondent declared that she did not intend to return to her husband. I returned to Radom in December 1945 and the respondent and I saw each other until the last minute. At the request of the plaintiff, I sought news of the respondent from my cousin who lives in Stuttgart and received the answer that she is not there.[166]

Mojżesz Bojm was granted a divorce.[167] Living in Radom after the war, he was single, like the majority of survivors residing in the city.[168] Immediately after his return to Radom, Bojm began working on the Jewish Committee. In mid-February 1945, he was one of its fourteen activists. On March 2, 1945, during the extraordinary general meeting of the Jewish Committee, a conflict arose between board members and chairman Obstler. In the course of the meeting, both the chairman and his critics presented their lists of candidates for membership on the new board. The name of Mojżesz Bojm appeared on both lists.[169] Clearly, his candidacy did not awaken any concerns. The following day, Bojm was unanimously elected the new chairman of the Jewish Committee.[170] In April 1945, Bojm, together with Ichiel Leszcz, a member of the Committee's board, became a delegate of the Radom community of survivors to the Provincial Jewish Committee in Kielce.[171]

Bojm fulfilled the function of chairman of the Radom Committee until his departure for Warsaw, which most likely occurred in December 1947 or January 1948. That a man who had never before been a well-known figure in the city held the position of chairman for so long probably can be ascribed to two factors. First, Bojm remained in Radom for a longer time. This distinguished him from almost all other individuals active on the Jewish Committee, including those who, like Ichiel Leszcz, possessed much greater experience in political and social activism. Second, Bojm turned out to be a skillful civil servant. "He is the most active of all the Jews and carries out his tasks excellently," a UB officer noted while describing the leader of the Radom community of survivors in the spring of 1947.[172] Management of the Committee must have been very difficult, especially in the initial period, since the number of Jews coming to the city was constantly increasing. The American journalist Samuel Margoshes described the Jewish Committee chairman in an article published in March 1946 in *Der Tog*. In his story, Mojżesz Bojm is a still young, energetic man dressed in a leather jacket concealing a revolver. Reporting a brief visit in Radom and a conversation with survivors who were living there, Margoshes noted the authority Bojm enjoyed among the Radom Jews. The Committee chairman's entrance into a room could calm every complaint. "A leader's power over people remains a great mystery," Margoshes concluded in his article.[173]

Although Bojm without a doubt ran the Jewish Committee skillfully, he did not escape conflicts and accusations of abuse. In 1946, together with other members of the Committee, he was suspected of irregularities in distributing aid sent from abroad. A group of more than twenty survivors defended Bojm and the members of the commission charged with the distribution of gifts. They sent a letter to the Joint:

It has become known to us that several local inhabitants wrote letters of complaint to the Landsmen Organization in America that allegedly we are dishonestly dividing both in-kind and cash allocations, directing their complaint first of all against the Chairman of the local Jewish Committee M. Bojm, wishing in that way to defame our local activists.

In connection with the above, we, the signatories, attest the following: Allocations received from the Landsmen's Organization directly or through the intermediary of the Joint, both in kind and in cash, are shared with the Jewish Denominational Congregation with help from the Citizens' Commission of local Jews, which decides how much should be allotted and to whom. The most important citizens of Radom city sit disinterestedly on the Distribution Commission.

It is possible that despite this there are, alas, nasty people dissatisfied with what they received according to the Commission's discretion and who desire to blacken through insidious means the reputations of people who have nothing on their conscience.

The local citizens whose signatures appear below know precisely that all accusations directed against the local social activists and also against the person of Engineer Bojm are false and motivated by resentment caused by not recognizing them [the authors of the accusations] as requiring [aid].[174]

On the letter were the signatures of members of the "Citizens' Commission for the Distribution of Landsmen Society Gifts" and "Jewish Citizens of Radom City." This document testifies to the considerable respect and support Bojm enjoyed among survivors residing in the city. The description in the letter of the procedure for the allocation of gifts received by the Committee also points to the fact that the chairman was concerned that decisions would be arrived at collectively. During the period of his activism in Radom, Bojm collaborated with many individuals who, often only briefly, were engaged in the Committee's work. He coped exceptionally well with managing the continually changing institution. Such an attitude may have resulted from his prewar experiences of work in the Bliska foundry, which probably functioned on cooperative principles.[175] Sources support the idea that Mojżesz Bojm was capable of working with people, not just managing them. This was the source of Bojm's undoubted success, for which one must recognize not so much his holding the position of chairman as the relatively professional operating of the Committee under his administration. The style of management represented by Bojm turned out to be very successful in the face of the constant changes taking place in the Committee and in the entire community of survivors living in the city, as well as the unfavorable reality in which they had to function. Bojm proved to be a good administrator, and in the course of his tenure his social activist character came out. Although everything points to the fact that this important role landed on him quite unexpectedly, by managing the Jewish Committee, the shelter, and the soup kitchen and by coordinating all other activities undertaken by the Committee, he fully earned the name of leader of the community of survivors in Radom.

For at least several months, Bojm nursed the idea of leaving the Committee. In March 1947 at a meeting of the board, "the chairman declared that he was leaving Radom, taking a health break, and would not return to that position. . . ."[176] The committee board expressed its approval of a leave but did not relieve Bojm of his position. At the end of November 1947, after almost three years of work on the Committee, Bojm sent a handwritten letter of resignation to the Department of Organization and

Control of the CKŻP.[177] He left for Warsaw, where he later worked in the Central Economic Office Solidarność and the National Union of Transport Cooperatives. In 1949 he officially changed his first and last names, becoming Mieczysław Boleński. That same year, he married, and two years later a son was born. The entire family emigrated to Israel in 1957.[178]

In his letter of resignation, Bojm nominated as his successor the secretary of the Committee: "I recommend that this function be entrusted to Citizen Stellman Leon, my current co-worker, and that Citizen Fuks A[bram] B[erek] be named to the post of clerk."[179] The CKŻP used Bojm's departure to reduce the number of salaried positions in the District Jewish Committee. From then on, the sole employee and last chairman of the Radom District Jewish Committee was Leon Stellman.[180] Very little is known about him. The Stellman family had moved to Radom from Przysucha, a small town about forty kilometers away, at the turn of the century. Leon Stellman was born either before their move or right after it. Before September 1939, he was living in Radom. His postwar registration card states that he completed six years of high school. Like Bojm, Stellman did not belong to the Radom elite. Before the war and during the first years of the occupation he worked as a clerk in an iron foundry in Radom.[181] In his application for an identity card in 1941, he wrote that he was an office worker. On his postwar registration card, under "occupation filled before the war," he entered "Industrialist."[182]

During the German occupation, Leon Stellman was sent to the Radom ghetto. From November 1943 he was in a forced labor camp at the Hasag ammunition factory in Skarżysko-Kamienna. After the liquidation of the camp in August 1944, he, along with other prisoners, wound up in Buchenwald, where he remained until its liberation by American troops.[183] His wife and daughter perished in Radom, shot in a mass execution on Biała Street in November 1943 when the Germans finally liquidated what remained of the ghetto along with the labor camp located inside the ghetto on Szwarlikowska Street.[184] Although Stellman gave evidence during the 1947 trial of Wilhelm Joseph Blum, the liquidator of the Radom ghetto, there is no reference in his testimony to his personal experiences. Stellman's statements, like Mojżesz Bojm's testimonies, are a listing of facts documenting the successive stages of the annihilation of Radom's Jews.[185]

There are more questions than answers connected with Stellman's postwar life. It is not known when exactly he returned to the city or what his life was like after his return. At the time he was chairman of the Committee, he most likely lived in the same apartment in which the institution he directed was located. It appears that Stellman was still residing in Radom in 1950. At that time, he was chairman of both the Jewish Committee and the Jewish Denominational Congregation (he had been fulfilling the latter function at the very least since June 1948).[186] The combining of both positions in such a small (and continually diminishing) community of survivors only supports the argument that in Radom the division between the Committee and congregation was almost completely theoretical.

Toward the end of 1950, Stellman disappeared. A document confirming his registration in the Jewish Committee in Radom has been preserved in the Archive of the Jewish Historical Institute in Warsaw.[187] Jews who wished to emigrate legally from Poland presented documents of this type to the authorities. In October, Stellman received a passport.[188] It is possible, however, that his "disappearance" was connected with his entanglement in criminal dealings. His name appears in an investigation conducted in Radom in 1950 in connection with the suspicion that several dozen individuals, among them several Radom survivors, were illegally trading foreign currency. Among the incomplete documents of the investigation, an "incarceration card" from the end of November 1950 has been preserved. It carries an entry reporting that Leon Stellman was detained on orders of the County Headquarters of the MO in Radom.[189] Most likely, soon afterward, in January 1951, Stellman left for Israel. After a year and a half of life in the Middle East, he attempted to return to Poland, but the Polish authorities denied him the right to enter.[190] Everything indicates that with Stellman's departure from Radom, the activity of the District Jewish Committee in the city came to an end.[191]

The last chairman of the Committee no longer played as significant a role in the community of survivors as did his predecessor. This was connected with the decline in significance of the Committee as the group of Jews residing in the city and its vicinity shrank. The institution directed by Leon Stellman was only a shadow of the Committee under the chairmanship of Mojżesz Bojm (especially in its initial period). With the fading of the District Jewish Committee's activity, it is difficult to say anything about the style of management practiced by Stellman. The fragmentary bits of information concerning the last chairman of the Jewish Committee in Radom appear to confirm that Leon Stellman was also not a natural leader of the Jewish community. Like Bojm, the last chairman of the Committee became the representative of the survivors living in Radom due more to the lack of other candidates for the post than to his high qualifications or authority. Bojm and Stellman must be recognized as "accidental" leaders; were it not for the Holocaust, most likely they would never have become such significant figures among the Radom Jews. Despite this, both coped competently with their responsibility and duties as leaders of the community of survivors residing in the city.

The careers of Bojm and Stellman become even more "accidental" when one notes the fact that at least two other survivors residing in the city were known before the war for their political activism. In addition, neither of the two had any accusations hanging over them about collaboration with the Germans. Both engaged in the work of the Jewish Committee, but only to a limited extent. The first of these was Ichiel Leszcz. Before 1939, he was a city councilor, a dedicated political activist, one of the leaders of the Zionist revisionists in the city.[192] After the war, until his departure from Radom, he participated actively in the Committee. He resided in the city, however, for only a few months, and left Radom after the murder in the "Praca" Cooperative in August 1945. The circumstances in which Leszcz left the city are brought into clearer focus by the report of the audit the CKŻP inspector conducted in the District Jewish Committee: "the accounts were handled by Citizen Leszcz, who, yielding to the general panic among the Jewish population caused by the known incidents in Radom [i.e., the murders in the cooperative], fled without handing over the funds."[193]

The second prewar political activist who survived the war and returned to Radom was the shoemaker Bajnysz (Bajnyś) Kamer.[194] His political road most likely began in the Bund. In 1922, he transferred to the Communist Workers' Party of Poland (Komunistyczna Partia Robotnicza Polski, KPRP), and then he continued his activism in the Communist Party of Poland (KPP).[195] At the beginning of the 1920s, Kamer "functioned as distributor of the press and liaison with the Jewish street" in the circle of

Radom communists.[196] His activity in the city broke off in the years 1924–1931 because of his arrest. As Kamer wrote: "In the interwar years I was sentenced to 7 years' imprisonment by the Sanacja regime for my communist activity. Our older son, Jakub Kamer, was also sentenced for communist activity to 3 years' imprisonment."[197]

After he was released, Bajnysz Kamer became the head of the Trade Union of Leather Industry Workers in Radom. According to Sebastian Piątkowski, in 1938, as "one of the best known communist activists," Kamer was nominated by the Provisional Administrative Board of the Radom Jewish Community to the position of community president. It was just a strategic move, since it was obvious the county government would not approve that choice. In the absence of an approved president, the provisional administration could continue its work.[198] Kamer was active in the community of Radom workers until September 1939 when he fled east with his family. He returned to Radom from the USSR as a repatriated citizen in May 1946.

Very few details are known about the prewar political and social activity of Kamer, but even the little we know testifies that he was a familiar figure in Radom, at least in the lower strata of the city's Jewish society. From the point of view of the postwar authorities, Kamer had an undoubtedly praiseworthy record as a communist activist for many years and a political prisoner. There was probably no other such individual in the community of survivors residing in the city. This prewar distinguished communist could have been an important figure in the Jewish community's relations with the new authorities. However, although Kamer served on the Radom Jewish Committee for a time, his name rarely appears in the documents of that institution and his duties there remain unknown.[199] A CKŻP representative who conducted an audit of the Radom Committee in the autumn of 1946 wrote in his report only that "Kamer Bajnyś, a 54-year-old worker, fulfilled the function of member of the board from the PPR."[200] Kamer did not play an important role in the internal affairs of the Jewish Committee, nor did he act as a go-between with the authorities. His signature does not appear at the bottom of any of the discovered letters addressed by representatives of the Radom survivors to local authorities or institutions. In the second half of December 1946, the Committee excluded him from its membership.[201] Although Kamer belonged to the PPR, and later to the Polish United Workers' Party (Polska Zjed-noczona Partia Robotnicza, PZPR), everything indicates that in the postwar period he did not engage in political activity, neither within the Jewish milieu nor outside it. The absence of Kamer in the postwar land-scape of Radom might have been due to poor health. The authors of an occasional publication devoted to the Radom KPP noted: "Unfortunately, a serious illness dating to the period of moving from one prison to an-other deprived him of strength and has currently made his full participa-tion in party work and public life impossible. Bajnyś Kamer paid with his health for his participation in the struggle for social and national liberation."[202]

It is possible that Kamer's health was ruined not by the prewar Polish prisons, as the authors of his biographical sketch suggest, but by his time in Soviet forced labor, followed by exile in Kazakhstan.[203] Supplying in-formation in 1946 for the CKŻP register of survivors, Kamer answered questions about arrest and prison: "Imprisoned before the war politically, and during the war served 14 months in a labor camp in the USSR."[204] He was one of thousands of Polish citizens who fled German occupation to the East and lived under Soviet rule (see Figure 3.5). The Soviet au-thorities viewed these refugees with suspicion and deported many of them as so-called special settlers to the depths of the Soviet Union.

In the first weeks of the German occupation, Kamer left Radom with his family for Lwów, where he worked as a shoemaker. They remained there until April 1940. Kamer's son Chaim wrote down the later fate of the family:

Entirely unexpectedly we were deported by the NKVD [Narodnyi Komissariat Vnutrennikh Del; People's Commissariat for Internal Af-fairs (the Soviet security police)] in cattle cars to the Ivanovskii region of Gorkovskaya oblast. There, Father [Bajnysz Kamer] and my two brothers [Jakub and Kelman (Karol) Kamer] were employed at felling trees; I was a water carrier for the bakery where my mother [Rywa Kamer] was employed. In this way, I, too, earned the crumb of bread that I received from the bakery's manager. We lived and worked there until the agreement between Stalin and Gen. Sikorski was arrived at in 1941. At that time, they liberated us from forced labor and each of

Figure 3.5 Members of the Kamer family in Alma-Ata [today, Almaty], Kazakh-
stan, March 1946. Seated: Rywa and Bajnysz Kamer with their grandson, Leon
Kamer. Standing: their son Karol Kamer with two local men. Courtesy Julia
Linkowski.

us could set off in our chosen directions. My family, persuaded by other
families we'd befriended, escapees from Poland, decided to head to Kazakhstan, drawn by its warm climate. We received train tickets and
dry provisions and set off for Alma-Ata [today, Almaty] in cattle cars.
The journey lasted about a month.[205]

During that wartime wandering, the Kamers encountered Ola and
Aleksander Wat, a Polish-Jewish poet and writer, and former communist
who, like Bajnysz Kamer, spent time in interwar Polish prisons. In the reminiscences of both Wats, the family of the shoemaker from Radom appears several times. In conversation with Czesław Miłosz (the Nobel prize-
winning Polish poet), Aleksander Wat remembered: "The greatest
Polish patriot in that settlement that numbered 500 Jews was Kamer, a
shoemaker from Radom, who had two sons, excellent shoemakers, too.
He was something out of a ballad, that Kamer. An old communist with

an excellent political mind."[206] Aleksander Wat's reminiscences also contain information suggesting that Bajnysz Kamer remained an activist even during the period of his forced stay in the USSR. Still, Wat notes, Kamer's political sympathies underwent a change: "We lived very poorly there and no more than four people could have fit into our small room, but that shoemaker was well off; it was at his place that our meetings against the Soviet authority took place. And he was one of the most passionate."[207]

Ola Wat's narrative about that period suggests that Kamer was imprisoned in the labor camp due to his refusal to accept Soviet citizenship.[208] While her suggestion cannot be proved wrong, it seems more likely that Kamer was not imprisoned in the camp but deported to the Soviet heartland as a special settler. The strict regime and exceptionally hard labor to which the deportees were assigned were in fact not that far from life in a labor camp. Regardless of the details of Kamer's trajectory in wartime Soviet Union, his experience there could have disillusioned the old communist. Thus, it cannot be ruled out that Kamer's lack of engagement in political activity after his return to Radom in May 1946 was not caused by his poor health alone but also by the impact of what he had seen of life in the Soviet Union. In addition, even if Kamer remained a communist at heart, he could not reconnect with the Jews among whom he had conducted his political work before the war. Most of the working class who were the natural political base of the communists had perished during the Holocaust. Communist ideas did not enjoy great popularity among the survivors. For that reason, even had Kamer wanted to continue his political activity, it is possible he would not have met with a positive response from the Jews living in Radom after liberation.

World War II influenced the shape of postwar elites in Poland, Jewish elites above all, as they were fundamentally shaped by the experience of the Holocaust. We can see this in the fates of those surviving members of Radom's Jewish community who were leaders before the war and those who became leaders only as a result of the devastation brought about by the Nazi genocide. The Holocaust resulted in the physical destruction of the majority of the members of the former elites; those who remained alive were uprooted from their prewar social milieu. Some

lost legitimacy because of their involvement in alleged or actual collaboration with the Nazis. The Holocaust deprived these individuals of the
legitimacy necessary for becoming leaders in the city in which they were
active before and during the German occupation. In this context it is
possible to point to the radical change inflicted on the social structure
of the Jewish community by the Holocaust. Leaders of the survivors'
community in Radom were individuals who, were it not for the war,
would never have played a leading role in the community or, most likely,
in any other Jewish social or political organization. As a result of the
Holocaust, an almost complete rupture of continuity among the former
elites and the postwar community leaders occurred. Such a social change
also took place in many other medium-sized cities in postwar Poland. It
seems this phenomenon affected large centers to a substantially lesser
degree. Prewar Jewish elites were more numerous there, and after the
war much larger numbers of surviving representatives of the Jewish
intelligentsia—both natives and new arrivals from other localities—lived
in the few major cities.

"Not to Feel Alone in Painful Memories": Remembrance of the Murdered

All the survivors were marked by the Holocaust. Even individuals who
lived through the war in the depths of the USSR were touched by the experience through the fates of their nearest and dearest. Thus, the culti-
vation of remembrance of the victims of the Final Solution played a
pivotal role in integrating the Jewish community in postwar Radom.
Organizing annual commemorations and amassing proof of the crimes
committed against the Radom Jews during the German occupation served
this need. Such activities were undertaken by the District Jewish Committee and two institutions connected with it: the District Jewish Historical Commission, a division of the Central Jewish Historical Commission
(Centralna Żydowska Komisja Historyczna, CŻKH); and the Committee
for the Celebration of the Memory of the Jewish Martyrs of Radom. It is
difficult to determine what the formal relations were between these two
institutions and the District Jewish Committee. Both organizations

functioned under the same address as the District Committee, and at various times the same individual, journalist Lejzor Fiszman, led the historical and the commemorative organizations.[209] The activities undertaken under the aegis of the Radom District Jewish Historical Commission and the Committee for the Celebration of the Memory of the Jewish Martyrs of Radom should therefore be analyzed in connection with the District Jewish Committee. Most likely the Committee for the Celebration of the Memory of the Jewish Martyrs of Radom established in June 1947 simply succeeded the District Jewish Historical Commission, which had been active in the city since February 1945. The fundamental aim of the Committee for the Celebration of the Memory of the Jewish Martyrs of Radom was the construction of a monument commemorating the Radom victims of the Holocaust and the enclosure of the devastated Jewish cemetery.[210]

Activities connected with commemoration were very important not only for the integration of the community of Radom survivors but they also made its presence in the postwar city visible. As in Jewish Committees in all of postwar Poland, in Radom annual observances were organized to commemorate the beginning of the so-called Great Action (*Grossaktion Warschau*)—the largest deportation from the Warsaw ghetto (July 22, 1942) and the outbreak of the Warsaw ghetto uprising (April 19, 1943).[211] The Jewish Committee in Radom organized the first formal ceremony commemorating the beginning of the liquidation of the Warsaw ghetto on July 22, 1945, several months after liberation and three years after the tragic events in Warsaw. After the victims were commemorated by a moment of silence, a lecture was delivered describing the Great Action. A report about this ceremony informed that the speaker ". . . concludes his lecture with profound reverence for the memory of the mothers of children, the heroes of unprecedented events in the history of the world, and draws the only conclusion so dearly paid for in blood—that Jews must have their own country in order to stand on an equal footing with other peoples. Afterward, Tuwim's letter 'We, the Polish Jews,' . . . and Broniewski's poem, 'To the Polish Jews,' were read."[212] It is worth recalling that Julian Tuwim's passionate essay is a manifesto of the poet's double Polish-Jewish identity, and Władysław Broniewski's poem contains this message:

This is what must be carved, as if in stone, into Polish memory:
They destroyed our common home, and our shed blood made us
    brothers.
We are united by the execution wall, by Dachau, by Auschwitz,
By every nameless grave and every prison grille.
The sky above demolished Warsaw will shine down on us
    together . . .[213]

That the commemoration program contained a lecture with a distinct
Zionist accent as well as two literary works in which the connection of
Jews with Poland and Polishness was underlined confirms Irena Hurwic-
Nowakowska's thesis about the frequent appearance among survivors of
a dual identity, with their ideological fatherland being a Jewish state, and
their private fatherland—Poland.[214] According to Hurwic-Nowakowska,
Polish Jews who survived the Holocaust understood these concepts par-
ticularly well.[215]

Of all the ceremonies commemorating the Holocaust, most likely it was
the observance of the anniversaries of the liquidation of the Radom ghetto
that held the greatest significance for the local community of survivors.
The records of the District Jewish Committee indicate that the anniversaries of the main liquidation action of the small ghetto in Glinice (August 4–5, 1942) and of the large ghetto in the city center (August 16–17,
1942) were both observed. In addition to that, the anniversaries of the other
deportations of Jews from the city were also remembered.[216] The fifth
anniversary of the liquidation of the Radom ghetto, in August 1947, had
a particularly poignant character. It coincided with the trial of Wilhelm
Joseph Blum, the man directly responsible for carrying out Operation
Reinhardt (*Aktion Reinhardt; a* mass annihilation of the Jewish population of the General Government) in the Radom district. As the plenipotentiary of Odilo Globocnik, a top Nazi official directing Operation
Reinhardt, Blum personally supervised the deportation of the majority of Radom ghetto inhabitants to the Treblinka extermination camp.[217]
The coincidence in the timing of the German war criminal's trial and
the ghetto liquidation anniversary was not accidental. At the end of
June 1947, the Jewish Committee submitted an official letter to the prosecutor of the District Court in Radom:

As we are aware, Wilhelm Blum, an SS-man and former higher official of the Polizeiamt in Radom district, a monstrous executioner and the direct co-liquidator of the ghettoes in Radom, is in the Radom prison. On the 16th and 17th of August we will observe the fifth anniversary of the annihilation of the Radom Jews to which the above-mentioned executioner contributed so significantly. We humbly request of the Honorable Citizen Prosecutor that he arrange it so that the trial of Blum might take place symbolically on the day of the observance of that sad anniversary, i.e., the 16th of August 1947.[218]

The Central Jewish Historical Commission addressed the court on the same matter.[219] The request of the Jewish community met with a positive response. Blum's trial before the District Court in Radom began on Saturday, August 16, 1947 (see Figure 3.6). Three days later, the former deputy chief of the SS and police in the Radom district was sentenced to death.[220] The local press wrote about the trial and recalled the history of the Holocaust in Radom. In one of the daily newspapers, two texts written

Figure 3.6 Trial of Wilhelm Joseph Blum, former deputy chief of the SS and police in the Radom district. District Court in Radom, August 16–19, 1947.
Archiwum Państwowe w Radomiu, 207/169.

by Lejzor Fiszman appeared. He described in detail the liquidation of the Radom ghetto.[221]

Blum was not accused of any crimes committed against Christian citizens. The document listing the charges shows that the prosecution was concerned exclusively with his participation in the annihilation of the Jewish population of Radom and his membership in the SS.[222] Survivors living in the city as well as Jews from Radom residing in other regions of the country were mobilized to participate in the trial. The Committee for the Celebration of the Memory of the Jewish Martyrs of Radom requested that the Legal Department of the CKŻP send a lawyer to participate in the trial in the role of auxiliary prosecutor: "Blum was the liquidator of the ghetto in Radom and personally directed all the actions against the Jews in Radom and the surrounding area. *This trial has a distinct 'Jewish' character and must be monitored,* especially because the public prosecutor is still young."[223] Furthermore, the District Jewish Committee strove to ensure that among the individuals who would judge Blum there would be a representative of the community of survivors. The Committee addressed the president of the Municipal National Council in Radom: "The miraculously surviving Radom Jews wish to have moral satisfaction for these uncompensated losses so that in the composition of the judicial bench there should be a fellow citizen of the Jewish nationality. We therefore request . . . that a Jewish citizen of the city of Radom be named as a juror who will be enabled to participate in the trial."[224] The Committee proposed its chairman, Bojm. In the end, however, no representative of the CKŻP was appointed auxiliary prosecutor nor was any member of the Jewish community added to the judicial bench adjudicating Blum's case. Nevertheless, the efforts undertaken by the Radom survivors testify to the importance they ascribed to the conviction of the Nazi criminal. The trial of Blum became itself a form of commemoration of the victims of the Radom ghetto liquidation.[225]

In order to participate in the observation of the anniversary of the ghetto liquidation and the trial of the German war criminal, surviving Radomers residing in other parts of the country came to the city. The Committee for the Celebration of the Memory of the Jewish Martyrs of Radom sought witnesses who could testify to Blum's guilt and coordinated their travel to the city.[226] Two days before the opening of the trial, the committee appealed to the Municipal Administration to reserve at least fifteen beds in two Radom hotels for individuals expected to arrive in the city.[227] The District Jewish Committee received from the authorities seventy cards permitting entry to the trial hall.[228] The interest in Blum's trial, however, was so great that those seventy cards did not suffice to meet the demand for entry to the courtroom. Long before the start of proceedings, a crowd of people gathered in front of the District Court building.[229] It is difficult to find hard proof in the archives, but it appears that the survivors came to Radom not only to testify but motivated by the need to be together. The anniversary of the liquidation of the ghetto was a moment of unity for Radom Jews—for those who lived in their native city after the war or had briefly returned to it and for those who had left the Radom phase of their lives behind. For all of them, the world had collapsed in August 1942 with the deportation of their families to the extermination camp at Treblinka. On the anniversary of these events, they felt the need for communal mourning. Letters and telegrams sent to the District Jewish Committee testify to this. Survivors living in Lower Silesia sent this telegram:

WE RADOM JEWS LIVING IN PIOTROLESIE[230] DZIERŻONIÓW BIELAWA ON THE DAY OF THE FIFTH ANNIVERSARY OF THE TRAGIC ANNIHILATION OF OUR DEAR ONES ARE UNITED WITH YOU BY THE MUTUAL FEELING OF GREAT PAIN STOP IN DEEP MOURNING WE BOW OUR HEADS BEFORE THE HOLY REMAINS OF THE MARTYRS THE INNOCENT VICTIMS OF BARBARIC GERMAN FASCISM STOP MAY MEMORY BE ALIVE IN OUR HEARTS AND THEIR INNOCENTLY SPILLED BLOOD UNITE US FOREVER WITH THE LAND SOAKED THROUGH WITH THAT BLOOD STOP.[231]

Similar feelings are expressed in a poem by Nella Gutman, one of the surviving Radom young women. Four days before the anniversary observation, she wrote from Kudowa:

Dear Brothers and Sisters joined in pain!
Let us honor today those who perished at bestial hands

Those who were near to us in soul and body
Wherever the wind carries us, let us unite on this day
so as not to feel alone in painful memories
despite our loneliness.
　　　Sister NG[232]

On Sunday, August 17, 1947, the day after the opening of Blum's trial, the Radom survivors organized a ceremony dedicated to the memory of the victims of the ghetto's liquidation. The press reported:

Yesterday, on the fifth anniversary of the murder of thirty thousand Radom Jews by the Germans, there took place in the TUR hall a solemn Ceremony of Mourning. The hall was beautifully decorated with artistic inscriptions. Each of them mentioned a specific date and indicated the number of Jews murdered on that day. On the main wall was a memorial plaque; below it, a large death candle; on either side, immense, seven-armed carved candelabras. Greenery and shroud-wrapped lamps completed the mournful solemnity.

The hall was filled to overflowing; representatives of the municipal authorities, with vice-president Budulski at the head, were there, also members of the political parties, the bar, Professional Unions, the army.[233]

One of the main guests at the anniversary observation was supposed to be the Jewish communist Paweł Zelicki (until October 1946, the secretary general of the CKŻP), who grew up in Radom.[234] Several days before the ceremony, the Committee for Celebration of the Memory of the Jewish Martyrs of Radom sent Zelicki the plan for the event and suggested, "Perhaps you would like to be in court at the hearing of Blum, the executioner, which will begin on Saturday, the 16th of this month."[235] It is not clear from the records, however, whether Zelicki did attend the commemoration or showed up in court.

The trial of Wilhelm Joseph Blum was not the only postwar trial arousing the interest of Jews in Radom. In June 1947, the District Jewish Committee sent a letter to the Legal Department of the CKŻP in connection with a different case:

On the 16th of the present month the criminal trial of Józef Fijał [actually, Fijoł] for participation in the murder of three Jews during the time of the German occupation took place before the Radom District Court.

In the course of the hearing new details were revealed about the participation [in crime] of an entire group of men, even from among the witnesses, which will bring about new arrests. This hearing was postponed until June 27 of the present year for questioning of new witnesses. The hearing will continue in Radom in the building of the District Court at 10 Piłsudski Street.

We consider it our duty to report about this and we are of the opinion that the civil plaintiff's presentation on behalf of the murdered individuals' children would make an important point, *which will enrich the material about the martyrology of the Jews during the time of the occupation.*[236]

This letter proves that the postwar trials of individuals accused of crimes against Jews were perceived not only as a means of achieving justice (often quite imperfect) but also as an occasion for documenting the Holocaust. Attempts at including Jewish organizations in ongoing trials could arise both from a lack of trust in the justice system and from the conviction that contributing to the punishment of individuals who had Jewish blood on their hands was the moral duty of those who had survived. The following letter, sent by the Jewish Committee to the CKŻP, indicates that this was so:

We did not write to you in order to receive advice as your answer but so that in the hall of the District Court in Radom, at the hearing in question there would be a Jewish lawyer, such as, alas, does not exist in Radom. *In our opinion, such matters should not be made light of, but this type of crime should be stigmatized appropriately from the Jewish point of view.*[237]

There is no official indication in the documents of Fijoł's trial that a delegate from the Legal Department of the CKŻP or the Radom Jewish Committee participated in the judicial procedure. Committee correspondence proves, however, that the community of survivors in Radom monitored this and other postwar trials, including those of local Polish perpetrators. The District Jewish Committee, acting at the request of the Central Jewish Historical Commission, sometimes also gathered proof of the guilt of individuals against whom legal proceedings were underway in other cities.[238]

Among the various actions undertaken by the Jewish Committee to document the Holocaust there were, unfortunately, unsuccessful efforts to discover the secret archive of the Radom ghetto. The archive's author, Chaskiel Rozenbaum, was murdered in 1942. His surviving son informed the Committee about the place where the documents were supposed to be hidden. In November 1945, the site he indicated was excavated but nothing was found.[239] More often than hidden documents, the survivors sought bodies of Holocaust victims. As Marcin Zaremba notes, "Throughout the country exhumations of the killed and the murdered took place. On the one hand, they psychologically extended the time of the war, while on the other, they were an effort at symbolic overcoming of the trauma. In general, families themselves exhumed their relatives insofar as they knew where to search."[240] The majority of Jewish victims left no surviving family members who might have searched for the wartime graves of their loved ones. For this reason and because of religious restrictions in Judaism concerning the exhumation of human remains, many nameless bodies of Holocaust victims lie forever in provisional, often mass, graves dug by the murderers or by the local peasants or the victims themselves at the murderers' command. Sometimes the Jewish committees substituted for the nonexistent families of Jewish victims and attended to the transfer of remains from burial pits to decent places of interment (see Figure 3.7). In April 1949, the Radom Jewish Committee informed the Committee for the Protection of the Graves of the Fallen in Defense of Freedom and Independence in Radom:

We inform you that as a result of searches for the graves of Jews murdered by the Nazis on the territory of the State Gunpowder Mill in Pionki, remains of 37 people were exhumed and were placed into 5 coffins. Submitting this to your information, we request consideration of the matter relative to a funeral and the setting of a date. The coffins are secured until burial in a barrack on the Gunpowder Mill property and

Figure 3.7 Exhumation of Jews murdered in Pionki, initiated and carried out by the Radom District Jewish Committee. Pionki, April 5, 1949. Yad Vashem Photo Archive, Jerusalem, 9652/61.

will be delivered to Radom at the appointed time. We mention that in consideration of religious law these remains will be buried in the Jewish cemetery in Radom.[241]

Survivors residing in Radom participated in the burial of the victims exhumed on the property of the Pionki factory. This type of ceremony could be very important for people, many of whom had had no chance to bury their own loved ones. The date for the funeral of the thirty-seven nameless victims was planned, perhaps not accidentally, for May 9, Victory Day, observed throughout the entire eastern bloc. The Jewish Committee printed invitations containing the information that "the funeral procession will set off from the square on ul. Bóżnicza [Synagogue Street] in Radom, to the local Jewish Cemetery."[242] On the day of the burial, the local press published a short note containing this appeal: "The Municipal National Council summons all councilors to stand in front of the Town Hall building at 17:00 with the purpose of taking part in the funeral observance."[243] The participants in the ceremony started their procession at the central point of the prewar Jewish quarter, where until recently the Radom synagogue had stood, and then, to the sound of the funeral march, they walked through the center of the city along Żeromski Street:

> The funeral procession was preceded by an honorary company of the Polish Army and by delegations, each of which carried a wreath. At the head of the delegations marched representatives of the KM PZPR [Municipal Committee of the PZPR (Komitet Miejski PZPR)].
>
> The coffins with the remains of the murdered were transported on three trucks behind which walked representatives of the Central Jewish Committee [most likely members of the OKŻ], the county authorities, county governor, and the chairman of the PRN [County National Council (Powiatowa Rada Narodowa)], the municipal authorities with the Mayor and the chairman of the MRN, the political parties with the first secretary of the KM PZPR at the head, and delegations from Radom workplaces.
>
> The funeral procession proceeded to First of May Street, from where the participants were driven in automobiles to the Jewish cemetery.[244]

In the documents I found, there is no information about the participation of "ordinary" inhabitants of Radom in this ceremony. Perhaps only members of official delegations and a few Radom Jews walked in the procession. It is incontestable, however, that the funeral of the exhumed victims was a very clear manifestation of the Jewish presence in Radom, even though it focused attention on the Jews among Radom's murdered citizens rather than among the living inhabitants of the city.

Another attempt to memorialize the victims of the Holocaust and at the same time to symbolically mark in the space of the city the existence of a Jewish community was the building of a monument. This initiative was carried out by the Committee for the Celebration of the Memory of the Jewish Martyrs of Radom, which operated from the summer of 1947.[245] It announced to the municipal authorities its intention to erect a monument: "In connection with the fifth anniversary of the bestial annihilation by the Nazi thugs of Jews, the fellow citizens of Radom, on August 17 of this year those who remained alive, the Jews saved by a miracle, wish to honor the memory of the martyrs by erecting a monument in the place where this terrible tragedy played out, in the space of the former synagogue—the heart of the ghetto—on Bóżnicza and Perec Streets."²⁴⁶ In the second paragraph of the same letter, the Committee for the Celebration of the Memory of the Jewish Martyrs of Radom justified to the authorities the point of erecting a monument. The committee referred to the participation of the Jewish community in the life of the city before the war. It appears that the committee members were anxious to demonstrate to the authorities that the murdered Jews were also Radom citizens, and it was proper that their annihilation should be remembered:

> The Radom Jews contributed to the development of the city, the growth of industry, trade and crafts. In the years of contending with the tsars' rule in the fight for freedom, Jewish workers and intelligentsia fought equally with the Polish working class. Later, in Reborn Poland [i.e., after 1918], on the grounds of the municipal government representatives of Radom Jewry walked hand in hand with . . . representatives of the Polish world of labor, for the general good of our city, which contemporary social and political activists remember well.²⁴⁷

The plan was for the monument to be "architecturally and artistically imposing," and the costs of its construction were to be covered by funds contributed by the survivors. The committee also counted on the authorities' financial and organizational participation in the undertaking.²⁴⁸ To be sure, the city agreed to clean up the grounds on which the monument was to stand, but most likely the majority of the costs connected with construction were borne by Radom Jews. In the District Jewish Committee's documentation, there is no information about the authorities helping to obtain the necessary permissions. That, most likely, is why it took as long as three years for the monument to arise. The Ministry of Culture and Art approved the project only in the middle of 1950. Sculptor Jakub Zajdensznir, a Radomer Holocaust survivor, was commissioned to do the work.²⁴⁹ He planned a sculpture representing the figure of a woman at whose feet stand five Jewish tombstones. Below, an inscription in Polish and Yiddish was placed: "To the Jews of Radom, the victims of Hitlerite crimes." Fragments of Jewish gravestones found in various parts of the

Figure 3.8 Ceremony unveiling the monument commemorating the Radom victims of the Holocaust. Standing on the right beside the monument are Jakub Zajdensznir and Pola Wajsfus (later Zajdensznir). Counting from the right, the second man is Bajnysz Kamer. Radom, August 17, 1950. Courtesy Barbara Fundowicz-Towarek.

city and rubble from the demolished Radom synagogue were used in the construction.[250] The monument was ceremoniously unveiled on the anniversary of the liquidation of the large ghetto, August 17, 1950 (see Figure 3.8). The local daily newspaper, *Życie Radomskie,* announced the ceremony and printed an article that discussed in detail the history of the deportation of the Jews from the Radom ghetto, together with the observances of the anniversary of the events in the current political context:

> Today is the eighth anniversary of the terrible annihilation of the Radom Jews. The perpetrator of that massacre, the deputy SS chief for the Radom district, Sturmbannführer Wilhelm Blum, appeared in Radom before the Republic's court and received the death sentence. However, his worthy successors remaining in West Germany together with their imperialist patrons are dreaming of new military turmoil.

Against them stands a united front of peace. Peaceful, creative work will
succeed in thwarting the plans of the imperialists from beyond the ocean.

In solidarity with the world front of defenders of Peace, today Radom
society once again will document its will in the struggle for peace,
taking mass participation in the ceremony of the unveiling of the Monument in Honor of the Radom Jews, the Victims of Hitlerite Crimes.[251]

Two days later, in the same newspaper, a brief informative piece describing
the ceremony of the unveiling of the monument appeared:

On the square where the synagogue once stood at the intersection of
Bóżnicza and Peretz Streets crowds had gathered. In front of the monument, which was veiled in mourning crepe, stood representatives of
political, community, and youth organizations, color guards, delegations carrying wreaths, and invited guests.

The chairman of the Municipal National Council, Citizen
Wrocławski, took his place on the podium and in a few words sketched
the history of the Radom ghetto, the hunger that reigned there, and the
bloody liquidation when nearly 30 thousand Radom Jews found their
deaths at the hands of the Nazi perpetrators.

"Rich in sad experience," Citizen Wrocławski said in closing, "acquired during the time of the occupation, we must exert all our strength
with the aim of averting by peaceful, creative work, a new military aggression so that in this way our children will be spared the necessity
of erecting monuments like this for us . . ."

Next, Citizen Wrocławski performed the ceremony of the unveiling
of the monument. Those gathered there honored the murdered Jews
with a minute of silence. The orchestra of the ZZWM No. 1 [United
Metal Products Plants (Zjednoczone Zakłady Wyrobów Metalowych)]
played Chopin's funeral march.

After speeches by Citizen Kwaterko, the representative of the Central Committee of Polish Jews, and by Editor Metera, a representative
of the Union of Fighters for Freedom and Democracy, the delegations
of Radom institutions and workplaces laid wreaths beside the monument. During this ceremony the funeral march was performed by a different orchestra, "The Railwaymen's."[252]

According to the author of the article, the monument was paid for with contributions from people who were prewar inhabitants of Radom or who had spent time in the ghetto there during the occupation. Surprisingly, there is hardly any mention of Jews currently residing in Radom, as if they did not exist. Only in the final sentence does the author note: "At the conclusion, a representative of the Jewish Committee in Radom, Citizen Zajdensznir, handed over the legal document that transferred the monument."[253] A copy of this document is preserved among the District Jewish Committee's papers: "In the name of the Jewish Committee, Community, and Landsmen Organization of the City of Radom, I have the honor to entrust to the City in the person of its Leader, the Chairman of the Municipal National Council, Citizen Wrocławski, this square and monument erected on the eighth anniversary of the annihilation of the Radom Jews by the Hitlerite thugs. We are confident that we are handing over the present monument, along with the square, into worthy, dependable and vigilant hands."[254]

The act of transferring the monument to the authorities can be seen as the symbolic conclusion of the District Jewish Committee's activities, and of the presence of Jews as a group in Radom society. As Sebastian Piątkowski writes, the unveiling of the monument was "the last event during which Jews residing in Radom appeared at a public forum as a religious and national group."[255] Also, their representatives, the Jewish Committee, precisely at that moment ceded their rights and obligations to the municipal authorities. By handing over the ground on which the Radom synagogue had stood along with the monument they had erected upon it, the community gave a clear signal that it was in no condition to take care of the memory of the slaughtered Radom Jews without external assistance. It was, after all, a shattered community, which from the moment the war ended had been living in almost complete isolation and detachment from both its non-Jewish fellow citizens and the administrative structures of the city. Thus, the ceremony of unveiling the monument dedicated to the victims of the Holocaust was a turning point, ending the postwar existence of the survivors in Radom as a community.

The local authorities apparently had not noticed the need to honor the Jewish victims. Nor did they perceive the significance of what had just taken place. In *Słowo Ludu* (The people's word), a daily that was the organ of the Provincial Committee of the PZPR, not a single article devoted to the eighth anniversary of the liquidation of the Radom ghetto appeared, nor was there even a mention of the newly built monument. More important were the war in Korea, the "struggle for peace" (one of the anti-western propaganda leitmotivs at the time), and even a discussion about the necessity of enhancing the quality of molds produced in the Kielce region.[256] The District Jewish Committee and the community of survivors living in Radom were silently retreating into nonexistence, unnoticed by the authorities and the non-Jewish citizens of the city. Barely eight years from the deportation of the majority of the inhabitants of the ghetto to the Treblinka extermination camp and five years from the end of the German occupation, the sole visible traces of the city's many thousands-strong prewar Jewish community and the handful of Radom Jews who had survived the Holocaust were the monument in the city center and the totally devastated cemetery at its outskirts (see Figure 3.9).[257]

Figure 3.9 Jakub Zajdensznir beside the demolished tombstone of his father in the Radom Jewish cemetery. Today there is no trace of this tombstone. Radom, 1946 or later.
Courtesy Barbara Fundowicz-Towarek.

Emotions in the Community of Survivors

The Radom Jewish community in which the District Jewish Committee operated was small, divided, and torn by very powerful emotions. Those who returned at times accused other survivors of the death of loved ones. Many individuals felt jealousy and a desire for revenge, and justice was sought in judicial trials. Tuwia Frydman learned about the death of his mother and sister from his surviving sister, Bela. He described that moment and the emotions accompanying it in his memoir: "I sat on the bed and listened as Bela told me about what took place. When she spoke about Szenderowicz, I felt a cold anger in my chest. 'I'll kill him,' I said to Bela. 'I have to take revenge.'"[258]

The survivors were haunted by a profound sense of guilt because of their own survival and the deaths of their families. Some of them were envious of the survival of the loved ones of someone they knew. A Polish émigré writer and a child survivor himself, Henryk Grynberg described such a situation. He and his mother were the only surviving members of the family. His younger brother and father had perished. Immediately after liberation, nine-year-old Grynberg and his mother were living in her native town in the Mazowsze region. A married couple, bakers with a young son, also returned to that locality, as did another couple, Frymka and Nusen, who had escaped from a transport to Treblinka. Their children, however, had remained in the train car.[259] As Grynberg writes, "Everyone thought that Frymka shouldn't have jumped from the train without her children. But, of course, they never said so to her. Frymka said she wanted to save them and everyone believed her. Who wouldn't want to save one's children? If she didn't save them, it means she couldn't. But still . . ."[260] Living in the same apartment house with the couple who lost their children, Grynberg seems to have witnessed a quarrel between his mother and Frymka:

"So why did you jump? Why didn't you stay on the train like all the rest? . . ."
"You begrudge me my life?"
"I don't begrudge you anything! But you envy me because I saved my child!"

"No, you envy me. . . . And you know what you envy me for? My
husband, that's what! You think I don't see how you look at
him? . . . You think I don't know what you tell people, that it
wasn't his fault. That it wasn't him who left the children, but me!
That I'm the one that's to blame!"[261]

Although it can't be ruled out that the scene is the author's literary creation, from a psychological point of view it seems very authentic.

Naum Szenderowicz, struggling with postwar accusations, believed
that he had fallen victim to envy: "I repeat that all the accusations are a
result of envy, that my family was saved, and others' weren't."[262] In the testimonies of individuals defending the doctor during his trial, suggestions were made that the former president of the Judenrat might have been
accused by people motivated by envy. Henryk Zameczkowski, in a letter
to Szenderowicz, presented his interpretation of the accusations put forward against the Radom doctor: "I have given a good deal of thought to
what motivations guide these denouncers of various calibers. It is not only
a desire to immediately find the perpetrator of their misfortune, or a desire to find satisfaction in a scapegoat; very often it is also jealousy that
someone else survived. These are the results of a general moral devastation. Alas, the best people perished."[263]

Romana Fargotsztejn-Fastmanowa also pointed to envy as one of the
causes of the accusations against the former chairman of the Radom Judenrat: "So I believe that the people who slander the name of Dr. Szenderowicz are definitely doing this out of meanness and jealousy. That his
family survived is pure chance, since his wife and daughter and his
mother-in-law were together with me in Auschwitz, and there were no
'privileged' people there."[264] Of course, there is no way to judge whether
there was even a grain of truth in Zameczkowski's and Fargotsztejn-
Fastmanowa's suggestions, but jealousy aroused by the survival of relatives and the envy connected with it must have been familiar to members
of the community of survivors.

Already in the late 1940s there was a lively argument among Jews about
the role played by Jewish elites in the Holocaust as well as their responsibility. The documents of the proceedings before the Citizens' Tribunal
of the CKŻP against the officials from the Radom ghetto contain also

general reflections about the Jewish leaders' behavior. One of the people who spoke out on this matter was Anna Gecow, a physician working in the Radom ghetto during the occupation:

> I experienced the Ghetto deeply, I saw tragic blindness and not only now but also when we all were facing destruction, I considered the behavior of our "authorities" to be fundamentally mistaken. Our people were doomed by paying a ransom to the Germans that could cover just a handful of people. And the handful who survived were by no means the most valuable people. Those with protection and money were situated at Kromołowski[265] and in the workshops; the poor and the hopeless went to Szydłowiec.[266] Determining the fate of our people was not a heavy duty but, alas, a privilege giving the possibility of saving oneself and one's dear ones in the first place.[267]

In the profoundly atomized community of survivors living in Radom, the collective search for traitors and the memorialization of victims had not only a therapeutic but also an integrative function. These two activities served to rebuild and strengthen ties in a group full of tension and insecurity. The majority of the Jews who returned to the city had gone through traumatic experiences: life in constant danger, the death of family—parents, spouses, children. These experiences were very often accompanied by feelings of powerlessness and guilt. A settling of scores, the search for justice, and even revenge for wounds sustained, as well as the commemorating of victims, to a certain degree must have given the survivors the feeling of reasserting their agency, of taking their fate into their own hands. But there was another way survivors manifested their agency: by making efforts to regain their property.

4

PROPERTY

THE FATE OF Jewish property in Poland immediately after World War II does not have known photographic documentation. Transfers of ownership, which began during the German occupation and continued in the first postwar years, were ubiquitous but rarely occurred in front of a camera lens. All the more valuable, then, are several photographs made in Radom in August or September 1942, after the deportation of the residents of the large ghetto to the Treblinka extermination camp. They are at the end of an album documenting the Holocaust in Radom and Szydłowiec. In the 1960s, the album reached the archive of the Yad Vashem Institute in Jerusalem. Little is known about the individual who took the pictures. That person may have been Heinrich Moepken, a German policeman stationed in Radom or its vicinity during the war.[1]

What is certain, however, is that the photographer was able to move about freely with a camera in the emptied Radom ghetto and document scenes encountered there. What did the photographer see? On the main street of the ghetto, peasant carts are crowded together, packed to the limits of possibility with Jewish property. In a moment, Jewish property had become "post-Jewish." All the doors and windows of the houses are open, as if welcoming intrusion. Property is piled up against the walls of the apartment houses: wardrobes, credenzas, washtubs, stools, cracked mirrors (see Figure 4.1).

In the tangle of furniture, wagons, and people, the Germans are almost absent. Men are loading furniture into the wagons. A woman appears to

Figure 4.1 Looting of Jewish property after the inhabitants of the ghetto were deported to the Treblinka death camp. Radom, August or September 1942. Yad Vashem Photo Archive, Jerusalem, FA76/98.

be trying on a dress she has extracted from the mounds of things (see Figure 4.2). One can sense the hurried, feverish atmosphere, but not fear.

The moments captured by the photographer document the irreversibility of the change of ownership tied to the Holocaust. The deported people were never supposed to return; their property became "ownerless" and very quickly found new owners who would not have to give it back to anyone. The finality of this change was obvious. Thus, when the few Holocaust survivors did return, those individuals who had taken Jewish property were both astonished and fearful of possible repercussions. Survivors' presence was a reminder of the origin of things that for several years had managed to feel at home in Polish hands.

THE FRONT, which ran through Radom at the beginning of 1945, did not bring serious destruction. The streets and buildings in the city remained unchanged since 1939. At first glance, then, the war had not left an imprint on the city. But that was only the surface appearance. The majority of Jews who came back to Radom did not find their prewar homes,

Figure 4.2 Looting of Jewish
property after the inhabitants of
the ghetto were deported to the
Treblinka death camp. Radom,
August or September 1942. Yad
Vashem Photo Archive, Jerusalem,
FA76/102.

apartment houses, stores, workshops, and factories waiting for their return. They had abandoned them either at the beginning of the war by
fleeing east to the Soviet Union or in the spring of 1941, when they moved
into the ghetto by order of the occupation authorities. Even up to the
summer of 1942, a portion of the Radom Jews had remained in their original apartments and workplaces if they were located in the ghetto or in
places where it was difficult for the Germans to replace Jews with non-
Jewish workers. Returning after liberation, survivors could assume that
they would settle into their own apartments, work once again in their own
shops, resume administration of apartment houses and enterprises.

Very quickly, it turned out that driving out the German occupier from
the city did not mean a return to pre-September 1939. The war had up-
ended property relations. During the war, many owners lost the possibility to dispose of their properties. Many were forced to abandon their
apartments and enterprises. Many had died. All these statements describe
Polish society in general after World War II, but they gather particular
force in relation to Polish Jews. In the face of the unprecedented scale of
destruction, Jewish survivors, as a group, experienced loss of property

in a most painful manner. Most of the returnees had nothing. Many made efforts to regain property that had belonged to them or their relatives before the war. In order to fully understand these efforts and the difficulties connected with the restitution of Jewish property immediately after liberation, it is necessary first to look closely at what happened to the property of Polish Jews during the German occupation.

The Property of Radom Jews during World War II

In the first months of the war, as Jan Grabowski notes, the Germans confiscated and assumed control over "state enterprises, private plants that were important for the defense of the German state, and all firms belonging to Polish Jews and to 'enemies of the Reich.' In addition, 'unowned structures' and real properties belonging to Polish citizens of Jewish origin were subject to confiscation."[2]

The law introduced by the German occupier in the territory of the General Government (GG) differentiated the citizens of the defeated state. It specifically singled out Jews from the rest of the inhabitants. Under this law, non-Jewish Polish citizens had their enterprises taken from them if the work had significance for the wartime economy of the Reich. Jewish citizens, in contrast, lost their enterprises and all their real property only because they were Jews. Already in January 1940, Jewish property was subject to registration. All real and movable property (with the exception of objects for personal use that were of little value) belonging to Jewish Polish citizens and their spouses (whether or not they, too, were Jews), as well as the properties belonging to enterprises owned by Jews, had to be reported to the German authorities. If at least 25 percent of the shares in an enterprise were owned by Jews, the business came under the new law. Goods that were not declared were treated as ownerless and subject to automatic confiscation.[3]

It is difficult to determine the ultimate number of properties taken over from the Polish state and private citizens by the German authorities in Radom. Given the high degree of industrialization of the city and the fact that almost one-third of the inhabitants of Radom before the war were Jews, property confiscations carried out in the city by the occupier undoubtedly took place on an enormous scale.[4]

In the course of so-called Aryanization, Radom Jews lost not only their businesses but also their dwellings and undeveloped plots of land. The confiscated factories and apartment houses were administered by trustees (*Treuhänder*) appointed by the German authorities. Jan Grabowski has determined that in light of "the enormous number of confiscated Jewish apartment buildings and insufficient number of German volunteers, permitting Poles to take on the work of trustees was a necessary condition for the efficient processing of ownership changes."[5] As Grabowski points out, Poles also played a significant role in administering the confiscated Jewish industrial plants.

In an account given in May 1945, Ichiel Leszcz spoke about what happened to Jewish property in Radom during the period before the creation of the ghetto in the spring of 1941:

> The liquidation of Jewish enterprises began. According to a newly published law, Jews were not allowed to direct their own enterprises. They had to hand them over to *freihendler* [*sic*] commissars [i.e., *Treuhänder*], Poles and Germans. Some Jews, who maintained contact with Germans through money, remained in their factories as office workers. But their entire wealth was looted. The Judenrat, not wanting Germans to go into houses, declared that it would take it upon itself to pass the wealth along to the Germans. The Judenrat had a wagon on which every morning furniture, objects, etc. were driven away from Jewish apartments. People were afraid of that wagon in which Jewish porters were seated. People fled their homes. In that case, the porters tore out the locks, knocked out windows, and collected whatever they wanted. With the help of German acquaintances, Jews were able to save some of their things. During the collection of furniture and other things various tricks were employed. The Germans demanded 50 davenports, the Judenrat collected 100. The "Judenrat" caused terrible bitterness among the Jews.[6]

The confiscation of movable property in Radom was also recalled by Maria Frydman: "Furniture, furs, crystal, bed linens, carpets were collected from Jewish apartments; day and night, wagons filled with Jewish belongings filed down the street."[7]

Alongside the official and organized robbery of Jewish property conducted by the occupation authorities in Radom, as happened throughout
German-occupied Poland, incidents of individual German officials and
soldiers robbing city inhabitants and exploiting their work were also com-
monplace (see Figure 4.3). Jews, singled out, deprived not only of privi-
leges but also of legal protection, were most at risk of "confiscations"
carried out on the private initiative and in the private interest of officials
of the Third Reich. Robberies committed by individual German soldiers

Figure 4.3 A Jewish carpenter and his helpers on business on Żeromski Street
(Reichstrasse). Movement of Jews in the city center had been restricted since
November 1940. It is likely the carpenter had been commissioned by a German
institution or a German resident of the city. Radom, between December 1939 and
August 1942. Courtesy Łukasz Biedka.

began in Radom immediately after the front divisions of the Wehrmacht
took the city, even before the occupation administration was firmly in
place: "Looting of shops by soldiers and officers of the Wehrmacht also
began, as the Nazis and SS-men were not yet here. They went into jewelry shops and workshops primarily, selected what they liked, and ordered
that it be packed up. A Mrs. Najman told one of these guys that it's not
right that an officer should steal. A few hours later a car drove up and they
took her, and she never came back."[8]

Not only ordinary soldiers but also high-placed Nazi officers personally looted Jewish property. It was usually wealthy Jews who fell victim
to such "confiscations." During the trial of Herbert Böttcher in 1949,
Ludwik Fastman described how SS officers serving in Radom selected
furniture for themselves from his apartment:

> It became clear to me later why Blum visited me. He looked over my
> furniture attentively. I had beautiful furniture. The defendant, Böttcher,
> took my dining room furniture, and Schippers took the bedroom. I was
> not present at the collection of my furniture. The Jews who were em-
> ployed to take away the furniture told me about it, however, as did two
> young women who polished my furniture pieces at the defendant's
> quarters. These young women were summoned wherever there was a
> need for furniture polishing. It was precisely from them that I found
> out where my furniture was located because they did their polishing
> here and there.[9]

In his study of the plundering of Jewish property in Europe in the years
1933–1945, Martin Dean writes that the decrees touching on the confiscation of Jewish property were often used for embezzlement. Both agen-
cies and individual Germans embezzled. Dean refers to the statement by
a German trustee who administered a Jewish tannery in Radom and who,
in the 1960s, admitted that only a small part of the money from the autumn 1939 confiscation was transferred to the firm's blocked account. As
a Jew, the man who had owned the firm had no access even to that sum.[10]
The official economic exploitation of the Jewish population created a climate conducive to appropriating Jewish property by individual representatives of the occupation regime. Although German law prohibited

such thefts, it was concerned not so much with the harm caused to the owners as with the lost profit of the Third Reich.

In Radom, as in other localities, Jews attempted to evade confiscation of their property, concealing it or transferring it to Polish friends, but it quickly became apparent that not everyone could be trusted. As Maria Frydman recounted after the war, "Jews immediately began giving items for safekeeping to Poles they knew. There were already instances when later, those people did not want to return those things, so others [Jews] buried their belongings."[11] The transferring of part of their property to non-Jewish acquaintances who agreed to keep it at home for a while was an effort at insuring the future. Many Radom Jews surely tried it. In doing so, it was necessary to divide the property so that it reached the largest possible number of trusted individuals. If it became impossible to gain access to assets in one of the hiding places, Jews could still dispose of belongings deposited somewhere else. Some of the Polish "safekeepers" discovered in preserving Jewish things an easy means of enriching themselves and did not fulfill the obligation they had agreed to. Certainly, there also existed safekeepers who acted in good faith, and the Jewish property ultimately remained in their hands only if the rightful owners had perished and no one appeared to claim the property. Although we are frequently dealing here with widely varying attitudes deserving different moral judgment, the result of transferring things to non-Jews was the same. Jewish property remained in the hands of Poles after the Holocaust and in fact changed owners—Jewish property was becoming de facto "post-Jewish" from the outset.

In addition to handing over movable property for safekeeping, Jews also transferred enterprises and workshops to Poles. Usually, such safekeepers had been partners in the business or employees, or they were other non-Jews who enjoyed the trust of the Jewish owners. In that way, Jews expected to evade the Aryanization of private firms. The transfers were sometimes carried out under fictional transactions. Certainly, some individuals deliberately sold their firms, counting on the money acquired to make it possible to save themselves. It is not possible to determine what percent of Jewish entrepreneurs attempted to evade confiscation by donations to non-Jewish acquaintances or concluded fictitious or factual agreements to sell their property. Sometimes, traces of such escapes from

Aryanization can be observed in the proceedings of civil trials after the war.[12] Distinguishing true transactions from fictional ones was a serious difficulty immediately after the war, too. However, many acquisitions of Jewish property by non-Jewish Poles left no trace in the record. If neither the former owners nor any of their family survived (and it is legitimate to assume that most often that was the case), the people who newly possessed that property could avoid revealing the circumstances in which they had taken over administration of an enterprise.

The property of Jews landed in the hands of their non-Jewish fellow citizens as a result of trade transactions, too. Both before the creation of the Radom ghetto and during its existence, the sale or exchange of property for food, medicine, or fuel was often a means of survival. As Maria Frydman recounted after the war, "[Jews] no longer found any source of income and everyone lived on the sale of objects to the 'Aryan' population of the city."[13] For some of the non-Jewish inhabitants of Radom, the ghetto was a place in which it was possible to strike a deal or acquire needed objects. Stefan Posyniak, a young forced-laborer, bought an overcoat in the Radom ghetto; someone had advised him that there were cheap clothes in the ghetto.[14] Non-Jews not only purchased objects sold by the people crowded into the closed district, they also profited from supplying foodstuffs and other goods for which there was a demand in the ghetto. Obviously, various objects and products were exchanged depending on the wealth of the individuals doing the trading and the period when the transaction was concluded. The most desired hard currency was gold coins and jewelry. As Jerzy Kochanowski writes, "A huge percentage of the contraband supplied to the Warsaw ghetto was paid for in hard currency . . . or works of art."[15] The Radom ghetto might have differed in this only in scale and average value of transactions, but the general trend was certainly the same. "Inflation, the enormous profits of both parts of the occupation apparatus and of the local community (including the black market sharks), and also the danger of sudden loss of all one's property drove the demand for objects that could accrue value."[16] Because many individuals did not have jewelry, the hard currency used in exchange for food was also books, clothing, and various household items.

In the General Government, a system based on planned scarcity of food for the native populations of occupied lands was in effect. As Kazimierz

Wyka noted, the inhabitants of the General Government faced a dilemma: "to eat only what was permitted and die of hunger, or—*somehow to make do*. Naturally no one seriously entertained the first alternative, so the only important question was: *how to survive despite the regulations*."[17] Villages located close to cities were in the best position to profit from the situation. Peasants could enrich themselves through trading in foodstuffs. To the extent that the non-Jewish population often traveled to the countryside for food, the Jews, in contrast, after the closing of the ghettos, were forced to use a network of smugglers and intermediaries. This escalated prices considerably, making trade with the ghetto a lucrative occupation. In the best case, the ghetto inhabitants could count on direct exchange with a peasant who, tempted by the possibility of higher profit, would come to the city and risk direct contact with the closed district. In this way, even before the liquidation of the ghettos, some Jewish objects of daily use wound up under cottage roofs in villages on the outskirts of cities. In Radom, trading contacts were probably easier with the small ghetto. Glinice was a typical suburb with a partially rural character and scattered development. Contact with individuals from the "Aryan" side was relatively easy there. At the same time, the large majority of the Radom Jewish elite who still had remnants of property lived in the large ghetto located in the city center. Hence, trade with the large ghetto could potentially bring more profit.

The mass transfer of movable and real Jewish property into the hands of the Christian inhabitants of Radom began in April 1941 when the German authorities first created the small and large ghettos. Jews living outside the designated areas had to leave their homes and move into the ghetto. Each person being resettled was officially permitted to bring only twenty-five kilograms of belongings; the rest had to be left behind.[18] In turn, non-Jewish Poles had to leave the territory that had now become part of the ghetto. The Judenrat oversaw the relocation of people in the closed districts, and the displaced Poles were settled in apartments assigned to them by the city administration. Sometimes the German administration was bypassed; Jews and non-Jews exchanged real property on their own. Furniture merchant Henoch Gotfryd, who lived with his family on Wąska Street in Radom (outside the ghetto), made use of his years-long acquaintance with some Polish women who were his clients to arrange for an exchange of apartments. The women, a mother and two daughters, moved to an apartment outside the ghetto that the merchant transferred to them, and the Gotfryds moved to the two-room little house that the women had occupied inside the newly established closed district. Transactions of this type increased one's chances for settling in a better place in the ghetto—there was a small garden next to the Gotfryds' little house in which the new tenants attempted to grow vegetables.[19]

In August 1942, the Germans carried out the main liquidation action in the two Radom ghettos, in Glinice and in the city center. Abandoned apartments, furniture, and other objects of daily use remained after the Jews were deported. The most valuable items from the closed districts were collected by the Germans. The less valuable also changed owners; their new possessors were the numerous non-Jewish inhabitants of the city and surrounding areas. Throughout Poland, Germans organized auctions and sales of Jewish belongings, in some places just a few days after the local Jews were deported. According to one Polish witness, "The auction committee went from house to house with a table which they set up on the street right in front of a house and they auctioned off literally everything."[20] Although I have not encountered documents directly referring to such a practice in Radom, there is no doubt that the non-Jewish inhabitants of the city could officially purchase some Jewish objects such as furniture from the Germans (see Figure 4.4).

Even though unauthorized access to the area of the former ghetto was forbidden and thus dangerous, some non-Jews scouted the neighborhood on their own. Stefan Kozieł, in an interview he gave for the United States Holocaust Memorial Museum, recalled that right after the liquidation of the small ghetto in Glinice, local youth thoroughly searched the area. Several days after the deportation, then twelve-year-old Kozieł also went there: "Because my friends told me that they found candlesticks there . . . and other such things, so I went to see. Well, when I looked into one house and there was an incredible mess there, because after all it was such a moment that the Germans surrounded the entire ghetto and in the course of a few hours they drove everyone into the square, they shot some of them there. . . . Curiosity propelled me to see what it was like there."[21] In an empty street, Kozieł happened upon an old woman who apparently had

Figure 4.4 Looting of Jewish property after the inhabitants of the ghetto were deported to the Treblinka death camp. Radom, August or September 1942. Yad Vashem Photo Archive, Jerusalem, FA76/103.

managed to live through the liquidation of the ghetto in hiding. She seemed to have lost any awareness of her surroundings; there was no connecting with her. Dressed only in a nightgown, she was wandering about the deserted area. The boy took fright and escaped to his home. Several weeks later, in September 1942, Mieczysław Wośko, also a twelve-year-old at the time, accompanying his mother Wiktoria, legally entered the emptied large ghetto:

> As we entered the space of the ghetto it was . . . a horrifying sight: silence, emptiness, no one there. Literally a surreal landscape. And we are walking. We can hear our footsteps. Every so often German patrols and Polish police would emerge from the side streets and each patrol checked if we have a pass allowing us to be there. . . . There really were almost no people there. Wide-open windows . . . wide-open shops . . . it was full of papers, cards, and those feathers blowing about . . . a thoroughly terrifying image . . . as we entered that ghetto, such large, horse-drawn wagons were circling. The Germans removed everything

that might be of use to them, so they removed furniture, materials. . . .
But those were individual wagons, and above all there was that striking
silence, from that traffic on Żeromski Street, when one entered there,
another land, completely other, as if one were in a completely other
place; it was completely horrifying.[22]

After the emptying of both Radom ghettos, many unoccupied dwelling
places were used by various types of wartime migrants, including Jews
who were hiding. The Goldman family, who had fled the Kraków ghetto
and were living under an assumed identity, arrived in Radom in the late
summer of 1942. They settled into an abandoned store in the territory of
the former small ghetto in Glinice.[23] In another case, an individual connected with Radom and involved in the underground was seeking a hiding
place for a physician, Dr. Józef Jabłoński, who was hiding on the "Aryan"
side. The member of the underground wrote in a letter to the doctor's son-
in-law: "An apartment would present serious difficulty, but I trust that
now, after the liquidation of the ghetto, it should be possible to find a
place."[24]

The German authorities rehoused Poles who had been evicted from
other parts of the city, assigning them housing in what remained after the
liquidation of the large ghetto in the center of Radom. Mieczysław Wośko
lived with his mother until 1942 in the so-called municipal blocs—a relatively modern complex of buildings located on the edges of the city center.
In autumn, these buildings were occupied by Germans, and their former
residents were assigned housing in the territory of the large ghetto, which
by then was empty. Wośko witnessed how the move to the former ghetto
was arranged:

> With that apartment, it was this way, that initially we . . . the first
> apartment we received, we received . . . it was on Starokrakowska
> Street . . . a room and a kitchen, that's what the Germans were
> giving for two people. And we wanted to move in there, but . . . And
> it had probably been a dentist's apartment, or a dental technician's.
> Because my mama, working in the health service administration
> there, she saw that there was equipment there . . . of some sort,
> there were no valuable things, but instruments like a dentist's. . . .[25]

Before the Wośkos transferred to the apartment, the Municipal Authority disinfected it. Mieczysław's mother paid for this service and then delayed the move until the place aired out from the unpleasant chemical smell. When she went to check if the apartment was ready, she encountered a crowd of people in the stairway. In the attic of the building, where the Wośkos received a room with a kitchen, a walled-in cache of textiles had been discovered, and the people, who were also being resettled in the former ghetto, began looting bales of cloth, which had great value during the occupation. The thread of "Jewish treasure" hidden in the grounds of the former ghetto appears again in Wośko's narrative:

> . . . I was laughing then, like this, "So that's how it is here, surely he hid some treasures here, so I will begin searching for these treasures here." Well. First, we carried out that disinfection. . . . Finally, we go look over the apartment after airing it out for another few days after Mama was there. We look: there was only a padlock—the padlock is ripped off. What happened? Someone broke in. But why break in to such an apartment? After all, there was nothing there. Poverty. We enter—nothing. The crummy junk that was there—still there. And there was a toilet in this apartment. We look. I go into the toilet room, and in it, over the tank . . . a large . . . hole was cut out—that's where it was hidden, some sort . . . maybe he had gold or something . . . , the owner of that apartment either he told someone, true, because he couldn't come himself, because at that time they [took] all those Jews . . . there were still a few Jews there, such a tiny number, around the Market Square [the reference is to the camp on Szwarlikowska Street] there was an enclave, some workshops there. So, he must have given it to someone. And there was nothing more there. So, about that apartment, Mama said, "Since it's like this here, I'll go over and maybe they'll give me another one." And then they gave us this apartment on Starokrakowska Street, on the other side of the street. . . . First of all, it was larger—the first one was very small, and we had all this stuff . . . from a three-room apartment. . . . [26]

In the end, the Wośkos settled in the second apartment assigned to them, in an apartment house on one of the larger streets of the former ghetto. Several months later, in this building, too, a concealed storage place was discovered in the attic: ". . . suddenly a truck pulls up in front of our building. A group of maybe 5–6 Jews gets out with German gendarmes and they rush up to the fourth floor. Damn, to us? They go up one more flight to the attic and again in the attic there was . . . an entire treasure of skins there. . . . They carried out entire bales of those skins for hours . . . those big ones for shoe soles. . . . And they loaded the entire truck with skins. They looked around some more and drove off."[27]

The apartment house to which the Wośkos were moved belonged to Jewish owners, and as confiscated Jewish property, it was managed by the administration installed by the occupation authorities.[28] When Wiktoria Wośko and her son entered the second apartment assigned to them, they found some worthless furniture and other objects from the previous tenants who had been deported to an extermination camp several weeks before. The Wośkos did not keep those things. The mother and son brought their own furnishings from the "municipal blocks" to the small apartment. They lived on Starokrakowska Street until the end of the German occupation of Radom. After the Warsaw uprising, which broke out on August 1, 1944, and lasted for sixty-three days, relatives from the capital moved in with them. Shortly after the Russians entered the city, thanks to the efforts of Wiktor Jaworski, Wiktoria Wośko's brother, a member of the PPS who became vice-mayor of Radom, mother and son received an apartment similar to the one they had occupied until 1942.

Items hidden by Jews during the war were found in the city after liberation, too. Sometimes, it was the lawful owners or their relatives who found them. One of the men who returned to Radom from a camp in 1945 dug up gold, silver, jewelry, and British pounds hidden in a cellar by his father during the war. A year later, he visited Radom again, and again he dug up valuables.[29] Non-Jews also discovered hiding places with "Jewish treasures." In 1951, a former Security Service (UB) officer testified that during his service in Radom, "Gold was dug up in the Ghetto; also it was divided up among ourselves [i.e., appropriated by the UB officers]."[30]

Information about such incidents undoubtedly contributed to strengthening among the non-Jewish population of Radom the myth about the Jews' wealth. People who believed it saw proof that Jews, even in the extreme conditions of the ghetto, were able to keep and hide valuable objects. Such convictions vanished slowly, and the discovery of "treasures" in the area of the former ghetto must have influenced the attitude of non-Jewish Poles toward Jews who appeared in Radom right after the war. The returnees looked poor, but after all, Jews from the ghetto had also looked as if they had nothing, yet after their deportation valuable objects and goods hidden by them were found. Most likely, many non-Jewish inhabitants of the city found such an explanation plausible.

In occupied Poland, Jewish assets had been transferred to the German state, and management of these assets was carried out by the occupation administration through trustees—both Germans and Poles. But a large portion of the property of Polish Jews wound up in the possession of their non-Jewish neighbors, either through the German authorities (the reassignment of apartments taken away from Jews, organized sale and auctions) or without intermediaries (trade exchanges or the appropriation of things entrusted for safekeeping). Confiscation, the establishment of trustee administration over the assets of Polish Jews by the occupation authorities, and the transfers of ownership from the period of the war, began the process of moving Jewish property into non-Jewish hands. This process in Poland did not conclude with the end of World War II. In the new postwar reality, it continued until the late 1940s. In 1945, Jewish real property, as well as that portion of movable property not taken out of Poland, was under the control of the Polish state or private Polish individuals.

Nobody's Property: The Moment German Occupation Ended

As the scales of victory tilted to the Allies' side, it became clear that the authorities of postwar Poland would have to confront from the very outset the confusion in matters of property ownership that the war had introduced. Many owners had lost their assets. Many had perished or disappeared without a trace, leaving their assets without a guardian. As the Soviet troops advanced, the real properties confiscated by the Germans were discarded by those who until then had administered them. It is not at all surprising that questions of ownership were among the first matters that the communists, who were assuming de facto power in the territory occupied by the Red Army, promised they would deal with. Already in the July 1944 Manifesto of the Polish Committee of National Liberation (Polski Komitet Wyzwolenia Narodowego, PKWN), they announced: "Property stolen by the Germans from individual citizens, peasants, merchants, craftsmen, petty and medium industrialists, institutions and the church, shall be returned to their lawful owners. German assets will be confiscated. . . . National assets, concentrated today in the hands of the German state and individual German capitalists, thus, the great industrial enterprises, trade, banking, transport and forests, will be transferred to the Provisional State Administration. As economic relations are regulated, the return of ownership will ensue."[31]

Thus, from the very beginning, a distinction was made concerning classification of assets into those belonging to Germans and those the Germans had taken from Polish citizens. The PKWN manifesto proclaimed that German assets (i.e., property formerly owned by the German state and German individuals) would come under government administration. The assets of Polish citizens would be returned to their rightful owners, while major enterprises and large industrial firms were to go under state administration. From the start, the new authorities were preparing for the nationalization of the enterprises that later would be recognized as belonging to the "key branches of the national economy."

Considering the ostensibly democratic tone of the entire PKWN manifesto and the joyful mood (underlain, to be sure, with uncertainty and fear) that prevailed in the liberated territories with the end of the German occupation, one can assume that many owners or their heirs held out hope that they would regain their property and the freedom to dispose of it. In the part of the manifesto devoted to questions of ownership, its authors also included an announcement that "Jews, after being bestially eradicated by the occupier, will be guaranteed the rebuilding of their existence and legal and actual equal rights." The manifesto itself obviously was only a political declaration, a propagandistic proclamation whose goal was to win the support of the inhabitants of Poland for the communists and their pursuit of the official assumption of power. The fact that questions of property already appeared in such an early document most likely expresses not so much the political will of the new authorities as their recognition of the burning problems that were troubling society immediately after the front crossed.

Recovery of Property Immediately
after the War: The Law

Many Jews returning to Radom right after the war did not yet know what they would do next. Some wanted to leave as quickly as possible the land that was for them only a cemetery for their loved ones.[32] Others planned to begin anew, in the city, lives that the war had so brutally interrupted. All were linked by a need for money, whatever their future might be and wherever it might be located. Therefore, many people undertook efforts to regain the property that had belonged to them or their families. These efforts should also be seen as attempts by the survivors at returning to the prewar order, at securing at least a partial connection with the prewar world, and as a reassertion of agency, of control over their own lives. The war turned everything upside down. Initially, many survivors held out hope for the return of the former order. Soon, hope was followed by the feeling of a rupture in continuity and of suspension in a postwar void. Although this experience had become the lot of millions of citizens, not only of Poland but of other countries as well, it must have been especially profound among Polish Jews. Many of them had lost all their relatives, all their acquaintances, coworkers, and neighbors. In the face of such devastation and the social void surrounding them, the survivors of the Holocaust turned to the courts to regain ownership of their estates. But the postwar reality differed greatly not only in social and political terms but also legally from the one they had known before September 1, 1939.

Fundamental questions connected with the restitution of property, both movable and real, were regulated in Poland after the war by three legal acts: two decrees with the power of a law, and one law. They were the Decree on Abandoned and Discarded Properties, issued March 2, 1945; the Law on Abandoned and Discarded Properties of May 6, 1945; and the Decree on Abandoned and Post-German Properties from March 8, 1946.[33] These laws did not complement each other; they succeeded one another. The law that was in effect from March 1945 changed twice in barely one year, in itself proof that the new authorities were still working out their approach to private property and to the owners who had lost possession of their properties as a result of the war.

The first of the legal acts systemizing questions of restitution, the Decree of March 2, 1945, concerning abandoned and discarded properties introduced a defining distinction between "abandoned" and "discarded." Any property that had been the property of the German state, German citizens, or individuals "who flocked to the enemy" was declared discarded and as such was to become state property.[34] All property over which the rightful (non-German) owners had lost control as a result of the war that began on September 1, 1939, on the other hand, was recognized as "abandoned" and was to be recovered by those who possessed it before the war.[35] In addition, properties confiscated by the German occupation authorities or transferred by their owners to third parties with the aim of avoiding confiscation were all considered "abandoned." The next two legal acts sustained the distinction between "abandoned" and "discarded" property. In the title of the decree of March 1946, the designation "discarded" property was replaced by the more literal designation "post-German" property. In contrast, the term "post-Jewish" did not enter the legal system. However, both terms—"post-Jewish" and "post-German"—came into common usage not only in the postwar street but also by organizations and representatives of the state administration. Both terms can easily be found in official bureaucratic correspondence from the second half of the 1940s. As Jan Tomasz Gross observes, the two phrases "are immediately understandable to a native speaker of Polish as 'leftover Jewish,' or 'leftover German' property."[36]

Immediately after the end of the German occupation of Poland, "abandoned" and "discarded" properties remained in the possession of private individuals or units of local administration. In March 1945, with the goal of regularizing such properties, the Central Office of the Provisional State Administration, which reported to the Ministry of the Treasury, was created.[37] This institution was eliminated one year later and, in its place, the Central Liquidation Office (Główny Urząd Likwidacyjny, GUL) was established. It was supposed to cooperate with its local branches in overseeing the administration of "abandoned" and "discarded" properties until they were taken over by particular state institutions (in the case of "abandoned" properties, also, returned to their lawful owners). In addition to that, GUL was responsible for leasing, for rental, and in certain situations for the sale of property.[38] In accordance with the law then in effect, trustees and other individuals holding "abandoned" or "discarded" property were obliged to make themselves known to the authorities.[39] People who, as a result of the war, had come into possession of the properties of dispossessed individuals could not legally retain those properties for themselves after the war's end. The Polish state was to play the role of intermediary in everything done after the war with "abandoned" and "discarded" property. At least in theory, no room was made for the "spontaneous transfer of ownership." Nonetheless, that became the norm, especially in the case of movable property; most often such items were not reported to authorities by the new possessors.

Proceedings for the Restoration of Possession

Since Roman times, there has existed in law the distinction between legal control and actual control. The former signifies the legal title to property and the latter, the possibility of the free use of it, with physical holding equaling possession.[40] The introduction immediately after the war in Poland of a law regulating matters of "abandoned" property made it possible for Polish citizens—owners or their relatives—who had lost control of property as a result of the war to petition the city courts for restoration of possession.[41] Restoration of possession did not include judgment as to the legal ownership of a property.[42] If, after some time, a different individual appeared who had the right to voice a claim, that individual, too, could regain actual control. In that way, at least from the viewpoint of the legal regulations, rapid decisions establishing the right of ownership whose results would have been difficult to overturn later on were avoided. Claimants who were not owners also avoided the lengthy, difficult, and costly procedure of a civil inheritance proceeding, which could also be undertaken at that time.[43] Relatives of prewar owners to whom possession of a property was returned, or the State Treasury, could acquire the ownership right of an "abandoned" property by prescription.[44]

The next two legal acts, passed during the first year after the enactment of the March 2, 1945, Decree on Abandoned and Discarded Properties, were perhaps aimed at clarifying the enacted solutions or correcting legislative errors revealed in the course of enforcing the regulations.[45] Regardless of the intentions of the authorities, it seems that the changes introduced by the law of May 6, 1945, actually led to the narrowing of the group of potential claimants. From May 1945, in the absence of the owner, only his or her closest relatives—parents, siblings, children, or spouse—could try for the return of property declared "abandoned."[46] Survivors noted the severity of the changes introduced by the law. In May 1945, Marceli Najder, a pharmacist at the time in Izbica, wrote in his diary:

> *A propos* a wrong. Two months ago, a law was enacted by the Polish
> Council of Ministers about abandoned properties [i.e., the Decree of
> March 2, 1945]. It was a very liberal law, allowing for inheritance to
> the 12th degree of kinship. . . . in a case in which someone has already
> entered into possession of a property and a second person has been
> found with greater rights, that person has the right to pursue claims.
> It was a law that gave the possibility of "recovery from loss"—for ex-
> ample, to Jews who were, after all, financially entirely broken. This law
> was based, after all, on Polish civic codes that are in effect. But what
> happened? That law was salt in the wounds of many people—for Jews
> could not so much enrich themselves as at least financially recompense
> all that they lived through. . . . And the KRN [State National Council]
> issued a new law: inheritance can only be on a direct line, that is, father,
> mother, daughter, son between each other. The matter is simplified:
> Jews won't have anything (for why should they?) and the [State] Trea-
> sury will take everything.
>   . . . Is it possible to recompense with money the slaughter of mil-
> lions? They should have been left at least this tiny equivalent—even if
> only for comfort. But that, too, was a disappointment.[47]

Najder was clearly mistaken in his belief that any of the postwar laws allowed inheritance to the 12th degree of kinship or that according to the changed law only direct relatives could recover property—siblings and spouses of the owner could file claims, too. This entry from the pharmacist's diary, however, should be read as a text documenting a survivor's emotions and perception of the legal changes, rather than as a source of information about the exact legal rules.

The exclusion of cousins and more distant relatives from the circle of individuals given the right to pursue the return of property was particularly painful for Polish Jewish citizens. It often happened that of an extensive family only one or two individuals survived who, from May 1945 on, could not get back properties lost by their murdered relatives. Consequently, such properties remained under the administration of the state, and in time became its property. True, during the war many Polish Christian citizens also lost their properties, but in their case, in absence of the owner, there was a much greater likelihood that someone from among the closest relatives would be found who could submit an application for return of possession. Thus, as a consequence, the state kept control over a much larger number of Jewish than non-Jewish properties.

The Decree of March 8, 1946, introduced further restrictions. It stipulated that applications for the return of possession had to be made before the end of 1947.[48] From the moment the decree came into effect in the second half of April 1946, individuals desiring to regain possession had no more than a year and a half to complete documents, find money for an attorney and judicial fees, and appeal to the proper city court. This term was extended by one year under pressure from the Central Committee of Jews in Poland (CKŻP) and the World Jewish Congress, with the final date for accepting applications designated as the end of 1948.[49] Despite these changes, it was obvious that many eligible individuals would not succeed in submitting claims within the term dictated by the law, and former owners or their families would lose the possibility of recovering properties, which would remain under the control of the Polish state.

Some owners or their relatives who had survived the Holocaust were living abroad. They may have emigrated before September 1939, escaped from Poland during the war, or left the country right after it. Such individuals required more time to put their property affairs in order. They had first to make often difficult attempts at establishing what was happening with their real property and what its actual condition was. To do this, most often they corresponded with the Legal Department of the CKŻP or local Jewish committees. The District Jewish Committee in Radom received letters of inquiry not only from private individuals but also from institutions acting on their behalf.[50] If a petitioner was living outside of Radom, usually the next step was naming a plenipotentiary.

In most instances, plenipotentiary rights were assigned to an attorney practicing in the city who pursued the case. Jews who wished to regain possession in Radom often turned to attorney Bronisław Hassenbein. His name was on the list of Jewish lawyers sent by the Paris bureau of the Joint Distribution Committee to headquarters in New York in December 1947.[51] Hassenbein had had a practice in Radom before the war. During the occupation, he was in hiding in Lublin.[52] He was a Lutheran, but everyone in the city knew about his Jewish background. Perhaps his heritage and wartime experience awakened trust in Hassenbein among some of the survivors. He was not, however, the sole Radom attorney employed by Jews applying for the return of their properties.

Regardless of which law was in effect at any given moment, throughout the entire period of 1945–1948, the most straightforward cases were those in which the claimant was both the legitimate owner and the prewar possessor of the real property the claim concerned. It was necessary in such a case to address a letter to the appropriate city court and document the legal title to the real property, preferably by presenting a copy from the land registry. After receiving an appeal for the return of possession, the court was obligated to post in its offices a notice with relevant information that would allow for eventual claims by other parties. The court would set a date for consideration of the case at which the claimant (or his plenipotentiary) and a representative of the state administration (or of the General Counsel to the Polish Republic representing the state) would participate. More often, however, it was the family of the prewar owner who sought the return of property. Then, prior to submitting a claim for return of possession, it was necessary to conduct a separate proceeding before the city court in which the owner would be officially declared deceased. If documents confirming the death were lacking, witnesses were called who testified that they saw the owner perish during the occupation or witnessed the owner being deported by the Germans.

Relatives or spouses making a claim also had to prove they were related by blood or marriage to the owner of the real property. To this end, it was best to present copies of birth certificates or marriage licenses. If that turned out to be impossible, as was often the case in postwar conditions, the court also accepted different types of testimony. Maria Frydman, the widow of Abram Hersz Frydman, petitioning for the return of part of an apartment house in the center of Radom that belonged to her husband, presented to the court a certificate issued by the Jewish Committee in Radom. That document asserted on the basis of a prewar registry of residents and the testimonies of witnesses that Maria and Abram Hersz were a married couple, that Abram Hersz was deported by the Germans, and that, as of the time of submitting her petition, Maria Frydman was the only co-owner of the real property who had returned to Radom.[53] Frydman, before the war a teacher in one of Radom's elementary schools, also tried to obtain written testimonies from the education authorities. In response to her request, the schools inspector testified that in 1938 Maria Frydman had deposited with the school authorities her marriage license, which, along with other documents, was destroyed during the war.[54] Three weeks after she filed her claim, on May 18, 1945, the City Court in Radom returned to her possession of the apartment house.[55] Only two years later, in June 1947, this decision was handed over to the General Counsel to the Polish Republic, representing the interests of the state in the court, which lodged a complaint in the District Court in Radom. The counsel correctly observed that before the war the apartment house was not the exclusive property of Abram Hersz Frydman. In 1945, Mrs. Frydman was therefore entitled to recover only one-eighth of the building, but she now held possession of the entirety. The counsel demanded that the part of the real property belonging to the co-owners be taken from her and transferred to the management of the District Liquidation Office (Okręgowy Urząd Likwidacyjny, OUL).[56] It turned out, however, that the City Court had already corrected the error it had committed, and in 1946 the court had changed the decision in the Frydman case. Therefore, the General Counsel withdrew the complaint.

In this case, one can see two characteristic features of the court cases for the return of possession that took place in the immediate aftermath of the war. First, the frequent lack of documents that would allow a definitive confirmation of the facts meant witnesses and their testimonies often played a decisive role. This created opportunities for various types of errors and abuses. Second, the institutional landscape in the first postwar years was very unclear; legal procedures were just being worked out. It is difficult to explain in any other way several facts from the Frydman case, including that the court did not inquire about the co-owners of the real property, nor did it send its findings to the Counsel until almost two years after the decision was handed down. It is likely that immediately after the war all the documents that became accessible after a year or two had not yet been found. After the decision was made in 1945, documents in the Radom city land registry and a separate set of documents attesting to marital status were discovered, for in later documentation related to the case, there is a copy of the Frydmans' marriage license and the statement presented by the Mortgage Department of the District Court in Radom.[57] As Maria Frydman's case shows, after the war the possibilities of confirming the legal state of property of Polish Jews, the victims of the Holocaust, changed as documentation was found and organized.

Real property as the subject of postwar proceedings for the return of possession can be divided into those in which the state, loosely construed (local administration, offices, industrial unions, social organizations), was interested, and those to which it was completely indifferent. A separate, intermediate category was made up of properties that were of interest to individuals who were often connected to the new authorities but were neither the prewar owners nor their heirs. To a great extent, the success of a claim submitted to the court for the return of possession of specific real property depended on whether that property was of interest to the state or to certain well-connected individuals.

Recovered Real Properties and Execution of Court Decisions

If the state did not oppose the return of possession to a prewar owner or owner's family, the courts most often rendered their decision in favor of the claimants, as happened in the case of Maria Frydman. After a city court issued a favorable ruling, the claimant then turned to the Provisional State Administration (in a later period, to the Liquidation Office) with a request for execution of the decision. It is difficult to state what such an execution looked like in practice on the basis of preserved documents of the courts and the District Liquidation Offices. I have also not found any description of it in narratives and memoirs. One can assume, however, that execution differed depending on the particular case at hand. If the real property was empty, the administration simply turned it over to the legal possessors, who were then free to make use of it. When individuals to whom possession of real property was returned were already occupying it at the time of their appeal, the execution of the court decision was only a matter of legalizing the existing state of affairs. Individuals regaining possession of real properties inhabited by new tenants were in a much more difficult situation. Many residents had already settled in during the occupation, with or without permission from the German authorities. Similarly, the postwar administration managing the real property could rent it out or lease it. Termination of such agreements was possible, to be sure, but in practice was limited by regulations protecting the interests of leaseholders.[58] Therefore, it was possible to regain possession of a real property in the legal sense but at the same time still be unable to dispose of it freely. An individual to whom possession was restored had to cope with the consequences of decisions taken by the provisional administration in a period when real estate remained under state administration.

If new residents had occupied the real property without a contract, the individual who regained possession theoretically could try for eviction of the "wild" tenants. However, as one might guess, petitioning the court with an appeal for eviction could turn out to be not only a difficult decision but also a dangerous one, doubtless creating many enemies. It is in this context that one should understand a comment by Inspector Zeliwski, who was authorized by the CKŻP to conduct in-person audits in the Jewish committees of Kielce province in May 1945:

[The safety of the Jewish population was improved by] the swift and focused political-economic orientation of the local Jewish element expressed in a conscious reluctance to repossess real estate, properties, shops, goods, apartments, etc. *Relatively rare instances of reclaiming properties are carried out in a conciliatory manner, practically without the authorities' interference.* In the opinion of the most well-connected and well-informed members of the Local Committees in the territory of the entire province, a relatively conditional and problematically peaceful residence in the villages and towns can be bought only *at this price.*[59]

A lack of money, the desire to leave, and the difficulty of taking over actual management meant that for the most part, survivors who regained possession of real property sold it quickly, often at prices far below market value. Tosia Lastman, having returned to Radom in the spring of 1945, sold half of a three-story apartment house located in the center of the city for three gold twenty-dollar coins.[60] Honorable transactions also took place at times. In 1948, Aleksander Wajselfisz sold real property belonging to his family, recalling that he got a good price, just what he had wanted, and the buyer did not bargain.[61] In theory, an individual to whom possession was restored, if not previously the owner of the real property, had only de facto ownership and could not sell the property. However, immediately after the war such transactions were a daily occurrence. Often, properties were sold even before the owner's relatives applied to the court for the return of possession of the real property. If the seller and the buyer wanted to conclude a contract, legal distinctions were a secondary matter. Those who acquired houses and lots sold by survivors were not, of course, Jews. Sometimes it was the buyers who approached the Provisional State Administration (or the Liquidation Office) requesting legal recognition of their right to the property. That was the case with the lot belonging to Bajla Lerman. In August 1945, by ruling of the City Court, Lerman regained possession of half of a lot located near Piwna Street in Radom.[62] Two weeks later, she sold the property to a married couple, Maria and Józef Badeński.[63] Two years later, in September 1948, the Badeńskis applied to the Radom branch of the OUL in Kielce to sanction their possession of the real property. In addition to documents certifying their ownership, both had to submit certificates issued by the Municipal National Council testifying that each of them "is well regarded. During the German occupation he/she did not declare German nationality or German descent. He/She did not work for or in behalf of the occupier nor did he/she take actions damaging to Polish interests."[64] This was standard procedure for everyone applying to the Liquidation Office to be granted possession of a property. Testimony about being well regarded and confirming noncollaboration with Germans took various forms. Aside from a document issued by the local authorities, it could be a transcript of witness statements made before an employee of the Liquidation Office.[65]

Originally, individuals pursuing claims before the city courts for return of possession were generally excused from paying judicial fees. In

March 1946, relatively low fees for filing a claim were introduced.[66] This does not mean, however, that the process for regaining real property was cheap. For the majority of survivors, scraping together even the small sum to make a claim could pose a problem. Additionally, before actually taking possession of the real property, it was necessary to settle accounts with the institution that had managed it until then. To this end, the state administration created a balance of costs expended and the potential income gained from the given property. The costs were supposed to be covered by income, but often the income was insufficient. In such a case, the individual receiving possession of the property had to pay off the state's liabilities. This rule applied to everyone who wanted to take possession of real property regardless of whether possession was returned to them as the result of a procedure created by the postwar legal regulations or if they had acquired the property through inheritance. Lejzor Cymbalista, among others, found himself in that situation. In December 1948, he received a house and lot in Radom as part of an inheritance ruling. When, in the summer of 1949, Cymbalista petitioned to be granted possession of the property, the Department of Abandoned and Discarded Real Properties of the Municipal Authority in Radom, at the request of the Liquidation Office, drew up a balance of the income and expenses borne while it held the building. Ultimately, wanting to take possession of the property, the heir had to pay more than three times the income derived from it by the Municipal Authority.[67] It should be noted that management of "abandoned" properties was not always linked to direct profits for the new state administration. Some of these properties required immediate renovation work with large financial outlays attached. Buildings left without the oversight of an owner thus created a real problem for the postwar administration, especially in the first months after the end of the occupation when the municipal treasury was almost empty.

Those individuals who took possession of real property in which the state had made some investments had to contend with even greater costs. In accordance with the Decree of March 8, 1946, the state also had the right to demand repayment of expenditures borne by the German occupation authorities in connection with investments made by them.[68] If the owner was not able to pay down the entire amount requested, the decree permitted securing the owner's liability through an entry in the land registry for the property.[69] Because of this, many properties, possession of which had been restored to private individuals, were encumbered with mortgages. By executing charges for investments made during the period of the German occupation, the Polish state in this fashion not only legitimized de facto the Nazi administration of real properties, later referred to as "abandoned," but also placed itself in the position of heir or continuator of the German administrators.

The local administration managing "abandoned" property that before the war had belonged to Polish citizens who were Jews took over these structures from the analogous German institutions. There is a good deal of evidence that in Radom the postwar Polish administration not only established its headquarters in the same building at Legions Square 13 (Plac Legionów; Rathausplatz during the German occupation)—a Jewish-owned building before the war—but also inherited documentation from its German predecessor.[70] A "Card Catalog of Post-Jewish Real Properties Located on Various Radom Streets in 1945" has been preserved in the Radom State Archive.[71] Although the name of the card catalog is certainly postwar, it is hard to say when exactly the evidentiary cards for particular properties it consists of were created. The majority of them were filled out by hand in Polish; one handwriting is dominant, but there are also cards filled out in German, and in different handwriting. There is no consistency as to the names of streets—German occupation–era names appear, but there are also Polish names that were in use both before and immediately after the war. A definite answer about when the card catalog arose is not particularly important, however, since "post-Jewish" real properties had existed in the city at least since 1942, and an apartment house that was "post-Jewish" in 1943 remained the same in January 1945. Thus, the Polish administration inherited from the German administrators not only their headquarters and part of their documentation but above all a property the Polish institutions would have to manage from then on. The card catalog encompasses over 700 buildings located in Radom. Without a doubt, it is not a complete list of "post-Jewish" real properties in the city. The index, therefore, does not fully represent the extent of properties that fell under the administration of the city after the war.

Unrecovered Real Property

In general, applications by the owners (or their relatives) for the return of
assets considered "abandoned" properties of industrial firms and enterprises were doomed to failure. The first of the three immediate postwar
legal acts regulating property included an article stating that "no one can
be brought into possession of property that is of particular significance
for the interests of the state."[72] In such cases, the law vested in the Provisional State Administration (Tymczasowy Zarząd Państwowy, TZP) the
right to appeal for the exclusion of a property from the effect of the decree. The TZP could do this at any time during an ongoing procedure.
A declaration of a justified objection by the TZP was binding on the court,
and procedures regarding the return of property claimed by the TZP were
subject to automatic suspension.

In February 1946, the Law on State Appropriation of the Main Branches
of the National Economy came into effect; it made possible the nationalization of the majority of private enterprises and industrial firms in Poland. The minister whose portfolio included relevant types of enterprise
was authorized to rule on the nationalization of similar properties in accordance with the law.[73] His decision was final and not subject to appeal.
The ministers thus gained a great deal of power over private enterprises
in the sectors of the economy that were subordinate to them. Under the
authority of this law, all private industrial enterprises capable of employing
over fifty workers during one shift would become the property of the
state. Similarly, all enterprises from the mining, energy, and armaments
branches; metal plants, coke works, sugar refineries, printing plants; poli-
graphic, communication, and telecommunication firms were transferred
to state ownership. Larger water-supply firms, textile plants, distilleries,
breweries, mills, and oil mills were also nationalized.[74] In practice, almost
every private enterprise could be nationalized by a minister's decision.[75]
The owners of enterprises seized by the state were entitled to indemnities, the amount to be set by specially appointed commissions. Compensation was to be paid out basically in securities, only exceptionally in cash
or other values.[76] It can be assumed that the indemnifications paid in securities served to give nationalization the appearance of legality rather
than provide actual compensation for losses borne by the private owners.

In the documents of cases connected with "abandoned" property, I came across no information about indemnities paid to owners of property destined for nationalization. This may mean that judgment about possible indemnification was conducted in separate proceedings, but it is probable that at least at times indemnification simply was not paid. In March 1946, when the Decree on Abandoned and Post-German Properties was adopted, the Law on State Appropriation of the Main Branches of the National Economy was already in force. Therefore, the last of the bills regulating questions of "abandoned" property included a notation that clearly stated possession of properties subject to nationalization in accordance with the law could not be restored.[77]

Traces of the transfer of Jewish enterprises to state property can be found in the records of cases concerning the restoration of possession to former owners. The Provisional State Administration (and later, District Liquidation Office) was informed about every ongoing proceeding. If it concerned an industrial firm, the TZP (later, the District Liquidation Office) sought the opinion of the local authority that supervised the industry or an appropriate industrial association for the type of firm. In April 1945, an application was submitted to the City Court in Radom by co-owners Alicja-Sara Żabner and Edyta-Estera Aronson requesting the return of ownership of the Rubinsztein Foundry—Heirs factory (the site, the factory premises, the warehouses, the furnishings, and the materials). The TZP requested an opinion from the Radom County Industrial Department.[78] The department declared that "the factory is currently up and running, and since it is fulfilling state orders it is of particular significance for the interests of the State."[79] In light of this information, the court dismissed Żabner and Aronson's application.[80] However, during the course of the proceedings, the law had changed, and a new law allowing petitioners to appeal a decision to the Ministry of the Treasury came into effect.[81] The two women appealed, but nothing indicates that their protest yielded a positive result. Rubinsztein Foundry–Heirs became a state firm producing farming machinery.

In a separate case, Rywka Ejzman, a survivor who was attempting to regain the Markant tannery operating in Radom, also appealed to the Ministry of the Treasury.[82] Her grandparents had leased the industrial firm before the war to Jerzy Cieński. He administered the tannery in 1945, too, only now he was paying rent not to its private owners, since they had perished during the Holocaust, but to the Provisional State Administration.[83] Ejzman's attempt to regain the tannery did not succeed, and her appeal to the Ministry of the Treasury was unsuccessful. After consultation with the Leather Industry Association, the Industrial Department of the Kielce Provincial Authority declared that the tannery was subject to seizure as state property.[84]

To understand the position of surviving Jews who attempted to recover enterprises, it is essential to look at the atmosphere surrounding the efforts of the prewar owners or their heirs. The Polish Workers' Party weekly paper in Radom, *Świt*, published in the summer of 1945 a front-page article titled, "Who Wants to Snatch Their Rights from the Worker? Disturbing Machinations in Radom Industry." The anonymous author referred directly to efforts undertaken by the co-owners of Rubinstein Foundry–Heirs, Alicja-Sara Żabner and Edyta-Estera Aronson:

> When two of the co-owners returned and submitted a complaint to the court, the workers, having found out about this, called a general meeting. The position of the workers at the meeting was unhesitating. A resolution was adopted unanimously (with one abstention) [*sic*] that the former owners have no right now to the firm, which is a state good. In the resolution it is emphasized, that *"a capitalist, who earned for so many years from the blood and sweat of the workers, long ago used up the capital he invested and now no longer has any rights."*
>
> One of the speakers raised an appropriate motif: *If land is taken back from landowners, why should industrialists whose property exceeds by many times the value of parceled out farms be privileged?*
>
> . . .
>
> The workers do not want to hear anything about making their foundry, for which they have presented so many proofs of devotion and initiative, into a private enterprise again. *The firm is of the highest social usefulness and must be a state property.*[85]

At the very least, some of the workers employed at the foundry and at other Radom factories did not want a return to former owners. Perceiving the wartime and postwar change of ownership as a positive thing, they counted on an improvement in their situation if the firm remained under state control. Communist propaganda made use of these attitudes, representing the efforts of private owners to regain industrial firms as a manifestation of "class enmity," which posed a direct threat to workers.

The practice of an administrative body seeking the opinion of industry authorities with respect to "the significance for the state's interest" in enterprises declared "abandoned" property was employed with small factories as well, even though their products could hardly be deemed goods with strategic significance. An example of this is Józef Frydman's carbonated water plant in Radom. In this case, it was stated that the firm could return to private hands without damage to the interests of the Polish state.[86] A different stance, at least initially, was taken in relation to a Radom comb factory and a paper products factory, both belonging to Ita Gutman. The Industrial Department of the Provincial Authority in Kielce informed the TZP that these firms, located on the same premises, "considering their production, are important for the interests of the State" and as such were not subject to reprivatization.[87] It is difficult to resist the impression that in arriving at a decision about whether certain smaller enterprises should remain under state control or be returned to their owners, a good deal of arbitrariness came into play. These decisions were often dependent on the subjective approach of an individual official.

Public Institutions in "Post-Jewish" Real Property

The law concerning "abandoned" and "discarded" ("post-German") assets made it possible for state administrations to transfer some properties to institutions of public utility, cooperatives, "social institutions, cultural and educational organizations, and organizations helping population groups particularly persecuted by the [German] occupier."[88] But even before the first legal regulations arose, that is, before the Decree of March 2, 1945, came into effect, the local administration allocated apartments in "abandoned" buildings to various organizations.[89] In August 1945, the Provincial Headquarters of the Union of Polish Scouting (Związek Harcerstwa Polskiego, ZHP) turned to the state administration for permission to use free of charge a five-room apartment located in an "abandoned" apartment house on Witold Street in Radom. From the contents of the letter, it appears that at the time the request was submitted, scouts were already occupying the apartment and had established in it the office of the Provincial Headquarters, the offices of the Boy Scouts and Girl Scouts, a room for cub scouts, and a day room for the scouts. Requesting relief from payment for use of the apartment, the Provincial Headquarters referred directly to the ruling addressing the transfer of "abandoned" real property for use by social institutions and educational organizations.[90] In support of the request, information was included about the way the apartment would be used by the ZHP and about the fact that "the premises are located in a post-Jewish house." In addition, reference was made to the guidelines of the Ministry of Public Administration (MAP) about allocating apartments to "democratic organizations of youth" and "giving the ZHP every support."[91] The fact that the scouts' letter speaks openly about an apartment in a "post-Jewish house" is one more proof that it was common knowledge where these "abandoned" properties came from. In all likelihood, after the war the non-Jewish inhabitants of Radom and many other Polish cities were convinced that the Jews would not return. Therefore, in the consciousness of ordinary inhabitants of the city and officials, the property that remained behind was "post-Jewish" property. The use of this designation in official correspondence indicates that taking over Jewish property was not seen as shameful. Not only was it permitted, it also, most likely, met with approval on the part of the authorities and a significant part of local society, who saw the undertaking as practical use of goods left behind by their slaughtered fellow citizens.

The precise provenance of "abandoned" real property was no secret; in some official documents, in addition to the annotation "post-Jewish," the surnames of the prewar owners were written down. In the records of the OUL in Kielce is preserved a "List of Real Property Discarded and Abandoned . . . in Use by the Postal Bureau in Radom County." The list indicates that one of the Radom telephone and telegraph offices was located in the "post-Jewish" property of Pinkus and Szaps Frydman, and the post office building in Szydłowiec—a town in the vicinity of Radom—belonged previously to Izaak Pinkert and Zyndel Zelberg. In Radom itself, the postal authority made use of four other "post-Jewish" properties.[92] The names of the former owners also appear in correspondence concerning the new seat of the City Court in Zwoleń, a small town located thirty kilometers east of Radom. The court building there had been burned during the war and could not be used. Therefore, already in January 1945 the mayor of Zwoleń allocated to the City Court seven rooms in an unfinished apartment building. The presiding officer of the court described the status of the building in a letter to the president of the District Court in Radom:

> The owners of this property are Jews who were deported by the German occupiers, and at present the property is in the possession of the Provisional State Administration.
>
> In connection with my conversation with the Citizen President and also in conformity with art. 13 of the law of 6 May 1945 about properties abandoned [and discarded] . . . , I humbly ask the Citizen President to address the Main Office of the Provisional State Administration with an appeal to hand over for management and use by the City Court in Zwoleń the post-Jewish property, located in Zwoleń, . . . *which is the property of the married couple Drajzla and Mordka-Dawid Braun and also the married couple Chaja-Mariem and Rachmil Kierzberg, Jews not present in Poland, and most probably murdered by the Germans.*[93]

The new users of these properties thus had no illusions as to who had "abandoned" them and under what circumstances. The correspondence of offices and institutions interested in "abandoned" property makes it clear that the taking of Jewish property by state institutions and social organizations was an open act that did not require "camouflage."

Jewish organizations, too, profited from the regulation permitting transfer of "abandoned" property to organizations assisting groups particularly persecuted by the Nazis. It appears that here, too, the legal ruling only confirmed a practice that had already existed for some time. The mayor of Radom allocated to the Jewish Committee space for its office at 45 Traugutt Street and a small building at 50 Traugutt Street, even before the first decree regulating the questions of "abandoned" and "discarded" property went into effect.[94] Before the war, a Jewish charitable organization, Ezra, had been housed in the second of these properties, where the Committee now established a shelter and a soup kitchen.[95] In the summer of 1945, the Jewish Committee also undertook efforts to recover and restart the Jewish hospital that had operated in Radom before the war:

> One of the greatest problems for those of the Jewish population returning from various concentration camps to Radom and surrounding towns is the lack of a Jewish hospital. The medical condition of the returning Jewish camp inmates, after all, is pitiful, and due to the lack of a hospital, the Jewish Committee cannot receive them with the help they require.
>
> The referral of gravely ill camp inmates to the municipal hospitals in Radom with the assistance of the Municipal Health Center, or the Polish Red Cross in Radom, encounters great difficulties due to the lack of free spaces in those hospitals.
>
> The Jewish Committee, therefore, seeking to aid the returning Jewish camp inmates, in particular with medical aid, in the broadest scope and the most effective manner, turns to the Mayor of Radom city with a respectful plea for the gracious return of the hospital on Starokrakowska Street in Radom, which for about 50 years was designated for the sick Jews of Radom city and the surrounding towns and was the pride of the local Jewish community.
>
> Should the hospital be returned, the Jewish Committee will make every effort to organize qualified medical and nursing personnel in the shortest possible time. It should be emphasized that the existence of a Jewish hospital is in the interest not only of the Jewish population itself, but of the entire population of Radom, since to a considerable extent it will relieve the municipal hospitals and other institutions of the burden of providing medical assistance (Municipal Health Center, Polish Red Cross, etc.).[96] (See Figure 4.5.)

The state administration did not agree, however, to return the hospital to the Committee. The property was occupied by the Municipal Authority, which in the middle of February 1945 was already planning to set up a city infectious diseases hospital in the building.[97] In the meantime, the municipal authorities had difficulty acquiring funds to renovate the building. Because of this, they agreed to a proposal by the Jewish Committee to seek support from abroad, but after renovation the hospital

Figure 4.5 Building that housed the Jewish hospital in Radom. Photo by Lukasz Krzyzanowski.

was to be managed by the Municipal Authority.[98] Most likely due to the rapidly diminishing number of survivors living in Radom, the Committee ultimately did not have the ability to provide aid in carrying out the necessary work. The hospital building, without changing its function, remained under the authority of the state after the war. In September 1946, the pulmonary department of the city hospital was established there.[99]

In the initial period after liberation, there was a conviction among Jewish committees and Jewish religious associations (later, Jewish denominational congregations) that they were the obvious heirs and had the greatest rights to property belonging to the prewar Jewish communities, other Jewish organizations, and private Jewish individuals. In the winter of 1945, the Ministry of Public Administration took up this question, issuing a circular on February 10 informing the provincial governors that

all movable property and real property remaining after the former Israelite Religious Communities will remain for the time being under

the management of the State Administration until the law about abandoned property comes into effect. The property is intended in the first
place for the aims of Jewish charitable, cultural, and other similar
organizations.

. . . With the goal of making it possible for Jewish Religious Associations to carry out their practices . . . county governors are obligated
forthwith to grant the board of the local Association *access* to any real
property that previously was the property of the former Israelite Religious Communities, such as synagogues, religious seminaries, ritual
baths, cemeteries, and also objects connected with the religious cult,
namely Talmuds, Torahs, etc.

. . . In localities where there are no buildings that serve exclusively
the aims of the Jewish religious cult, but other buildings remain that
until now were the property of the Israelite Religious Communities,
the county governors are required to the extent possible to permit use
of these premises with the goal of making their [i.e., postwar Jewish
religious organizations'] activity feasible for them.[100]

Like other regulations concerning "abandoned" property, the MAP
circular also spoke only about granting access to real properties, but the
properties remained under state control all the time. There is no mention of returning real property to the Jewish organizations or of issues related to the right of ownership. It was the state, not the postwar Jewish
organizations, that was the legal and de facto holder of the property belonging to prewar Jewish institutions and Jewish citizens of Poland who
had lost control of that property as a result of the war. The Department
of Productivization of the CKŻP underscored that truth to the Radom
Jewish Committee in no uncertain terms: "In answer to your letter . . .
we communicate that we do not have any legal foundations for laying claim
in the matter of allocating to you, free of charge, 40 post-Jewish sewing
machines lent to you by the OUL in 1945. The lack of legal foundations
derives from the fact that *the Polish state and not the Jewish Committee is
the heir of post-Jewish property.*"[101]

The state decided that "post-Jewish" real property would be allocated for use (not ownership) to the Jewish Committee, the Jewish Denominational Congregation, or other Jewish organizations, or it would

be assigned as an office or a place for scout assemblies or—like the
Radom synagogue—it would be torn down. The fate of the Radom synagogue demonstrates that the law and the orders of the central authorities were interpreted by the local administration in a rather loose manner.
The synagogue and house of prayer in the center of the city had survived
the war although they were in ruins. The District Jewish Committee described the postwar condition of the buildings in a letter to the mayor of
the city at the end of June 1945: "The Synagogue and House of Prayer on
Bóżnicza Street which are the property of the former Jewish Religious
Community were requisitioned by the German occupiers and destroyed in a barbaric fashion. After the withdrawal of the occupiers the
above-mentioned buildings remained without protection, and various individuals are profiting from this, tearing them apart completely, collecting all the metal and wood."[102]

The Jewish Committee turned to the city powers at least several times
with a request for protection of the buildings from further theft of materials by the local population and the ensuing destruction. The state administration in charge of the synagogue as "abandoned" property clearly
was not performing its duties. It also did not assign these buildings to the
Jewish community of Radom, which was reemerging at the time, as would
have accorded with the MAP circular. Without considering the religious
needs of the Jews returning to Radom, the city authorities decided to tear
down the synagogue.[103] It appears that this decision was made without
the participation or even the knowledge of the representatives of the community of survivors: "The Synagogue and Prayer House in Radom on
Peretz and Bóżnicza Streets survived the Nazi Occupation. Already
during the time of Reborn Poland these buildings, with their historic
character, were destroyed on order of the Magistrate under the pretext of
the danger of collapse, without prior warning to agents of the Jewish community about the necessity to secure these buildings."[104]

In 1947, the Jews residing in Radom decided to build a monument on
the square where the synagogue had stood. In a letter to the Municipal
Authority, the Jewish Committee informed the authorities that the monument would memorialize the murdered Radom Jews, and at the same
time, "this place, so holy for the Jewish population, will be protected in
this way from possible profanation."[105] The monument actually did stand

in this location, but before it was built, a rumor arose that the Municipal Authority wanted to establish a marketplace on the synagogue square.[106] It was easy to believe the rumor, since the local administration treated "abandoned" real property as its own and instead of administering it in the name of the absent owners, freely disposed of it.

The Radom Jewish cemetery was another area that had belonged to the Jewish community before the war and whose security survivors in the city tried to ensure. In June 1945 in a letter to the mayor of the city, the Jewish Committee described the condition of the graveyard: "On the Kozienice highway, 4 kilometers more or less from Radom, near the Rajec grove, is the Jewish cemetery, which was destroyed by Hitlerite vandalism with the removal of all the monuments. Independently of this, the brick fence of the cemetery was taken down and the bricks given away to build a marmalade factory."[107]

After the war, inhabitants of villages close by used the cemetery to pasture their cows.[108] The District Jewish Committee sent the mayor of the city a request to "issue a recommendation to fence in the cemetery with the goal of protecting it from further destruction and trampling by cattle passing through there."[109] The mayor refused, citing a lack of funds. He agreed only that the Committee could fence in the cemetery at its own cost.[110] Also, the District Jewish Committee itself was to finance the installation of signs forbidding cutting through the cemetery and ruining it, another arrangement the authorities were asked to undertake.[111] It is unknown whether the community of survivors residing in Radom succeeded in achieving these aims. Although plans for the inscriptions on plaques and a purchase order for building a cemetery fence with concrete posts and netting, prepared in early 1950, are preserved in the Committee's files, there is no information confirming that these jobs were actually carried out. The grounds of the Jewish cemetery were cleaned up and fenced in with a wall only after 1989.[112]

Survivors, Fellow Citizens, and "Post-Jewish" Property

Jews who returned to Radom and attempted to regain their property not only met with obstacles on the part of the state and the local administration but also encountered resistance from fellow citizens. Some of the non-Jewish inhabitants had no intention of returning to prewar property relations. It is difficult to establish the number of individuals who, already during the occupation, were resettled in, or of their own volition occupied, Jewish apartments and remained in them after the end of the war. Others received assigned living quarters in "abandoned" real properties administered by the city after the war. Many places required repairs, and the new tenants carried them out with their own funds. Leon Różewicz, an employee in the Municipal Authority in Radom, received a two-room apartment in a "post-Jewish" building in the city center on Wałowa Street. He renovated it at his own expense. In the autumn of 1945, Różewicz attempted to have the cost of renovation counted toward his rent, though it is unclear if he succeeded.[113] The new tenants of "abandoned" real properties also bore costs connected with ongoing maintenance and repairs of the entire buildings in which they lived. On July 22, 1945, a storm that passed through Radom tore the roofs off several "post-Jewish" houses under state authority. An inspector from the TZP, having performed an inspection of the damages, obligated the buildings' tenants to cover the cost of repairs to the roofs out of their own pockets.[114] Considering that the new inhabitants had settled in and made investments in their residences, it is easy to imagine that even had the court returned possession to the prewar owners, the court's ruling would have been very difficult to execute. Many "post-Jewish" buildings were simply swallowed up by the new reality.

The inhabitants of the city and the officials treated "abandoned" real property as a reservoir of free apartments, all the more valuable because in Radom (as in many other Polish cities after the war) there was great congestion and new people kept arriving, both from distant parts of the country and from nearby villages. Apartments left behind by the annihilated Radom Jews were also attractive for officials who moved to Radom for work. The competition for "abandoned" property could get fierce, with new tenants displaying enmity toward each other. Sometimes, applications for assignment of a "post-Jewish" apartment had the clear character of denunciations, like this one concerning an apartment for an inspector of the Provisional State Administration:

In Radom on Piłsudski Street . . . there is a 4-room apartment which is occupied by some Citizeness Ćwiekiewicz without assignment and without registration, despite the fact that she possesses in Radom another apartment and does not use that place.

This apartment is located in a house that is an abandoned property remaining under the administration of the Provisional State Administration in Radom.

Inspector of the Provisional State Administration for the city and county of Radom, Citizen Fijałkowski Józef, has been on duty in Radom for several weeks and does not have an apartment, and his family, consisting of his wife and three grown children, is forced to live in Busko [a town over 100 kilometers away] because their husband and father does not yet have a place to live in Radom.

Considering the onerous and responsible work of our inspector and the impossibility of maintaining two homes, I humbly request that the above-mentioned apartment be assigned as quickly as possible to Citizen Fijałkowski and to organize with the participation of a representative of the Municipal Housing Office, an organ of the TZP, as well as Citizeness Ćwiekiewicz, the immediate vacating of the apartment under consideration. In the event that Citizeness Ćwiekiewicz should fail to appear, to organize the placement of her things for the time being into one room until their definitive removal at the owner's cost and risk.[115]

Another official, the director of the elementary school in Wieniawa in the vicinity of Radom and clerk in the Office of Information and Propaganda, requested to be assigned a "post-German" or "post-Jewish" house in the summer of 1945. He received in answer from the Kielce division of the State Repatriation Office (Państwowy Urząd Repatriacyjny) an explanation that in accordance with the law and regulations in effect "post-German households are designated exclusively for resettlement of populations from the other side of the Bug River."[116] So the clerk appealed directly to the administration of "abandoned" property with a request that he be assigned "post-Jewish real property possibly in Częstochowa (a house or a villa with a garden)."[117] For many officials of the new regime, getting an "abandoned" house or apartment was a chance to improve their living conditions. Taking into consideration the reality in Poland immediately after the war, cases initiated by Jewish owners who aimed to reclaim possession of properties occupied by officials were most likely doomed to failure.

Ownership changes that were the result of sales agreements concluded during the occupation were also difficult to reverse. In March 1945, two brothers, Wiktor and Szlama Ajzner, appeared in Radom. They were cousins of Szyja and Syma Buszacki, sibling photographers who before the war ran a studio in the center of Radom, on Witold Street. Right after the war broke out, Szyja Buszacki and his children had left for Warsaw, where they wound up in the ghetto. In April 1943, they were transported to the concentration camp in Majdanek (KL Lublin) and most probably perished there. Syma Buszacka, his sister, remained in Radom, sold her business to Stanisław Soborski, and worked for him as a lab technician until the liquidation of the ghetto. During the main liquidation of the large ghetto in August 1942, she was deported to the extermination camp at Treblinka. As the only living heirs of the Buszackis, the Ajzner brothers attempted to regain the photography firm, relying on the March 2, 1945, Decree on Abandoned and Discarded Properties. In their appeal to the City Court in Radom requesting that possession of the Buszackis' property be taken from Stanisław Soborski and assigned to them, the Ajzners challenged the validity of the transaction concluded between Buszacka and Soborski in February 1941 regarding the sale of the firm:

> There is no precise information about under what conditions and on what principle Soborski assumed ownership of the Buszackis' photography firm. According to his testimony, he allegedly purchased it for 1,500 złotys. Taking into consideration:
> a) the unbelievably low price of acquisition,
> b) the circumstance that Syma Buszacka worked in the firm until the moment of her deportation and thus did not dispose of her possession,
> c) the coerced position of the Buszackis, who according to German statutes were threatened with confiscation of their property, must lead to the conclusion that whatever may have been stated in the contract that Soborski holds and which he will undoubtedly present to the Court, it was a fiction intended

> to protect the property from loss in connection with the
> occupation, and thus in the given instance the regulation . . .
> from the Decree of 2.III.45 applies.
>
> The property of the Buszackis is abandoned property and as such . . .
> must be returned to the owners or to their presumed heirs.[118]

The Ajzners' application referred not only to the space in which the photographic studio was housed but also (perhaps above all) to the firm's equipment. Soborski refused to voluntarily hand over the disputed property to the Ajzners. He submitted testimony that in addition to the studio's equipment he had purchased, "there are objects in my possession which I did not purchase from Syma Buszacka, namely: one camera size 30×40 with a Görtz lens with an aperture of f/7.7 and one small arc lamp. In addition, Syma Buszacka left with me for safekeeping: an old, broken gold watch with watchcases and 2 gold rings without stones as well as a woolen dress and a gramophone. All the above-mentioned objects I am prepared to return at any moment without any compensation to the lawful heirs of Syma Buszacka."[119] The Ajzner brothers appealed to the court for measures securing their claim by taking custody of objects that were part of the photography firm's equipment and located in the disputed premises. The brothers argued that, fearing the loss of the studio, Soborski might attempt to remove the firm's equipment that was housed there.[120] Stanisław Soborski tried to raise doubt as to the Ajzners' relationship with the Buszackis. He presented in court the contract for sale of the firm and the testimony of the well-known Radom photographer Stanisław Sybilski. He stated that Soborski purchased the firm in 1941 and had managed it since then.[121] Both sides summoned many witnesses, but unfortunately their testimonies are not preserved in the case file. In the end, the Ajzners did not succeed in regaining the Buszackis' firm, but that was due to a change in the law and not the effectiveness of Soborski's argument. In the course of the trial, the May 6, 1945, Law on Abandoned and Discarded Properties had come into effect, no longer making it possible for relatives, other than siblings, in a collateral branch of a family to recover the property of prewar owners. Thus, as cousins, the Ajzners were not entitled to pursue the case. The City Court in Radom discontinued the proceedings on the Buszackis' photography studio.[122] Stanisław Soborski remained the owner of the firm "S. Buszacki"; in accordance with the buy-sell agreement, he was able to use the firm's old name. He had already done so during the occupation. On July 14, 1942, a month before the liquidation of the ghetto, this announcement appeared in the "reptilian" press (as German newspapers published in Polish language were commonly referred to), in *Dziennik Radomski* (The Radom daily): "The photographic establishment under the firm 'Buszacki,' proprietor Soborski, Radom, Witold Street. . . ."[123] The Jewish photography studio became the non-Jewish photography studio still preserving the name that was recognizable in the city.[124]

The case of the Ajzner brothers is one of very few incidents when survivors appealed to the Radom court for the return of possession of movable property. Although the three foundational legal acts regulating restitution of property in Poland right after the war pertained to both real property and movable property, the majority of cases before the Polish courts related to buildings and land. If the survivors made attempts to regain movable property, they did so most often without recourse to the courts. Certainly, it was more difficult to prove one's right to movable property than to land and buildings; objects do not have counterparts to registries of deeds. Another reason may have been the fact that unlike real property, the movable property of Polish Jews, lost during the Holocaust, was for the most part in private hands right after the war, not under state management. An appeal to a court requesting the return of such objects would have meant, therefore, a suit against specific individuals. It is easy to imagine that that fact alone may have dissuaded many survivors. Bringing suit against Poles who had grown accustomed to using Jewish furniture, chandeliers, or cutlery could turn out to be fatal for returning Jews. Many survivors did not even attempt to negotiate the recovery of property. When eighteen-year-old Tosia Lastman returned to Radom from a concentration camp in Germany, she went to visit the apartment house in which she had lived with her parents. Passing through the gate of the building, she stopped at the janitor's. The man recognized her and would not let her into his apartment. The young woman was able, however, to see through the half-open door familiar furniture in the janitor's lodgings—a sideboard, table, and chairs from her parents' living room. Describing this encounter, Tosia declared that she felt then "just as during the German times."[125] The Lastmans' furniture remained with the new owner. Mendel (Menachem) Gotfryd, another returnee to Radom after the war, also went to his family home. A Polish woman he did not know opened the door of his parents' apartment. She was friendly and invited him inside. A clock that belonged to the Gotfryd family was hanging in the same place on the wall. The man mentioned the happiness he felt knowing that the clock had survived the hell of the occupation, but he did not attempt to get it back. Years later, he told me that to do so would have been unpleasant and awkward.[126]

Very likely, in order to avoid such unpleasantness and awkwardness, survivors who wanted to take back movable property from Poles sometimes asked for help from Jewish acquaintances who were serving in the army or the UB. A man dressed in a Polish uniform or embodying the authority of the Security Service would certainly have encountered less resistance than a civilian. Authority and a weapon served as persuasive arguments for returning property to the rightful owners and at the same time offered protection. The writer Józef Hen described such a situation in one of his published interviews:

> In 1944, when I was in the Rzeszów region, in the theater of the 10th Division [of the Polish Army], a certain surviving Jew offered me money to go with him to his village because he wanted to take back the furniture he had left with peasants for safekeeping. I said that I would go there with a wagon, but with a colleague who recently was very active in the AK underground—he with a rifle, I with a revolver. There were those who immediately gave things back, but there were also those who resisted. After all, if that Jew had not survived, the things would have been theirs.[127]

Sometimes survivors were invited to buy back "post-Jewish" objects: ". . . in our town every so often Aryans turn to the Jewish Committee with propositions about buying back from them religious books, Torah scrolls, and books with secular content in the Yiddish or Hebrew language."[128] Not having funds for this purpose, the Committee borrowed from private individuals and bought back valuable books. It is difficult to say how frequently such "offers" were made. Most likely, they related to objects not useful to the non-Jews who possessed them, such as Torah scrolls or books in Hebrew or Yiddish, but whose sale could be profitable.[129]

The survivors sometimes knew about objects hidden by someone else and attempted to retrieve them. In June 1945, Tuwia Frydman, who was working at the time in the UB in Gdańsk under an assumed name, on his own initiative and accompanying another survivor, staged a search in a Radom apartment. In a request that Frydman be reprimanded, his superior reported that

> Jasiński Tadeusz [i.e., Tuwia Frydman], an employee of the WUBP [Provincial Office of the Security Service] in Gdańsk, while on leave in Radom on 4.6.1945, at the request of his colleague Birenbaum Jeremi of Radom, went to the apartment of Citizen Zaremba Jan [actually, Marian] in Radom, Stare Miasto Sq. . . . , identifying himself as a Security officer, and declared that there are buried weapons in this apartment and he has come with his colleague to dig it up. The true aim was to dig up fur coats that had been buried in the apartment by a Jewish family which had occupied the apartment before the incursion of the Germans [actually, before the liquidation of the ghetto].[130]

Frydman's interrogation has been preserved in the files of the investigation initiated after this incident. The day after conducting the illegal search, he explained,

> I am currently on leave in Radom. On 4.6. of the current year [1945] my colleague Birenbaum Jarmia [Jeremi] of Radom met me, I don't know the exact place where he lives, asking me to go with him to Stare Miasto to an apartment that some young ladies had pointed out to him, because they had lived there previously with their family, furriers by trade, and that two boxes of fur coats ought to be buried there which the family of these young ladies had buried. I set off for the indicated apartment, identifying myself with my [Security] Service identification card, informing the man of the house that he should bring in the caretaker as a witness, but for some reason, I don't know why, the caretaker did not come; then I asked the man of the house to remove the boards and dig a hole one meter deep.[131]

As the testimony of the tenant in the apartment describes it, Frydman attempted to threaten him, pretending that he had appeared there in an official capacity: ". . . took out his official identification card from the Security Service with the stamp of the State Seal, asking me if I know what that means, telling me at the same time that it means the same as the German Gestapo. At that time, interrogating me officially, he asked me where I served in the army, to what organization I belong, the source of my income."[132]

In the end, Frydman and his acquaintance were interrupted by a policeman who lived in the neighborhood. Birenbaum fled. Frydman was detained, but later he, too, fled. Two days after the incident, MO officers actually found under the kitchen floor a wooden box with fur pieces that were damaged as a result of having been stored underground. Apparently, news of the dug-up "Jewish treasure" had circulated through the city, and the policemen who were searching the apartment were attacked on the spot by an unidentified armed group. After confirming that the furs were useless, the armed attackers themselves began digging in search of gold. Their searches turned out to be unsuccessful.[133]

Frydman and Birenbaum's invasion of the apartment was likely motivated by a simple desire for profit. However, objects lost by survivors and their families during the Holocaust also had great sentimental value for many of the returnees. Sometimes, indeed, the items could be completely worthless, and getting them back would not have materially changed the survivors' lives. Objects such as a mother's sugar bowl, a father's cufflinks, or a clock from the family home were physical confirmation of the existence of a world before the Holocaust, the only material proof of the existence of family members who had perished. If survivors succeeded in getting them back, they could keep them close by, even when they decided to leave the city.

Invalid Restitution

The huge number of buildings and undeveloped lots without owners, as well as the complicated postwar judicial procedures for repossessing "abandoned" properties, created great opportunities for abuse. Some of the Jews attempting to repossess real properties belonging to them or their relatives encountered obstacles created by organized criminal groups. In many of Poland's cities right after the war, specialized gangs existed that, thanks to false testimony and documents, fraudulently obtained "post-Jewish" real properties from state administration, and then profited from their sale. Mordechai Tsanin, a Jewish writer and a journalist who traveled around Poland in 1946 and 1947 reporting for the New York Yiddish daily *Forverts,* noted this criminal activity in one of his articles: "There are some Jews riding around in the cities and towns, selling Jewish houses that have no heirs or ones whose heirs have not made themselves known. Fraudulent witnesses present themselves, fraudulent trials are conducted, and the houses are sold as their own property. It's referred to as 'hogwash' [*lipa*]. A 'hogwashed house' worth a million złotys is sold for three- or four-hundred thousand and the seller disappears."[134]

There has been no major study to this day of this criminal activity, which was specific to the postwar period.[135] The phenomenon is difficult to study; individuals engaged in the business of invalid restitution relied on their cases not differing in any way from ordinary attempts at reclaiming possession, thousands of which went before the courts throughout Poland. It can be deduced, then, with high probability, that we will not find out about many successful instances of fraud of this type. An additional difficulty is the degree of preservation of court documents—they are often incomplete. Nonetheless, inquiries carried out by historians in recent years testify that traces of the existence of invalid restitution of Jewish property immediately after the war can be found in many (if not the majority) of cities and small towns in Poland.[136] A group of *li-piarze* ("hogwashers"), as survivors referred to individuals profiteering in this way, was active in Radom, too.[137] The District Jewish Committee informed the Presidium of the CKŻP in February 1948 about the existence of this gang:

> In our city, as, most likely, in other cities, too, there are individuals who in a criminal fashion are selling abandoned post-Jewish real properties. In Radom there are few Jews (around one hundred), and those who engage in this shameful process number a dozen or so individuals. With such a small number of Jews the uselessness of these vermin is only too apparent to the population of the city. Their uninhibited lifestyle, con-

stant public rows against a background of mutual scores to settle, as well as the scandals arising with new purchasers after claims are raised by the legal heirs is what slanders the good name of a Jew.[138]

There is little information about the members of this group. In addition to a desire for rapid enrichment and readiness to break the law, it was necessary to have knowledge, ability, and contacts. Certainly they were Jews who were well informed about ownership situations in the given territory. They also must have had extensive networks, which allowed them to find collaborators, especially false witnesses, among the surviving Jews but also to establish contact with individuals (non-Jews) eager to purchase "recovered" real property. No doubt, acquaintances among the members of the Security Service and in the Provisional State Administration, and later in the District Liquidation Office, could help carry out invalid restitution.

The modus operandi of the *lipiarze* rested on simple enough foundations. They made use of judicial procedures that made possible the recovery of "abandoned" property by owners or their close relatives. The group carrying out the "restitution" brought an individual pretending to be the owner or, more safely, the owner's heir to the City Court to claim the return of real property. To lessen the risk, the entire procedure was conducted by intermediaries. The alleged owner or "relative of the owner" gave power of attorney to an individual who subsequently appeared on the owner's behalf at the City Court or the District Liquidation Office. In the event that the fraud was revealed, the use of intermediaries made it possible for the authorized agent to pretend to be unaware and to cast all the blame on a person who was not in the city and had been impersonating an individual legally entitled to reclaim the estate.

Pretending to be the owner or heir of real property was possible because at least some of the register books of the Jewish population in Radom, as in many other municipalities, were destroyed during the war or had been misplaced and were not yet found. Therefore, when ascertaining kinship, the courts had to rely on the witness statements. Criminals exploited this fact: "And if necessary, an impostor testifies by way of mutual services before the Court that with his own eyes he saw the deceased testator. This is commonly spoken of as 'putting an end to him,' and in reality, the 'witness' during the occupation was far, far away, beyond the woods, over the seas . . ."[139]

It sometimes happened that the true owner or heir of illegitimately obtained real property would submit an appeal for return of their house only to discover it had already been reclaimed or even sold. Such a fate likely befell Jack (Icek-Ber) Rosenstein, the son of the prewar owner of an apartment house in Radom's city center. Living in Paris, Rosenstein was the sole individual in his family who survived the war. In December 1946 he wrote a letter to the Radom District Jewish Committee inquiring about his father's property.[140] Two months later, the Committee responded to Rosenstein that the house his father had owned "was sold by a son" and advised him to contact the legal department of the Polish Embassy in order to report the possible fraud.[141] Mordechai Tsanin reported encountering one of the fraud victims during his travels: "Also, the young man who is showing me around intends to sell his parents' house. Some unrelated individuals had already sold two houses that belonged to his closest relatives one year before his return from Russia."[142] There were more such incidents in Radom and other Polish cities. Following the return of some family members, frauds and impersonations of dead owners came to light:

Judges serving in our district as well as officials in the Liquidation Office and attorneys are aware of incidents in which lawsuits about granting rights to inheritance or to recognize ownership of a piece of real property arrive almost simultaneously, which causes endless problems for these institutions: one lawsuit is instituted by the owner's son or daughter, and an identical lawsuit arrives supposedly in the name of the living owner of the property, or vice versa. . . . A son who saw his father die in front of him is claiming his inheritance, and finds out in court that his father "is alive." . . . Quite frequently such an heir confronts an accomplished fact, because everything is "in order"; a "plenipotentiary" had appeared carrying a counterfeit power of attorney produced by a notary in some small town who had relied on a declaration by "trustworthy witnesses," and presented an identity card. If necessary, one can find in the documents of the case even proofs confirming the registration of the "plenipotentiary." More than one Radom attorney has already been led into error in this way.

. . . And these resurrected corpses are mixing with the living on the
streets of Radom and laughing up their sleeves. . . .[143]

Considering the possibility of complications if the rightful owner or
heir to the real property returned, the criminal group, having obtained
the property fraudulently, would immediately sell it. The speed of the entire operation certainly influenced the reduction in price, which in turn
would have motivated potential buyers. Historian Krzysztof Persak, who
studied several invalid restitutions in Jedwabne, noted that after a sale the
group shared among its members the money gained. Everyone counted
on a quick conclusion of the sale.[144] There seems to be no record of any
member of the gang operating in Radom being brought before the court
in connection with these swindles, so there is a lack of detailed information about this particular group's activity. However, one can assume that
the *lipiarze*'s scheme was similar everywhere. As observed by Tsanin in
Łuków, a town 130 kilometers northeast of Radom, the gangs were also
selling former communal property:

> So, a few young people from Łuków appeared and sold the synagogue
> for seventy-five thousand złotys. That's the equivalent of five pairs of
> shoes. . . . The synagogue was purchased by the municipality and now
> the town's main warehouse will be there. The synagogue is only one
> of many "hogwashes" [i.e., properties recovered and sold by *lipiarze*],
> because the same group of swindlers had already sold one third of
> Łuków's Jewish houses. Two members of this group live in Łuków; they
> sell whatever they can get their hands on. Those two individuals lead
> a dissolute, drunken life.[145]

Apparently, sale of the synagogue was concluded before the municipality
officials learned that the new laws sanctioned their power over "abandoned" property and that they did not need to purchase it in order to
administer it as they pleased.

Probably we will never know who exactly were the people engaging in
invalid restitution in Radom. It is possible to deduce from the Jewish
Committee's documents that these people had money and felt they could
get away with the illicit activity: "These individuals (the so-called *lipiarze*)

have available huge profits from those disgraceful transactions, so that they feel self-assured and are more and more aggressive and shameless in their actions. This matter was the subject of our Committee's deliberations. Despite our strongest desire to combat these vermin in our own domain, unfortunately we are in no condition [to do so] since the danger to our lives must be taken into account."[146]

Actions aimed at stigmatizing and excluding from the Jewish community people involved in the process of invalid restitution in the city were discussed in December 1946 during a conference, held in Wrocław, of survivors who hailed from Radom but were living in various corners of Poland:

> The National Conference [of Jewish delegates who were former inhabitants of Radom] recommends to the Board of the Federation [of Radom Landsmen Associations] the compilation of a list of those swindlers, and also of the individuals collaborating with them, and that copies of the list should be sent to all Jewish committees in Poland with the goal of public announcement. It likewise recommends to the Board that it request the Central Committee of Jews in Poland to deprive the named individuals of the right to make use of any community assistance and to institute a boycott of them in the broadest meaning of this word.[147]

Nothing, however, indicates that such a list actually was compiled. I also did not find any documents confirming that individuals who dealt in invalid restitution were stigmatized. The only individuals who met with any kind of punishment in Radom for their participation in the shady business of taking real property were two members of the Jewish Committee. In the second half of December 1946, they were removed from membership in the Committee because "they testified in court on the sale of properties of unlawful owners."[148] The two expelled members of the Committee were most likely not the core of the criminal group, however. Considering the lack of sufficient data, it is difficult to guess whether the *lipiarze* were above all professional criminals or, rather, individuals whom the war had deprived of family and conscience. Perhaps some considered that they had a greater right to apartment houses of exterminated Jews than the Polish state had or the Poles occupying "post-Jewish" apartments.[149] Regardless of the motivation of the swindlers, the few preserved documents indicate that invalid restitution was considered by the Radom survivors to be an exceptionally shameful undertaking— directly benefiting from the Holocaust and preying on its victims:

> On the ruins of the destroyed life of the fellow citizens of the Jewish people of our city and region several individual co-religionists are building a happy life for themselves with the help of unheard-of swindles, schemes, and other shameful methods. . . . Probably a well-organized gang of social vermin is engaged in this shameful and unheard-of procedure. . . . These individuals can often be seen in the offices of vital records, land registries, [and] notary offices, and everywhere they feel like "Adam in paradise." . . . there is no place in the New Poland for such parasites who gnaw at the social organism. These "cemetery hyenas" should not escape without punishment.[150]

Transfer of Ownership and Attempts at Reversing It

Polish Jewish survivors had lost loved ones, families, and community. Their property had been taken from them during the occupation by order of the German administration. It also wound up in the hands of many private Germans and Poles by less official routes—the result of confiscations, looting, appropriations, and black market transactions, and by being entrusted to them for safekeeping. At the moment the occupation ended, these goods passed into administration by the Polish state, but they also remained (or only then wound up) in the possession of many Poles who were private citizens. The first situation mainly affected real property; the second, movable property. The state, officially only the administrator of the property of Polish Jews who had perished in the Holocaust, in reality behaved as if it were the actual owner and protected it like its own property. Thus, the charge that the state increased its ownership with the property of its Jewish citizens appears to be well founded. An unusually drastic illustration of this process is supplied by a communique issued in February 1946 by the Polish head of the Bełżec village community where the Nazi extermination camp had been located: "Digging up graves of individuals murdered by the Germans in search of valuables is a crime, *for it is an attempt at appropriation of objects which are the property of the State.*"[151] It was not a question here of condemning and ending the looting of the graves of Holocaust victims at the site of a former death camp, but only of ensuring that the state did not lose potential profit by these actions. The property of victims of the Holocaust, including whatever remained with them in their graves, was on the one hand seen as belonging to the state, and on the other, treated by many representatives of the Polish administration, as well as by individual Poles, as belonging to no one and available to be appropriated. Often, this was not accompanied by any moral reflection concerning the circumstances in which the former owners had lost control of their property.[152] The state, like its non-Jewish citizens, did not especially conceal the provenance of the property at its disposal. Evidence of this can be found in the designation "post-Jewish property" and the listing of the names of prewar owners in official correspondence relating to the "adopting" of Jewish properties after the war. By their very reappearance, surviving Jews who returned to their native places brought into question the transfer of ownership that had taken place during the German occupation and immediately afterward, the benefits to which a large portion of the non-Jewish community had by then grown accustomed.[153]

Wishing to rebuild their lives in Poland or abroad, survivors made numerous attempts at regaining properties that had belonged to them or their families before the war. They did this in various ways depending on the type of property and the circumstances. In the case of movable property, informal efforts predominated without recourse to the judicial apparatus. In the case of real property claims survivors often made use of the legal path, submitting to the court appeals for the return of possession or, more rarely, requests for inheritance proceedings. Sometimes, survivors were interested not so much in specific objects or real property as in a return to their prewar situation, the return of a former order—if that was, indeed, possible. Dr. Ludwik Fastman's case can be viewed in this light. During the war, he had lost his well-equipped doctor's office and five-room apartment in Radom. In 1945, having left Radom, he took advantage of the opportunity to rebuild his life by settling in Wałbrzych, in Poland's "post-German" western territory, where he resumed work as a physician. There he received a five-room apartment that had belonged to a German doctor.[154]

During the first dozen or so months after liberation, when the majority of survivors were leaving Poland illegally, avoiding all formalities connected to their departure, attempts at recovering property by legal means were the only level on which many Polish Jewish citizens had relatively lengthy contact with the Polish state and its officials.[155] These interactions were not easy. The law on the basis of which many survivors appealed for return of property changed twice during the first year after liberation. The changes that were introduced created additional obstacles on the road to regaining properties. This law applied to all Polish citizens who, as a result of the war, had lost their property. But considering the degree of devastation of the Jewish community, the survivors encountered many more difficulties than those faced by the majority of their non-Jewish fellow citizens. Despite this, very many surviving Jews, although it is difficult to ascertain numbers absolutely, decided to pursue their rights in Polish courts. Many surviving Jewish owners or their relatives did not, however, succeed in regaining their property. It turned out to be difficult or altogether impossible after the war to regain real properties that had been designated for public use, as well as those containing enterprises or industrial plants. It was relatively easier to regain possession of residential buildings. But even in this latter category, Jews lost their property even when they regained it. Holocaust survivors to whom the court restored ownership of an apartment house, a single house, or a lot very often had to sell it immediately out of financial considerations if they wished to emigrate, or to provide security for themselves. Thus, their property wound up once again in non-Jewish hands.

One should consider the efforts at restitution undertaken by returning Jews in the Polish courts as a manifestation of prewar thinking which allowed them to place their trust in the law and instructed them to seek justice in the courts. At the same time, these were attempts by the survivors to actively oppose and reverse the material consequences of the Holocaust. Analysis of judicial documents shows very clearly that right after the war Jews were not passive victims but were attempting to reassert control of their lives. Even if rulings by the courts and offices were unfavorable for the survivors, the proceedings for return of possession were one way many Polish Jews affirmed and manifested their agency. Regardless of the efforts undertaken, in reality the returning Jews were in no condition to counteract the results of the two powerful processes taking place before their eyes: the transfer of Jewish property into non-Jewish hands and the surrender of private property to the state. Both these processes had begun on Polish territory in the period of German occupation and were continued afterward.

EPILOGUE

THE SURVIVORS OF THE HOLOCAUST who found themselves in Radom immediately after the war were castaways on a familiar-looking island that soon turned out to be completely alien and hostile. For many of them, arrival in the city meant a return in the strict sense of the word. They recognized the streets and houses, but the world after the Holocaust was entirely different from the one they remembered. Every aspect of their postwar existence was marked by the Nazi genocide. These people had lost everything—their families, workplaces, homes, and often, too, the entire social milieu in which they had lived before the war. They came back from the abyss and no one was expecting their return.

The distance between Christian and Jewish Poles, citizens of one country that already existed in prewar times became a chasm during the German occupation. Although both groups were tragically tested during World War II, their experiences often were extremely different. All Polish Jews—men, women, and children—were condemned to death only because they were born Jews (or considered as such by the Nazis). By the power of Nazi law and occupation policy, they were excluded from the human community. Broad strata of non-Jewish Poles quickly and willingly accepted the fate the Germans inflicted on Jewish fellow citizens. It was even worse; many Polish Christians looked upon the successive stages of the extermination of the Jews with unconcealed satisfaction. The war elicited what was best from people—remarkable examples of heroism and a readiness to help another person without regard to religious or cultural differences. But the war also revealed the darkest aspects of human nature. Across the entire territory of occupied Poland, blackmail, denunciation, and even murder of Polish Jews by their fellow Poles were a part of daily life. During the occupation, in the minds of a large portion of the non-Jewish inhabitants of Poland, Jews had finally been expelled beyond the margins of society. Perishing in ghettos and camps, in villages and cities, Jews found themselves outside the community of fellow human beings. The moral commandment to help those in distress, or at least to sympathize and refrain from doing harm, no longer applied to them. With this heavy moral baggage, Polish society entered the postwar period, and to such a society Jews who had survived the Holocaust returned or attempted to return. Often, they came back despite the universal conviction among non-Jewish Poles (expressed at times with complete satisfaction) that the presence of Jews in the Polish landscape had been ended once and for all.

Analyzing the situation of survivors of the Holocaust through the example of Radom, it is easy to see that these people experienced an environment full of indifference, dislike, enmity, and outright violence. It was precisely the violence accompanied by the suffocating atmosphere that proved to be the fundamental factor shaping the postwar Jewish community in Radom and most likely the communities of survivors living in other medium-sized cities in central Poland. The killings and assaults to which the Jews in Radom fell victim were perceived by them as elements of a wave of anti-Semitism that was engulfing the entire country. Unable to obtain help from the authorities, the survivors living in the city were forced to create their own defensive strategies. Many individuals left. Others attempted to acquire weapons. For those Jews who did not want to, or could not, leave the city, the only realistic prospect for remaining in Radom was to live their lives not within the Polish community but alongside it.

The survivors in Radom created a small, closed community. It was centered around the District Jewish Committee, one of many institutions of that type that arose across postwar Poland. The war had deprived the Radom Jews of experienced leaders; most of the prewar activists had perished, while others did not return to the city or were discredited by the roles they had played during the Holocaust. In that situation, new, "accidental" leaders appeared. The small, constantly

changing, and conflict-ridden community was not able to create sufficiently powerful institutions to partner with the local authorities. The
community and individual Jews were almost invisible in postwar Radom.
Many survivors could not return to the social roles they had played and
the occupations they had engaged in before the war. While many of
these people remained in the city they used to know, their return in a
social sense turned out to be impossible. They were "ghost citizens," for
their physical presence in the postwar city did not bring with it their full
participation in the life of the city and its society.

This gloomy conclusion does not mean that the survivors of the Holocaust were passive victims or that they remained apathetic in response to
the surrounding reality. On the contrary, they acted their agency and actively tried to re-create a community. Their reconstruction of institutions and social ties within the group of survivors bears witness to that.
While the rebirth of the Jewish community in its prewar form was not possible, the survivors definitely created their own community. They did so
despite the very difficult conditions which they faced. Survivors sought
to take control over their own lives. The efforts undertaken by Jews to
regain property lost during the war make this very clear. The fate of Jewish
properties demonstrates the complicated legal and social reality to which
these people returned. Their efforts, however, were incapable of reversing
the proprietary changes initiated during the German occupation and
maintained after liberation. As a result of the transfer of ownership, which
was carried out on an unimaginable scale, the property of Polish Jews became "post-Jewish" property remaining under the control of the Polish
state or its non-Jewish citizens. The transfer of Jewish property to non-
Jewish hands was largely irrevocable and accompanied by another
powerful process; that is, placement of private property into state
ownership.

In Polish society and in Polish cities, the traces left by the Holocaust
of Jewish citizens are still visible. Most Poles today are unaware that to
this day the social and material consequences of the mass murder of the
Jews influence their daily lives. Many are still unwilling to accept the bitter
fact that they live in a post-genocidal land. And yet the Holocaust is still
present in contemporary Poland. It keeps coming back as a topic in most
heated historical and political debates, inhabits fine arts and literature,

and remains present in private conversations. Succeeding generations of residents of Radom and other Polish cities still walk along the same roads down which several decades ago survivors of the Holocaust—Polish citizens—used to walk. Their fates and suffering are the history of this land, too. If one acknowledges this, it becomes obvious that the Holocaust was both the most tragic and the most important event to impact Polish society in the twentieth century and beyond.

ABBREVIATIONS

AK Home Army (Armia Krajowa)

AL People's Army (Armia Ludowa)

CKŻP Central Committee of Jews in Poland (Centralny Komitet Żydów w Polsce)

CŻKH Central Jewish Historical Commission (Centralna Żydowska Komisja Historyczna)

D.O.W.S. Leader of the Freedom Force, Falcon (Dowódca Oddziału Wolności Sokół)

GG General Government (*Generalgouvernement*, Generalne Gubernatorstwo)

GUL Central Liquidation Office (Główny Urząd Likwidacyjny)

Joint American Jewish Joint Distribution Committee

KBW Internal Security Corps (Korpus Bezpieczeństwa Wewnętrznego)

KC PPR Central Committee of the Polish Workers' Party (Komitet Centralny Polskiej Partii Robotniczej)

KL concentration camp (*Konzentrationslager*)

KM MO Municipal Headquarters of the Citizens' Militia (Komenda Miejska Milicji Obywatelskiej [MO; police])

KM PZPR Municipal Committee of the PZPR (Komitet Miejski PZPR)

KPP Communist Party of Poland (Komunistyczna Partia Polski)

KPRP Communist Workers' Party of Poland (Komunistyczna Partia Robotnicza Polski)

KRN State National Council (Krajowa Rada Narodowa)

KW MO Provincial Headquarters of the Citizens' Militia (Komenda Wojewódzka Milicji Obywatelskiej [MO; police])

MAP Ministry of Public Administration (Ministerstwo Administracji Publicznej)

MO Citizens' Militia, police, MO police (Milicja Obywatelska)

MRN   Municipal National Council (Miejska Rada Narodowa)

MUBP   Municipal Office of the Security Service (Miejski Urząd Bezpieczeństwa
             Publicznego)

n.d.   no date

NKVD   People's Commissariat for Internal Affairs (Narodnyi Komissariat Vnutrennikh
             Del)

N.N.   nomen nescio

NSZ   National Armed Forces (Narodowe Siły Zbrojne)

OKŻ   District Jewish Committee (Okręgowy Komitet Żydowski)

ONR   National-Radical Camp (Obóz Narodowo-Radykalny)

OUL   District Liquidation Office (Okręgowy Urząd Likwidacyjny)

PKWN   Polish Committee of National Liberation (Polski Komitet Wyzwolenia
             Narodowego)

PPR   Polish Workers' Party (Polska Partia Robotnicza)

PPS   Polish Socialist Party (Polska Partia Socjalistyczna)

PRN   County National Council (Powiatowa Rada Narodowa)

PUBP   County Office of the Security Service (Powiatowy Urząd Bezpieczeństwa
             Publicznego)

PZPR   Polish United Workers' Party (Polska Zjednoczona Partia Robotnicza)

SB   Security Police (Służba Bezpieczeństwa)

SOK   Railroad Security Police (Służba Ochrony Kolei)

TOZ   Society for Safeguarding the Health of the Jewish Population (Towarzystwo
             Ochrony Zdrowia Ludności Żydowskiej)

TZP   Provisional State Administration (Tymczasowy Zarząd Państwowy)

UB [UBP]   Security Service (Urząd Bezpieczeństwa [Publicznego])

WiN   Freedom and Independence (Wolność i Niezawisłość)

WKŻ   Provincial Jewish Committee (Wojewódzki Komitet Żydowski)

WP   Polish Army (Wojsko Polskie)

WRN   Provincial National Council (Wojewódzka Rada Narodowa)

WUBP   Provincial Office of the Security Service (Wojewódzki Urząd Bezpieczeństwa
             Publicznego)

ŻAP   Jewish Press Agency (Żydowska Agencja Prasowa)

ZHP   Union of Polish Scouting (Związek Harcerstwa Polskiego)

NOTES

In the archival references, an abbreviation "f." signifies folio. Due to changes in the archival collections in Poland (especially those in the Archives of the Institute of National Remembrance) and a practice of merging into a single folder documents that originally came from separate files, pagination is often not consistent within individual folders. Some of the documents in a file may contain references to folios, while others use page numbers. In the endnotes for this book, the number that follows "f." in references to archival material always indicates the number that appears on the document. Depending on how the particular folder (or its part) has been organized, the number can refer to folio or page number.

Introduction

1. Archiwum Instytutu Pamięci Narodowej w Kielcach (Archive of the Institute of National Remembrance in Kielce; hereafter, IPN Ki), 016/5, f. 53, 54 [explanatory note concerning documents of the former Jewish Committee in Radom, January 3, 1974].
2. IPN Ki 016/5, f. 29, 30 [information pertaining to the archive of the former District Committee of Jews in Radom, May 18, 1974].
3. Pola Zajdensznir died in Radom in 1998. It is not known what became of the objects from the District Jewish Committee's collection that were in Pola Zajdensznir's possession. I did not find any trace of them in Polish or foreign archives or museums.
4. Digital copies of this collection are also accessible in the Archive of the United States Holocaust Memorial Museum (hereafter, USHMM) in Washington, DC (RG-15.137).
5. Conversation with former officer of the Security Police N. K., Poland, 2014.
6. See IPN Ki 016/5, f. 30. Despite my attempts at finding the card index, I had no success in coming upon even a trace of it either in the archive of the Institute of National Remembrance, where the documents might have been found had the Security Police

kept them for their own purposes, or in the archive of the Emanuel Ringelblum Jewish Historical Institute, where card indexes from other committees wound up.

7. Robert E. Stake, *The Art of Case Study Research* (Thousand Oaks, CA: SAGE Publications, 1995), 3.

8. Emil Marat and Michał Wójcik, *Made in Poland: Opowiada jeden z ostatnich żołnierzy Kedywu, Stanisław Likiernik* (Warsaw: Wielka Litera, 2014), 108, 109.

9. Zygmunt Bauman, *Modernity and the Holocaust* (Cambridge: Polity Press, 1989), xiv.

10. Gunnar S. Paulsson, *Secret City: The Hidden Jews of Warsaw* (New Haven, CT: Yale University Press, 2002), ix–xi.

11. Liisa Malkki, "Speechless Emissaries: Refugees, Humanitarianism, and Dehistoricization," *Cultural Anthropology* 11, no. 3 (1996): 378, 385–388.

12. Nicholas Stargardt, *Witnesses of War: Children's Lives under the Nazis* (London: Jonathan Cape, 2005) and "Children of Hitler's War," 30th Annual Vanderbilt University Holocaust Lecture Series, November 1, 2007 (https://www.youtube.com/watch?v=HoRHQXhLLFs, accessed September 29, 2014).

13. Irena Hurwic-Nowakowska, *A Social Analysis of Postwar Polish Jewry* (Jerusalem: Zalman Shazar Center, 1986); Irena Hurwic-Nowakowska, *Żydzi polscy (1947–1950): Analiza więzi społecznej ludności żydowskiej* (Warsaw: IFiS PAN, 1996).

14. Jan Tomasz Gross, *Neighbors: The Destruction of the Jewish Community in Jedwabne, Poland* (Princeton, NJ: Princeton University Press, 2001); Jan Tomasz Gross, *Upiorna dekada: Trzy eseje o stereotypach na temat Żydów, Polaków, Niemców i komunistów, 1939–1948* (Kraków: Universitas, 1998); Jan Tomasz Gross, *Fear: Anti-Semitism in Poland after Auschwitz; An Essay in Historical Interpretation* (Princeton, NJ: Princeton University Press, 2006); David Engel, "Patterns of Anti-Jewish Violence in Poland, 1944–1946," *Yad Vashem Studies* 26 (1998): 43–85; Joanna Tokarska-Bakir, *Legendy o krwi: Antropologia przesądu* (Warszawa: WAB, 2008).

15. Anna Cichopek-Gajraj, *Beyond Violence: Jewish Survivors in Poland and Slovakia, 1944–1948* (Cambridge: Cambridge University Press, 2014), 4–5.

16. Cichopek-Gajraj, *Beyond Violence*, 7.

1. The City

1. *Mały rocznik statystyczny 1938* (Warsaw: GUS, 1938), 12, 22. I have rounded up the census figures.

2. Piotr Tusiński, "Katolicy w Radomiu w latach 1938–1939: Organizacja kultu i najważniejsze przejawy życia religijnego," *Życie codzienne w międzywojennym Radomiu, Biuletyn Kwartalny Radomskiego Towarzystwa Naukowego,* ed. Grażyna Łuszkiewicz-Dzierżawska, 2009, vol. 43: 4, 38.

3. Sebastian Piątkowski, *Dni życia, dni śmierci: Ludność żydowska w Radomiu w latach 1918–1950* (Warsaw: Naczelna Dyrekcja Archiwów Państwowych, 2006), 33–36.

4. Ben-Zion Gold, *The Life of Jews in Poland before the Holocaust: A Memoir* (Lincoln: University of Nebraska Press, 2007), 2.

5. Piątkowski, *Dni życia,* 38.

6. Stefan Witkowski, "Struktura współczesnego przemysłu radomskiego," in *Radom: Szkice z dziejów miasta,* ed. Jerzy Jędrzejewicz (Warsaw: Arkady, 1961), 137. During the German occupation, many armaments factories were located in the Radom district. Often, Jewish laborers were forced to work in them. There were factories in Radom, Pionki, Kielce, Skarżysko-Kamienna, and Częstochowa. As military actions increased, the need for an involuntary labor force in factories administered by Germans in the territory of the General Government grew, which paradoxically led to the survival of many Jewish forced laborers.

7. Sebastian Piątkowski, "Żydowscy robotnicy przymusowi w radomskiej fabryce obuwia 'Bata' (1941-1943)," *Kwartalnik Historii Żydów* 3 (2008): 323.

8. Piątkowski, *Dni życia,* 59, 60; Witkowski, "Struktura," 140. According to Piątkowski, at the beginning of 1939, 2,265 people worked in twenty-four factories of the leather-and-shoemaking industry, 4,960 people in the twenty factories of the metallurgical industry, the ten plants in the food-supply industry employed 1,058 workers, and the same number of plants producing construction materials gave work to 592 city residents.

9. Piątkowski, *Dni życia,* 65, 66.

10. Piątkowski, *Dni życia,* 68.

11. Piątkowski, *Dni życia,* 71-73.

12. Jolanta Żyndul, *Państwo w państwie? Autonomia narodowo-kulturalna w Europie Środkowowschodniej w XX wieku* (Warsaw: Wydawnictwo DiG, 2000), 106.

13. Sebastian Piątkowski, "Żydowska Gmina Wyznaniowa w Radomiu w latach 1918-1939," *Życie codzienne w międzywojennym Radomiu, Biuletyn Kwartalny Radomskiego Towarzystwa Naukowego* 2009, vol. 43: 4, 124-130.

14. Piątkowski, "Żydowska Gmina Wyznaniowa," 130-132.

15. Grażyna Łuszkiewicz-Dzierżawska, "Przedstawiciele społeczności polskiej we władzach samorządowych Radomia (1916-1939)," *Życie codzienne,* 135-270. In her text, the author is concerned with "Polish" groupings as distinct from "Jewish" parties, which she analyzed in a different article (see note 17). That at the beginning of the twenty-first century it is possible to write and publish two entirely separate texts about "Jewish" and "Polish" councillors who served, after all, in one city council demonstrates on one hand the deep divisions existing in the interwar period and, on the other hand, their continuation in contemporary historiography.

16. Piątkowski, *Dni życia,* 77-98.

17. Grażyna Łuszkiewicz-Dzierżawska, "Przedstawiciele społeczności żydowskiej we władzach samorządowych Radomia (1916-1939)," in *Społeczność żydowska Radomia w I połowie XX wieku: Kultura, Zagłada, Rozproszenie,* ed. Zbigniew Wieczorek (Radom: Radomskie Towarzystwo Naukowe, 2008), 48.

18. Łuszkiewicz-Dzierżawska, "Przedstawiciele społeczności żydowskiej," 48

19. "Czy w Radomiu jest za dużo szpitali?," *Trybuna: Tygodnik Radomski,* October 8, 1937, no. 41.

20. Łuszkiewicz-Dzierżawska, "Przedstawiciele społeczności żydowskiej," 48.

21. The reference is to the boycott of Jewish shops and craftsmen that the right-wing Polish political groupings were promoting in the 1930s.

22. "8 Żydów na robotach miejskich!," *Trybuna: Tygodnik Radomski,* May 20, 1938, no. 20.

23. "Niedopuszczalne metody 'Falangi,'" *Trybuna: Tygodnik Radomski,* October 8, 1937, no. 41.

24. Piątkowski, *Dni życia,* 144–147.

25. "Najście chuliganów," *Trybuna: Tygodnik Radomski,* October 8, 1937, no. 41.

26. Conversation with S. K., Poland, 2013, incomplete interview, not recorded. Also, Piotr A. Tusiński, *Postawy polityczne mieszkańców Radomia w latach 1918–1939* (Radom: Radomskie Towarzystwo Naukowe, 1991), 141.

27. Piątkowski, *Dni życia,* 148. The publication of photographs of individuals who were not observing the boycott called for by nationalist circles in a provincial city like Radom definitely should be seen as an example of the use, during the interwar period, of new technologies in a political struggle. The titles of both papers are also telling about their perspective: *Pod Pręgierz* can be translated as "To the Pillory" and *Pod Kropidło* as "By the Aspergillum." Hence, the first contains a reference to physical violence; the latter, to symbolic violence.

28. "Kto finansuje bojkot handlu żydowskiego w Radomiu," *Trybuna: Tygodnik Radomski,* October 1, 1937, no. 40 (emphasis in the original).

29. "Odebrać żydom przemysł garbarski: Żydowskie garbarnie w Radomiu piekłem polskich robotników," *ABC—Nowiny Codzienne,* September 23, 1937.

30. "Odebrać żydom przemysł garbarski."

31. "Endeccy kamienicznicy organizują się," *Trybuna: Tygodnik Radomski,* October 1, 1937, no. 40.

32. Piątkowski, *Dni życia,* 149.

33. Tusiński, *Postawy polityczne,* 139 and the following pages.

34. Piątkowski, *Dni życia,* 148, 149.

35. Marcin Kula, "Duński historyk pyta o Jedwabne," in *Uparta sprawa: Żydowska? Polska? Ludzka?* (Kraków: Universitas, 2004), 142.

36. Gold, *Life,* 76.

37. Sarah Bender, "The Jews of Radom in Forced Labor Camps, 1941–1944," in *The End! Das Ende! Radom and Szydłowiec through the Eyes of a German Photographer,* ed. Bella Gutterman and Nina Springer-Aharoni (Jerusalem: Yad Vashem, 2013), 58.

38. Piątkowski, *Dni życia,* 154, 155.

39. See Czesław Madajczyk, *Polityka III Rzeszy w okupanowanej Polsce,* vol. 1 (Warsaw: PWN, 1970), 99–102.

40. After Germany attacked the USSR in 1941 and the fifth district of the GG was established with the capital in Lviv [Lwów], the territory of the GG rose to one-third of the territory of prewar Poland and the population rose to 45 percent of the prewar state. See Jan Tomasz Gross, *Polish Society under German Occupation: The Generalgouvernement, 1939–1944* (Princeton, NJ: Princeton University Press, 1979), 45.

41. It is important to note particular differences among the districts of the General Government over the course of the occupation and Holocaust. These differences stemmed from the specific characteristics of particular areas and the populations inhabiting them, as well as from the occupation politics of Nazi Germany and its local officials. On the theme of the history of the Radom district and the annihilation of the Jews in that district, see Robert Seidel, *Deutsche Besatzungpolitik in Polen: Der Distrikt Radom 1939–1945* (Paderborn: Ferdinand Schöningh, 2006); Jacek Młynarczyk,

Judenmord in Zentralpolen: Der Distrikt Radom im Generalgouvernement 1939–1945 (Darmstadt: Wissenschaftliche Buchgesellschaft, 2007).

42. Idit Gil, "From Radom to Vaihingen via Auschwitz: Testimonies and Memoirs of a Transport of Jewish Slave Laborers," *Holocaust and Genocide Studies* 28, no. 2 (2014): 310.

43. Piątkowski, "Żydowscy robotnicy," 322–324.

44. Marcel Goldman, *Iskierki życia* (Kraków: Arcana, 2006), 33.

45. Madajczyk, *Polityka III Rzeszy,* 561.

46. Gross, *Polish Society,* 48–50.

47. In documents relating to this individual, other versions of his first name also appear: "Chil" and "Chiel."

48. "Judgment Day" is a popular name for Yom Kippur. In 1939, the holy day fell on September 23.

49. Archiwum Żydowskiego Instytutu Historycznego im. Emanuela Ringelbluma w Warszawie (Archive of the Emanuel Ringelblum Jewish Historical Institute in Warsaw; hereafter, AŻIH), 301/56, Ichiel Leszcz.

50. Raul Hilberg, *The Destruction of the European Jews,* rev. and definitive ed., (New York: Holmes & Meier, 1985), 1:53.

51. Regulation about the definition of the concept of "Jew" (Żyd) in the General Government July 24, 1940, "Dziennik Rozporządzeń Generalnego Gubernatora dla Okupanowanych Polskich Obszarów," pt. 1, no. 48, August 1, 1940, p. 231, 232.

52. Martin Dean, *Robbing the Jews: The Confiscation of Jewish Property in the Holocaust, 1933–1945* (Cambridge: Cambridge University Press, 2010), 187.

53. Sebastian Piątkowski, "Radom," in *Encyclopedia of Camps and Ghettos 1933–1945,* vol. 2, pt. A, ed. Martin Dean (Bloomington: Indiana University Press, USHMM, 2012), 289.

54. Piątkowski, *Dni życia,* 188, 189.

55. I refer here to the forced labor camp (*Arbeitslager Belzec*) and not the death camp (*Vernichtungslager Belzec*) that operated in that very locality from March to December 1942.

56. Piątkowski, *Dni życia,* 162–165.

57. Bender, "Jews of Radom," 58; Piątkowski, "Radom," 290.

58. Piątkowski, *Dni życia,* 188–191.

59. Hans Kujath's announcement, April 4, 1941, in *Społeczność żydowska Radomia,* 173.

60. Piątkowski, *Dni życia,* 178–180.

61. Piątkowski, "Radom," 290, 291. See Sebastian Piątkowski, *Radom w latach wojny i okupacji (1939–1945)* (Lublin: IPN, 2018), 428, 449.

62. Piątkowski, *Dni życia,* 219; USHMM, RG-15.183M [District Court in Radom], reel 3, frame 467 [indictment, July 29, 1947]. In the autumn of 1943, Blum was promoted to the rank of Sturmbannführer (the equivalent of a major); USHMM, RG-15.183M [District Court in Radom], reel 3, frame 154.

63. On Polish "Blue" Police, see Jan Grabowski, "The Polish Police: Collaboration in the Holocaust," Ina Levine Annual Lecture, November 17, 2016 (Washington, DC: USHMM, 2017); Jan Grabowski, *Na posterunku: Udział polskiej policji granatowej i kryminalnej w Zagładzie Żydów,* unpublished manuscript (forthcoming, Wołowiec: Czarne, 2020).

64. USHMM, RG-15, 183M [District Court in Radom], reel 3, frame 44 [transcript of the main trial: testimony of Ludwik Fastman, August 16, 1947].
65. Piątkowski, *Dni życia,* 220, 221.
66. In documents and narratives, there occasionally appears information that the deportations began on August 17. Sebastian Piątkowski gives that date (*Dni życia,* 222). The indictment against Wilhelm Blum, who oversaw the deportation from the Radom ghetto, contains this formulation: "On the night of August 16–17, 1942 and on the following days" (AŻIH, CKŻP, Wydział Prawny 108, f. 15). Piątkowski and several narratives relate that the deportation action of the large ghetto began on a Sunday; that information points unambiguously to the date of August 16. Also, in documents of the Jewish Committee, one most frequently comes upon information that the deportation was conducted over the course of the two nights, August 16–17 and 17–18 [for example, Archiwum Państwowe w Radomiu (State Archive in Radom; hereafter, AP Radom), OKŻ, 13, k. 4].
67. Piątkowski, *"Radom,"* 291, 292; Piątkowski, *Dni życia,* 293, 294. Sarah Bender, in "The Jews of Radom," gives the number as 2,000 victims shot at the time of the liquidation of the large ghetto in Radom.
68. AP Radom, OKŻ, 12, f. 8, 18.
69. Piątkowski, *Radom,* 292.
70. Gil, "From Radom," 310; USHMM, RG-15.183M [District Court in Radom], reel 3, frame 389 [transcript of the hearing of witness Leon Stellman, July 18, 1947]. The vestigial ghetto (it encompassed Szpitalna, Żytnia, Ciasna, Szwarlikowska, and Brudna Streets, and parts of Rej Street) and the later camp on Szwarlikowska Street at times was called the "little ghetto." For clarity in my presentation, I reserve this name for the Jewish residential district that existed in the Glinice district before August 5, 1942.
71. Piątkowski, *Radom w latach wojny,* 454.
72. Gil, "From Radom," 310. Many of the men who reached Vaihingen from Radom in 1944 managed to survive until liberation. That is why, after the end of the war, in a DP (displaced persons) camp in nearby Stuttgart there existed a relatively large and strong community composed of Radom Jews. See Joanna Wiszniewicz, *And Yet I Still Have Dreams: A Story of a Certain Loneliness,* trans. and with a foreword by Regina Grol (Evanston, IL: Northwestern University Press, 2004).
73. USHMM, RG-15.183M [District Court in Radom], reel 3, frames 448, 449 [transcript of the main trial, August 16, 1947].
74. I raise this topic also with an eye to the opinion, frequently shared in contemporary Poland even by educated people whose attitude is far removed from anti-Semitism, that the Holocaust was carried out only far from the eyes of Polish witnesses, in the gas chambers of camps that were distant from human settlements. That conviction appeared even during the discussion after a debate, "Do Poles Still Look Poorly at the Ghetto? From Moral Witnessing to an Ethics of Memory," which took place in the POLIN Museum of the History of Polish Jews in Warsaw, on April 28, 2013. Testimonies like those of the railroad workers I cited and a closer analysis of the extermination of Jews in the territory of the GG forcefully rebut such an opinion.
75. Antonina Kłoskowska, "Polacy wobec zagłady Żydów polskich: Próba typologii postaw," *Kultura i Społeczeństwo* 4 (1988): 111–127.

76. Kłoskowska, "Polacy wobec zagłady Żydów polskich," 117.

77. Gross, "Sprawcy, ofiary i inni," *Zagłada Żydów: Studia i Materiały* 10 (2014): 887.

78. Jan Grabowski, *Rescue for Money: Paid Helpers in Poland, 1939–1945,* Search and Research—Lectures and Papers (Jerusalem: Yad Vashem, 2008), 17.

79. AŻIH, 302/274, Bogdan Kowalski, f. 14.

80. Jan Tomasz Gross, "Sprawcy," 886 (emphasis mine). One of the more frequent rationalizations, the creation of which serves to reduce the dissonance engendered by breaking the command to oppose violence, is the assertion that the individual to whom one was obliged to extend assistance did not actually deserve it or did not need it. Nonetheless, it should be noted that sometimes it is difficult or completely impossible to help—even if one wishes to. Thus, it appears that "doing/acting" in this context should be understood rather as an act of will independently of whether its results are visible to others.

81. Visual History Archive USC Shoah Foundation (hereafter, VHA), 16666, interview: Ada Birecka-Jaworska.

82. Goldman, *Iskierki życia,* 21–34.

83. *The Encyclopedia of the Righteous among the Nations,* vols. 1 and 2, editor-in-chief Israel Gutman (Jerusalem: Yad Vashem, 2004).

84. Database of Righteous among the Nations; Yadvashem.org (accessed September 19, 2019). This calculation results from entering "Radom" into the database search tool and selecting from the search results people who provided assistance to Jews in the city of Radom itself. https://righteous.yadvashem.org/?search=radom&searchType=righteous_only&language=en

85. Kazimierz Wyka, "The Excluded Economy," in *The Unplanned Society: Poland during and after Communism,* ed. Janine R. Wedel (New York: Columbia University Press, 1992), 40.

86. Tadeusz Kotarbiński's daughter and son.

87. Połączone Biblioteki Wydziału Filozofii i Socjologii UW, Instytutu Filozofii i Socjologii PAN oraz Polskiego Towarzystwa Filozoficznego, Dział Zbiorów Specjalnych (hereafter, BWFiS UW), Rps U 594, *Dzienniki Tadeusza Kotarbińskiego,* vol. 1, notebook 2, f. 22, 23.

88. Jan Jasek, "Moje przeżycia wojenne," manuscript in my own collection, p. 58.

89. Maria Fołtyn, *Żyłam sztuką, żyłam miłością . . .* (Warsaw: Instytut Technologii Eksploatacji, 1997), 14.

90. Interview: Mieczysław Wośko, Poland, 2012.

91. Yad Vashem Archive in Jerusalem (hereafter, YVA), O.5, 79, f. 145 [T. Friedman Collection—Radom, Danzig, Wien: Przeżycia i działalność Tadka F. od roku 1939–1947]. After emigration, the author used the surname Friedman, under which he published his reminiscences in English: Tuvia Friedman, *The Hunter* (London: Anthony Gibbs & Phillips, 1961). In this book, I cite both the typescript of his reminiscences written in Polish [in the collections of the Yad Vashem Institute], and the reminiscences published in English since there are differences between the two texts.

92. Quoted in Helena Kisiel and Jan Boniecki, "Początki władzy ludowej w Radomiu," in *Rozwój Radomia 1945–1964,* ed. Stefan Witkowski (Radom: Radomskie Towarzystwo Naukowe, 1964), 1:15.

93. Archiwum Akt Nowych w Warszawie (Central Archives of Modern Records in Warsaw; hereafter, AAN), Grupy Operacyjne Komitetu Ekonomicznego Rady Ministrów i Ministerstwa Przemysłu, 240, f. 12. The copy of the document, which I cite here, bears the date "February 18, 1945" but most likely refers to January 18, 1945.

94. Muzeum im. Jacka Malczewskiego w Radomiu (Jacek Malczewski Museum in Radom; hereafter, MJM), H.772/61/78, Ogłoszenie Kiełczewskiego [January 18, 1945].

95. Grzegorz Miernik, "Wydarzenia radomskie 30 października 1945 roku—geneza, przebieg, konsekwencje," in *Młodzież w oporze społecznym 1944-1989*, ed. Monika Kała and Łukasz Kamiński (Wrocław: IPN, 2002), 40. On the topic of the formation of authority and state administration in Radom and its vicinity immediately after the war, see Piotr Chojnacki, "Miasto Radom i powiat radomski w latach 1945-1956: Życie polityczne i społeczno-gospodarcze," unpublished doctoral dissertation (Lublin: UMCS, 2014). I thank the author for allowing me access to a printout of his work.

96. In 1946, the county that included Radom had a population of 69,455 people. The population density in this county was the highest in Kielce province and exceeded 2,776 people per square kilometer (*Rocznik statystyczny 1946* [Warsaw: GUS, 1947], 15, 21).

97. Interview: Mieczysław Wośko, Poland, 2012.

98. Piątkowski, *Dni życia*, 259.

99. Marcin Zaremba, *Wielka trwoga: Polska 1944-1947; Ludowa reakcja na kryzys* (Kraków: Znak, 2012), 456.

100. Dziennik Ustaw (hereafter, Dz. U.), 1945 no. 1, item 2; Zaremba, *Wielka trwoga*, 457.

101. BWFiS UW, Rps U 594, *Dzienniki Tadeusza Kotarbińskiego*, vol. 1, notebook 2, f. 23.

102. Miernik, "Wydarzenia radomskie," 39.

103. Zaremba, *Wielka trwoga*, 456-463.

104. Archiwum Państwowe w Kielcach (State Archive in Kielce; hereafter, AP Kielce), Akta Powiatowych i Miejskich Oddziałów Informacji i Propagandy woj. kieleckiego, 75, f. 78 [March 14, 1946].

105. AP Kielce, Akta Powiatowych i Miejskich Oddziałów Informacji i Propagandy woj. kieleckiego, 76, f. 178 [reporting questionnaire for the month of November 1945]. At the time, the monthly salary of laborers working in industrial plants managed by the state ranged from 2,000 to 4,000 złotys.

106. Miernik, "Wydarzenia radomskie," 41-43.

107. Miernik, "Wydarzenia radomskie," 44, 45.

108. Piątkowski, *Dni życia*, 259.

109. Miernik, "Wydarzenia radomskie," 39.

110. Kisiel and Boniecki, "Początki władzy," 14.

111. Zaremba, *Wielka trwoga*, 237.

112. Kisiel and Boniecki, "Początki władzy," 14.

113. *Rocznik statystyczny 1948* (Warsaw: GUS, 1949), 30.

114. Kisiel and Boniecki, "Początki władzy," 16.

115. Quotation in Wojciech Lubelski, *Wajda* (Wrocław: Wydawnictwo Dolnośląskie, 2006), 26.

116. Most likely the person referred to was Władysław Bieńkowski (1906-1991), a member of the Central Committee of the Polish Workers' Party [KC PPR], Minister of Educa-

tion 1956–1959, and after 1976 a coworker of the democratic opposition—the Committee for Defense of Workers [KOR].

117. BWFiS UW, Rps U 594, *Dzienniki Tadeusza Kotarbińskiego,* vol. 1, notebook 2, f. 31, entry on April 23, 1945.

118. Roman Loth, *Wspomnienia Kochanowskie, czyli Radom sprzed półwiecza* (Radom: Społeczny Komitet Ratowania Zabytków Radomia, 2007), 16, 17, quoted in Zaremba, *Wielka trwoga,* 144.

119. Jasek, "Moje przeżycia wojenne," p. 59.

120. Jasek, "Moje przeżycia wojenne," p. 56–59, and unnumbered pages.

121. Jasek, "Moje przeżycia wojenne," p. 117; AP Radom, OKŻ, 12, f. 47 [statement issued by the OKŻ, October 6, 1950].

122. Russian Liberation Army (Russkaja Osvoboditel'naja Armija)—a formation collaborating with the Germans and composed mainly of Russians.

123. "Raport I. Sierowa dla Ł. Berii o działaniach NKWD ZSRS na tyłach I Frontu Białoruskiego z 29 stycznia 1945 r.," *Teczka specjalna J. W. Stalina, Raporty NKWD z Polski 1944–1946,* selected and edited by Tatiana Cariewskaja, Andrzej Chmielarz, Andrzej Paczkowski, Ewa Rosowska, and Szymon Rudnicki (Warsaw: ISP PAN, IH UW, Oficyna Wydawnicza Rytm, Archiwum Państwowe Federacji Rosyjskiej, 1998), 188.

124. Zaremba, *Wielka trwoga,* 381; also, "Wyzwolenie / zniewolenie Radomia," interview of Łukasz T. Prus with Sebastian Piątkowski, *Gazeta Wyborcza,* January 16, 2015, *Gazeta w Radomiu* supplement.

125. BWFiS UW, Rps U 594, *Dzienniki Tadeusza Kotarbińskiego,* vol. 1, notebook 2, f. 24, entry from January 28, 1945.

126. Ryszard Śmietanka-Kruszelnicki, *Podziemie poakowskie na Kielecczyźnie w latach 1945–1948* (Kraków: IPN, 2002), 26, 90.

127. AP Kielce, Akta Powiatowych i Miejskich Oddziałów Informacji i Propagandy woj. kieleckiego, 76, f. 113 [report for autumn 1945]. The description of the group as "NSZ" does not necessarily mean that the group was affiliated with the National Armed Forces (NSZ). The name NSZ was sometimes used to label all the divisions of the armed underground fighting against the new authorities.

128. Archiwum Instytutu Pamięci Narodowej w Warszawie (Archive of the Institute of National Remembrance in Warsaw; hereafter, IPN BU) 578/108, f. 32 [n.d.]; Stefan Bembiński, "Harnaś," *Te pokolenia z bohaterstwa znane* (Radom: Instytut Technologii Eksploatacji, 1996), 125–127.

129. IPN BU 01480/932 [the sole document in this file, September 19, 1945].

130. To be sure, these statistics also take into account victims of ordinary crimes; however, one can accept with great likelihood that the majority of those working for the new authorities perished in connection with the ongoing political conflict in the region.

131. IPN BU 01265/107/J, f. 490. [total number of attacks in Kielce province for the period June 6–December 20, 1945.]

132. IPN Ki 29/131, f. 184 [daily information report, October 30, 1945].

133. Ryszard Śmietanka-Kruszelnicki, "Problem 'bandycenia się' podziemia na przykładzie Kielecczyzny," *Polska 1944/45–1989: Studia i Materiały* 1999:4, 61–70.

134. Archiwum Instytutu Pamięci Narodowej w Radomiu (Archive of the Institute of National Remembrance in Radom; hereafter, IPN Ra) 14/1 [repository of the prosecutor's office in Radom 1941–1946].

135. IPN Ki 29/131, f. 249–250 [compilation of the more serious cases and crimes for the period from June 25, 1946, to July 25, 1946, of the KM MO in Radom].

136. IPN Ki 29/134, f. 2, 3 [statistical listing and description of the most serious crimes carried out in the city of Radom from December 1, 1947 to January 1, 1948]. According to the document, in November 1947, not a single attack was recorded in the city of Radom. The rise in criminality in December 1947 is explained by an influx of the criminal element into the city before the Christmas holidays (f. 6).

137. IPN Ki 29/134, f. 6.

138. AP Kielce, Akta Powiatowych i Miejskich Oddziałów Informacji i Propagandy woj. kieleckiego, 76, f. 273 [January 4, 1946].

139. Zaremba, *Wielka trwoga*, 199; Stefan Czarnowski, "Ludzie zbędni w służbie przemocy," in *Dzieła*, ed. Nina Assorodobraj and Stanisław Ossowski (Warsaw: PWN, 1956), 2:186–193.

140. In Poland, a county (powiat) headed by a county governor (starosta) is a smaller administrative unit. A province (województwo) headed by a provincial governor (wojewoda) consists of several counties. After World War II, Kielce province consisted of thirteen counties; Kielce county was one of them.

141. AP Kielce, Urząd Wojewódzki Kielecki II (hereafter, UWK II), 1299, f. 34, 35 [July 21, 1945]; Zaremba, *Wielka trwoga*, 179.

142. AP Kielce, UWK II, f. 33 [July 21, 1945]; Zaremba, *Wielka trwoga*, 179.

143. Zaremba, *Wielka trwoga*, 163.

144. IPN Ki 29/135, f. 99 [incident report of the Investigative Department of the KM MO in Radom, September 27, 1945].

145. IPN Ki 29/131, k, 202 [October 2, 1945]; IPN Ki 29/28, f. 48 [extraordinary incident report, June 13, 1946].

146. AP Kielce, UWK II, 1300, f. 72 [May 10, 1946].

147. Interview: Henry R., Canada, 2013. After having emigrated to Canada, Henryk changed his first name. When I interviewed him, he had been known for years as Henry.

148. See Albert Stankowski, "How Many Polish Jews Survived the Holocaust," in *Jewish Presence in Absence: The Aftermath of the Holocaust in Poland, 1944–2010*, ed. Feliks Tych and Monika Adamczyk-Garbowska (Jerusalem: Yad Vashem, 2014), 207.

149. Alina Cała and Halina Datner-Śpiewak, *Dzieje Żydów w Polsce 1944–1968: Teksty źródłowe* (Warsaw: ŻIH, 1997), 166; Stankowski, "How Many Polish Jews," 208.

150. Barbara Engelking and Jan Grabowski, "Wstęp," in *Dalej jest noc: Losy Żydów w wybranych powiatach okupowanej Polski*, ed. Barbara Engelking and Jan Grabowski (Warsaw: Stowarzyszenie Centrum Badań nad Zagładą Żydów, 2018), 1:28–29.

151. Cała and Datner-Śpiewak, *Dzieje Żydów*, 166. Cała and Datner-Śpiewak report that during the Holocaust, 90 percent of the prewar population of Jews in Poland lost their lives.

152. See nine detailed studies examining Jewish survival strategies applied by individuals attempting to survive in nine different counties in German-occupied Poland in Engelking and Jan Grabowski, *Dalej jest noc*.

153. Michael C. Steinlauf, *Bondage to the Dead: Poland and the Memory of the Holocaust* (Syracuse, NY: Syracuse University Press, 1997), 46.

154. Natalia Aleksiun, *Dokąd dalej? Ruch syjonistyczny w Polsce (1944-1950)* (Warsaw: Centrum Badań i Nauczania Dziejów i Kultury Żydów w Polsce im. Mordechaja Anielewicza, Trio, 2002), 66.

155. Grzegorz Berendt, "A New Life: Jewish Institutions and Organizations in Poland from 1944 to 1950," in *Jewish Presence in Absence: The Aftermath of the Holocaust in Poland, 1944-2010,* ed. Feliks Tych and Monika Adamczyk-Garbowska (Jerusalem: Yad Vashem, 2014), 226.

156. August Grabski, "Kształtowanie się pierwotnego programu żydowskich komunistów w Polsce po Holokauście," in *Studia z historii Żydów po 1945 r.,* ed. Grzegorz Berendt, August Grabski, and Albert Stankowski (Warsaw: ŻIH, 2000), 67.

157. AP Radom, OKŻ, 16, f. 4 [letter from the Municipal Administration in Radom to the Administration of the Jewish Gmina, February 11, 1947].

158. Steinlauf, *Bondage to the Dead,* 46. In addition to survivors residing in the territory of Poland, there was a large concentration of Polish Jews in Germany. At the end of 1945, about 18,000 people were living in the displaced persons camps in Germany administered by the United Nations Relief and Rehabilitation Administration (UNRRA) (Lucjan Dobroszycki, *Survivors of the Holocaust in Poland: A Portrait Based on Jewish Community Records 1944-1947* [Armonk, NY: M. E. Sharpe, 1994], 67, 71, 76-83). The number of survivors in the territory of Germany rose rapidly in connection with the departures of Jews from Poland. For many of them, the DP camps in Germany were a temporary stop on the road to further emigration. A particular place where Jews from Radom were concentrated in Allied-occupied Germany was the displaced persons camp in Stuttgart. The majority of its inhabitants in the second half of 1945 were Radomers. The camp was informally called "Radom Center" ("Radomer Center") (Alfred Lipson, ed., *The Book of Radom: The Story of a Jewish Community in Poland Destroyed by the Nazis* [New York: United Radomer Relief for U.S. and Canada, 1963], 85).

159. Zaremba, *Wielka trwoga,* 99.

160. Zaremba, *Wielka trwoga,* 357.

161. Today it is the Holy Virgin Mary Cathedral, known in the city also as the Mary Church [Kościół Mariacki].

162. Jasek, "Moje przeżycia," p. 117.

163. Quoted in Aleksiun, *Dokąd dalej,* 82n138.

164. Interview: Henry R., Canada, 2013.

165. Interview: Aleksander Wajselfisz, Israel, 2015, not recorded.

166. YVA, 0.5, 79, f. 146. [T. Friedman Collection—Radom, Danzig, Vienna. Przeżycia i działalność Tadka F. od roku 1939-1947].

167. YVA, 0.5, 79, f. 146.

168. Interview: Henry R., Canada, 2013.

169. Marceli Najder, *Rewanż* (Warsaw: Karta, 2013), 221, entry dated May 12, 1945.

170. Mietek Pachter, *Umierać też trzeba umieć . . . ,* ed. Barbara Engelking (Warsaw: Stowarzyszenie Centrum Badań nad Zagładą Żydów, 2015), 644.

171. Pachter, *Umierać,* 644.

172. Maria Orwid, *Przeżyć . . . I co dalej? Rozmawiają Katarzyna Zimmerer i Krzysztof Szwajca* (Kraków: Wydawnictwo Literackie, 2006), 74.

173. Pachter, *Umierać*, 634.

174. Jan Tomasz Gross, *Strach: Antysemityzm w Polsce tuż po wojnie: Historia moralnej zapaści* (Kraków: Znak, 2008), 47. This Polish edition of Gross's book *Fear* appeared later and differs from the English edition. In this book, as here, I occasionally quote from the Polish edition when a corresponding fragment does not appear in *Fear*.

175. AŻIH, CKŻP, Wydział Ewidencji i Statystyki, 631, f. 5–10 [list of the Jewish population after liberation January 1945. Register until February 2, 1945.]. The list is not legible in several spots. It seems, too, that several individuals were listed twice. The number I give here of 281 survivors does not include obvious repetitions.

176. Helena Datner, "Children in the Polish-Jewish Community from 1944 to 1968," in Tych and Adamczyk-Garbowska ed., *Jewish Presence in Absence*, 284.

177. See Sara Bender, *In Enemy Land: The Jews of Kielce and the Region, 1939–1946,* trans. Naftali Greenwood and Saadya Sternberg (Boston: Academic Studies Press, 2018), 235.

178. AŻIH, 301/58, Emil Karpp (Ofer).

179. AŻIH, 301/59, Mojżesz Bojm.

180. VHA, 20375, interview: Harry Hendel.

181. AŻIH, 302/290, Icek Heider, "Wspomnienia z czasów okupacji 1939–1945."

182. AP Radom, Akta miasta Radomia (hereafter, AmR), Wydział Aprowizacji i Handlu, 9736, f. 9 [February 19, 1945], f. 12 [March 10, 1945].

183. Bender, *In Enemy Land,* 235.

184. Dobroszycki, *Survivors of the Holocaust,* 70. Dobroszycki also gives the number 810 Jews in Radom toward the end of 1945 (p. 77). This figure seems significantly elevated, however.

185. YIVO Institute for Jewish Research (Yidisher Visnshaftlekher Institut) in New York (hereafter, YIVO), RG 335.7, box 32, file 802, not paginated [American Jewish Joint Distribution Committee, Landsmanshaftn Department—List of Jews residing in Radom on October 30, 1946].

186. IPN Ki 016/4, f. 50 [letter from the chief of the Office of the Security Service for Radom City and County to the Head of Department V of the Provincial Office of the Security Service in Kielce, February 2, 1950].

187. This phenomenon was not limited to Radom only. It occurred also in other medium-sized Polish cities at the time. See Lukasz Krzyzanowski, "An Ordinary Polish Town: The Homecoming of Holocaust Survivors to Kalisz in the Immediate Aftermath of the War," *European History Quarterly* 48, no. 1 (2018): 106–108.

188. The person with number 1,756, the highest number issued in the index of survivors registered in Radom, was a child of survivors, Chaja Pesa Markowicz, born in Radom in 1948, and registered there on November 20, 1949 [AŻIH, 303/V/425Mbn1195]. Mieczysław Cymbalista, who was issued number 1,752, was registered later—on December 10, 1949. It is unclear why the later-issued number would have been lower than Markowicz's registry number [AŻIH, 303/V/425Cbn1531].

189. Małgorzata Melchior, *Zagłada a tożsamość: Polscy Żydzi ocaleni "na aryjskich papierach"; Analiza doświadczenia biograficznego* (Warsaw: IFiS PAN, 2004), 322–359.

Daniel Blatman draws attention to the fact that there were also individuals who returned to their Jewish identity only in the presence of other Jews, but maintained their wartime identity for their Polish environment. The Jewish journalist Henryk Shoshkes called them "new Marranos" (Daniel Blatman, "The Encounter between Jews and Poles in Lublin District after Liberation, 1944–1945," *East European Politics and Societies* 20, no. 4 [2006]: 608). Irena Hurwic-Nowakowska wrote more broadly about the phenomenon of maintaining a "dual" identity in her book *A Social Analysis of Postwar Polish Jewry* (Jerusalem: Zalman Shazar Center for Jewish History, 1986), 126.

2. Violence

1. David Engel, "Patterns of Anti-Jewish Violence in Poland, 1944–246," *Yad Vashem Studies* 26 (1998): 43–85; Jan Tomasz Gross, *Strach: Antysemityzm w Polsce tuż po wojnie; Historia moralnej zapaści* (Kraków: Znak, 2008) and the somewhat different English edition, published earlier, *Fear: Anti-Semitism in Poland after Auschwitz; An Essay in Historical Interpretation* (New York: Random House, 2006); Joanna Tokarska-Bakir, *Okrzyki pogromowe: Szkice z antropologii historycznej Polski lat 1939–1946* (Wołowiec: Czarne, 2012); Joanna Tokarska-Bakir, *Pod klątwą: Społeczny portret pogromu kieleckiego,* vol. 1–2 (Warsaw: Czarna Owca, 2018); Andrzej Żbikowski, "The Post-War Wave of Pogroms and Killings," in *Jewish Presence in Absence: The Aftermath of the Holocaust in Poland, 1944–2010,* ed. Feliks Tych and Monika Adamczyk-Garbowska (Jerusalem: Yad Vashem, 2014), 67–94.

2. The Citizens' Militia (Milicja Obywatelska, MO) began as more or less a popular force, but within weeks it became a regular police force. The communist regime kept the name "Militia." One reason for this decision may have been that it differentiated the new force from the prewar police, and the Polish Blue Police subordinated to the Nazi apparatus. Another reason could have been the will to emphasize a connection between the police force and the people, which certainly aligned with the regime's ideology. Regardless of the difference in the name, Citizens' Militia was a regular police force. In this book, therefore, the Polish term "milicja" has been rendered as "the police" or occasionally as "MO" or "the MO police" when referring to the Citizens' Militia. For the same reason, the Polish term "milicjant," denoting an officer of this force, has been translated as "policeman," occasionally also as "MO policeman." The full name of the force has been kept only in the names of institutions and citations from the sources.

3. IPN Ki 29/131, f. 173–176, 183, [daily information report of the KM MO Radom, October 29, 1945]; 184 [daily information report of the County Headquarters of the Citizens' Militia in Radom, October 30, 1945].

4. IPN Ki 29/131, f. 176.

5. IPN Ki 29/131, f. 183 [daily information report of the KM MO Radom, October 29, 1945].

6. IPN Ki 30/35, f. 3 [transcript of the report of a crime committed, Radom, November 14, 1945].

7. Gross, *Strach,* 64n37.

8. IPN Ki 29/131, f. 1 [extraordinary report of the KM MO in Radom to the Provincial Headquarters of the Citizens' Militia(Komenda Wojewódzka Milicji Obywatelskiej; KW MO)] in Kielce, December 27, 1945]. In the second half of 1945, most likely also at the end of the year, there were four movie theaters in Radom (one of them, exclusively for members of the military, so most likely it was excluded from the "disarming of viewers" action). The three civilian movie theaters—Ojczyzna, Bałtyk, and Hel—together held about 2,000 seats (AP Kielce, Akta Powiatowych i Miejskich Oddziałów Informacji i Propagandy woj. kieleckiego, 76, f. 59).

9. Eli Gat, *Not Just Another Holocaust Book*, trans. Lidya Gosher (Tel Aviv: Yerushalayim, 2006), 234.

10. Interview: Eli Gat, Israel, 2012. Eli Gat is Ludwik Gutsztadt's elder son.

11. AP Radom, OKŻ, 15, f. 1 [letter from the Administrative Department of the Municipal Administration in Radom to the First Police Station, June 20, 1945].

12. Interview: Eli Gat, Israel, 2012.

13. Gat, *Not Just Another*, 101.

14. Interview: Eli Gat, Israel, 2012.

15. Interview: Eli Gat, Israel, 2012.

16. Gat, *Not Just Another*, 227, 228; also, interview: Eli Gat, Israel, 2012.

17. Seeing Ludwik Gutsztadt opening his store in May 1945, Henryk R., nineteen years old, who had returned to the city, expressed his astonishment: "Ludwik, where did you come from; you already even have your own store?" (interview: Henry R., Canada, 2013. After emigration from Poland, he used the name "Henry"). Gutsztadt's activity must have been noticed not only by his neighbors, but acquaintances who were returning to the city.

18. Interview: Eli Gat, Israel, 2012.

19. IPN BU 00231/146/1, f. 167 [report of the Department for Jewish Minority Affairs from Kielce, Radom, and Częstochowa, February 22, 1945].

20. IPN Ki 29/131, f. 83 [report of the Investigative Department KM MO in Radom, November 7, 1945].

21. YIVO, RG 104, ser. 1, file 1020 [Eyewitness Accounts of the Holocaust Period Collection—Anna Hendel, January 31, 1946].

22. USHMM, RG-15.153, file 4 [Biuletyn ŻAP, November 12, 1945, no. 99/109], f. 1.

23. IPN Ki 29/131, f. 83 [November 7, 1945].

24. YIVO, RG 104, ser. 1, file 1020.

25. YIVO, RG 104, ser. 1, file 1020.

26. USHMM, RG-15.153, file 3 [Biuletyn ŻAP, August 30, 1945, no. 67/77], f. 3; Alina Cała, *Ochrona bezpieczeństwa fizycznego Żydów w Polsce powojennej: Komisje Specjalne przy Centralnym Komitecie Żydów w Polsce* (Warsaw: ŻIH, 2014), 32, 33.

27. To a certain extent, a similar mechanism was at work in the case of a series of ten murders of immigrants from Turkey and Greece in Germany in the years 2000–2007. For a long time, the police asserted that the crimes were the result of debt-settling among members of the Turkish mafia. Only accidentally did it come out that a trio of neo-Nazis was behind the murders, and the sole motive for the crimes was racial hatred ("The Brown Army Faction: A Disturbing New Dimension of Far-Right Terror," Spiegel Online International, November 14, 2011, http://www.spiegel.de/international

/germany/the-brown-army-faction-a-disturbing-new-dimension-of-far-right-terror-a-797569.html, accessed January 3, 2014).

28. VHA, 20375, interview: Harry Hendel. After emigration from Poland, Chaskiel Hendel used the name "Harry."

29. AP Radom, OKŻ, 19, f. 73.

30. The colloquial Polish term used by their host, *melina,* translated here as "hole," refers to a honky-tonk or a thieves' den. In the interview he gave to the USC Shoah Foundation, Harry Hendel emphasizes that the owner of the apartment used the word *melina* (VHA, 20375, interview: Harry Hendel).

31. VHA, 20375, interview: Harry Hendel.

32. Jan Grabowski, *Rescue for Money: Paid Helpers in Poland, 1939–1945,* Search and Research—Lectures and Papers (Jerusalem: Yad Vashem, 2008).

33. Gross, *Fear,* 39–47.

34. AP Radom, Rejonowy Urząd Likwidacyjny (hereafter, RUL), 510, not paginated [announcement of the City Court in Radom].

35. AP Radom, RUL, 510, not paginated [announcement of the City Court in Radom; letter from the City Court in Radom to the Provincial Department of the Provisional State Administration of Abandoned and Discarded Properties in Kielce, June 12, 1945].

36. AP Radom, RUL, 510, not paginated [letter from a TZP inspector to the Industrial Department of the County Governor in Radom, June 20, 1945].

37. AP Radom, RUL, 510, not paginated [letter from TZP inspector Fijałkowski to the Industrial Department of the County Governor in Radom, July 21, 1945].

38. AP Radom, RUL, 510, not paginated [letter from TZP inspector Fijałkowski to the Delegated Unit of the General Counsel of the RP in Kielce, October 20, 1945].

39. AP Radom, RUL, 510, not paginated [information sent by the TZP to the Delegated Unit of the General Counsel of the RP in Kielce, November 27, 1945].

40. MJM, H.925/334/79.

41. AP Radom, OKŻ, 19, f. 67.

42. AP Radom, OKŻ, 19, f. 68.

43. IPN Ki 30/3, f. 11 [transcript of witness interview: Bogda Jasińska, October 30, 1945].

44. In the testimonies, the name was spelled "Chendel" (just as in several documents related to the later murder), but there is no doubt that it refers to the same person. For the sake of clarity, I use the spelling "Hendel" throughout, since it is most likely that Aron Hendel himself used that version.

45. Probably, "double" refers to gold plating. An inscription like that was placed on watch cases to distinguish them from those made entirely of gold. "Anker" was a system, not a brand. Most likely, the stolen watch was not especially valuable, although in 1945 every watch was a valuable object.

46. IPN Ki 30/3, f. 7, 8 [transcript of witness interview: Maria Cyna, October 30, 1945].

47. IPN Ki 30/3, f. 7, 8.

48. IPN Ki 29/131, f. 183[daily information report of the KM MO in Radom, October 29, 1945].

49. IPN Ki 30/3, f. 10 [transcript of witness interview: Eliasz Birenbaum, October 30, 1945].

50. IPN Ki 30/4, f. 7 [testimony of the janitor: Sieradz Józef]; IPN Ki 30/4, f. 6 [transcript of report about a crime committed: Imieński Teodor-Teofil, November 2, 1945]. On November 8, 1945 also, five attackers robbed the office of the Agricultural-Trading Cooperative in Radom.

51. IPN Ki 30/3, f. 8, 9 [transcript of witness interview: Maria Cyna, October 30, 1945].

52. IPN Ki 30/3, f. 12 [transcript of witness interview: Bogda Jasińska, October 30, 1945].

53. IPN Ki 30/3, f. 10 [transcript of witness interview: Eliasz Birenbaum, October 30, 1945].

54. AP Kielce, UWK II, 1283, f. 117 [correspondence, November 15, 1945].

55. AP Kielce, UWK II, 1281, f. 7 [report, August 9, 1945].

56. IPN Ki 013/2644, f. 19 [testimony of Zofia Siwiec, September 25, 1945].

57. IPN BU 0173/63, f. 24. In documents related to Władysław Kozłowski the first name "Włodzimierz" also appears at times [f. 230, 247].

58. IPN BU 0173/77, f. 14 [biography].

59. IPN Ki 013/2644, f. 18 [testimony of Zofia Siwiec, September 25, 1945].

60. Documents of the investigation begun after the murder certainly would have provided valuable information about the circumstances of Bolesław Gaut's death, but at the present stage of cataloging the IPN's archival hoard, they appear not to be discoverable. There is also the possibility that they were discarded.

61. In the documents, there is information that Władysław Kozłowski died in 1953. IPN BU 0173/77, f. 14. [biography of Wladysław Kozłowski, May 6, 1985].

62. IPN BU 0173/63, f. 3 [report no. 94, November 8, 1982], 54 [personnel questionnaire: Cichoński aka Galicz Eugeniusz, pseud. "Strumień," November 11, 1982].

63. Ryszard Śmietanka-Kruszelnicki, *Podziemie poakowskie na Kielecczyźnie w latach 1945–1948* (Kraków: IPN, 2002), 109; *Atlas polskiego podziemia niepodległościowego: The Atlas of the Independence Underground in Poland 1944–1956,* ed. Rafał Wnuk et al. (Warsaw: IPN, 2007), 274.

64. IPN BU 0173/63, f. 208 [card 15 on a criminal act, November 8, 1982].

65. IPN BU 0173/63, f. 16 [report no. 94, November 8, 1982].

66. IPN Ki 022/76, f. 63 [personnel questionnaire: Drozdowska-Siwiec Zofia].

67. IPN BU, copies of a card from the index of former officers: Bolesław Gaut.

68. Ryszard Śmietanka-Kruszelnicki, "Podziemie antykomunistyczne wobec Żydów po 1945 roku—wstęp do problematyki (na przykładzie województwa kieleckiego)," in *Z przeszłości Żydów polskich: Polityka—gospodarka—kultura—społeczeństwo,* ed. Jacek Wijaczka and Grzegorz Miernik (Kraków: IPN, 2005), 256.

69. IPN BU, copies of a card from the index of former officers: Bolesław Gaut. This document also indicates that Gaut was born in Chełm on May 15, 1924. His father was named Jan-Josek. This information is also confirmed by a short biographical note placed in a list of officers of the service who perished in the course of "solidifying" the people's authority in Poland. There is also this laconic confirmation: "He gave his life . . . at the hands of an unidentified fighter of the reactionary underground" (*Polegli w walce o władzę ludową: Materiały i zestawienia statystyczne* [Warsaw: Książka i Wiedza, 1970], 152).

70. Śmietanka-Kruszelnicki, "Podziemie antykomunistyczne," 255, 256.

71. See Jan Tomasz Gross, "Żydokomuna," *Gazeta Wyborcza,* December 1–2, 2012.

72. Gross, *Strach,* 288n1; Gross, *Fear,* 228.

73. Dariusz Libionka, "The Life Story of Chaim Hirszman: Remembrance of the Holocaust and Reflections on Postwar Polish-Jewish Relations," *Yad Vashem Studies* 34 (2006): 246–247.

74. On October 13, 1945 in the Radom suburbs, Corporal Witold Słomczyński, an MO policeman from Wałbrzych, was shot. He was on leave, visiting his parents in the city. It is most likely, however, that his death arose from the fact that he attempted to defend himself in the course of an attack on the house where he was staying (IPN Ki 29/131, f. 174).

75. IPN Ki 29/28, f. 56 [list of policemen from the KM MO in Radom killed from January 15, 1945, to January 3, 1946].

76. AP Kielce, UWK II, 1281, f. 7 [report, August 9, 1945].

77. USHMM, RG-15.153, file 3 [Biuletyn ŻAP, August 23, 1945, no. 65/75], f. 3. Thank you to Bożena Szaynok for drawing my attention to this document.

78. *Dziennik Powszechny,* July 18, 1945.

79. AP Kielce, UWK II, 1281, f. 10 [letter from the vice governor to the KW MO in Kielce concerning the omission of an official funeral of a deceased partisan, September 19, 1945].

80. IPN Ki 01/1076 pt. 3, f. 252 [report of Second Lieutenant Henryk Mazur, March 23, 1947].

81. IPN Ki 01/1076 pt. 3, f. 256 [transcript of examination of a witness: Stanisław Bączek, May 10, 1947].

82. Archiwum Państwowe w Kaliszu (State Archive in Kalisz; hereafter, AP Kalisz). Spuścizna Tadeusza Martyna, 430, not paginated.

83. Mietek Pachter, *Umierać też trzeba umieć* . . . , ed. Barbara Engelking (Warsaw: Stowarzyszenie Centrum Badań nad Zagładą Żydów, 2015), 660n289.

84. Marcin Zaremba, *Wielka trwoga: Polska 1944–1947; Ludowa reakcja na kryzys* (Kraków: Znak, 2012), 263, 266, 267.

85. IPN Ki 01/1076 pt. 3, f. 256 [transcript of examination of a witness: Stanisław Bączek, May 10, 1947].

86. Other names for the cooperative also appear in the documents: Work Cooperative "Praca," "Praca" Cooperative of Tailors and Boot Leather Stitchers, Cooperative "Praca." There is not, however, any doubt that the same institution is referred to.

87. YIVO, RG 104, ser. 1, file 1017 [Eyewitness Accounts of the Holocaust Period Collection—Mojżesz Kirszenblat, January 31, 1946].

88. Sebastian Piątkowski takes a different position on this matter in his book, writing that "the course of the attack points . . . to its having been a robbery" (Sebastian Piątkowski, *Dni życia, dni śmierci: Ludność żydowska w Radomiu w latach 1918–1950* [Warsaw: Naczelna Dyrekcja Archiwów Państwowych, 2006], 274.) At the time he was working on his book, Piątkowski most likely did not have access to the report by Mojżesz Kirszenblat, which I cite.

89. AP Kielce, UWK II, 1299, f. 274 [report of offenses of units of the Red Army and terrorist attacks, n.d.] The document gives a form of the first name of one of the victims: "Tuchen"—most likely the reference is to "Tanchem." The report for the month of August 1945 of the Clerk for Matters of Aid for the Jewish Population in the Ministry of

Labor and Social Welfare refers to five victims of the attack (four civilians and one military), but no other document confirms this information. In the light of the archival materials I was able to access, it is possible to assert with almost complete certainty that the attack on the "Praca" Cooperative took four victims (IPN BU 00231/146/1; I thank Dr. Aleksander Namysło of the IPN branch in Katowice for providing the copy of this document); YIVO, RG 104, ser. 1, file 1017 [Eyewitness Accounts of the Holocaust Period Collection—Mojżesz Kirszenblat, January 31, 1946]. Information concerning the murdered Red Army officer: *Polegli w walce o władzę ludową,* 487; in this publication it says that Getłach "died at the hands of an unidentified armed group of the reactionary underground" (I thank Dr. Sebastian Piątkowski for bringing this publication to my attention). In the cemetery record of the Orthodox Parish of St. Mikołaj in Radom, he appears as A. Petlach, b. April 20, 1912, d. August 1, 1945 (the mistaken day of death probably is the result of a clerical error). Despite contacting the cemetery administration and the Municipal Office in Radom that cares for the graves of Soviet soldiers, I did not succeed in gaining additional information about the individual I was interested in.

90. Database of individuals buried in the Cemetery of the Parish of St. Mikołaj in Radom, http://www.polskie-cmentarze.com/radom.cerkiew/grobonet/start.php?id =detale&idg=149&inni=0&cinki=1, accessed July 20, 2014.

91. Nella Gutman-Laks, "A Personal Story," in *Voice of Radom: 50th Anniversary of Liberation Edition* (Toronto: B'nai Radom, 1995), 19; VHA, 8976, interview: Marie Snyder.

92. AP Radom, OKŻ, 22, f. 13 [report]; AP Radom, OKŻ, 19, f. 68. In the document, the first name appears in the form of "Josek."

93. Interview: Henry R., Canada, 2013.

94. YIVO, RG 104, ser. 1, file 1017. Ryszard Śmietanka-Kruszelnicki's suggestion that the murdered Red Army soldier was an officer of the NKVD has no confirmation in the sources (Śmietanka-Kruszelnicki, "Podziemie antykomunistyczne," 256).

95. VHA, 9002, interview: Elias Snyder. The funeral of Tanchem Gutman took place on a different date, most likely also in the Jewish cemetery in Radom. I thank Monika Sznajderman for drawing my attention to Elias Snyder's testimony.

96. YIVO, RG 104, ser. 1, file 1017.

97. The majority of sources indicate that the murder occurred on the evening of August 10, 1945, which means it was a Friday.

98. Quotation in Zaremba, *Wielka trwoga,* 616.

99. Nella Gutman-Laks, "Some Memories of Radom after the Holocaust," *Voice of Radom* 31, no. 1 (1986): 7.

100. Stanisław Benski, *Ocaleni* (Warsaw: Czytelnik, 1986), 83.

101. Joanna Tokarska-Bakir, "Cries of the Mob in the Pogroms in Rzeszów (June 1945), Cracow (August 1945), and Kielce (July 1946) as a Source for the State of Mind of the Participants," *East European Politics and Societies* 25 no. 3 (2011): 568n42.

102. "Anti-Jewish Terror in Poland Increases: Jews Continue to Flee in Panic," *Jewish Telegraphic Agency,* September 12, 1945, http://www.jta.org/1945/09/12/archive/anti -jewish-terror-in-poland-increases-jews-continue-to-flee-in-panic, accessed March 10, 2014. On the murder during the Kraków pogrom see: Łukasz Krzyżanowski, "'To było

między pierwszą a drugą': Zabójstwo Róży Berger podczas pogromu w Krakowie, 11 sierpnia 1945 r.," *Zagłada Żydów: Studia i Materiały* 15 (2019): 409-445.

103. Krystyna Kersten, *Narodziny systemu władzy: Polska 1943-1948* (Poznań: SAWW, 1990), 192; also Piątkowski, *Dni życia,* 274.

104. See Gross, *Strach,* 130.

105. On the subject of ritual murder, see Joanna Tokarska-Bakir, *Legendy o krwi: Antropologia przesądu* (Warsaw: WAB, 2008).

106. USHMM, 1999.25, file 3 [Rachela Rottenberg papers]; also, AP Radom, OKŻ, 5, f. 11 (here, the document is addressed to "The Jewish Community in Jedlińsk"). The fact that the word "Jews" is lacking capitalization in this and many other documents from the period was intentional and was a form of symbolic violence.

107. YIVO, RG 104, ser. 1, file 1019 [Eyewitness Accounts of the Holocaust Period Collection—Henryk Griffel, Mendel Goldberg, January 31, 1946].

108. Śmietanka-Kruszelnicki, "Podziemie poakowskie," 89, 90.

109. Śmietanka-Kruszelnicki, "Podziemie antykomunistyczne," 264.

110. Śmietanka-Kruszelnicki, "Podziemie antykomunistyczne," 264. The words "Jews" and "Russians" are not capitalized in this document. See note 106.

111. Śmietanka-Kruszelnicki, "Podziemie poakowskie," 111.

112. Joanna Tokarska-Bakir, "The Figure of the Bloodsucker in Polish Religious, National and Left-Wing Discourse, 1945-1946: A Study in Historical Anthropology," *Dapim: Studies on the Holocaust* 27 no. 1 (2013): 92-93.

113. Tokarska-Bakir, "The Figure of the Bloodsucker," 96.

114. Tokarska-Bakir, "The Figure of the Bloodsucker"; Gross, *Fear.*

115. In the original version of "Jewish questions in the country," written by Karski during his first mission as a courier from occupied Poland to France, this assertion can be found: "The people hate their mortal enemy [Germans]—but this question [attitude toward Jews] nevertheless creates something like a narrow footbridge on which the Germans and a large part of Polish society meet in agreement" [as cited in Jan Tomasz Gross, *Upiorna dekada: Eseje o stereotypach na temat Żydów, Polaków, Niemców, komunistów i kolaboracji 1939-1948* (Kraków: Austeria, 2007), 16-17].

116. Zaremba, *Wielka trwoga,* 269.

117. Zaremba, *Wielka trwoga,* 269.

118. Gross, *Strach,* 61.

119. Bożena Szaynok, *Pogrom Żydów w Kielcach 4 lipca 1946* (Warsaw: Bellona, 1992), 40.

120. Cited in Tokarska-Bakir, "Cries of the Mob," 559.

121. Szaynok, *Pogrom Żydów,* 44.

122. Tokarska-Bakir, "Cries of the Mob," 559.

123. IPN BU 00231/146/1, f. 162 [Ninth Report of the Office for Matters of Aid for the Jewish Population for March 1945].

124. IPN BU 00231/146/1, f. 167 [report of the Department for Jewish Minority Affairs from Kielce, Radom, and Częstochowa, February 22, 1945]. Only the initial letter of Rubinstein's first name appears in the document. August Grabski assisted me in determining the full first name.

125. IPN BU 00231/146/1, f. 162.

126. IPN BU 00231/146/1, f. 162.

127. IPN BU 00231/146/1, f. 147 [Twelfth Report of the Office for Matters of Aid for the Jewish Population, Ministry of Labor and Social Welfare (transcript written down in the Provincial Jewish Committee [Wojewódzki Komitet Żydowski, WKŻ] in Kielce) June 30, 1945].

128. Police statement, August 9, 1946. A copy of the document received from Frymer's daughter, in my own collection.

129. Interview: Eli Gat, Israel, 2012.

130. IPN Ki 01/1076 vol. 3, f. 315 [transcript of witness interview: Maria Wac, November 19, 1948].

131. IPN Ki 01/1076 vol. 3, f. 303 [official note, November 11, 1948].

132. IPN Ki 01/1076 vol. 3, f. 312 [transcript of witness interview: Jan Wac, November 19, 1948].

133. IPN Ki 01/1076 vol. 3, f. 253 [transcript of witness interview: Stanisław Bączek, April 10, 1947] (emphasis mine).

134. IPN Ki 01/1076 vol. 3, f. 254 [transcript of witness interview: Stanisław Bączek, April 10, 1947].

135. IPN Ki 6/5265, f. 2 [decision about punishment in a disciplinary way, January 15, 1949].

136. IPN Ki 30/3, f. 5.

137. IPN Ki 6/4024, f. 73 [profile of Second Lieutenant Skałbania, n.d.], f. 77 [information about his nomination, August 26, 1946].

138. IPN Ki 6/4719, f. 38–39 [petition of Jan Wac to the Military Regional Prosecutor's Office in Kielce, n.d.].

139. ". . . wife and three children, the oldest daughter, Rajzla, was 12; Jankiel, the son, was 5; and the younger daughter, Chana, was 1½; [they and my] wife Jochweta, née Kaufman, were murdered by Gestapo officials on October 16, 1942. Also my mother and three sisters came to stay with me to hide after the murder of my father, and were also murdered on the same day." IPN Ki 6/4719, f. 44, 47 [biographical sketch of Jan Wac, n.d.].

140. IPN Ki 6/4719, f. 39 [petition of Jan Wac to the Military Regional Prosecutor's Office in Kielce, n.d.].

141. Żbikowski, "Post-War Wave of Pogroms and Killings," 72; Alina Skibińska, "The Return of Jewish Holocaust Survivors and the Reaction of the Polish Population," in *Jewish Presence in Absence: The Aftermath of the Holocaust in Poland, 1944–2010,* ed. Feliks Tych and Monika Adamczyk-Garbowska (Jerusalem: Yad Vashem, 2014), 41.

142. IPN Ki 6/4719, f. 40 [petition of Jan Wac to the Military Regional Prosecutor's Office in Kielce, n.d.].

143. IPN Ki 6/4719, f. 41 [petition of Jan Wac to the Military Regional Prosecutor's Office in Kielce, n.d.].

144. IPN Ki 6/4719, f. 41, 42 [petition of Jan Wac to the Military Regional Prosecutor's Office in Kielce, n.d.].

145. IPN Ki 41/2218, f. 133 [judicial opinion, August 18, 1950].

146. IPN Ki 41/2218, f. 120 [main trial transcript, August 18, 1950].

147. IPN Ki 41/2218, f. 173 [petition, November 25, 1950].

148. IPN Ki 41/2218, f. 173.

149. IPN Ki 41/2218, f. 174 [petition, November 25, 1950] (emphasis in the original).

150. IPN Ki 41/2218, f. 262–265 [sentence, January 24, 1952].

151. IPN Ki 41/2218, f. 276–278 [decision, February 25, 1952].

152. Joanna Tokarska-Bakir, "Proces Tadeusza Maja: Z dziejów oddziału AL 'Świt' na Kielecczyźnie," in Tokarska-Bakir, *Okrzyki pogromowe,* 55.

153. Tokarska-Bakir, "Proces Tadeusza Maja, 55; IPN BU 0703/1132, f. 56 [report, Adam Bakalarczyk, June 19, 1951], f. 60 [transcript of witness interview: Józef Bugajski, September 22, 1949]. At least one more member of the detachment who participated in the shooting of Jews lived in Radom after the war. Wacław Tracz, pseud. "Skóra," in 1951 was an employee in the personnel office of the Provincial Firm MHD. One may consider it an irony of fate that at the time he was testifying, that is, in 1951, Tracz was living in the same apartment building in which, in 1945, the Jewish Cooperative "Praca" was located, and where the murder of Jews discussed earlier in the text was carried out. IPN BU 0703/1132, f. 63 [transcript of witness interview: Wacław Tracz, March 27, 1951]; IPN BU 0703/1132, f. 78 [transcript of witness interview: Adam Bakalarczyk, June 28, 1951].

154. IPN BU 0703/1132, f. 39. After the merger of the MUBP (Municipal Office of the Security Service) and PUBP in Radom in January 1946, Bakalarczyk became a section director. In June 1946, he was transferred to the WUBP in Kielce, and then to the Central School of the MBP in Łódź. In addition, in the spring of 1944, before the murder of ten to twelve Jews committed by members of the "Świt" detachment, that detachment was merged with a detachment led by Czesław Byk (later: Borecki), pseud. "Brzoza." From August 1945 to September 1946, he fulfilled the duties of chief of the MUBP in Radom.

155. Tokarska-Bakir, "Proces Tadeusza Maja," 52, 76.

156. Tokarska-Bakir, "Proces Tadeusza Maja," 74.

157. Tokarska-Bakir, "Proces Tadeusza Maja," 74, 75.

158. Transcript of an interview with Jan Barszcz, quoted in Tokarska-Bakir, "Proces Tadeusza Maja," 65.

159. IPN BU 00231/146/1, f. 166 [report of the Department for Jewish Minority Affairs from Kielce, Radom, and Częstochowa, February 22, 1945].

160. IPN BU 00231/146/1, f. 167 [report of the Department for Jewish Minority Affairs from Kielce, Radom, and Częstochowa, February 22, 1945].

161. Gross, *Strach,* 71.

162. AP Radom, OKŻ, 1, f. 2 [February 23, 1945].

163. AP Radom, OKŻ, 23, f. 7 [January 21, 1946].

164. Quoted in Gross, *Strach,* 72.

165. Gross, *Strach,* 72n55.

166. IPN BU 00231/146/1, f. 153 [Eleventh Report of the Office for Matters of Aid for the Jewish Population, Ministry of Labor and Social Welfare for May 1945, May 31, 1945].

167. AP Kalisz, Akta Miasta Kalisza, 10, f. 13, 14; Joanna Tokarska-Bakir, "Następstwa Holokaustu w relacjach żydowskich i w pamięci polskiej prowincji w świetle badań etnograficznych," in Tokarska-Bakir, *Okrzyki pogromowe,* 102. Skibińska, "Return of Jewish Holocaust Survivors," 58.

168. AP Radom, OKŻ, 2, f. 13 [transcript of the Conference of Jewish committees of Kielce province, May 14, 1945]; also Adam Penkalla, "Sytuacja ludności żydowskiej na terenie województwa kieleckiego w maju 1945 roku," *Kieleckie Studia Historyczne* 13 (1995); Gross, *Strach,* 70, 71 (emphasis mine).

169. Bożena Szaynok, "Kościół katolicki w Polsce wobec problematyki żydowskiej (1944–1989)," *Następstwa zagłady Żydów,* 557.

170. Bożena Szaynok, "'Tuż po zagładzie': Kościół katolicki wobec problematyki żydowskiej (VII 1944–VII 1946)," *Zagłada Żydów: Studia i Materiały* 5 (2009): 138, 139.

171. Szaynok, *Pogrom Żydów,* 97.

172. Uwagi Kardynała Augusta Hlonda, wobec dziennikarzy amerykańskich w Warszawie, dnia 11 lipca 1946 [Remarks of Cardinal August Hlond, primate of Poland, to American journalists in Warsaw, July 11, 1946], in Szaynok, *Pogrom Żydów,* 116.

173. Uwagi Kardynała Augusta Hlonda, 116.

174. Gross, *Strach,* 186, 191. Another exception can be pointed out: the declaration of the bishop of Katowice, Stanisław Adamski, who in the spring of 1946 declared during a meeting with delegates from a Jewish committee that "he knows the martyrology of Polish Jews during the period of the Nazi occupation and in accordance with the principles of Christian ethics of the Catholic Church he condemns as sharply as possible all murders committed against the innocent Jewish population" (Szaynok, "Tuż po Zagładzie," 138).

175. AAN, Ministerstwo Informacji i Propagandy (hereafter, MIiP), 295, f. 26 [copy of a letter from the Provincial Office of Information and Propaganda in Lublin, July 23, 1946]. I thank Marcin Zaremba for giving me access to this document (Szaynok, "Tuż po Zagładzie," 128).

176. Szaynok, "Tuż po Zagładzie," 128.

177. IPN BU 170/52/3, f. 252–253 [Doniesienie agenturalne, March 12, 1954]. I thank Bożena Szaynok for drawing my attention to that document.

178. "Biskup Lubelski do Przewielebnego Duchowieństwa w sprawie cmentarzy, mogił i miejsc straceń," *Wiadomości Diecezjalne Lubelskie,* no. 8, August 1946, 296. I thank Bożena Szaynok for drawing my attention to that letter.

179. "Dokument 35. 1946, lipiec, 18, Warszawa. Sprawozdanie instruktorów Komitetu Centralnego Polskiej Partii Robotniczej z pobytu w województwie kieleckim w czasie od 4 do 15 lipca 1946 r.," in *Antyżydowskie wydarzenia kieleckie 4 lipca 1946 roku: Dokumenty i materiały,* ed. and prepared for printing by Stanisław Meducki, (Kielce: Kieleckie Towarzystwo Naukowe, 1994), 2:140.

180. Szaynok, "Tuż po Zagładzie," 128.

181. Robert K. Merton, *Social Theory and Social Structure,* rev. and enl. ed. (Glencoe, IL: Free Press, 1968), 475–476.

182. Żbikowski, "Post-War Wave of Pogroms and Killings," 70.

183. YIVO, RG 104, ser. 1, file 1020 [Eyewitness Accounts of the Holocaust Period Collection—Anna Hendel, January 31, 1946]. In reality, the attack on Maria Cyna took place before the murder of Aron Hendel.

184. Joseph Freeman, *Job: The Story of a Holocaust Survivor* (St. Paul, MN: Paragon House, 2003), 97. When Joseph Freeman was living in Radom after the war, he most likely used the name Józef Friedman; however, I have been unable to establish that beyond any

doubt. Therefore, throughout the text I am using the name under which he published his memoir.

185. USHMM, RG-50.029*0010, interview: Sally Chase (Zylbersztajn at the time).

186. Fortunoff Video Archive for Holocaust Testimonies, Yale University Library (access at Stiftung Denkmal für die ermordeten Juden Europas, Berlin, hereafter, HVT), HVT-2613, interview: Bertha G.

187. Lejzor Fiszman, "Uzupełniamy akt oskarżenia przeciw Wilhelmowi Blumowi," pt. 2, *Życie Radomskie: Pismo Codzienne Ziemi Kieleckiej,* August 18, 1947.

188. Quoted in Zaremba, *Wielka trwoga,* 584 (emphasis mine).

189. AP Radom, OKŻ, 20, f. 13 [letter from the OKŻ to the MUBP in Radom, August 31, 1945].

190. AP Radom, OKŻ, 23, f. 5 [October 25, 1945].

191. AP Radom, OKŻ, 23, f. 9 [letter from the OKŻ to the KM MO in Radom and the KW MO in Kielce, February 22, 1946].

192. AP Radom, OKŻ, 23, f. 8 [February 15, 1946].

193. YIVO, RG 104, ser. 1, file 1020. The number of graves corresponds to the number of Jews murdered in Radom right after the war, which I established in the course of my archival search. However, one of the victims of the murder in the "Praca" Cooperative was buried in another location. If the number of graves is correct, there seems to be no information about the seventh person buried at the Jewish cemetery in Radom after the war. In Christopher Browning's book *Remembering Survival: Inside a Nazi Slave-Labor Camp* (New York: W. W. Norton, 2010), 360n35, one can find information about the murder in Radom of Szaja Langleben, who was said to be "the most hated camp policeman." According to individuals whom Browning interviewed, Langleben was to have been murdered in one of the Radom restaurants as vengeance for his activity in the camp. It seems, however, that the information about the murder of Langleben is false. In 2006, an article appeared in the Radom-Kielce daily containing information about Szaja Langleben, who lived in Radom above the Teatralna coffee shop. In that text, there is no mention of a murder and only that the old man died in isolation and was buried in the Jewish cemetery in Warsaw (Krzysztof Żmudzin, "Jej Żydzi," *Słowo Ludu,* May 11, 2006, http://www/slowo.com.pl/?dod=11&id=6483, accessed April 13, 2014). In the cemetery on Okopowa Street in Warsaw (a functioning Jewish cemetery closest to Radom), there is only one grave of an individual with the name Szaja Langleben (sector 2a, row 7, no. 16). That man died on February 14, 1991. It is unlikely that after the war two individuals with the name Szaja Langleben were living in Radom. Browning himself, in conversation with me, stated that the information about the alleged murder of Langleben could have been the product of wishful thinking by the individuals whom he interviewed.

194. Clara Thomas Archives and Special Collections, York University, Toronto (hereafter, CTASC), Sam and Manya Lipshitz Fonds, 2003-061/011(1), not paginated.

195. Halina is the name she used until her emigration from Poland.

196. Interview: Helen H., USA, 2013. Until she emigrated from Poland and married, she used the name: Halina Wajsbord.

197. YIVO, RG 104, ser. 1, file 1018 [Eyewitness Accounts of the Holocaust Period Collection—Aron Łęga, January 31, 1946].

198. YIVO, RG 104, ser. 1, file 1018.

199. YIVO, RG 104, ser. 1, file 1018.

200. YIVO, RG 104, ser. 1, file 1018.

201. Elliot Aronson, Timothy D. Wilson, and Robin M. Akert, *Social Psychology,* 8th ed. (Boston: Pearson, 2013), 315.

202. YIVO, RG 104, ser. 1, file 1018 [Eyewitness Accounts of the Holocaust Period Collection—Aron Łęga, January 31, 1946].

203. AP Kielce, Akta Powiatowych i Miejskich Oddziałów Informacji i Propagandy woj. kieleckiego, 76, f. 411 [monthly report, July 1946].

204. Szaynok, *Pogrom Żydów,* 65.

205. Cited in Joanna Tokarska-Bakir, "Figura Krwiopijcy w dyskursie religijnym, narodowym i lewicowym Polski w latach 1945–1947," in Tokarska-Bakir, *Okrzyki pogromowe,* 347n74. This note does not appear in the English version of the text: Tokarska-Bakir, "The Figure of the Bloodsucker."

206. "Radom protestuje przeciw zbrodni kieleckiej," *Dziennik Powszechny,* July 15, 1946.

207. AP Kielce, Akta Powiatowych i Miejskich Oddziałów Informacji i Propagandy woj. kieleckiego, 76, f. 411–413 [monthly report, July 1946] (emphasis mine).

208. "Dokument 35. 1946, lipiec, 18, Warszawa. Sprawozdanie instruktorów . . . ," 138, 139.

209. "Dokument 28. Lipiec 1946 r., Warszawa. Raporty agentów Urzędu Bezpieczeństwa do centrali dotyczące nastrojów społecznych w Kaliszu, Dęblinie i Łodzi," in *Dzieje Żydów w Polsce 1944–1968: Teksty źródłowe,* ed. Alina Cała and Helena Datner-Śpiewak (Warsaw: ŻIH, 1997), 71.

210. "Dokument 44. 1946, sierpień, Skarżysko-Kamienna, Sprawozdanie Miejskiego Oddziału Informacji i Propagandy w Skarżysku za lipiec 1946," in Meducki, *Antyżydowskie wydarzenia kieleckie,* 152, 153. It should be noted that the resolutions were adopted during a series of other rallies, mass meetings, and assemblies that took place in the town. Four days later, on July 12, 1946, a repeat mass meeting was organized in the "Kamienna" factory; an official of the Municipal Office of Information and Propaganda noted that this time the mood of the assembly was good.

211. "Dokument 35. 1946, lipiec, 18, Warszawa. Sprawozdanie instruktorów," 139.

212. Żbikowski, "Post-War Wave of Pogroms and Killings," 70.

3. Community

1. My thanks to Matan Shefi for help in accessing information about Michał Guzawackier.

2. AP Kielce, Akta Powiatowych i Miejskich Oddziałów Informacji i Propagandy woj. kieleckiego 76, f. 89 [Sprawozdanie Miejskiego Oddziału Informacji i Propagandy za sierpień 1945, September 6, 1945].

3. Interview: Helen H., USA, 2013. Helen H. asserts that the murder happened in December 1945; however, the circumstances of the crime indicate that she is referring to the attack on the Jewish cooperative in August 1945.

4. AP Radom, OKŻ, 9, f. 6. [letter from OKŻ to the Kielce Provincial Governor, August 25, 1945], 7 [letter from OKŻ to the County Governor of Radom, August 25, 1945], 8 [Letter from OKŻ to the Mayor of Radom, August 25, 1945].

5. AP Radom, OKŻ, 1, f. 24.

6. AP Radom, OKŻ, 20, f. 13, 14. There is no further information about the attack on Lewental. Not even the first name of the victim is known.

7. AP Radom, OKŻ, 9, f. 6, 7, 8 [August 25, 1945] (emphasis mine).

8. AP Radom, OKŻ, 23, f. 5 [October 10, 1945].

9. AP Radom, OKŻ, 23, f. 6 [November 3, 1945].

10. AP Radom, OKŻ, 23, f. 9 [February 22, 1946].

11. Jan Tomasz Gross, *Fear: Anti-Semitism in Poland after Auschwitz: An Essay in Historical Interpretation* (New York: Random House, 2006), 99.

12. AP Radom, OKŻ, 23, f. 10 [February 25, 1946]. After the pogrom in Kielce, the CKŻP established the Special Commission, whose task was to ensure the physical security of survivors in Poland. It appears, however, that this decision was taken too late to have any effect on the lives of survivors residing in Radom. In the course of my inquiry, I did not come across even the slightest mention that would allow me to link the activity of the Special Commission of the CKŻP with Radom. See Alina Cała, *Ochrona bezpieczeństwa fizycznego Żydów w Polsce powojennej: Komisje Specjalne przy Centralnym Komitecie Żydów w Polsce* (Warsaw: ŻIH, 2014).

13. AP Radom, OKŻ, 23, f. 8 [February 15, 1946]. The document in the Committee's files has no heading; it is unknown to whom the shelter residents' request was addressed.

14. AP Radom, OKŻ, 20, f. 6 [May 26, 1945].

15. The first murders in the cited fragment most likely were the attack against the "Praca" Cooperative. An attempt to determine what incident was meant in the murder of two Jews mentioned by the man was not successful. It is possible that those people were murdered not in Radom but in one of the neighboring localities. Samuel Margoshes, "A Nacht in Radom," *Der Tog,* March 21, 1946. Thanks to Rivka Schiller for help in translating this text from Yiddish.

16. Margoshes, "A Nacht in Radom."

17. HVT-2613, interview: Bertha G.

18. Adam Kopciowski, "Zajścia antyżydowskie na Lubelszczyźnie w pierwszych latach po drugiej wojnie światowej," *Zagłada Żydów. Studia i materiały* 3 (2007): 187. This was not the only instance of an attack against Jews in a hospital. There was a similar event in Bełżyce, as Kopciowski writes in his detailed study of instances of anti-Jewish violence in the Lublin region. It also happened that the hospital personnel themselves treated the Jewish patients with hostility and contempt; that is what individuals wounded in both the Kraków and Kielce pogroms experienced (see Gross, *Fear,* 81–82, 100, 101–103).

19. Interview: Aleksander Wajselfisz, Israel, 2015.

20. Marcin Zaremba, *Komunizm, legitymizacja, nacjonalizm: Nacjonalistyczna legitymizacja władzy komunistycznej w Polsce* (Warsaw: Trio, ISP PAN, 2005), 201. Zaremba writes about the name changes adopted by individuals in the top leadership of the party and administration in 1951. However, name changes were also made before then.

21. The term "ghost citizens" was coined by my friend from graduate school at the University of Warsaw and now a fellow academic, Dominika Michalak, during one of our lengthy discussions about my research.

22. AŻIH, CKŻP, Wydział Ewidencji i Statystyki, 631, f. 5–10 [List of the Jewish population after liberation, January 1945. Register up to February 5, 1945]; YIVO, RG 335.7, box 32, file 802, not paginated [American Jewish Joint Distribution Committee, Landsmanshaftn Department—List of Jews Residing in Radom on October 30, 1946].

23. AP Radom, AmR, Wydział Aprowizacji i Handlu, 9736, f. 1, 3.

24. Sebastian Piątkowski, *Dni życia, dni śmierci: Ludność żydowska w Radomiu w latach 1918–1950* (Warsaw: Naczelna Dyrekcja Archiwów Państwowych, 2006), 261.

25. Natalia Aleksiun, *Dokąd dalej? Ruch syjonistyczny w Polsce (1944–1950)* (Warsaw: Centrum Badań i Nauczania Dziejów i Kultury Żydów w Polsce im. Mordechaja Anielewicza, Trio, 2002), 52.

26. Irena Hurwic-Nowakowska, *A Social Analysis of Postwar Polish Jewry* (Jerusalem: Zalman Shazar Center for Jewish History, 1986), 47.

27. AŻIH, CKŻP, Prezydium, 8, f. 18 [February 21, 1945].

28. IPN BU 00231/146, vol. 1, f. 167 [February 22, 1945]. In the section referring to Radom, the report covers the period "until February 18, 1945." In the document, only the first letter of the investigator's first name can be seen. I thank Dr. Aleksandr Namysło for bringing this file to my attention and making archival copies available to me.

29. The found documents contain no more information about Obstler. Even his first name remains unknown.

30. The religious-conservative Agudath Israel Party was not legalized after the war. In reality, however, this party conducted open activity and even published newspapers in postwar Poland (August Grabski, *Działalność komunistów wśród Żydów w Polsce (1944–1949)* [Warsaw: Trio, ŻIH, 2004], 19, 105).

31. IPN BU 00231/146, file 1, f. 166 [February 22, 1945].

32. AP Radom, OKŻ, 2, f. 1 [transcript of extraordinary meeting, February 3, 1945; extract from board session, March 3, 1945].

33. IPN BU 00231/146, file 1, f. 167 [February 22, 1945]; AŻIH, CKŻP, Wydział Organizacji i Kontroli, 104, f. 4 [personnel staff, November 1, 1946].

34. AŻIH, CKŻP, Wydział Opieki Społecznej, 404, f. 1 [report, November 8–10, 1946]. In May 1948, the Radom branch of Ichud counted twenty-two members (that is how many individuals purchased membership cards). Among them was also the then-president of the Committee, Leon Stellman (AŻIH, Organizacje syjonistyczne, 86, f. 8).

35. Archiwum Państwowe w Poznaniu, Komitet Miejski PPR w Kaliszu, 19, f. 7 [transcript, November 15, 1947].

36. David Engel, "The Reconstruction of Jewish Communal Institutions in Postwar Poland: The Origins of the Central Committee of Polish Jews, 1944–1945," *East European Politics and Societies* 10, no. 1 (1996): 106.

37. AP Radom, OKŻ, 1, f. 9 [May 21, 1945]. Adam Penkalla reports that in May 1945 in Kielce province itself there were as many as forty-eight Jewish committees, which reported to the WKŻ in Kielce (Adam Penkalla, "Władze o obecności Żydów na terenie Kielecczyzny w okresie od wkroczenia Armii Czerwonej do pogromu kieleckiego," *Kwartalnik Historii Żydów* 2003:4, 558). It appears that that is actually information about the number of localities in the province in which there were groups of survivors. Many of those "committees" most likely did not undertake work at all or swiftly abandoned their activity.

38. Bożena Szaynok, *Pogrom Żydów w Kielcach 4 lipca 1946* (Warsaw: Bellona, 1992), 45, 70.

39. AAN, Urząd do Spraw Wyznań, 13/415, f. 3.

40. AŻIH, CKŻP, Wydział Opieki Społecznej, 404, f. 1 [report of activity audit of the OKŻ in Radom for the period January–October 1946].

41. AŻIH, CKŻP, Wydział Organizacji i Kontroli, 104, f. 1 [February 10, 1949]; AP Radom, OKŻ, 22, f. 53 [March 6, 1950].

42. AP Radom, OKŻ, 10, f. 6 [May 17, 1945]; Adam Penkalla, "Stosunki polsko-żydowskie w Radomiu (kwiecień 1945–luty 1946)," *Biuletyn Żydowskiego Instytutu Historycznego* 95 no. 3–96 no. 2 (lipiec 1995–czerwiec 1996): 59.

43. AP Radom, OKŻ, 12, f. 6 [August 10, 1945].

44. AP Radom, OKŻ, 11, f. 34 [October 5, 1945]; AŻIH, TOZ, 119, f. 4 [October 18, 1945].

45. AP, Radom, OKŻ, 11, f. 33.

46. AP Radom, AmR, Wydział Aprowizacji i Handlu, 9736, f. 12 [March 10, 1945].

47. AP Radom, AmR, Wydział Aprowizacji i Handlu, 9736, f. 5.

48. AP Radom, AmR, Wydział Aprowizacji i Handlu, 9736, f. 9 [February 19, 1945].

49. AP Radom, Wydział Aprowizacji i Handlu, 9736, f. 11 [February 28, 1945].

50. AP Radom AmR, Wydział Aprowizacji i Handlu, 9736, f. 14 [May 17, 1945].

51. AP Radom, AmR, Wydział Aprowizacji i Handlu, 9736, f. 3 [letter from OKŻ to Municipal Authority in Radom, January 27, 1945].

52. AP Radom, OKŻ, 11, f. 2 [March 10, 1945].

53. AP Radom, OKŻ, 11, f. 5 [April 4, 1945].

54. The Jewish shelter at 52 Traugutt Street existed almost until the end of the Jewish Committee's activity in Radom. The OKŻ decided to close the shelter on February 10, 1949. The cause of this decision was, most likely, the lack of a demand for shelter services [AP Radom, OKŻ, 2, f. 10 (transcript of OKŻ session, February 10, 1949)].

55. AP Radom, OKŻ, 11, f. 7 [May 12, 1945].

56. AP Radom, OKŻ, 11, f. 8 [May 17, 1945].

57. In March 1945, the Jewish Committee submitted an appeal to the Municipal National Council for the admission of their own delegate to the Housing Commission. It appears, however, that it was one more unsuccessful attempt at influencing the policies of the local authorities toward survivors residing in the city (AP Radom, OKŻ, 11, f. 6).

58. His name might also have been spelled "Żeliwski"; postwar documents created on a typewriter often lack Polish diacritical signs. This was a result of two things: German typewriters were in general use and the individuals creating the documents often were not proficient at using typewriters.

59. AŻIH, CKŻP, Wydział Organizacji i Kontroli, 23, f. 37 [report, May 23, 1945]. Very bad conditions were also prevalent in Jewish shelters in other Polish cities. See Aleksiun, *Dokąd dalej?*, 74.

60. AP Radom, OKŻ, 11, f. 10 [June 4, 1945]; AP Radom, AmR, Wydział Aprowizacji i Handlu, 9736, f. 15 [June 4, 1945].

61. AP Radom, AmR, Wydział Aprowizacji i Handlu, 9736, f. 16 [July 13, 1945], 17 [August 7, 1945], 18 [August 30, 1945].

62. AP Radom, OKŻ, 19, f. 36 [July 24, 1945].

63. AP Radom, AmR, Wydział Aprowizacji i Handlu, 9736, f. 18 [August 30, 1945], 19 [October 2, 1945], 20 [November 3, 1945].

64. AP Radom, OKŻ, 2, f. 2 [May 15, 1946].

65. AŻIH, CKŻP, Wydział Opieki Społecznej, 404, f. 3 [report of activities audit of OKŻ in Radom for the period January–October 1946, n.d.]

66. AŻIH, CKŻP, Wydział Opieki Społecznej, 404, f. 6 [report of activities audit of OKŻ in Radom for the period January–October 1946, n.d.].

67. Aleksiun, *Dokąd dalej?*, 69.

68. Interview: Henry R., Canada, 2013.

69. Aleksiun, *Dokąd dalej?*, 61.

70. Aleksiun, *Dokąd dalej?*, 69.

71. Sara Zyskind, *Stolen Years* (Minneapolis, MN: Lerner Publications, 1981), 269.

72. Sam Lipshitz, "In Majn Geburt-Sztot," *Vokhnblat,* May 2, 1946. Thanks to Rivka Schiller for her help translating this text from Yiddish.

73. The goals of the CKŻP were published in the first number of the Jewish Press Agency's newsletter, *Biuletyn Żydowskiej Agencji Prasowej:* "Productivization of the surviving Jews and their active participation in the economic rebuilding of their country and the development of their creative powers on a foundation of legal and actual equality" belonged to the CKŻP's priority tasks. Cited after Grabski, *Działalność komunistów,* 59. See Piotr Kendziorek, *Program i praktyka produktywizacji Żydów polskich w działalności CKŻP* (Warsaw: ŻIH, 2016).

74. Kendziorek, *Program i praktyka produktywizacji Żydów polskich w działalności CKŻP,* 66.

75. IPN BU 00231/146, vol. 1, f. 167 [report, February 22, 1945].

76. Michał Grynberg, *Żydowska spółdzielczość pracy w Polsce w latach 1945–1949* (Warsaw: ŻIH, PWN, 1986), 15.

77. IPN BU 00231/146, vol. 1, f. 167 [report, February 22, 1945].

78. AP Radom, OKŻ, 3, f. 4 [independent workshops of Jews in Radom, n.d.].

79. AP Radom, OKŻ, 20, f. 4 [April 9, 1945].

80. AP Radom, OKŻ, 1, f. 62 [December 18, 1945].

81. Grynberg, *Żydowska spółdzielczość,* 15.

82. Anna Cichopek-Gajraj, *Beyond Violence: Jewish Survivors in Poland and Slovakia 1944–1948* (Cambridge: Cambridge University Press, 2014), 210.

83. AP Radom, OKŻ, 3, f. 4 [independent workshops of Jews in Radom, n.d.].

84. AP Radom, OKŻ, 20, f. 3; Piątkowski, *Dni życia,* 268.

85. AŻIH, CKŻP, Wydział Organizacji i Kontroli, 23, f. 40 [report, May 23, 1945].

86. Piątkowski, *Dni życia,* 67.

87. It is necessary to point out that the prewar designation of cooperative societies or enterprises as "Jewish" or "Christian" also existed in the first years after the war. The division between Jews and non-Jews existed in the consciousness of both, independently of the equality slogans proclaimed in the official propaganda of the new authorities. In this context, the demand that Jewish artisans join "Christian" cooperative societies was a form of repression.

88. AŻIH, CKŻP, Wydział Organizacji i Kontroli, 23, f. 39 [report, May 23, 1945] (emphasis in the original).

89. AŻIH, CKŻP, Wydział Organizacji i Kontroli, 23, f. 40 [report, May 23, 1945].
90. Grynberg, *Żydowska spółdzielczość*, 53.
91. AP Radom, OKŻ, 20, f. 5 [April 25, 1945].
92. Grynberg, *Żydowska spółdzielność*, 58, 59. The Central Economic Office "Solidarność" had nothing in common with the Independent Self-governing Labor Union "Solidarność," known as "Solidarity," and the social movement founded in 1980 in Gdańsk and led by Lech Wałęsa.
93. AŻIH, CKŻP, Wydział Opieki Społecznej, 404, f. 3 [report of activities audit of OKŻ in Radom conducted November 8–10, 1946].
94. AŻIH, CKŻP, Wydział Organizacji i Kontroli, 23, f. 37 [report, May 23, 1945].
95. AŻIH, 301/56, Ichiel Leszcz.
96. Eli Gat, *Not Just Another Holocaust Book,* trans. Lidya Gosher (Tel Aviv: Yerushalayim, 2006), 163. The roundup of Jews in Radom under the pretext of an exchange for German citizens interned by the Allies was part of a broader action also conducted in other cities of the General Government. See Agnieszka Haska, *"Jestem Żydem, chcę wejść": Hotel Polski w Warszawie, 1943* (Warsaw: IFiS PAN, 2006).
97. Piątkowski, *Dni życia,* 234.
98. AŻIH, 301/56, Ichiel Leszcz.
99. Piątkowski, *Dni życia,* 234, 235. Believing that being on the list afforded a chance of survival, many people attempted to enroll in it. Those who were initially not eligible for registration also attempted to join the transport. At least three individuals succeeded: Eli Gutsztadt (now Eli Gat), Bela Frydman, and her brother Tuwia Frydman (after emigration from Poland, Tuvia Friedman). All three managed to escape execution. They returned to the city together with the trucks carrying the belongings of those who were murdered. In their memoirs, Eli Gat and Tuvia Friedman give various counts of the murdered. One must accept that during that execution between 130 and 150 Radom Jews were shot.
100. AŻIH, 301/56, Ichiel Leszcz.
101. Saul Friedländer, *The Years of Extermination: Nazi Germany and the Jews, 1939–1945* (HarperCollins e-books, 2008), 40.
102. Piątkowski, *Dni życia,* 188, 189.
103. Piątkowski, *Dni życia,* 189. Szenderowicz also displayed political ambitions before the war. In 1934, he ran unsuccessfully for membership in the City Council [Grażyna Łuszkiewicz-Dzierżawska, "Przedstawiciele społeczności żydowskiej we władzach samorządowych Radomia (1916–1939)," *Społeczność żydowska Radomia w I połowie XX wieku: Kultura, Holocaust, Rozproszenie,* ed. Zbigniew Wieczorek (Radom: Radomskie Towarzystwo Naukowe, 2008), appendix, 99]. In several documents, Ludwik Fastman appears as Lipa Fastman.
104. AŻIH, TOZ, 1143, f. 145.
105. Piątkowski, *Dni życia,* 229.
106. AŻIH, Sąd Społeczny, 121, f. 6 [Naum Szenderowicz letter to TOZ, April 18, 1946].
107. AŻIH, TOZ, 1143, f. 145 [biographical sketch, Naum Szenderowicz].
108. AŻIH, TOZ, 754, f. 205.
109. AŻIH, TOZ, 1143, f. 67 [biographical sketch, Ludwik Fastman].
110. *Dziennik Powszechny,* July 15, 1945, July 18, 1945.

111. *Dziennik Powszechny,* August 13, 1945, August 14, 1945, August 15, 1945.

112. Piątkowski, *Dni życia,* 197.

113. Hannah Arendt, *Eichmann in Jerusalem: A Report on the Banality of Evil,* trans. Amos Elon (London: Penguin, 2006), 117.

114. Friedländer, *Years of Extermination,* xix–xx.

115. Raul Hilberg, *The Destruction of the European Jews,* rev. and definitive ed. (New York: Holmes & Meier, 1985), 1:218.

116. AŻIH, CKŻP, Prezydium, 7, f. 84 [transcript of session, June 29, 1945].

117. AP Radom, OKŻ, 11, f. 31.

118. AŻIH, TOZ, 396, f. 36 [questionnaire, September 19, 1946].

119. Seweryn Kahane, chairman of the Provincial Jewish Committee in Kielce, was murdered on July 4, 1946, during the Kielce pogrom.

120. AŻIH, Sąd Społeczny przy CKŻP (hereafter, Sąd Społeczny), 121, f. 40 [November 11, 1946].

121. AŻIH, Sąd Społeczny, 121, f. 5 [April 18, 1946].

122. AŻIH, Sąd Społeczny, 121, f. 80.

123. AŻIH, TOZ, 409, f. 122.

124. AŻIH, TOZ, 289, f. 104 [letter to CKŻP, January 1, 1947].

125. Andrzej Żbikowski, *Sąd Społeczny przy CKŻP: Wojenne rozliczenia społeczności żydowskiej w Polsce* (Warsaw: ŻIH, 2014); Gabriel Finder, "Judenrat on Trial: Postwar Polish Jewry Sits in Judgment of Its Wartime Leadership," *Jewish Honor Courts: Revenge, Retribution, and Reconciliation in Europe and Israel after the Holocaust,* ed. Laura Jockush and Gabriel Finder (Detroit: Wayne State University Press, 2015), 83–106.

126. The reference is to Romana Fargotsztejn, who married Dr. Ludwik Fastman after the war.

127. AŻIH, Sąd Społeczny, 121, f. 30 [testimony, November 3, 1946] (emphasis in the original).

128. AŻIH, Sąd Społeczny, 121, f. 37 [transcript, November 13, 1946].

129. AŻIH, Sąd Społeczny, 121, f. 79 [transcript, November 13, 1946]. Bela Frydman was one of the few people whose name was on the "Palestine list" who were not executed in Szydłowiec Jewish cemetery.

130. AŻIH, Sąd Społeczny, 121, f. 49 [transcript, November 13, 1946].

131. AŻIH, Sąd Społeczny, 121, f. 22 [letter from Gutharc to Marbach, October 30, 1946].

132. Untersturmführer SS Franz Schippers from the second half of 1942 until March 1943 was the commandant of the work camps for Jews on Szwarlikowska and Szkolna Streets in Radom (Piątkowski, *Dni życia,* 227).

133. AŻIH, Sąd Społeczny, 121, f. 45–47 [transcript of witness testimony, November 26, 1946] (emphasis mine).

134. AŻIH, Sąd Społeczny, 121, f. 53 [transcript, November 28, 1946].

135. AŻIH, Sąd Społeczny, 121, f. 54, 55 [transcript, November 28, 1946].

136. AŻIH, Sąd Społeczny, 121, f. 54 [transcript, November 28, 1946].

137. AŻIH, Sąd Społeczny, 121, f. 65, 66 [letter from Bolesław Sławiński aka Bencjon Szajnberg to Citizens' Tribunal, November 11, 1946].

138. AŻIH, Sąd Społeczny, 121, f. 51, 52 [letter from Naum Szenderowicz to Citizens' Tribunal, November 27, 1946].

139. AŻIH, Sąd Społeczny, 121, f. 1, 2 [testimony: Rózia Rywan, April 8, 1946]. Almost entirely identical in content is the testimony of Celina Nasielska [k. 3]—with the sole difference that the author worked in the hospital for infectious diseases.

140. AŻIH, Sąd Społeczny, 121, f. 10 [April 27, 1946].

141. AŻIH, Sąd Społeczny, 121, f. 69 [December 13, 1946].

142. AŻIH, Sąd Społeczny, 121, f. 70, 71 [December 13, 1946]. Also, Rachela Wajsbrot stated in her testimony: "For inclusion on the 'Palestine list' people paid, but that money went not to private pockets but to the Judenrat account" [k. 77].

143. AŻIH, Sąd Społeczny, 121, f. 72, 73 [transcript, December 16, 1946].

144. AŻIH, Sąd Społeczny, 121, f. 41 [November 25, 1946].

145. AŻIH, Sąd Społeczny, 121 f. 60 [December 4, 1946].

146. AŻIH, Sąd Społeczny, 121, f. 59, 60 [December 4, 1946]. Fargotsztejn-Fastmanowa did not mention, however, that she was Dr. Szenderowicz's cousin, which cast a somewhat different light on the help he gave her. That Dr. Szenderowicz saved Fargotsztejn-Fastmanowa as his cousin is known from the statements given by Irena Szenderowicz in the course of the trial of Wilhelm Blum (USHMM, RG-15.183 [Sąd Okręgowy w Radomiu], reel 3, frame 349).

147. AŻIH, Sąd Społeczny, 121, f. 60 [December 4, 1946].

148. AŻIH, Sąd Społeczny, 121, f. 60, 61 [December 4, 1946].

149. AŻIH, Sąd Społeczny, 121, f. 22 [letter from Gutharc to Marbach, October 30, 1946].

150. AŻIH, Sąd Społeczny, 121, f. 77 [transcript, December 28, 1946].

151. Interview with Ewa Cederbaum, Holocaust Survivors' Testimonies, Yad Vashem Archives 2008. Interview accessible on the Internet: http://www.google.com /culturalinstitute/asset-viewer/testimony-of-eva-cederbaum-born-in-radom-poland -1924-regarding-her-experiences-in-the-pionki-camp-and-additional-camps /zAG44Elh5RVOKA?hl=en&l.expanded-id=fQHTflG=c91aCA. Accessed June 15, 2014.

152. AŻIH, Sąd Społeczny, 121, f. 91 [letter from Irena Szenderowicz to Citizens' Tribunal, January 23, 1947].

153. AŻIH, Sąd Społeczny, 119, f. 1 [transcript, July 8, 1947], f. 4 [transcript, July 26, 1947].

154. AŻIH, Sąd Społeczny, 144, f. 122 [excerpt from court's decision, November 15, 1948].

155. AŻIH, Sąd Społeczny, 144, f. 16 [statement by Bencjon Sławiński aka Szejnberg, December 13, 1946]. The information about drinking alcohol with the Germans most likely should not be taken literally. It appears that it is, rather, a signal that the accused was on excessively "familiar terms" with the occupier.

156. AŻIH, Sąd Społeczny, 144, f. 115b [letter of Hersz London, n.d.]. See Ewa Koźmińska-Frejlak, "'I'm Going to the Oven Because I Wouldn't Give Myself to Him': The Role of Gender in the Polish Jewish Civic Court," in *Jewish Honor Courts: Revenge, Retribution and Reconciliation in Europe and Israel after the Holocaust,* ed. Laura Jockusch and Gabriel N. Finder (Detroit: Wayne State University Press, 2015), 260–263.

157. AŻIH, Sąd Społeczny, 121, f. 49 [transcript, November 27, 1946].

158. AŻIH, 301/59, Mojżesz Bojm. In the testimony another form of the first name is used: "Mojsze." The information about the testifying person says: "Technical director of the Jewish factory B-ka—a metal foundry."

159. AP Kielce, Okręgowy Urząd Likwidacyjny w Kielcach (hereafter, OUL w Kielcach), 49, f. 26 [letter from the Union of the Casting Industry in Radom, September 8, 1945]. In 1945, Bojm was trying, with no success, to recover control over the foundry.

160. AP Radom, Sąd Okręgowy, 1281, f. 4 [copy of marriage certificate]. In the documents, the first names appear as Rywka and Moszek, and the bride's maiden name appears in three different versions of its spelling: Gutsztad, Gutsztat, Gutsztadt.

161. AP Radom, Sąd Okręgowy, 1281, f. 1 [summons, April 7, 1948].

162. AŻIH, Sąd Społeczny, 121, f. 69 [transcript, December 13, 1946].

163. AŻIH, 301/59, Mojżesz Bojm. Testifying in the Szenderowicz trial, Bojm said that his task in the Bliżyn camp was the construction of a hydraulic pumping station [AŻIH, Sąd Społeczny, 121, f. 69].

164. AŻIH, 301/59, Mojżesz Bojm.

165. AP Radom, Sąd Okręgowy w Radomiu, 1281, f. 1 [petition for divorce, April 7, 1948].

166. AP Radom, Sąd Okręgowy w Radomiu, 1281, f. 15 [transcript, May 11, 1948].

167. AP Radom, Sąd Okręgowy w Radomiu, 1281, f. 16 [verdict, May 11, 1948].

168. In a passport questionnaire from 1956, Mojżesz Bojm also wrote that he had a sister, Sabina Tencer, who lived in Warsaw. It does not appear, however, that Tencer ever lived in Radom after the war (IPN BU 1547/659, f. 19).

169. AP Radom, OKŻ, 2, f. 1 [transcript, March 2, 1945].

170. AP Radom, OKŻ, 2, f. 1 [excerpt from board session, March 3, 1945].

171. AP Radom, OKŻ, 18, f. 3 [authorization, April 15, 1945].

172. IPN Ki 016/4, f. 137 [special report, May 8, 1947].

173. Margoshes, "A nacht in Radom."

174. AŻIH, American Jewish Joint Distribution Committee in Poland (hereafter, AJDC), 1335, f. 165 [September 3, 1946].

175. AŻIH, 301/59, Mojżesz Bojm.

176. AP Radom, OKŻ, 2, f. 4 [transcript of board session, March 6, 1947].

177. AŻIH, CKŻP, Wydział Organizacji i Kontroli, 104, f. 102 [letter, November 31, 1947].

178. IPN BU 1547/659, f. 19 [passport questionnaire, December 24, 1956]; RG-15.183M [Sąd Okręgowy w Radomiu], reel 13, frame 645. In Warsaw, Mieczysław Boleński married Anna Krengel of Kraków, an employee in the Railway Scientific-Research Institute (IPN BU 1547/659, f. 20). The wedding took place on November 16, 1949. Before the war and during the occupation, Anna Krengel lived in Kraków. Her parents and other family members perished during the Holocaust (https://www.ics.uci.edu /~dan/genealogy/Krakow/Families/Krengel.html, accessed October 17, 2017; http:// yvng.yadvashem.org/index.html?language=en&s_lastName=krengel&s_firstName =anna&s_place=krakow, accessed October 17, 2017). In 1951, a son, Stefan, was born to the couple. Starting in 1956, the Boleński family tried for passports to emigrate to Israel. A year later, they received documents legalizing their departure. Most likely, they left Poland in the second half of 1957 (IPN BU 1547/659, f. 6, 7, 15).

179. AŻIH, CKŻP, Wydział Organizacji i Kontroli, 104, f. 102.

180. Fuks did not receive a salaried position, but most probably he worked with the Committee pro bono for a time as a form of social service.
181. IPN Ki 016/4, f. 57.
182. AŻIH, CKŻP, Wydział Ewidencji i Statystyki, 425/Sz14662 [registration card: Leon Stellman, November 18, 1946]. Both of Leon Stellman's brothers completed higher education. Jakub Stellman (b. 1892) was a ceramicist, and Władysław Stellman (b. 1911) was a bacteriologist. Both perished during the Holocaust (USHMM, RG-15.114M [Naczelna Rada Starszych Ludności Żydowskiej Dystryktu Radomskiego w Radomiu, Dział Dowodów Osobistych], reel 17, folder 116, f. 62, 64, 66).
183. AŻIH, CKŻP, Wydział Ewidencji i Statystyki, 425/Sz14662 [registration card: Leon Stellman, November 18, 1946].
184. USHMM, RG-15.183M [Sąd Okręgowy w Radomiu], reel 3, frame 376 [transcript of witness interview: Izrael Dawid Kuperber, July 2, 1947]. The actual name of the witness was Kuperberg.
185. USHMM, RG-15.183M [Sąd Okręgowy w Radomiu], reel 3, frames 388, 389 [transcript of witness interview: Leon Stellman, July 18, 1947]. The age of the witness listed in the transcript, forty-seven, testifies to yet another possible date of Stellman's birth.
186. AP Radom, OKŻ, 22, f. 53 [transcript, March 6,1950].
187. AŻIH, CKŻP, Wydział Ewidencji i Statystyki, 425/Sz14662 [registration card: Leon Stellman, November 18, 1946].
188. IPN BU, PZ-26, copy of a card from the index of emigration departures: Leon Stellman.
189. IPN Ki 29/51, vol. 4, f. 5 [November 23, 1950].
190. IPN BU, PZ-26, copy of a card from the index of emigration departures: Leon Stellman.
191. In the files of the Jewish Committee there is one document dated June 6, 1956. It is an agreement concerning the territory of the Jewish cemetery and the meadow belonging to it in Szydłowiec. According to that agreement, two men, presenting themselves as representatives of the District Jewish Committee in Radom and the Jewish Denominational Congregation, handed over the immovable property to two farmers in a lease arrangement. The farmers could graze their cattle and mow the grass in the areas where there were no gravestones. In the document, the stamp of the Jewish Committee appeared in two places. Perhaps the contents of the agreement were an attempt at protecting the cemetery from further devastation. However, the stamp of an institution that had long since not existed was used. In 1956, there was no longer in Radom either a Jewish Committee or a Jewish Denominational Congregation (AP Radom, OKŻ, 22, f. 58).
192. Piątkowski, *Dni życia,* 86.
193. AŻIH, CKŻP, Wydział Organizacji i Kontroli, 104, f. 12 [March 14, 1946].
194. A different spelling of his first name occurs in several documents: Bajnyś.
195. Private Archive of Joanna Niewiadomska (Archiwum Prywatne Joanny Niewiadomskiej; hereafter, AJN), *40 lat KPP: Jednodniówka Komitetu Obchodu 40-lecia KPP w Radomiu* [December 1958].
196. Piątkowski, *Dni życia,* 99.
197. IPN BU 00170/464, f. 48 [appeal to the Ambassador of the Polish People's Republic in Berlin, July 8, 1954].

198. Piątkowski, *Dni życia,* 51. There also exists a reference to Kamer having been elected to the post of chairman by a one-vote majority (AJN, excerpt from Sefer Radom: Tel Aviv, 1961).

199. AP Radom, OKŻ, 11, f. 59; IPN Ki 016/4, f. 59.

200. AŻIH, CKŻP, Wydział Organizacji i Kontroli, 104, f. 3 [report of audit, November 1946].

201. IPN Ki 016/4, f. 59.

202. AJN, *40 lat KPP: Jednodniówka Komitetu Obchodu 40-lecia KPP w Radomiu* [December 1958].

203. AJN, Kopia karty rejestracyjnej CKŻP [May 28, 1946].

204. AJN, Kopia karty rejestracyjnej CKŻP [May 28, 1946].

205. AJN, Chaim Kamer's biographical sketch [December 10, 1997].

206. Aleksander Wat, *My Century: The Odyssey of a Polish Intellectual,* ed. and trans. Richard Lourie, with a foreword by Czeslaw Milosz (New York: W. W. Norton, 1990), 359. Actually, Bajnysz and Rywa Kamer had three sons: Jakub, Karol, and Chaim. All three were in the USSR.

207. Aleksander Wat, *Mój wiek, Pamiętnik mówiony,* (Warsaw: Czytelnik, 1990), 1:60.

208. Ola Watowa, *Wszystko co najważniejsze . . .* (Warsaw: Agora, 2011), 163.

209. AŻIH CKŻP, Wydział Organizacji i Kontroli, 104, f. 4 [report, March 14, 1946]; AŻIH, CKŻP, Wydział Opieki Społecznej, 404, f. 3 [report for the period January–October 1946, no date]; AP Radom, OKŻ, 13, f. 4 [July 1, 1947]. Lejzor Fiszman did not head the Historical Commission from its beginning. Later, the role of chairman of the Committee for the Celebration of the Memory of the Jewish Martyrs of Radom was filled by Jonas Kirszenbaum, who also was active in the Denominational Congregation (AP Radom, OKŻ, 13, f. 1).

210. AŻIH, CKŻP, Centralna Żydowska Komisja Historyczna (hereafter, CŻKH), 385, f. 1 [protocol, February 14, 1945]; AP Radom, OKŻ, 13, f. 4 [July 1, 1947].

211. Renata Kobylarz points to the memory of the uprising in the ghetto as forging a sense of unity among the survivors in Poland. Renata Kobylarz, *Walka o pamięć: Polityczne aspekty obchodów rocznicy powstania w getcie warszawskim 1944–1989* (Warsaw: IPN, 2009), 22.

212. AP Radom, OKŻ, 12, f. 6 [August 10, 1945].

213. Władysław Broniewski, "Żydom polskim," *Wiersze zebrane* (Warsaw: Książka i Wiedza, 1949), 199, 200. I leave aside the question of the political message of Broniewski's poem contained in its final three lines: "when we will end with victory our bloody many-year labor:/every man will gain freedom, a bite of bread, and rights,/and one race will arise, the highest one: noble people."

214. These categories were introduced into sociology by Stanisław Ossowski in "Analiza socjologiczna pojęcia ojczyzny," in his *O ojczyźnie i narodzie* (Warsaw: PWN, 1984), 15–46.

215. Hurwic-Nowakowska, *Social Analysis,* 77–78.

216. In 1948, a program was held commemorating the victims removed in the final deportation from the Radom ghetto, which took place on January 13, 1943. AP Radom, OKŻ, 13, f. 1 [mourning ceremony in memory of the murdered Jews, n.d.].

217. Piątkowski, *Dni życia,* 219.

218. AŻIH, CKŻP, CŻKH, 114, f. 83 [June 26, 1947].

219. AP Radom, OKŻ, 12, f. 15 [correspondence of the CŻKH to the OKŻ, July 3, 1947].

220. USHMM, RG-15.183M [Sąd Okręgowy w Radomiu], reel 3, frame 588. The Supreme Court dismissed the cassation complaint at the beginning of 1948. The President of Poland, Bolesław Bierut did not make use of his right to grant a pardon. The sentence was carried out in Radom in 1948. The execution was not public.

221. Lejzor Fiszman, "Uzupełniamy akt oskarżenia przeciwko Wilhelmowi Blumowi," *Życie Radomskie: Pismo Codzienne Ziemi Kieleckiej,* August 17, 1947 (pt. 1), August 18, 1947 (pt. 2). The postwar trials of the Nazis carried also certain potential for brief integration of Polish Jews and Christian Poles around a common goal of bringing to justice German war criminals. See Gabriel N. Finder and Alexander V. Prusin, *Justice Behind the Iron Curtain: Nazis on Trial in Communist Poland* (Toronto: University of Toronto Press, 2018), 212.

222. AŻIH, CKŻP, *Wydział Prawny,* 108, f. 14–17.

223. AP Radom, OKŻ, 12, f. 27 [August 13, 1947] (emphasis mine).

224. AP Radom, OKŻ, 12, f. 29.

225. In June 1949, the trial of Herbert Böttcher, a former chief of the SS and police in the Radom district, took place before the District Court in Radom. On June 18, 1949, he was sentenced to death. It appears that this trial produced a lesser echo among the surviving Radom Jews than the trial of Wilhelm Joseph Blum, which took place two years earlier. The reason for this difference may have been the diminishing of the community of survivors in the city but also the fact that the charges brought against Böttcher included crimes committed against Jews and Polish Christians, and not, as was the case of Blum, solely the annihilation of the Jewish population (USHMM, RG-15.183 [District Court in Radom], reel 14, frames 912, 913).

226. AP Radom, OKŻ, 12, f. 8 [letter to the Jewish Committee in Siedlce, July 30, 1947]; AP Radom, OKŻ, 13, f. 6 [letter to the Jewish Committee in Siedlce, August 6, 1947].

227. AP Radom, OKŻ, 12, f. 28.

228. AP Radom, OKŻ, 12, f. 30.

229. "Jak wygląda i co mówi Blum: Migawki z sali sądowej," *Życie Radomskie: Pismo Codzienne Ziemi Kieleckiej,* August 17, 1947.

230. Today the locality is called Pieszyce.

231. AP Radom, OKŻ, 13, f. 17 [n.d.].

232. AP Radom, OKŻ, 10, f. 26 [August 13, 1947].

233. "Smutna uroczystość: Akademia Żałobna ku czci pomordowanych Żydów," *Życie Radomskie: Pismo Codzienne Ziemi Kieleckiej,* August 18, 1947.

234. Grabski, *Działalność komunistów,* 68n24.

235. AP, Radom, OKŻ, 12, f. 25 [August 13, 1947].

236. AŻIH, Wydział Prawny, 108, f. 2 [June 19, 1947] (emphasis mine). Fijoł was sentenced to death. As grounds for the sentence, the court stated that in the apprehension of Moszek Feldman, his daughter Regina Feldman, and a man whose name is not known, and in handing them over to the German police, several other villagers took part equally with Fijoł. As an act of clemency, the President of Poland changed Fijoł's sentence to life imprisonment. Fijoł went free in 1957 thanks to an amnesty. Although he did not deny his role in apprehending the three Jewish fugitives, throughout his entire time in prison he made light of his deed, insisting that it was "allegedly a serious

crime" and that his first confessions were extracted from him by a beating during the interrogation. To the extent that one can believe that Fijoł was beaten by officers of the PUBP in Kozienice, his explanations about the circumstances of the deaths of the three Jews must be considered to be preposterous. Although the court confirmed the complicity in the crime of several other inhabitants of the village, most likely none of them were held liable (USHMM, RG-15.183M [District Court in Radom], reel 1, frames 355-599 [documents in the case of Józef Fijoł]).

237. AŻIH, Wydział Prawny, 108, Fijał Józef, f. 3 [June 25, 1947] (emphasis mine).

238. AŻIH, CŻKH, 115, f. 69, 70 [letters of the CŻKH to the OKŻ w Radom, May 22, 1947]. On the role of the Central Jewish Historical Commission in prosecuting Nazi war criminals, see Finder and Prusin, *Justice Behind the Iron Curtain*, 180–182.

239. AP Radom, OKŻ, 3, f. 12; Piątkowski, *Dni życia*, 265.

240. Marcin Zaremba, *Wielka trwoga: Polska 1944–1947; Ludowa reakcja na kryzys* (Kraków: Znak, 2012), 94.

241. AP Radom, OKŻ, 12, f. 44 [April 12, 1949].

242. AP Radom, OKŻ, 12, f. 46. It was probably the last interment in the Radom Jewish cemetery.

243. *Życie Radomskie*, May 9, 1949.

244. *Życie Radomskie*, May 11, 1949.

245. In documents touching upon the construction of a monument, this institution is often named the Organizational Committee for Construction of a Monument for the Celebration of the Jewish Martyrs in Radom (e.g., AP Radom, OKŻ, 13, f. 3).

246. AP Radom, OKŻ, 13, f. 5 [letter to the city mayor and the chairman of the MRN, July 3, 1947].

247. AP Radom, OKŻ, 13, f. 5.

248. AP Radom, OKŻ, 13, f. 5.

249. Piątkowski, *Dni życia*, 266. Zajdensznir was born in Radom in 1903 into a Jewish family. He studied at the École nationale supérieure des Arts Décoratifs in Paris, 1925–1928. He converted to Catholicism in the 1930s, joined the Cistercian order in France and became a monk, and was ordained a priest in 1942. He returned to Poland in 1946. In 1957 he married Pola Wajsfus, a Holocaust survivor and his relative. He lived in Warsaw and Radom, where he died in 1970. He was buried in the Roman Catholic cemetery on Limanowski Street in Radom.

250. CTASC, 2003-061/011(1), "Der fraynt fun Radom 1925–1950" (Paris, 1950), 71 [letter of L. Fiszman from Radom]; Penkalla, "Stosunki polsko-żydowskie," 59.

251. "8 rocznica zagłady Żydów radomskich stanie się manifestacją w obronie Pokoju," *Życie Radomskie*, August 17, 1950 (emphasis in the original).

252. "Społeczeństwo Radomia oddało hołd ofiarom zbrodni hitlerowskich: Odsłonięcie pomnika ku czci pomordowanych Żydów," *Życie Radomskie*, August 19, 1950. Both texts published in *Życie Radomskie* were signed with the same pseudonym, "gaj." A photograph documenting the unveiling of the monument printed in a Yiddish-language brochure in Paris in December 1950 presents a group of several dozen men with banners and Polish flags standing in front of the monument. Around the cleaned-up square, with flowers planted around it, stands a crowd of at least a few hundred adults and children. There is also an orchestra. It is not known who were the people grouped around the square. Were they "the Radom community paying respect to the victims

of Nazi crimes," as the article in *Życie Radomskie* cited suggests, or were the majority of them Radom Jews who came to the observation of the anniversary of the liquidation of the ghetto from other parts of Poland, as well as the few survivors still residing in the city? This question will perhaps remain always unanswered.

253. "Społeczeństwo Radomia oddało hołd ofiarom zbrodni hitlerowskich."

254. AP Radom, OKŻ, 13, f. 27 [August 17, 1950].

255. Piątkowski, *Dni życia,* 266.

256. *Słowo Ludu,* August 17, 1950; August 18, 1950; August 19, 1950.

257. The planned fencing around the Jewish cemetery in Radom did not succeed [CTASC, 2003-061/011(1), "Der fraynt fun Radom" (Paris, 1950), 71 (letter of L. Fiszman from Radom)]. Another attempt at marking the Jewish presence in the city also ended in failure. In 1947, together with the initiative to build the monument, the Committee for the Celebration of the Memory of the Jewish Martyrs of Radom undertook an effort to name Szwarlikowska Street "Martyrs of the Ghetto." Later, the Jewish Committee put forward an identical initiative in relation to Zatylna Street. In August 1950, the presidium of the MRN in Radom informed the Committee that no further action would be taken following the guidelines of the central authorities and the prepared General Population Census (AP Radom, OKŻ, 13, f. 5; AP Radom, OKŻ, 12, f. 48).

258. Tuvia Friedman, *The Hunter* (London: Anthony Gibbs & Phillips, 1961), 58. In the English text, a version of the surname appears, "Szendorowicz," but there is no doubt this is a spelling mistake and the reference is to Dr. Naum Szenderowicz.

259. Henryk Grynberg, *The Victory,* trans. Richard Lourie, in Grynberg, *The Jewish War and the Victory,* trans. Celina Wieniewska with the author and by Richard Lourie (Evanston, IL: Northwestern University Press, 2001), 68. Although Henryk Grynberg's work is not a typical memoir, its autobiographical character cannot be doubted.

260. Grynberg, *Victory,* 82–83.

261. Grynberg, *Victory,* 84–85.

262. AŻIH, Sąd Społeczny, 121, f. 8 [April 18, 1946].

263. AŻIH, Sąd Społeczny, 121, f. 9 [April 18, 1946].

264. AŻIH, Sąd Społeczny, 121, f. 42 [November 25, 1946].

265. Sebastian Piątkowski writes that at the time of the liquidation of the ghetto, it was calculated that the workers of several industrial plants supplying the Germans, among them former Kromołowski tannery workers, might evade deportation (*Dni życia,* 221). The Jews confined in barracks on the grounds of the Kromołowski tannery who were producing leather handgun holsters and belts for the Wehrmacht actually did avoid deportation in August 1942 (telephone conversation: Tosia Goldberg, Israel, 2016).

266. This is a reference to the mass execution of Radom Jews carried out by the Germans at the end of March 1943.

267. AŻIH, Sąd Społeczny, 121, f. 12, 13 [letter from Anna Gecow, June 2, 1946].

4. Property

Many of the legal references below include the following abbreviations: "no." (number), "art." (article), and "par." (paragraph).

1. Nina Springer-Aharoni, "A Photo Album of the Radom and Szydłowiec Ghettos: A Visual Document from the Days of the Nazi Occupation," in *The End! Das Ende! Radom and Szydłowiec Through the Eyes of a German Photographer,* ed. Bella Gutterman and Nina Springer-Aharoni (Jerusalem: Yad Vashem, 2013), 14–33.

2. Jan Grabowski, "Polscy zarządcy powierniczy majątku żydowskiego: Zarys problematyki," *Zagłada Żydów* 1 (2005): 253.

3. Monika Krawczyk, "The Effect on the Legal Status of Jewish Property in Post-War Poland on Polish-Jewish Relations," in *Jewish Presence in Absence: The Aftermath of the Holocaust in Poland, 1944–2010,* ed. Feliks Tych and Monika Adamczyk-Garbowska (Jerusalem: Yad Vashem, 2014), 794–797. It was different in the eastern part of the country occupied by the Germans from the summer of 1941 [i.e., the Galicia district of the GG]. These lands had been occupied by the Soviets since September 17, 1939, and all Jewish and non-Jewish businesses there were nationalized under Soviet rule. See Anna Wylegała, "About 'Jewish Things': Jewish Property in Eastern Galicia During World War II," in *Yad Vashem Studies* 44 no. 2 (2016): 85.

4. Sebastian Piątkowski, *Dni życia, dni śmierci: Ludność żydowska w Radomiu w latach 1918–1950* (Warsaw: Naczelna Dyrekcja Archiwów Państwowych, 2006), 168.

5. Grabowski, *Polscy zarządcy,* 254.

6. AŻIH, 301/56, Ichiel Leszcz.

7. AŻIH, 301/2161, Maria Fridman. In various documents, two versions of the spelling of her last name appear "Frydman" or "Fridman." Without a doubt, they refer to the same person. Therefore, I use a uniform spelling of her name in the text but when providing references, I write her name the way it is spelled out in the description of the particular collection to which I am referring.

8. AŻIH, 301/2161, Maria Fridman.

9. USHMM, RG-15.183M [District Court in Radom], reel 15, frames 165, 166.

10. Martin Dean, *Robbing the Jews: The Confiscation of Jewish Property in the Holocaust, 1933–1945* (Cambridge: Cambridge University Press, 2010), 179–181.

11. AŻIH, 301/2161, Maria Fridman.

12. AP Radom, Rejonowy Urząd Likwidacyjny, 501 [In the matter of the return of property: Wiktor and Szlama Ajzner], not paginated. Application to the City Court in Radom arrived April 5, 1945.

13. AŻIH, 301/2161, Maria Fridman.

14. USHMM, RG-50.488*0135, interview: Stefan Posyniak.

15. Jerzy Kochanowski, *Tylnymi drzwiami: "Czarny rynek" w Polsce 1944–1989* (Warsaw: Neriton, 2010), 41.

16. Kochanowski, *Tylnymi drzwiami,* 41.

17. Kazimierz Wyka, "The Excluded Economy," in *The Unplanned Society: Poland during and after Communism,* ed. Janine R. Wedel (New York: Columbia University Press, 1992), 25 (emphasis in original).

18. Piątkowski, *Dni życia,* 177–179.

19. VHA, 734, interview: Bernard Gotfryd.

20. Wojciech Skrodzki, "Żydzi z Wodzisławia," *Tygodnik Powszechny,* no. 28/2006, cited in Jan Grabowski, *Na posterunku: Udział polskiej policji granatowej i kryminalnej w zagładzie Żydów,* unpublished manuscript (forthcoming, Wołowiec: Czarne, 2020).

21. USHMM RG-50.488*0291 interview: Stefan Kozieł.
22. Interview: Mieczysław Wośko, Poland, 2012.
23. Marcel Goldman, *Iskierki życia* (Kraków: Wydawnictwo Arcana, 2006), 44.
24. Personal Archive of Nina Assorodobraj-Kula and Witold Kula (Archiwum Prywatne Niny Assorodobraj-Kuli i Witolda Kuli), letter from Tadeusz Kwaśniewski to Witold Kula, n.d. I thank Marcin Kula for providing me with a copy of the document.
25. Interview: Mieczysław Wośko.
26. Interview: Mieczysław Wośko.
27. Interview: Mieczysław Wośko. Another Radom resident, Stefan Kozieł, saw a German leading two Jews into the territory of the former ghetto. The men were digging up some kind of can from the ground (USHMN RG-50.488*0291, interview: Stefan Kozieł).
28. AP Radom, AmR, Wydział Finansowy, 9702 [Kartoteka Nieruchomości Pożydowskich znajdujących się na poszczególnych ulicach Radomia w roku 1945, S-T].
29. Joseph Freeman, *Job: The Story of a Holocaust Survivor* (St. Paul: Paragon House, 2003), 99, 101.
30. IPN BU 0703/1132, f. 52 [excerpt from the testimony of Władysław Czerwiński, June 1951].
31. Manifest Polskiego Komitetu Wyzwolenia Narodowego [July 22, 1944] (hereafter, Manifest PKWN). Cited according to *Źródła do historii Polski 1944-1956*, pt. 1, ed. Mieczysław Jaworski and Mieczysław Starczewski (Warsaw: Wojskowa Akademia Polityczna im. Feliksa Dzierżyńskiego, 1987), 18, 19.
32. See Document no. 20: "1946 kwiecień 10: Memorandum Centralnego Komitetu Żydów w Polsce do Komisji Anglo-Amerykańskiej dla Spraw Palestyny, m. in. żądanie wolnej emigracji do Palestyny," *Stosunki polsko-izraelskie (1945-1967): Wybór dokumentów*, ed. Szymon Rudnicki and Marcos Silber (Warsaw: Naczelna Dyrekcja Archiwów Państwowych, Archiwum Państwowe Izraela, 2009), 88, 89.
33. Dekret z dnia 2 marca 1945, o majątkach opuszczonych i porzuconych, Dz. U. 1945, no. 9, position 45; Ustawa z dnia 6 maja 1945, o majątkach opuszczonych i porzuconych, Dz. U. 1945, no. 17, position 97; Dekret z dnia 8 marca 1946, o majątkach opuszczonych i poniemieckich, Dz. U. 1946, no. 13, position 87.
34. Dekret z dnia 2 marca 1945, o majątkach . . . , art. 2, par. 1.
35. Dekret z dnia 2 marca 1945, o majątkach . . . , art. 1, par. 1.
36. Jan Tomasz Gross, *Neighbors: The Destruction of the Jewish Community in Jedwabne, Poland* (New York: Penguin Books, 2002), 185n4. Alina Skibińska points out that immediately after the war two similar designations were also used: "post-Ukrainian" and "post-Lemke"; Alina Skibińska, "Problemy rewindykacji żydowskich nieruchomości w latach 1944-1950: Zagadnienia ogólne i szczegółowe (na przykładzie Szczebrzeszyna)," in *Klucze i kasa: O mieniu żydowskim w Polsce pod okupacją niemiecką i we wczesnych latach powojennch 1939-1950*, ed. Jan Grabowski and Dariusz Libionka (Warsaw: Centrum Badań nad Zagładą Żydów, 2014), 496n13.
37. Dekret z dnia 2 marca 1945, o majątkach . . . , art. 5.
38. Dekret z dnia 8 marca 1946, o majątkach . . . , art. 7.3. See Skibińska, "Problemy rewindykacji," 509-512, for discussion of competence of the Liquidation Offices.
39. Dekret z dnia 2 marca 1945, o majątkach . . . , art. 11.

40. Kazimierz Kolańczyk, "Prawo rzymskie," updated by Jan Kodębski, 5th ed. (Warsaw: LexisNexis, 2001), 268.

41. Dekret z dnia 2 marca 1945, o majątkach . . . , art. 18, 19; Ustawa z dnia 6 maja 1945, o majątkach . . . , art. 19, 20; Dekret z dnia 8 marca 1946, o majątkach . . . , art. 15, 16. This last legal act, in addition to submitting a petition to the city court for restoration of possession, also created the possibility of turning directly to the Liquidation Office in the administrative course of action.

42. Kolańczyk, "Prawo rzymskie," 268.

43. In 1945, as many as five systems of civil law, depending on the region of the country, were in effect in Poland. Inheritance law was unified only in 1946 (personal correspondence with Krzysztof Persak, October 17, 2014). This does not mean, however, that attempts at gaining property through inheritance procedure did not take place. See Skibińska, "Problemy rewindykacji," 516.

44. Private individuals to whom possession had been restored acquired the right of ownership on the strength of a court's ruling after a ten-year prescription period (Dekret z dnia 2 marca 1945, o majątkach . . . , art. 35; Ustawa z dnia 6 maja 1945, o majątkach . . . , art. 36; Dekret z dnia 8 marca 1946, o majątkach . . . , art. 33). In the case of occupation by the State Treasury or by institutions to which the State had entrusted possession of an "abandoned" property, this period initially was twenty years for real property and ten years for movable property (Dekret z dnia 2 marca 1945, o majątkach . . . , art. 36; Ustawa z dnia 6 maja 1945, o majątkach . . . , art. 37). In 1946 these periods were shortened by half (Dekret z dnia 8 marca 1946, o majątkach . . . , art. 34).

45. Personal correspondence with Krzysztof Persak, October 17, 2014.

46. The law in truth made it possible for children born out of wedlock to put forward claims and for the spouses of owners, without regard to the form in which their union was concluded (art. 20), so this narrowing was not entirely unambiguous. The question demanding particular attention is what the practical consequences were of the replacement in the March 8, 1946, decree of "the owner of an abandoned property" with the designation "the individual, who in connection with the war begun on September 1, 1939, lost possession of his property." On the one hand, such a change could really broaden the circle of individuals to include leaseholders and tenants who, in accordance with the decree, now had the possibility of submitting a claim for return of possession. On the other hand, it is not clear what the actual consequences were of this designation for owners who before the war rented out their real property to third parties and after the war desired to take back possession of their property. On the basis of archival searches conducted in the documents of the city courts in Radom and Kalisz, it appears that the majority of cases concerning the return of possession were put forward by owners or individuals related to them, and not by prewar lessees or their relatives. Also, I have not come across any claim filed by an owner's child born out of wedlock (Krzysztof Persak, "Na Niemców wina i zbrodnia, dla nas klucze i kasa," *Gazeta Wyborcza,* September 27–28, 2014).

47. Marceli Najder, *Rewanż* (Warsaw: Karta, 2013), 226, 227, entry from May 18, 1945.

48. Dekret z dnia 8 marca 1946, o majątkach . . . , art. 15.2.

49. Michael Meng, *Shattered Spaces: Encountering Jewish Ruins in Postwar Germany and Poland* (Cambridge, MA: Harvard University Press, 2011), 52; Skibińska, "Problemy

rewindykacji," 519; Dekret z dnia 28 października 1947, w sprawie przedłużenia terminu, przewidzianego w art. 15.2 dekretu z dnia 8 marca 1946, O majątkach opuszczonych i poniemieckich (Dz. U. 1947, no. 66, position 402).

50. AP Radom, OKŻ, 9, f. 26, 28.

51. American Jewish Joint Distribution Committee Archives in New York (JDCA), AR 45/54 No. 762 [Poland—Lawyers 1947-1948].

52. IPN Ki 016/4, f. 69.

53. AP Radom, Sąd Grodzki w Radomiu, 44, f. 12 [testimony, April 30, 1945].

54. AP Radom, Sąd Grodzki w Radomiu, 44, f. 13 [testimony, n.d.].

55. AP Radom, Sąd Grodzki w Radomiu, 44, f. 20, 21 [decision, May 18, 1945].

56. AP Radom, Sąd Grodzki w Radomiu, 44, f. 31 [protest, June 26, 1947].

57. AP Radom, Sąd Grodzki w Radomiu, 44, f. 39, 42.

58. Dekret z dnia 8 marca 1946, o majątkach . . . , art. 17.2. Once the property was recovered by the owner or their relative, the lease rent was payable to that person.

59. AŻIH, CKŻP, Wydział Organizacji i Kontroli, 23, f. 35. [report by inspector Zeliwski on his inspection tour No. 2, May 7-17, 1945] (the first emphasis is mine; the second is in the original).

60. Telephone conversation: Tosia Goldberg, Israel, 2016. Getting from Radom to Stuttgart cost her two of those coins. Lastman changed her name to Goldberg.

61. Interview: Aleksander Wajselfisz, Israel, 2015, not recorded.

62. AP Kielce, Okręgowy Urząd Likwidacyjny w Kielcach (hereafter, OUL w Kielcach), 70, f. 25 [decision of the City Court in Radom, August 29, 1945].

63. AP Kielce, OUL w Kielcach, 70, f. 26–27 [copy of a contract in the registry book of mortgages of real property, September 11, 1945].

64. AP Kielce, OUL w Kielcach, 70, f. 9 [statement, September 23, 1948], 10 [statement, August 6, 1948].

65. AP Kielce, OUL w Kielcach, 76, f. 21 [protocol, June 13, 1949].

66. Dekret z dnia 8 marca 1946, o majątkach . . . , art. 28.1. Fees collected for making a claim for the return of possession equaled one-tenth of the comparable registration fee based on the estimated value of the property that was the subject of the case.

67. AP Kielce, OUL w Kielcach, 86, f. 16 [settlement of property, July 18, 1949].

68. Dekret z dnia 8 marca 1946, o majątkach . . . , art. 5.1.

69. Dekret z dnia 8 marca 1946, o majątkach . . . , art. 5.3.

70. Legions Square is today's Rynek (Market Square).

71. AP Radom, AmR, 9698–9703.

72. Dekret z dnia 2 marca 1945, o majątkach . . . , art. 24, par. 1.

73. Ustawa z dnia 3 stycznia 1946, o przejęciu na własność Państwa podstawowych gałęzi gospodarki narodowej, Dz. U. 1946, no. 3, position 17, art. 2.7.

74. Ustawa z dnia 3 stycznia 1946, o przejęciu na własność . . . art. 3.1.

75. Ustawa z dnia 3 stycznia 1946, o przejęciu na własność . . . art. 3.4.

76. Ustawa z dnia 3 stycznia 1946, o przejęciu na własność . . . art. 7.2. Cases where the seized enterprises were the property of the German Reich or its citizens did not qualify for indemnification.

77. Dekret z dnia 8 marca 1946, o majątkach . . . , art. 22.1.

78. AP Radom, Sąd Grodzki w Radomiu, 24, f. 1, 2 [petition for the restoration of possession, April 4, 1945].

79. AP Radom, Sąd Grodzki w Radomiu, 24, f. 27 [letter from the Head of the Industrial Department of the Municipal Authority in Radom to the Inspector's Office of the Provincial Branch of the TZP in Radom, April 25, 1945].

80. AP Radom, Sąd Grodzki w Radomiu, 24, f. 30 [decision of the City Court in Radom, May 11, 1945], 31 [justification of the decision, May 15,1945].

81. Ustawa z dnia 6 maja 1945, o majątkach opuszczonych . . . , art. 25, par. 3.

82. AP Kielce, OUL w Kielcach, 49, f. 123 [letter from the Ministry of the Treasury to the City Court in Radom, April 18, 1946], f. 126.

83. AP Kielce, OUL w Kielcach, 49, f. 140 [letter from the TZP branch in Radom to the TZP w Kielcach, September 17, 1945].

84. AP Kielce, OUL w Kielcach, 49, f. 125 [letter from the Industrial Department of the Provincial Authority in Kielce to the OUL, June 22, 1946].

85. "Kto chce wydrzeć robotnikowi jego prawa? Niepokojące machinacje w przemyśle radomskim," *Świt*, June 24, 1945, no. 11 (emphasis in original).

86. AP Kielce, OUL w Kielcach, 49, f. 142–152.

87. AP Kielce, OUL w Kielcach, 49, f. 177.

88. Dekret z dnia 2 marca 1945, o majątkach . . . , art. 13, par. 1. Later legal acts preserved a similar possibility.

89. During the occupation, the German authorities also turned some of the Jewish-owned property into public utility spaces. Beginning in April 1948, such property had been nationalized and as such could not be recovered by the prewar owners or their relatives. See Łukasz Krzyżanowski, "'Chcielibyśmy, by ten dom nie pozostał w obcych rękach': Sądowa restytucja prywatnego mienia żydowskiego w Polsce na przykładzie Radomia i Kalisza 1945–1948," in *Klucze i kasa,* 592.

90. Ustawa z dnia 6 maja 1945, o majątkach opuszczonych . . . , art. 13, par. 1.

91. AP Kielce, OUL w Kielcach, 34, f. 17 [letter from the headquarters of the ZHP to the Central Office of the Provisional State Administration in Łódź, August 8, 1945].

92. AP Kielce, OUL w Kielcach, 34, f. 3 [inventory of real property, n.d.].

93. AP Kielce, OUL w Kielcach, 34, f. 3 [letter of the presiding officer of the City Court in Zwoleń to the president of the District Court in Radom, September 22, 1945] (emphasis mine).

94. AP Radom, OKŻ, 11, f. 2 [allocation of apartment, March 10, 1945].

95. Radom, OKŻ, 11, f. 57 [letter from the OKŻ to the Extraordinary Housing Commission in Radom, October 5, 1946].

96. AP Radom, OKŻ, 16, f. 1 [June 9, 1945].

97. AP Radom, OKŻ, 16, f. 2 [August 21, 1945]; AP Radom, AmR, 9610, f. 8 [February 15, 1945].

98. AP Radom, AmR, 9610, f. 58 [July 24, 1945].

99. Adolf Tochterman, "O szpitalach i lekarzach radomskich," typescript, p. 38. The department was still functioning in this location toward the end of the 1990s.

100. AP Kalisz, Sąd Grodzki w Kaliszu, 1603, f. 3 [MAP circular in the matter of provisional regulation of confessional affairs of the Jewish population, February 10, 1945] (emphasis mine). For more on the property of Jewish communities after World War II

in Poland, see Julia Machnowska, *Jewish Communal Property in Postwar Poland (1945-1950)*, unpublished master's thesis, Institute of History, University of Warsaw, 2018; Yechiel Weizman, "Unsettled Possession: The Question of Ownership of Jewish Sites in Poland after the Holocaust from a Local Perspective," *Jewish Culture and History* 18, no. 1 (2017).

101. AŻIH, CKŻP, Wydział Produktywizacji, 144, f. 1 [letter from the Department of Productivization to the OKŻ in Radom, August 13, 1947] (emphasis mine). In the end, the Radom Committee had to pay to lease the machines.

102. AP Radom, OKŻ, 14, f. 1 [letter from the OKŻ to the Mayor of Radom, June 25, 1945].

103. Piątkowski, *Dni życia,* 264.

104. AP Radom, OKŻ, 14, f. 5 [letter from the OKŻ to the Municipal Authority in Radom, December 2, 1947].

105. AP Radom, OKŻ, 14, f. 5.

106. AP Radom, OKŻ, 14, f. 5.

107. AP Radom, OKŻ, 15, f. 2 [letter from the OKŻ to the mayor of Radom, June 25,1945].

108. AP Radom, OKŻ, 15, f. 1 [letter from the Administrative Department of the Municipal Authority in Radom to the First Station of the Citizens' Militia in Radom, June 20, 1945].

109. AP Radom, OKŻ, 15, f. 2. The use of Jewish cemeteries for pasturing cattle after the war was not limited to Radom. In that region alone, the phenomenon occurred also in Ostrowiec Świętokrzyski, Szydłowiec, and most likely in many other localities.

110. AP Radom, OKŻ, 15, f. 3 [letter from the mayor of Radom City to the OKŻ, August 16, 1945].

111. AP Radom, OKŻ, 15, f. 6 [letter of the City Community Authority to OKŻ, August 7, 1947].

112. Adam Penkalla, "Stosunki polsko-żydowskie w Radomiu (kwiecień 1945–luty 1946)," *Biuletyn Żydowskiego Instytutu Historycznego* 95, no. 3–96 no. 2 (lipiec 1995–czerwiec 1996): 59n20.

113. AP Kielce, OUL w Kielcach, 34, f. 20, 22, 23, 25.

114. AP Kielce, OUL w Kielcach, 34, f. 139.

115. AP Kielce, OUL w Kielcach, 34, f. 152 [letter to the Presidium of the Municipal National Council, September 23, 1945].

116. AP Kielce, OUL w Kielcach, 34, f. 156.

117. AP Kielce, OUL w Kielcach, 34, f. 155.

118. AP Radom, Sąd Grodzki w Radomiu, 25, f. 1 [motion, n.d.].

119. AP Radom, Sąd Grodzki w Radomiu, 25, f. 27.

120. AP Radom, Sąd Grodzki w Radomiu, 25, f. 1.

121. AP Radom, Sąd Grodzki w Radomiu, 25, f. 15 [transcript of court proceedings, April 13, 1945]; f. 18 [copy of sale agreement, 10.03.1941]; f. 27 [statement by Stanisław Sybilski, April 7, 1945].

122. AP Radom, Sąd Grodzki w Radomiu, 25, f. 68 [June 1, 1945].

123. *Dziennik Radomski,* July 14, 1942.

124. It is likely, however, that the photography studio run by Stanisław Soborski ceased functioning already in 1945.

125. Telephone conversation: Tosia Goldberg, Israel, 2016.

126. Telephone conversation: Michael Gotfryd, USA, 2013. After his emigration from Poland, Mendel (Menachem) Gotfryd changed his first name to Michael.

127. Józef Hen, "Cudowny kraj, ta Polska," interview with Donata Subotko, in Donata Subotko, *Wiem, co mówię, czyli dialogi uzdrawiające: Spotkania z Józefem Henem* (Warsaw: Iskry, 2013), 235. First published in *Gazeta Wyborcza,* April 16, 2013.

128. AP Radom, OKŻ, 22, f. 40 [June 21, 1948]. The use of the term "Aryans" in a postwar document is an example of the transfer of Nazi terminology into the colloquial language used after the war.

129. Unfortunately, the new owners sometimes demonstrated great "creativity" in finding a use for the Torah. The parchment from the Torah scrolls was used to make musical instruments and even served as inserts in shoes.

130. Archiwum Instytutu Pamięci Narodowej w Gdańsku (Archive of the Institute of National Remembrance in Gdańsk; hereafter, IPN Gd) 212/526DVD, f. 68 [July 20, 1945].

131. IPN Gd 212/526/DVD, f. 42, 43 [transcript of investigation of suspect, June 5, 1945].

132. IPN Gd 212/256/DVD, f. 41, 42 [transcript of investigation of Marian Zaremba, June 5, 1945].

133. IPN Gd 212/526/DVD, f. 46 [transcript of interrogation of a witness, June 6, 1945].

134. Mordechaj Canin, *Przez ruiny i zgliszcza: Podróż po stu zgładzonych gminach żydowskich w Polsce,* trans. Monika Adamczyk-Garbowska (Warsaw: Nisza, ŻIH, 2018), 210–211.

135. See Łukasz Krzyżanowski, "Chcielibyśmy," 595–600.

136. Krzysztof Persak, "Akta postępowań cywilnych z lat 1947–1949 w sprawach dotyczących zmarłych żydowskich mieszkańców Jedwabnego," in *Wokół Jedwabnego,* ed. Paweł Machcewicz and Krzysztof Persak (Warsaw: IPN, 2002), 2:375–413; Jerzy Kułak, "Faber i S-ka—Krótka historia pewnego przekrętu," in *Biuletyn IPN,* 16 no. 6 (June 2002): 80–83; Alina Skibińska, "Problemy rewindykacji," 586–588; Anna Cichopek-Gajraj, *Beyond Violence: Jewish Survivors in Poland and Slovakia 1944–1948* (Cambridge: Cambridge University Press, 2014), 85; also, information gained in conversations with Jan Grabowski and Jakub Petelewicz.

137. It is difficult to say how widely used was the term *lipiarze.* Supposedly its etymology derives from *lipa* or "hogwash"—a colloquial description of a false, untrue thing—like the claims put forward by members of a criminal group. This term appears in the correspondence of the Radom District Jewish Committee with the Central Committee of Polish Jews (CKŻP), which is why I am using it. AŻIH, CKŻP, Wydział Organizacji i Kontroli, 104, f. 96 [letter from OKŻ to Prezydium CKŻP, February 20, 1948]. However, this term was not used only locally. Mordechai Tsanin refers to it while describing the situation in Łuków [Canin, *Przez ruiny i zgliszcza,* 211].

138. AŻIH, CKŻP, Wydział Organizacji i Kontroli, 104, f. 96 [letter from OKŻ to CKŻP Presidium, February 20, 1948].

139. AP Radom, OKŻ, 23, f. 12 [what the public prosecutor's office or Special Commission have to say about this, n.d.].

140. AP Radom, OKŻ, 9, f. 15–16 [letter from Jack Rosenstein to OKŻ, December 17, 1946].

141. AP Radom, OKŻ, 9, f. 23 [letter of the OKŻ to Jack Rosenstein, February 13, 1947].

142. Canin, *Przez ruiny i zgliszcza,* 211.

143. AP Radom, OKŻ, 23, f. 11, 12 [what the public prosecutor's office or Special Commission have to say about this, n.d.] (emphasis mine).

144. Krzysztof Persak, "Akta postępowań," 379.

145. Canin, *Przez ruiny i zgliszcza*, 211.

146. *AŻIH*, CKŻP, Wydział Organizacji i Kontroli, 104, f. 96 [letter from the OKŻ to the Presidium of the CKŻP, February 20, 1948].

147. AŻIH, AJDC, 1335, f. 22 [protocol of the all-country conference of Radom Landsmen Associations delegates, December 25, 1946].

148. IPN Ki 016/4, f. 59 [letter of the Municipal Office of the Security Service in Radom to the Head of Department V of the Provincial Office of the Security Service in Kielce, April 30, 1947].

149. Łukasz Krzyżanowski, "Chcielibyśmy," 597, 598.

150. AP Radom, OKŻ, 23, f. 11, 13 [what the public prosecutor's office or Special Commission have to say about this, n.d.].

151. Quoted in Natalia Aleksiun, *Dokąd dalej? Ruch syjonistyczny w Polsce (1944–1950)* (Warsaw: Centrum Badań i Nauczania Dziejów i Kultury Żydów w Polsce im. Mordechaja Anielewicza, Trio, 2002), 85n150 (emphasis mine). Also worth noticing here is the lack of condemnation of digging up graves of Holocaust victims as a crime or at least as a morally reprehensible act.

152. As the journalist Paweł Piotr Reszka has recently shown, the absence of moral reflection travels through generations and is still present in the vicinity of former Nazi extermination camps in Poland. See Paweł Piotr Reszka, *Płuczki: Poszukiwacze żydowskiego złota* (Warsaw: Agora, 2019).

153. See Andrzej Leder, *Prześniona rewolucja: Ćwiczenia z logiki historycznej* (Warsaw: Krytyka Polityczna, 2014), 80-81.

154. AAN, Biuro Komisarza Rządu ds. Produktywizacji Ludności Żydowskiej w Polsce, 49, f. 75 [March 18, 1947].

155. Alina Cała and Helena Datner-Śpiewak, *Dzieje Żydów w Polsce 1944–1968: Teksty źródłowe* (Warsaw: ŻIH, 1997), 167.

ARCHIVES CONSULTED

American Jewish Joint Distribution Committee Archives in New York (JDCA)
Archive of the Emanuel Ringelblum Jewish Historical Institute in Warsaw (Archiwum Żydowskiego Instytutu Historycznego im. Emanuela Ringelbluma w Warszawie, AŻIH)
Archive of the Institute of National Remembrance in Gdańsk (Archiwum Instytutu Pamięci Narodowej w Gdańsku, IPN Gd)
Archive of the Institute of National Remembrance in Kielce (Archiwum Instytutu Pamięci Narodowej w Kielcach, IPN Ki)
Archive of the Institute of National Remembrance in Radom (Archiwum Instytutu Pamięci Narodowej w Radomiu, IPN Ra)
Archive of the Institute of National Remembrance in Warsaw (Archiwum Instytutu Pamięci Narodowej w Warszawie, IPN BU)
Archive of the United States Holocaust Memorial Museum in Washington, DC (USHMM)
Central Archives of Modern Records in Warsaw (Archiwum Akt Nowych w Warszawie, AAN)
Clara Thomas Archives and Special Collections, York University, Toronto (CTASC)
Fortunoff Video Archive for Holocaust Testimonies, Yale University Library (accessed at Stiftung Denkmal für die ermordeten Juden Europas, Berlin) (HVT)
Jacek Malczewski Museum in Radom (Muzeum im. Jacka Malczewskiego w Radomiu, MJM)
Personal Archive of Nina Assorodobraj-Kula and Witold Kula (Archiwum Prywatne Niny Assorodobraj-Kuli i Witolda Kuli)
Połączone Biblioteki Wydziału Filozofii i Socjologii UW, Instytutu Filozofii i Socjologii PAN oraz Polskiego Towarzystwa Filozoficznego, Dział Zbiorów Specjalnych (BWFiS UW)
Private Archive of Joanna Niewiadomska (Archiwum Prywatne Joanny Niewiadomskiej, AJN)
State Archive in Kalisz (Archiwum Państwowe w Kaliszu, AP Kalisz)
State Archive in Kielce (Archiwum Państwowe w Kielcach, AP Kielce)
State Archive in Radom (Archiwum Państwowe w Radomiu, AP Radom)
Visual History Archive USC Shoah Foundation (VHA)
Yad Vashem Archive in Jerusalem (YVA)
YIVO Institute for Jewish Research (Yidisher Visnshaftlekher Institut) in New York (YIVO)

ACKNOWLEDGMENTS

While writing *Ghost Citizens,* I experienced benevolence and support on the part of many individuals and institutions to whom I feel deeply grateful. First, I would like to express my gratitude to all the survivors who shared their often most painful memories with me. Meeting survivors is always a powerful experience for a Holocaust historian. Many of those I interviewed passed away in recent years. I was lucky to be there in time to talk with the last people who remembered and experienced the ordeals that became the fate of the community I wrote about. Many of these meetings would never have happened without the assistance of individuals who put me in touch with the survivors, offered trust, and sometimes provided necessary logistical support. I did not even meet many of these people in person, but only heard their voices on the phone or read their emails. These contacts, however, were essential. I also wish to thank private individuals and institutions that shared their photos with me and gave permission for publication.

Research for this book would not have been possible without the hard work of many archivists and librarians who assisted me throughout my studies. I am indebted to Vincent Slatt (USHMM), Aleksandra Bańkowska, Agnieszka Reszka (ŻIH), Renata Sowińska and Michał Rosenberg (IPN), and archivists from the State Archive in Radom as well as workers at all the institutions where I conducted my research.

I am grateful to the Claims Conference, National Science Center (NCN), and Institute of Sociology at the University of Warsaw for funding my research throughout the years. This book received its final shape during my more than two-year fellowship at the Institute for East European Studies at the Freie Universität Berlin. I was welcomed to the institute by Gertrud Pickhan, Halina Zeman-Castillo, and Agnieszka Wierzcholska, who together with Katarzyna and Martin

Schmidt greatly facilitated my transfer to Germany. I also owe my gratitude to Simon Lewis, with whom I shared an office and who offered his friendship (and consultation on translating Polish swear words). Without Simon, and one of the many lunches we ate together, this book would not exist in English. I am also grateful to Freie Universität Berlin for following Simon's idea and providing necessary funds for translation. My thanks to the Institute of Philosophy and Sociology, Polish Academy of Sciences in Warsaw for providing institutional support. I remain grateful to Andrzej Rychard for his warm welcome on my arrival at the institute.

Ghost Citizens is an English adaptation of my book that originally came out in Polish in 2016. Neither of the two books would exist without the constant support and real friendship I continue to enjoy from my university mentor Marcin Kula. My study of the Holocaust survivors' experience was facilitated by fellowships at the Faculty of History, University of Oxford, and the International Institute for Holocaust Research at Yad Vashem, and by working with individuals at both institutions who offered guidance and mentorship. I am deeply indebted to Nick Stargardt, David Rechter, David Silberklang, and Eliot Nidam-Orvieto. I also wish to thank Jan Grabowski and Marcin Zaremba for their constant support throughout the years. Eliana Adler, Sharon Grosfeld, and Krzysztof Persak read the manuscript and provided invaluable insight. The manuscript was also read and discussed at a seminar organized by Andrzej S. Kamiński in Kraków in 2018.

I would like to express my deepest gratitude to my translator, Madeline G. Levine. She is one of the most generous people I have ever met in my academic career. As a scholar herself, she was always open to discussing any problems arising in the course of translating my work. It was great not to travel alone through the publication process. Learning from Madeline and her friendship has been a real gift and honor. Tomaz Jardim and Michael Meng greatly supported me in my search for a publisher in the United States. At Harvard University Press, I was very lucky to work with Kathleen McDermott and Mihaela-Andreea Pacurar, who offered their commitment, expertise, and friendliness. Sherry Gerstein and Ellen Lohman patiently took care of the manuscript and guided me through the production stage.

Work on this book was a very long journey, and I am grateful to my companions: my friends Anna and Andrzej Cała, Kierra Crago-Schneider, Katarzyna Czerwonogóra, Tomasz Frydel, Dominika Michalak, Rivka Schiller, Matan Shefi, and Elsbeth van der Wilt. They assisted my studies in all sorts of ways, caring for the book and its author. My parents, Magdalena and Bogdan Krzyżanowscy, and our nanny, Jolanta Baranowska, were always ready to provide childcare when I was traveling for research.

I am incalculably lucky to be married to Dorota Woroniecka-Krzyżanowska, a fellow academic and an incredible person. It was her love for the Arabic language and culture that first brought me to the Middle East and allowed me to conduct research in Israel. Without her unconditional support, understanding, and intellectual partnership, my work would be much harder, if not impossible. Together with our son, she constantly reminds me that there is life beyond the horrors I encounter through archival documents. To Dorota I dedicate this work.

I am the only person responsible for all misjudgments, inaccuracies, or errors.

INDEX

Radom, Poland *(continued)*
employment of Jews in, 12; City
Council, 13–14; division between Jews
and Christians in, 14–15, 17–19,
265–266, 300n87; elimination of Jews
from economic and public life in,
17–18; under German occupation,
19–21; concentration of Jewish
population of, 23–25; deportation of
Jews from, 25–29, 118, 155–156, 164,
169, 172, 174, 190–195, 201–204,
278n66; Poles' attitudes toward Jews
in, 29–30, 31–32; isolation of Jews
from non-Jewish population in, 30–31;
aid for Jews in, 33, 74–75; liberation
of, 34–38; following liberation, 38–50;
Jews return to, 50–61; "pogrom" in,
91–96; Jews ordered to leave, 96–99,
128–129, 130
Radom prison, attack on, 45
Radom synagogue, 1, 13, 23, 199,
200–203, 246–247, 259
rape. *See* sexual violence
Red Army, 34–38, 42–44, 48–50
refugees, 7, 19, 186
remembrance of murdered Jews, 1–2, 190,
199–204, 246–247, 308–309n252
Reszka, Paweł Piotr, 317n152
R., Henryk (Henry), 50–51, 56, 92, 146,
282n147, 286n17
robberies, 63–80, 121–123, 213–214. *See also*
Jewish property
Rosenstein, Jack (Icek-Ber), 258
Rozenbaum, Chaskiel, 197
Rubinstein, Mojżesz, 100, 111, 137, 138,
148–149, 291n124
Rubinsztein Foundry–Heirs factory, 238,
239
Rywan, Rózia, 170–171
Rzeszów pogrom, 95–96

Saski, Jan, 77
"S. Buszacki" photography studio,
250–252
Schippers, Franz, 167, 168, 214, 302n132
Security Police (Służba Bezpieczeństwa,
SB), 4–5, 83, 273–274n6

Security Service (Urząd Bezpieczeństwa,
UB), 45, 46, 49, 64, 81, 99–110, 129,
133, 222, 253–255
Selivanovsky, Nikolai, 86
Serov, Ivan, 44
sexual violence, 48–49, 164, 165–167, 174
Shoshkes, Henryk, 284–285n189
Siwiec, Zofia, 82–83, 84
Skałbania, Stefan, 104
Sławiński, Bolesław, 168, 169, 174
Słomczyński, Witold, 289n74
Słowo Ludu, 203–204
Śmietanka-Kruszelnicki, Ryszard, 85–86,
97, 290n94
Sobczyński, Władysław, 108
Soborski, Stanisław, 250–252, 315n124
Society for Safeguarding the Health of the
Jewish Population (Towarzystwo
Ochrony Zdrowia Ludności
Żydowskiej, TOZ), 157, 163, 170
soup kitchen, 141–145
Soviet security police (NKVD), 43–44, 54,
186
Soviet soldiers, crimes committed by, 48–50
Soviet Union: and liberation of Radom,
34–38, 42–44; survival of Polish Jews
in, 51, 52, 186; Kamer deported to, 188;
German aggression against, 276n40
Special Commission of the CKŻP, 297n12
Stellman, Jakub, 305n182
Stellman, Leon, 182–184, 298n34,
305n182, 305n185
Stellman, Władysław, 305n182
"Świt" (Dawn) detachment. *See* Dawn
("Świt") detachment
Sybilski, Stanisław, 158, 251
synagogue, Radom. *See* Radom synagogue
Szajnberg, Bencjon. *See* Sławiński, Bolesław
Szaynok, Bożena, 113–114, 116
Szenderowicz, Irena, 173, 174–175,
303n146
Szenderowicz, Naum (Norbert), 156–159,
161–173, 175, 177, 205, 206, 301n103,
303n146
Szkolna Street camp, 27, 58, 77, 177,
302n132
Sznajderman, Eliasz (Snyder, Elias), 93
Sznajderman, Mania, 93